Contents at a Glance

Table of Contents

Introduction

Welcome to *1,001 GRE Practice Questions For Dummies*. Don't take the Dummies thing personally — you're obviously no dummy. You made it through high school with high enough grades and test scores to get into college. You then graduated to join the elite group of approximately 30 percent of U.S. citizens who hold bachelor's degrees, and some of you even have master's degrees. And now you're about to take your education further.

Between you and your goal is the GRE: a test designed solely to challenge your ability to remember everything you've forgotten since high school — material you haven't touched in years. To clear this hurdle, you need some practice along with pointers of how best to answer the questions. This book provides that and more: It goes beyond providing relevant practice questions by showing simple and effective ways to solve the seemingly challenging GRE problems.

What You'll Find

The GRE practice problems in this book are divided into six chapters: three verbal, two math, and one writing. Questions are grouped by topic. If there's a topic that you struggle with, you'll find a group of similar questions to practice and hone your skills. This book serves as an effective stand-alone refresher of GRE basics, or as an excellent companion to *GRE For Dummies*, 8th Edition, written by yours truly (with invaluable help from Joe Kraynak) and published by Wiley. Either way, this book helps you identify subject areas you need to work on so that you can practice them until you're a pro, and thus prepare yourself for test day.

If you get a problem wrong, don't just read the answer explanation and move on. Instead, come back to the problem and solve it again, this time avoiding the mistake that you made the first time. This is how you improve your skills and learn to solve the problems correctly and easily.

Whatever you do, stay positive. The challenging problems in this book aren't meant to discourage you. Rather, they're meant to show you how to solve them so that you can practice and master them.

How the Questions Are Organized

The test is divided into three main parts: verbal, math, and writing.

Verbal

The verbal questions in this book cover the following topics:

- ✔ **Sentence completion:** These questions have sentences with one, two, or three words missing, and you have to select the word or words that logically complete the sentence.

- ✔ **Reading comprehension:** The GRE gives you a reading passage along with two to five questions based on the passage. The questions challenge your ability to discern the purpose of the passage and the significance of the details.

- ✔ **Argument analysis:** The GRE provides a short argument in the form of a passage and then asks you to select an answer that would either strengthen or weaken the argument. You may also have to define the roles of bolded sentences or select a sentence that serves a specific purpose.

Math

The math questions in this book cover the following topics:

- ✔ **Arithmetic:** These questions are based on core arithmetic concepts, including prime numbers, absolute value, decimals, fractions, and ratios. Don't be fooled by the simple nature: these questions can be as challenging as any that you find on the GRE.

- ✔ **Geometry:** Geometry covers basic shapes, such as triangles, circles, and squares. These questions also go into basic 3-D shapes, including cylinders and boxes, but no prisms, spheres, or cones. The GRE sticks to its limited scope of math concepts.

- ✔ **Argument analysis:** The GRE provides a short argument in the form of a passage and then asks you to select an answer that would either strengthen or weaken the argument. You may also have to define the roles of bolded sentences or select a sentence that serves a specific purpose.

- ✔ **Algebra:** These questions are extensions of arithmetic, going into exponents, square roots, and numeric sequences. They also explore variations of solving for x and linear equations having x and y.

- ✔ **Word problems:** No set of word problems is complete without the two trains coming from Chattanooga. These questions cover those, along with weighted averages, probability, Venn diagrams, permutations, and combinations.

- ✔ **Graphs and data interpretation:** The GRE problems feature variations of median, range, and standard deviation concepts. It also asks challenging tables and graphs questions where, like the reading comprehension, you are given a set of graphs along with three questions based on those graphs.

- ✔ **Comparing quantities:** About 8 of the 20 math questions in each section rehash the topics mentioned previously, but they're in the format where you compare Quantity A to Quantity B and determine whether one is greater, they're the same, or the relationship can't be determined.

Writing

You are tasked with writing two different essays on the GRE, and these pages provide plenty of practice:

- ✔ **Analyze an issue essay:** For your first essay, the GRE gives you an issue statement and asks you to declare and support your position on that issue. The GRE asks for *your opinion,* so be sure to state what you think — as long as you can support it.

- ✔ **Analyze an argument essay:** For your second essay, the GRE gives you an argument that is typically flawed or incomplete. Your job is to analyze the argument and its reasoning and evidence and describe why the argument is either faulty or sound, and what information or evidence is needed to validate the argument.

Beyond the Book

Your purchase of this book gives you so much more than just several hundred problems you can work on to improve your understanding of the topics on the GRE. It also comes with a free, one-year subscription to hundreds of practice questions online. Not only can you access this digital content anytime you want, on whichever device is available to you, but you can also track your progress and view personalized reports that show you which concepts you need to study the most.

What you'll find

The online practice that comes free with this book offers you the same questions and answers that are available here along with hundreds more. And online, they're in a multiple-choice format. What's great about this format is that it allows you to zero in on the details that can make or break your solution. Sometimes one (or more) of the incorrect answer options is the result of a calculation error. When you catch yourself making such a common error, you'll know not to take the same approach with similar problems on a graded test, when the right answers really count.

Of course, the real beauty of the online problems is the ability to customize your practice. In other words, you get to choose the types of problems and the number of problems you want to tackle. The online program tracks how many questions you answer correctly versus incorrectly so you can get an immediate sense of which topics need more of your attention.

This product also comes with an online Cheat Sheet that helps you increase your odds of performing well on the GRE. Check out the free Cheat Sheet at www.dummies.com/cheatsheet/1001GRE. (No access code required. You can benefit from this info before you even register.)

How to register

To gain access to practice online, all you have to do is register. Just follow these simple steps:

1. **Find your PIN access code.**

   • **Print-book users:** If you purchased a print copy of this book, turn to the inside front cover of the book to find your access code.

   • **E-book users:** If you purchased this book as an e-book, you can get your access code by registering your e-book at www.dummies.com/go/getaccess. Go to this website, find your book and click it, and answer the security question to verify your purchase. Then you'll receive an email with your access code.

2. **Go to** studyandprep.dummies.com.

3. **Enter the access code.**

4. **Follow the instructions to create an account and establish your own personal login information.**

Now you're ready to go! You can come back to the program as often as you want — simply log on with the username and password you created during your initial login. No need to enter the access code a second time.

For Technical Support, please visit http://wiley.custhelp.com or call Wiley at: 1-800-762-2974 (U.S.), +1-317-572-3994 (international).

Where to Go for Additional Help

The solutions to the practice problems in this book are meant to walk you through how to get the right answers; they're not meant to teach the material. If certain concepts are unfamiliar to you, you can find help at www.dummies.com. Just type "GRE" into the search box to turn up a wealth of GRE-related information.

If you need more detailed instruction, check out the previously referenced *GRE For Dummies*.

Part I
The Questions

Visit www.dummies.com for free access to great *For Dummies* content online.

In this part . . .

*B*ecome familiar with the ways the GRE asks you to read sentences and paragraphs, and brush up on the vocab that you're likely to see. You also get to work on hundreds of math problems so that you recognize the common GRE traps and tricks. Finally, you get some practice writing the essays.

- ✔ Sentence Completion (Chapter 1)
- ✔ Reading Comprehension (Chapter 2)
- ✔ Argument Analysis (Chapter 3)
- ✔ Arithmetic (Chapters 4 and 5)
- ✔ Geometry (Chapters 4 and 5)
- ✔ Algebra (Chapters 4 and 5)
- ✔ Word Problems (Chapter 4)
- ✔ Graphs and Data Interpretation (Chapters 4 and 5)
- ✔ Quantitative Comparisons (Chapter 5)
- ✔ Analyze an Issue Essay (Chapter 6)
- ✔ Analyze an Argument Essay (Chapter 6)

Chapter 1

Sentence Completion

· ·

Sentence Completion refers to Text Completion and Sentence Equivalence questions. Text Completion questions have one, two, or three words missing, and you choose one word for each blank. Sentence Equivalence questions have one word missing, and you choose two words for the blank.

Half the challenge is interpreting the sentence, and the other half is sorting through the vocabulary. With practice, you learn to easily interpret the sentence, and with exposure, you recognize the commonly-used GRE vocabulary words.

The Problems You'll Work On

When working through the questions in this chapter, be prepared to

- ✔ Look for clues in the sentence to determine its meaning.
- ✔ Recognize irony, figures of speech, and formal diction.
- ✔ Use transition words ("but, however, therefore") to get the gist of the phrases.
- ✔ Break the sentence into smaller pieces.
- ✔ Check one word blank at a time to eliminate answer choices.

What to Watch Out For

The meaning of the sentence is not always clear, and the vocabulary can be tricky, so watch out for trap word-choice answers that

- ✔ Appear to fit the sentence but don't support its meaning
- ✔ Support the meaning of the sentence but aren't used properly
- ✔ Appear to have one meaning but actually mean something else, such as "condone," which means "approve"

For questions 1–90, each of the following sentences has a blank indicating that a word or phrase is omitted. Choose the two answer choices that best complete the sentence and result in two sentences most alike in meaning.

1. The crowd applauded the dancer, despite her odd ways, finding brilliance in the _____ of her movements.

    [A]   offensiveness

    [B]   anomaly

    [C]   irregularity

    [D]   mastery

    [E]   grotesquery

    [F]   banality

2. I read every political blog I found to _____ as many facts about the state of the world as I could before my interview with the foreign service.

    [A]   accrete

    [B]   eradicate

    [C]   garner

    [D]   jettison

    [E]   comprise

    [F]   accumulate

3. The dedication highlighted Dr. Carter's Nobel Prize in mathematics as the _____ of his career, which hardly acknowledges the honor of such a distinction.

    [A]   zenith

    [B]   apex

    [C]   plateau

    [D]   median

    [E]   pedestal

    [F]   foundation

4. Tracy thought James was a perfect match for her in every way except for his _____ taste in food, with her palette not as adventurous as his.

    [A]   humdrum

    [B]   dazzling

    [C]   eclectic

    [D]   lackluster

    [E]   diverse

    [F]   inspired

5. Mr. Horton turned beet red after Ricky failed to show the proper _____ at Kim's graduation.

    [A]   unruliness

    [B]   tranquility

    [C]   majesty

    [D]   violence

    [E]   decorum

    [F]   tact

6. Considering how outlandish the pop star's wardrobe is when she is on stage, her gown at the music awards was very _____.

    [A]   extraordinary

    [B]   banal

    [C]   predictable

    [D]   derivative

    [E]   conventional

    [F]   unique

7. As much as Carl wanted to buy the mountain bike, he felt that it wasn't a _____ decision.

[A] trustworthy

[B] risky

[C] pragmatic

[D] corrupt

[E] precarious

[F] rational

8. Downhill skiers are some of the most _____ in the Olympics, reaching speeds of up to 80 miles per hour.

[A] coy

[B] plucky

[C] tentative

[D] egotistical

[E] fearless

[F] haughty

9. John thought that he and Kim had made amends after the disagreement last week, but based on the way she continued to _____ at him, it was clear John was wrong.

[A] beam

[B] glower

[C] contort

[D] smirk

[E] scowl

[F] mope

10. The fact that Nichelle made it into Harvard was _____, considering that she had such a low GPA.

[A] enlightening

[B] furtive

[C] incoherent

[D] enigmatic

[E] explicable

[F] mysterious

11. The bistro was known for its lobster bisque, so when the kitchen ran out, the cooks had to come up with a suitable replacement dish to _____ the angry diners.

[A] annoy

[B] placate

[C] remedy

[D] provoke

[E] improve

[F] appease

12. The cheating scandal would likely _____ the football team's reputation for a long time.

[A] extol

[B] heighten

[C] sully

[D] belittle

[E] tarnish

[F] boost

13. The scene in the stadium was becoming increasingly _____ as the fans grew angrier about calls made against the home team.

[A]   explosive

[B]   vulnerable

[C]   tenuous

[D]   volatile

[E]   steady

[F]   weak

14. Tommy's _____ manners were far below Sarah's parents' high-class lifestyle.

[A]   polished

[B]   plebeian

[C]   abrasive

[D]   naughty

[E]   refined

[F]   coarse

15. Karen refuses to _____ for a raise.

[A]   crave

[B]   pray

[C]   inquire

[D]   grovel

[E]   request

[F]   plead

16. The Jones family acts like it doesn't seek attention, but then it does something wholly _____, such as when Mrs. Jones wore a mink coat to the little league football game.

[A]   modest

[B]   salient

[C]   trivial

[D]   prominent

[E]   unobtrusive

[F]   palpable

17. The students loved the teacher's _____ style of teaching because they never knew what the lesson would be like on any given day.

[A]   humdrum

[B]   knowable

[C]   trite

[D]   whimsical

[E]   capricious

[F]   innovative

18. Jackie had been saving her frequent flyer miles for ten years, and her patience paid off when she was able to book the _____ suite in Las Vegas fit for a king. There was even a chandelier in the bathroom.

[A]   unique

[B]   moderate

[C]   palatial

[D]   pedestrian

[E]   lavish

[F]   unparalleled

19. The _____ of the intervention trial was more than the researchers had hoped for, with results far beyond what they had hypothesized.

[A]   ineptitude

[B]   efficacy

[C]   shortcoming

[D]   tolerability

[E]   effectiveness

[F]   acceptability

20. Karen was shocked hearing her dad tell friends how proud he was of her, as all he ever did was make _____ comments.

[A] profane

[B] caustic

[C] sarcastic

[D] encouraging

[E] blasphemous

[F] supportive

21. Rather than discuss the issues at hand, the speaker _____ all day about how right he was and how wrong everyone else was.

[A] pondered

[B] opined

[C] consulted

[D] preached

[E] deliberated

[F] reflected

22. Jason took Carol to dinner and a movie, which she felt was a _____ activity and not impressive at all.

[A] tasteless

[B] imaginative

[C] dreary

[D] thrilling

[E] prosaic

[F] pedestrian

23. Having the play produced was the _____ of Charlotte's college career, with the rest of the experience passing by without anything else significant occurring.

[A] standard

[B] makeup

[C] quality

[D] acme

[E] pinnacle

[F] peculiarity

24. The success of the hit comedy *Seinfeld* was mainly due to the _____ dialogue between the characters, with each being capable of cleverly delivering humorous lines.

[A] droll

[B] witty

[C] obvious

[D] dense

[E] obtuse

[F] classic

25. By _____ the immoral behaviors of celebrity professional athletes, society is sending a negative message to our youth.

[A] punishing

[B] praising

[C] condoning

[D] lauding

[E] rebuking

[F] pardoning

26. Trying to get a picture of white storks in migration is tricky because of their _____ travel patterns.

[A] erratic

[B] transparent

[C] obvious

[D] intermittent

[E] foreseeable

[F] unimagined

27. Although Johnny Depp is best known as a major Hollywood celebrity, he is also well known for his _____ personality, frequently socializing in the communities where he is shooting films.

[A]   confident

[B]   gregarious

[C]   introverted

[D]   extroverted

[E]   pompous

[F]   reluctant

28. The Congressional Medal of Honor is given to exceptionally _____ soldiers who place themselves in the most terrifying situations to save the lives of others.

[A]   proficient

[B]   resolute

[C]   established

[D]   intrepid

[E]   gallant

[F]   clever

29. Being confident in your ideas is a good characteristic for a boss, but if you possess a _____ attitude, you hinder your ability to learn from others and improve yourself or the business.

[A]   lenient

[B]   doctrinaire

[C]   dogmatic

[D]   prejudiced

[E]   generous

[F]   partisan

30. By providing tax incentives for small business startups, the president _____ economic growth and reduced unemployment.

[A]   engendered

[B]   obstructed

[C]   allowed

[D]   inhibited

[E]   certified

[F]   stimulated

31. Google is considered to be the _____ of a positive workplace environment, with ample vacation time and nap pods for every employee.

[A]   deficiency

[B]   surplus

[C]   paragon

[D]   exemplar

[E]   shortcoming

[F]   intemperance

32. Because Jordan quickly noticed his wallet was missing, the damage to his bank account was _____, with most of his money remaining untouched.

[A]   microscopic

[B]   nominal

[C]   immense

[D]   significant

[E]   petite

[F]   negligible

33. As the semester progressed, the attendance in Professor Landsburg's class diminished due to his _____ character, as the professor often shed tears while reciting poetry.

    [A] composed

    [B] maudlin

    [C] mawkish

    [D] affectionate

    [E] impassive

    [F] neurotic

34. St. Mary's Catholic School has been teaching students for more than 100 years, and it takes great pride in the _____ that guide(s) it, in that each day starts and ends the same way, and any student who does not act accordingly is subject to expulsion.

    [A] agendas

    [B] mores

    [C] authority

    [D] strategies

    [E] norms

    [F] formulas

35. The coaches agreed to _____ to determine the outcome of the game after the last play was too close for the referees to call.

    [A] analyze

    [B] dispute

    [C] concur

    [D] parley

    [E] squabble

    [F] confer

36. Poor grades are _____ among the basketball team players because of all the classes they miss for games.

    [A] endemic

    [B] native

    [C] measly

    [D] sparse

    [E] exclusive

    [F] rife

37. The hiker showed _____ by rationing his water for the long hike.

    [A] prudence

    [B] destiny

    [C] providence

    [D] retrospection

    [E] fortune

    [F] hindsight

38. The barn cat created _____ with the farmer by keeping mice out of the horse feed, for which the farmer gave it food and water and let it sleep in the barn.

    [A] sovereignty

    [B] symbiosis

    [C] enslavement

    [D] freedom

    [E] mutualism

    [F] addiction

39. J. D. Salinger was famous for the way in which he moved into a remote cabin and lived a _____ life; therefore, there are few accounts of his personal life.

    [A] hermetic

    [B] forsaken

    [C] lonely

    [D] derelict

    [E] deserted

    [F] reclusive

40. The only reason Henry passed English this fall semester was that his professor was extremely _____, believing every story for why assignments were never finished.

[A] seasoned

[B] credulous

[C] gullible

[D] immature

[E] inept

[F] cunning

41. Davis was naïve to think that Ms. Miller would change her _____ behavior, as she was in the middle of a con when he met her.

[A] stony

[B] honorable

[C] wily

[D] sincere

[E] unemotional

[F] crafty

42. The sheriff almost fired the deputy for committing such a _____ act, when the deputy ran from the building after discovering the bomb.

[A] craven

[B] feeble

[C] valiant

[D] heroic

[E] pitiable

[F] pusillanimous

43. Emily Post is a famous author whose name has become synonymous with _____ after writing a number of books teaching young women how to be respectable ladies in society.

[A] insolence

[B] sympathy

[C] audacity

[D] propriety

[E] sensitivity

[F] etiquette

44. Steve Martin made many movies during his career, but despite his serious and dramatic roles, he will be remembered best for his _____ characters in his early comedies.

[A] irresponsible

[B] puerile

[C] infantile

[D] mature

[E] petty

[F] wise

45. The comedian was not well liked by the audience, which felt that his _____ jokes were offensive.

[A] heartfelt

[B] duplicitous

[C] dishonest

[D] sardonic

[E] hypocritical

[F] mordant

46. Bill's dad had to pay the neighbor $150 to _____ the disturbance, and Bill wasn't allowed to play drums in the backyard anymore.

[A]   exacerbate

[B]   redress

[C]   alleviate

[D]   recuperate

[E]   remedy

[F]   enrich

47. The voters were _____ as they stood in line, primarily because the latest polls had shown that their representative was way ahead of his opponent in the elections.

[A]   cynical

[B]   sanguine

[C]   suspicious

[D]   insistent

[E]   adamant

[F]   optimistic

48. The _____ appetite of the Great White Shark causes it to consume almost 500 pounds of food a day, but it can survive for two weeks without eating.

[A]   replete

[B]   temperate

[C]   satiated

[D]   implacable

[E]   unappeasable

[F]   abounding

49. Jenny had a style that fit the punk scene, but the preppy kids at school treated her like she was a(n) _____ and barely spoke to her.

[A]   pariah

[B]   offscouring

[C]   colleague

[D]   interloper

[E]   counterpart

[F]   expatriate

50. Though initially successful, the art dealer had to close his gallery after word got out that he was a _____, having never seriously studied or worked with fine art to any significant extent.

[A]   proletarian

[B]   authority

[C]   specialist

[D]   dilettante

[E]   curmudgeon

[F]   amateur

51. The directors chose Lisa to _____ her former supervisor after they caught the supervisor printing Christmas cards with the company's equipment.

[A]   promote

[B]   invite

[C]   terminate

[D]   coordinate

[E]   supplant

[F]   displace

52. No one invites Monty to parties, because he drinks too much and becomes _____, arguing and picking fights.

[A] surly

[B] churlish

[C] insubordinate

[D] civil

[E] polished

[F] defiant

53. After the _____ actions of President Nixon involving the Watergate Hotel, the country was shocked and disillusioned, and his impeachment seemed imminent.

[A] fearsome

[B] unconscionable

[C] obscure

[D] bravura

[E] scandalous

[F] brilliant

54. The members of the jury couldn't come to a decision because of the defendant's moving testimony, with those believing the _____ of it voting to acquit.

[A] fraudulence

[B] equivocation

[C] veracity

[D] duplicity

[E] directness

[F] authenticity

55. The bank cut Tim off after his _____ use of credit cards exceeded the account limits.

[A] prodigal

[B] oblivious

[C] heedless

[D] selfless

[E] philanthropic

[F] extravagant

56. The stock market crash of 2008 led to the _____ of most banking activities, including mortgage loans and lending services, due to the levels of bankruptcy and the instability of fund balances.

[A] upsurge

[B] diminution

[C] abeyance

[D] suspension

[E] improvement

[F] escalation

57. Although the volcano Haleakala on the island of Maui is usually _____, it has erupted in a lava flow three times during the last 900 years.

[A] functional

[B] destroyed

[C] lively

[D] fallow

[E] immobile

[F] dormant

58. The school board was completely unprepared for the _____ by the cafeteria staff, which locked the doors and refused to accept delivery from the food vendor.

[A] riots

[B] insurrection

[C] complaints

[D] unrest

[E] uprising

[F] reconciliation

59. The playwright wrote a(n) _____ that depicted his mother as a neurotic control freak who rummages his drawers when he's not home, though he later said that he had exaggerated.

[A] cartoon

[B] tribute

[C] lampoon

[D] homage

[E] satire

[F] analysis

60. Training for the marathon while working 60 hours a week left Charlie feeling _____.

[A] frenzied

[B] enervated

[C] reinvigorated

[D] languid

[E] supported

[F] prohibited

61. Robin didn't agree with what her competitor said during the debate, but she couldn't help but feel sorry for him after the vicious _____ he received from the judge following his statement.

[A] docility

[B] commendation

[C] reticence

[D] vituperation

[E] condescension

[F] opprobrium

62. The _____ explanation Jeannine gave for being late only made her parents more suspicious of her whereabouts; she should have been brief.

[A] oblique

[B] persnickety

[C] earnest

[D] circuitous

[E] punctilious

[F] frivolous

63. Henry David Thoreau wrote *Walden* while living in a remote cabin in the woods, and although his philosophy and insights about getting back to nature are quite wise, most of modern society, with all the available indulgences, does not have what it takes to live that type of _____ life.

[A] monastic

[B] zealous

[C] equitable

[D] clement

[E] austere

[F] altruistic

64. Cherry tells the truth in such a way that people are taken aback by her _____ remarks.

[A] sincere

[B] amicable

[C] hypocritical

[D] deceitful

[E] ingenuous

[F] candid

65. In the horror movie *Carrie*, bullying hits a(n) _____ when the main character is doused in blood at the prom and is humiliated in front of the entire school.

[A] infamy

[B] crest

[C] distinction

[D] peak

[E] nadir

[F] depth

66. Nelson Mandela was held in great _____ by citizens and leaders of the world for his prudence in the fight for equal rights in South Africa, and as a result, more than 4,500 people attended his funeral.

[A] revulsion

[B] deference

[C] disdain

[D] regard

[E] infatuation

[F] allure

67. Finishing the book on time wouldn't have been so _____ if the publisher hadn't moved the deadline up by three weeks, causing Jane undue duress.

[A] convoluted

[B] facile

[C] onerous

[D] extraneous

[E] arduous

[F] paltry

68. Dale's friends were concerned about him because he'd become _____ since he was left at the altar, staring at the television in his basement day in and day out.

[A] derisory

[B] phlegmatic

[C] vigorous

[D] apathetic

[E] slothful

[F] pathetic

69. Although the teacher's _____ abilities come in handy, they can also trap him, as he doesn't always want to be responsible for every problem.

[A] assiduous

[B] perspicacious

[C] sagacious

[D] pensive

[E] erudite

[F] introspective

70. Debating the professor was a challenge, as he was such a(n) _____ that he would use the smallest detail of any point to invalidate the entire argument.

[A] pedant

[B] connoisseur

[C] obfuscator

[D] contender

[E] hair-splitter

[F] specialist

71. The outrage over the verdict was immense from the crowd, which could not believe that the jury had decided the crime was nothing more than _____ when so many people had been hurt.

[A] reputable

[B] wicked

[C] nefarious

[D] a peccadillo

[E] a misdemeanor

[F] culpable

72. The admissions committee was quick to narrow the field to only the most remarkable candidates, rejecting any application that was _____ in tone or content.

[A] quotidian

[B] unexceptional

[C] prestigious

[D] outlandish

[E] phenomenal

[F] inconsequential

73. Vera was so offended at her date's chauvinism that she stood up, delivered a _____ remark, and threw her drink in his face before storming off.

[A] straggling

[B] loutish

[C] pithy

[D] urbane

[E] sententious

[F] chivalrous

74. King Henry VIII was able to divorce his first wife, Catherine of Aragon, by forcing the clergy of the Catholic church to _____ its power and then claiming the role of supreme head of the church himself.

[A] congregate

[B] abdicate

[C] assent

[D] diverge

[E] renounce

[F] disperse

75. Matt shows off that he's a _____ whenever he can, as he spoke French to the cab driver and Portuguese to the hotel concierge, both of whom were American.

[A] polyglot

[B] genius

[C] linguist

[D] bilingual

[E] leader

[F] mastermind

76. The planners avoided the big picture by obsessing over _____ details.

[A] wooly

[B] ambiguous

[C] incongruous

[D] tangential

[E] peripheral

[F] divergent

77. Mr. Wentworth made his fortune as a(n) _____ businessman; when a farmer was in financial trouble, he would help out for a share of the profits.

[A] politic

[B] astute

[C] parsimonious

[D] munificent

[E] miserly

[F] charitable

78. The family searched for even the slightest _____ of something nostalgic from the tornado wreckage, but everything was gone.

[A] paucity

[B] vestige

[C] indication

[D] plethora

[E] trace

[F] glut

79. Shelly's _____ belief that she was going to sell her first novel and become a millionaire kept her from considering any other reality.

[A] recalcitrant

[B] quixotic

[C] idealistic

[D] obliging

[E] emphatic

[F] malleable

80. A sense of _____ helps one act according to what is right and with respect for others and the truth.

[A] clemency

[B] impiety

[C] commiseration

[D] malevolence

[E] probity

[F] integrity

81. It takes some degree of _____ to publish a daily personal blog because not everyone is able to talk about himself prolifically.

[A] ambivalence

[B] narcissism

[C] eloquence

[D] moderation

[E] hypocrisy

[F] conceit

82. Everyone who had the _____ to invest in Apple when it was cheap, in the '80s, is a millionaire now.

[A] circumspection

[B] prescience

[C] foresight

[D] negligence

[E] gumption

[F] imprudence

83. Egyptian tombs, being _____ and capable of protecting the dead from thieves and vandals, were burial sites for ancient religious figures and leaders.

[A] sacrosanct

[B] spindly

[C] inviolable

[D] bounteous

[E] meager

[F] resplendent

84. Frodo Baggins, with the success of his _____ pursuit of his mission to destroy the ring despite every possible obstacle, is an excellent example of fortitude.

[A] preventable

[B] unavoidable

[C] inexorable

[D] superfluous

[E] relentless

[F] obligatory

85. The topic of the lecture was interesting, but the audience was lulled into slumber by the speaker's _____ manner of delivery.

[A] invigorating

[B] repellant

[C] soporific

[D] charismatic

[E] restorative

[F] monotonous

86. With the job market the way it is, many professionals have _____ résumés, working in a variety of fields that are as different as night and day.

[A] analogous

[B] multifarious

[C] uniform

[D] synchronized

[E] disparate

[F] atypical

87. When the pressure of law school is too much, the _____ sounds of Mozart calm one down.

[A] sedative

[B] anguished

[C] analgesic

[D] heartening

[E] sorrowful

[F] palliative

88. Stephen King is such a _____ writer that he has to publish under several different names, lest the market become flooded with Stephen King titles.

[A] learned

[B] infertile

[C] cultivated

[D] fruitless

[E] fecund

[F] prolific

89. Celestial eclipses are considered special events because they are _____ in certain parts of the world, happening once every 100 years and lasting only a few hours.

[A]   colossal

[B]   infinite

[C]   eternal

[D]   transitory

[E]   ordained

[F]   ephemeral

90. Howard's fan base continues to _____ because of all the new website traffic from his restaurant critiques.

[A]   supplement

[B]   diminish

[C]   engorge

[D]   proliferate

[E]   convoy

[F]   burgeon

For questions 91–115, choose the one entry best suited for each blank from its corresponding column of choices.

91. Celebrities often travel with bodyguards due to the _____ of adoring fans constantly vying for their attention.

(A)   deficiency

(B)   bevy

(C)   tribe

(D)   remainder

(E)   clique

92. The police chief ordered a standard _____ into the actions of the officer who had accusations made against him.

(A)   experiment

(B)   analysis

(C)   application

(D)   observation

(E)   inquest

93. A marathon runner usually takes the day after the race off from work, knowing her body needs (a) major _____ from the strain.

(A)   breather

(B)   repose

(C)   recreation

(D)   agitation

(E)   support

94. The casting director told Tony that although he had a lot of charm, she was looking for someone with a bit more _____ in his demeanor.

(A)   meekness

(B)   panache

(C)   charisma

(D)   complexity

(E)   humility

95. Even on the tenth stop of the tour, the _____ singer meditated for an hour before she could bring herself to go on stage.

(A)   exhausted

(B)   relaxed

(C)   overwrought

(D)   timorous

(E)   tranquil

96. The police arrested two bank tellers after the manager overheard them _____ together to extort millions of dollars.

   (A) professing

   (B) colluding

   (C) improvising

   (D) adjoining

   (E) fabricating

97. The process Jessica used to _____ her Yorkshire Terrier in the backyard was solemn, after she had spent most of the morning building an ornate box for the occasion.

   (A) inter

   (B) harvest

   (C) unearth

   (D) banish

   (E) enclose

98. The meatpacking industry faced major changes in the late 20th century due to new restrictions requiring factory owners to _____ the working conditions on their production lines.

   (A) revolutionize

   (B) develop

   (C) ameliorate

   (D) depreciate

   (E) modernize

99. Wary of the protests of dissenting stakeholders, the CEO convened a meeting with a _____ of the top executives to go forward with the merger.

   (A) cabal

   (B) subordinate

   (C) clique

   (D) sect

   (E) class

100. The insecure team captain had a reputation for _____, and somehow the best players always got injured.

   (A) trickery

   (B) seniority

   (C) machination

   (D) prowess

   (E) athleticism

101. Tracy hates spending the holidays at her in-laws because the _____ remarks by her mother-in-law always bruise her self-esteem.

   (A) discordant

   (B) defamatory

   (C) amicable

   (D) pejorative

   (E) congruous

102. The tell-all book would have sold millions of copies, but because of the _____ marketing, the buzz was over by the time the book hit the shelves.

   (A) resolute

   (B) dithering

   (C) remarkable

   (D) cowardly

   (E) vacillating

103. The candidate's platform was exactly what the farming community needed. However, because of his _____ manner of speaking, they thought he was a snob.

   (A) diplomatic

   (B) affectionate

   (C) vicious

   (D) bombastic

   (E) circuitous

104. Naomi Judd eventually had to stop performing because of the severe _____ she felt as part of her chronic fatigue syndrome.

(A) lassitude

(B) dexterity

(C) ingenuity

(D) apathy

(E) ineptitude

105. As the popularity of Black Friday sales increases, the safety of shoppers decreases, as crowds of _____ shoppers rush past each other in search of the best deals.

(A) serene

(B) distracted

(C) fervent

(D) frenetic

(E) listless

106. The mountain pine beetle has wiped out more than 1.5 million acres of forest in Colorado by creating a _____ on pine and spruce trees in the Rocky Mountains.

(A) misfortune

(B) defacement

(C) blight

(D) infirmity

(E) affliction

107. New York Mayor Bloomberg proposed a ban on large-sized sodas to help promote better health in the city, but despite the good intentions behind it, critics were quick to _____ his plan due to its infringements on personal freedoms.

(A) commend

(B) sanction

(C) vilify

(D) slander

(E) deride

108. The seniors at McCarren High School held such _____ that the younger students had no say in school-related affairs.

(A) inferiority

(B) constraint

(C) hegemony

(D) evaluations

(E) expertise

109. It was bad enough that the rest of the team was upset with Joe for missing the last question at the quiz bowl, but when the coach _____ him in front of everyone, he really felt like a failure.

(A) branded

(B) violated

(C) congratulated

(D) castigated

(E) desecrated

110. The harsh way that Kelly depicted the people of her community in her book shed light on why she never talked to anyone or left her house. Before her book came out, everyone had thought the _____ was just quiet.

(A) misanthrope

(B) skeptic

(C) pessimist

(D) curmudgeon

(E) idealist

111. The government often refuses to address issues of the masses because of _____ attitudes of certain lawmakers, which can motivate actions such as the woman's suffrage and the civil rights movements.

(A) malleable

(B) obstinate

(C) desultory

(D) amenable

(E) methodical

112. The president angered many of his supporters when he read his _____ in his public address and deeply criticized Congress's stance on the bill.

    (A) homily

    (B) polemic

    (C) opus

    (D) proposal

    (E) masterpiece

113. Japanese honeybees efficiently protect themselves from the predatory hornet by forming a _____ around the hornet and literally cooking it to death with the heat generated from the mass of vibrating wings.

    (A) legion

    (B) cohort

    (C) phalanx

    (D) throng

    (E) consortium

114. Marie was finally ready to buckle down and pursue a career; however, because she used to chronically _____, she found she could not get any letters of recommendation from her former employers.

    (A) hesitate

    (B) meander

    (C) tarry

    (D) acquiesce

    (E) malinger

115. According to Aristotle, in order for a dramatic character to be a tragic hero, one must be able to juxtapose the magnitude of the character's downfall with the manner in which he was previously _____ by society, thus creating a pitying effect.

    (A) praised

    (B) decried

    (C) spurned

    (D) lionized

    (E) eulogized

For questions 116–150, choose the one entry best suited for each blank from its corresponding column of choices.

116. Cornelius Holtorf, an archaeologist whose theories often generate controversy in the scientific sphere, received great (i) _____ for his adverse statements that the past is a renewable resource in that it is never lost but is always being (ii) _____.

    Blank (i)

    (A) contempt

    (B) criticism

    (C) acclaim

    Blank (ii)

    (D) buried

    (E) wasted

    (F) created

117. Juniper was always chosen first for teams in gym class because of her (i) _____ nature and the fact that she was so (ii) _____ in her participation.

    Blank (i)

    (A) idle

    (B) sportive

    (C) eccentric

    Blank (ii)

    (D) ardent

    (E) dispassionate

    (F) furtive

118. Manuel was tired of always covering for his friends with the teacher because they never showed any appreciation. The (i) _____ never did anything nice for him to (ii) _____ his kindness.

Blank (i)

(A) allies

(B) champions

(C) ingrates

Blank (ii)

(D) ignore

(E) perceive

(F) reciprocate

119. The bawdy disc jockey took the (i) _____ phrase from the song and turned it into a rudimentary babble. His antics and lack of appreciation for such poignancy are indications of his (ii) _____ character.

Blank (i)

(A) garbled

(B) confident

(C) eloquent

Blank (ii)

(D) congenial

(E) sordid

(F) hostile

120. Margaret clearly demonstrated her (i) _____ nature when she steered her cousins toward the less expensive restaurant for dinner. Her uncle paid for her meal as a sign of (ii) _____.

Blank (i)

(A) hasty

(B) judicious

(C) discreet

Blank (ii)

(D) obligation

(E) gratitude

(F) vulgarity

121. The animal rights group set up a booth every year at the state fair next to the barn to promote its (i) _____ of no harm to animals. The hunters hold a lot of (ii) _____ for them.

Blank (i)

(A) dedication

(B) verdict

(C) dogma

Blank (ii)

(D) esteem

(E) mockery

(F) disdain

122. The wacky mirror at the carnival (i) _____ June's reflection so that June appeared ten times her normal size. This effect was contrary to her (ii) _____ nature.

Blank (i)

(A) constricted

(B) exposed

(C) dilated

Blank (ii)

(D) vain

(E) futile

(F) humble

123. Everyone could tell that the speaker wasn't really educated about the subject. He just used a lot of (i) _____ that people already knew, which made him a (ii) _____ in Paula's eyes.

Blank (i)

(A) mantras

(B) axioms

(C) expertise

Blank (ii)

(D) maverick

(E) charlatan

(F) conformist

124. Although Chad can be a (i) _____ in the way he insults people, he tends to have luck with employers, who seem to enjoy the bold and (ii) _____ side of his personality.

Blank (i)

(A) boor

(B) patrician

(C) wretch

Blank (ii)

(D) foolhardy

(E) audacious

(F) impudent

125. No one could believe the boys were twins; not only did they look nothing alike, but one was excessively (i) _____, always showing a certain artistry in his gestures and speech, whereas the other was more (ii) _____, showing little energy in his demeanor.

Blank (i)

(A) ostentatious

(B) diffident

(C) florid

Blank (ii)

(D) despondent

(E) pallid

(F) exultant

126. Sarah knew that moving to a big city to be more alone was a (i) _____, but it was easier to (ii) _____ her nature among so many strangers than in the small town where she grew up.

Blank (i)

(A) paradox

(B) farcicality

(C) enigma

Blank (ii)

(D) dissemble

(E) secrete

(F) articulate

127. The hardest part of a(n) (i) _____ life is making and leaving so many friends, but it can be nice getting to (ii) _____ a new version of oneself in each new place.

Blank (i)

(A) orthodox

(B) rousing

(C) itinerant

Blank (ii)

(D) simulate

(E) fashion

(F) parody

128. The referee's comments could not be heard over the (i) _____ of voices from the opposing side of the field, but his (ii) _____ was sufficient to express the penalty.

Blank (i)

(A) melodiousness

(B) cacophony

(C) scarcity

Blank (ii)

(D) demeanor

(E) gesticulation

(F) carriage

129. In only stating key concepts once before moving on, the professor was so (i) _____ in his lectures that the students were afraid there would be a (ii) _____ in their knowledge of the subject matter.

Blank (i)

(A) laconic

(B) predictable

(C) interminable

Blank (ii)

(D) dearth

(E) precision

(F) surfeit

130. Part of serving as a diplomat requires being (i) _____ when greeting visiting leaders, regardless of how much one (ii) _____ their political agendas.

Blank (i)

(A) doleful

(B) robust

(C) ebullient

Blank (ii)

(D) reveres

(E) espouses

(F) abominates

131. Cory's parents couldn't understand why their couch was suddenly giving off a (i) _____ stench until they found the rotten orange stuck behind the couch cushion. The way it was shoved in there suggested that it was intentional, meaning some (ii) _____ guest did it.

Blank (i)

(A) fetid

(B) despicable

(C) affable

Blank (ii)

(D) nefarious

(E) rancorous

(F) benevolent

132. The manager looked embarrassed after realizing his receptionist's (i) _____ about how he treated her had been emailed to the entire office. After that, his coworkers looked at him with (ii) _____.

Blank (i)

(A) diatribe

(B) dissertation

(C) sermon

Blank (ii)

(D) savagery

(E) approbation

(F) derision

133. The Dalai Lama's (i) _____ about living the simple life seems easy enough to follow, but many people find this notion (ii) _____ to their cushy lifestyles.

Blank (i)

(A) dictum

(B) cliché

(C) mandate

Blank (ii)

(D) opportune

(E) incommodious

(F) imprudent

134. Parent-teacher night at Jeff's school was particularly contentious; his teachers hated that Jeff was so (i) _____, refusing to do what he was supposed to, and they blamed his parents, who were thought of in the community as (ii) _____ because of their constant rejection of the town customs.

Blank (i)

(A) licentious

(B) scrupulous

(C) depraved

Blank (ii)

(D) iconoclasts

(E) mutineers

(F) fundamentalists

135. Richard put the wood through the steam press to (i) _____ it so that he could shape it into the hull of the boat. Because the birch was so (ii) _____, it required several passes to become pliable.

Blank (i)

(A) pacify

(B) mollify

(C) congeal

Blank (ii)

(D) permeable

(E) unequivocal

(F) durable

136. It is easy to tell when someone is driven by (i) _____: First, he digresses from topic to topic, and second, when he finally returns to his speaking point, he is so (ii) _____ that he speaks with wild abandon.

Blank (i)

(A) facetiousness

(B) levity

(C) intransience

Blank (ii)

(D) garrulous

(E) taciturn

(F) forthcoming

137. Ivy League legacies are more common in families with a long history of wealth than those with more (i) _____ riches; however, if a student is not (ii) _____ in his studies, a legacy won't help him meet the standards of these schools.

Blank (i)

(A) entrenched

(B) nascent

(C) moribund

Blank (ii)

(D) industrious

(E) vehement

(F) languid

138. The Weather Underground Organization (i) _____ the resistance movement in the '70s by creating a (ii) _____ faction from a once unified, peaceful movement.

Blank (i)

(A) disseminated

(B) bifurcated

(C) amassed

Blank (ii)

(D) purposive

(E) tractable

(F) pugnacious

139. More than 200 homes burn down each year from fires caused by Christmas trees that (i) _____ over time and become great kindling for the heat of the lights. Simply keeping these trees hydrated and healthy could thwart these (ii) _____ incidents.

Blank (i)

(A) desiccate

(B) evanesce

(C) wane

Blank (ii)

(D) innocuous

(E) injurious

(F) harmless

140. A typical successful pop star is surrounded by nauseatingly (i) _____ assistants who do not want to fall from the pop star's good graces, yet despite the lack of (ii) _____ in their positions, they still look down on others who lack the association with stardom.

Blank (i)

(A) tentative

(B) obsequious

(C) unctuous

Blank (ii)

(D) nobility

(E) ignominy

(F) rectitude

141. Although bees are (i) _____ to people, they are vital to farming. Yet, because of the (ii) _____ of the bee population, the world's food supply is becoming (iii) _____.

Blank (i)

(A) delinquents

(B) traitors

(C) menaces

Blank (ii)

(D) decimation

(E) phylogeny

(F) reversion

Blank (iii)

(G) abolished

(H) preserved

(I) imperiled

142. When the budget cuts forced a number of public schools in Chicago to close, the fallen districts were forced to (i) _____ with the remaining schools, which caused a significant (ii) _____ due to a lack of resources caused by overcrowding. This change also required students to travel great distances, sometimes more than 30 miles, to go to school, which (iii) _____ their ability to participate in after-school programs due to transportation issues. If students missed the bus, their parents would be responsible for making the lengthy commute.

Blank (i)

(A) secede

(B) coalesce

(C) separate

Blank (ii)

(D) burden

(E) obstruction

(F) benefit

Blank (iii)

(G) impeded

(H) improved

(I) postponed

143. The coach did his best to keep the assignment of players to teams (i) _____ so that each team in the league had the same chance as the others to get the best players. Yet, inevitably, one team always seemed to be (ii) _____ with the best players, as if they were magnets drawn to each other, which made the parents suspect (iii) _____ in the decision-making process.

Blank (i)

(A) irrational

(B) imbalanced

(C) arbitrary

Blank (ii)

(D) teeming

(E) vacant

(F) laden

Blank (iii)

(G) neutrality

(H) preference

(I) justice

144. At the end of the phone interview, the manager told Stacy that they would choose two finalists within the next week, but that was three weeks ago. The (i) _____ after the interview made Stacy very impatient. Her desperation for a job and interest in this particular position led her to make the (ii) _____ move of calling the manager, which only infuriated the manager and (iii) _____ him against choosing Stacy as a finalist.

Blank (i)

(A) inertia

(B) headway

(C) stasis

Blank (ii)

(D) adlibbed

(E) impetuous

(F) premeditated

Blank (iii)

(G) predisposed

(H) confined

(I) prejudiced

145. The cuts and bruises from Justin's motorcycle accident are (i) _____ but the phobia caused by his near-death crash is (ii) _____, and it is unclear whether he will ever ride his motorcycle again. Knowing how much riding means to Justin, his family wants him to see a therapist to (iii) _____ his apprehension.

Blank (i)

(A)   evanescent

(B)   succinct

(C)   everlasting

Blank (ii)

(D)   relenting

(E)   perpetual

(F)   procuring

Blank (iii)

(G)   annihilate

(H)   motivate

(I)   quell

146. The loss of the championship game had him reeling, and Thom (i) _____ his misfortune for a number of weeks after it was over. His team was undefeated going into the game, so the loss was (ii) _____. To make matters worse, he had already planned a victory celebration, so seeing the party decorations only (iii) _____ his anguish after the game.

Blank (i)

(A)   gloated

(B)   rejoiced

(C)   bemoaned

Blank (ii)

(D)   debauched

(E)   astounding

(F)   sensational

Blank (iii)

(G)   defended

(H)   disregarded

(I)   amplified

147. Despite John's best attempts to reveal his affection for Millie, she remained (i) _____ to his advances, showing no interest in return. It wasn't that she didn't like John, but her feelings were (ii) _____ compared to his, and she didn't want to lead him on by giving (iii) _____ to his feelings for her.

Blank (i)

(A)   impervious

(B)   compliant

(C)   disloyal

Blank (ii)

(D)   unreceptive

(E)   considerable

(F)   subdued

Blank (iii)

(G)   skepticism

(H)   credence

(I)   tenacity

148. The paparazzi have the ability to make or break a celebrity's career, but they don't take this responsibility seriously. In one moment, they (i) _____ a star's latest box office success for his style and popularity, but at the first chance, they turn the tables and print (ii) _____ that turn popular opinion away from the same celebrity. It is disgraceful how they (iii) _____ without any regard to the effect on someone's personal life.

Blank (i)

(A) venerate

(B) summon

(C) spurn

Blank (ii)

(D) invectives

(E) panegyrics

(F) liabilities

Blank (iii)

(G) wield their power

(H) brandish their weapons

(I) employ their benevolence

149. The attack on Pearl Harbor by the Japanese in 1941 (i) _____ the United States' entry into World War II. Prior to this attack, the U.S. government had only provided aid to European allies, but had not actually fought, due to the (ii) _____ sentiment of the American public against intervening in the overseas conflict. However, when the conflict landed on U.S. soil, that sentiment (iii) _____ , and war was officially declared on Japan the very next day.

Blank (i)

(A) encumbered

(B) precipitated

(C) abridged

Blank (ii)

(D) inescapable

(E) pervasive

(F) gratuitous

Blank (iii)

(G) besmirched

(H) abated

(I) warped

150. Gandhi was a (i) _____ among men, staunchly abiding to his ideals of nonviolent protests and modest living, and he often fasted as a form of protest for civil rights and social reform. This level of discipline helped him remain (ii) _____ in the face of adversity and personal suffering. His willpower, determination, and compassion for people have made him a symbol of (iii) _____ in the history of civil rights.

Blank (i)

(A) Spartan

(B) brute

(C) warrior

Blank (ii)

(D) stalwart

(E) biddable

(F) pusillanimous

Blank (iii)

(G) belligerence

(H) philanthropy

(I) affability

Chapter 2

Reading Comprehension

• •

Reading Comprehension questions on the GRE comprise almost half of the Verbal questions. The questions are grouped by passage, where a single passage has one to five questions on it. The screen is split, with the passage on the left side and the question on the right. If the passage has more than one question, you see one question at a time, and the passage stays while the question changes.

All Reading Comprehension questions are based directly on what's in the passage. You don't need to know anything about the subject outside the passage. If you're familiar with the topic, you may easily comprehend the passage, but be careful not to mix your own knowledge of the topic with what's in the passage.

The Problems You'll Work On

When working through the questions in this chapter, be prepared to

- Choose one answer from a multiple-choice selection.
- Choose two or more answers from a multiple-choice selection.
- Select a sentence in the passage to answer the question.
- Answer questions based on biological and physical science topics, including physics, astronomy, chemistry, and astronomy.
- Understand the impact of social science topics, including history, psychology, and business.
- Get the gist of humanities topics, including art, music, philosophy, drama, and literature.

What to Watch Out For

Trap answers include the following

- Facts that aren't mentioned in the passage
- Information that's partly accurate and partly inaccurate
- Subtle distinctions with words such as *mostly, best,* and *primarily*

Choose the correct answer(s) for each reading comprehension question.

Questions 151 through 153 are based on the following passage.

It would seem unlikely that anything weighing 45 tons would move easily, but that is just what the male humpback whale does every winter. With a deft gracefulness, the massive sea mammal travels from the Gulf of Alaska to Hawaii in less than two months. Part of the baleen whale species, the male humpback can stretch 40 to 52 feet in length and weigh up to 45 tons. Even with those dimensions, the whales are able to propel themselves out of the ocean in a breach, revealing 40% to 90% of their bodies. The purpose of the breach is not completely understood, but different theories abound to explain this behavior, such as assertions of dominance, warnings to other whales in the pod, or as a form of courting.

The latter explanation, perhaps, makes the most sense concerning the North Pacific male humpback population in that the purpose of their mission is to mate with the females. Approximately two-thirds of the whales residing in the Gulf of Alaska travel more than 3,000 miles to breed and nurse their newborns during a five- to six-month period. The migration is a fierce race among the male humpbacks, who may be tracking a female with other competing males in order to be first in line when they reach the breeding grounds off the coast of Hawaii. A female whale only breeds every two to three years, and the gestation period is 11.5 months. These courting rituals, although turbulent in the social structure of humpback whales, make for entertaining displays for human spectators watching as the pods of males gather and breach to win the female's attention.

151. What is the best title for this passage?

  (A) "Courting Rituals of the Humpback Whale"

  (B) "Popular Breeding Grounds for Different Whale Species"

  (C) "To Alaska and Back: The Treacherous Journey of the Whale"

  (D) "The Motivating Factors of Whale Migration Activities"

  (E) "Great Place to Whale Watch"

152. What are the possible reasons male whales breach out of the water?

  Consider each of the three choices separately and select all that apply.

  [A] To attract the attention of female whales

  [B] To take a breath of air

  [C] To make a stand against other whales in the pod

153. Why did the author provide information about the female whale's birthing process?

  (A) To set a timeframe for whale migration

  (B) To express the intense nature of competition between male whales

  (C) To show the superiority of the female whale

  (D) To explain why whale migration is entertaining

  (E) To highlight the main point of the passage

Questions 154 through 158 are based on the following passage.

Theodor Adorno believed that the true value in knowledge is partly owed to the struggle to attain it. As a philosopher, critic, and musicologist, he often praised works that were difficult to comprehend, attesting that the richness of what is gained when working through the information or movement is more beneficial than easily digested ideas.

Adorno was born in 1903 in Frankfurt, Germany. He was the son of an opera singer, which likely led to his appreciation and immersion in the study of music. He began publishing essays concerning the work of German composers in 1925 while studying to be a concert pianist. He eventually received his doctorate degree in music, as well as in sociology and psychology.

In the late 1920s, Adorno became heavily influenced by certain parts of Marxist theory, namely, the relationship between economically driven innovation and social structure divisions. He began to formulate his theories on self-preservation and the disparities between capitalist motivation and the equity of distribution among the social classes. His ideas were strengthened by the rise of the fascist movement in Germany at the time. In 1931, he and fellow philosopher Max Horkheimer created the Frankfurt Institute for Social Research, as a way to address these issues.

Adorno was forced to flee Germany in 1934 after Adolf Hitler and his Nazi party began their genocidal campaign. He was able to reestablish the institute in New York City in 1938, where his authoritative attack on advanced capitalist theory became rooted. Over the next 30 years, he would write five books relating to critical theory and capitalism, as well as a number of musical compositions, for which he never lost his passion or talent. His early critiques of music expanded to all forms of art later in life, and he began to purport art as an embodiment of the subjective and divergent characteristics that challenge the conforming and homogenizing dominance of society.

The basis for much of Adorno's argument stemmed from this concept of standardization of society through the delineation of thought through economic growth and uniform conceptualization of mass media. He argued that popular media is shaped by cultural industry to sustain the dominance of capitalism and social inequality. In keeping the population passive, social media is able to conjure the false sensation of needs in a culture, diverting any free thought of what exists outside of those needs. In this way, socialist theories are expunged, and economic production is able to continue its reign as the predominant effort of the culture.

This focus on the cultural aspects of social segregation differentiated Adorno's theories from those of Marxism, for which he inevitably came to attribute its failure in society. During the political unrest of the 1960s, Adorno found himself the target of student activists who once heralded his line of thinking as revolutionary and an affront to the bourgeoisie. However, his lack of support for actions such as protests and sit-ins quickly moved him into a position of opposition in the students' eyes. His life ended in 1969 in the midst of this rejection.

154. What is the main idea of the passage?

(A) Theodor Adorno was a Marxist with many musical talents.

(B) Theodor Adorno was a progressive philosopher whose ideas challenged the fabric of global society and economic policies.

(C) Marxism is socialist theory that was popularized by Theodor Adorno.

(D) Music composition is a format used to understand social policies and development.

(E) Even famous members of the Jewish faith were persecuted by the Nazis in Germany.

155. According to the passage, Adorno saw the expression of art as

(A) not being significant in the context of social action.

(B) the only logical connection between a free society and governmental law.

(C) a hindrance to the growth of social capital.

(D) exemplifying the civil rights movement in America.

(E) signifying individual thought beyond the collective ideals of society.

156. Select the sentence from the fifth paragraph (reproduced below) that most efficiently describes Adorno's belief that social constructs, such as media sources, are manipulated for the purpose of maintaining a discrepant class structure.

(1) The basis for much of Adorno's argument stemmed from this concept of standardization of society through the delineation of thought through economic growth and uniform conceptualization of mass media. (2) He argued that popular media is shaped by cultural industry to sustain the dominance of capitalism and social inequality. (3) In keeping the population passive, social media is able to conjure the false sensation of needs in a culture, diverting any free thought of what exists outside of those needs. (4) In this way, socialist theories are expunged, and economic production is able to continue its reign as the predominant effort of the culture.

(A) The basis for much of Adorno's argument stemmed from this concept of standardization of society through the delineation of thought through economic growth and uniform conceptualization of mass media.

(B) He argued that popular media is shaped by cultural industry to sustain the dominance of capitalism and social inequality.

(C) In keeping the population passive, social media is able to conjure the false sensation of needs in a culture, diverting any free thought of what exists outside of those needs.

(D) In this way, socialist theories are expunged, and economic production is able to continue its reign as the predominant effort of the culture.

157. Which of the following statements about the change in student attitudes toward Adorno in the 1960s can best be inferred from the passage?

(A) They saw his lack of actions against the oppressive laws of segregation as a symbol of his concession.

(B) They felt supported by his philosophies and actions toward equality.

(C) They thought his philosophies further supported the segregation of races.

(D) They were pleased with the manner in which Adorno spoke out and rallied against segregation.

(E) They were finally able to generate enough support to expose Adorno's negative policies.

158. Why does the author most likely discuss Adorno's passion for music in this passage?

(A) Because it was the driving force in his life to compose the music of his country.

(B) Because he used music to help convince the world of the validity of his theories.

(C) Because he used musical theory to explain his social theories.

(D) Because his appreciation for creative works was a contributing factor in many of his academic theories.

(E) Because philosophy was only a small part of his contributions to the world.

Questions 159 through 162 are based on the following passage.

A recent study by researchers from the University of New South Wales states that attempting to find ways to coexist with the animal kingdom's top predators could save the world's ecosystems from unforeseen detrimental effects. Impacts of declining predator populations may be felt at the regional level — the areas in which these species currently reside — but could also cause climate changes because of environmental instability. Although top predators, such as lions, wolves, and leopards, may pose threats to humans and livestock, as well as their wild mammalian prey, the loss of these animals due to competition for food among each other and land with the expansion of civilization has a significant cascading outcome on ecosystems.

Researchers pointed to the treatment of dingoes in Australia as an example of this impact. Because of rampant destruction of livestock populations in many heavy sheep-grazing regions of the country, a dingo-proof fence was erected to keep them out. However, the lack of dingoes in certain areas led to an increase in the fox population, which concurrently led to a number of smaller mammalian species becoming extinct because they are preyed upon by foxes. Conversely, the kangaroo population has flourished due to the lack of dingoes, which has disrupted the vegetation and ecology of certain plant species, such as grasses. Although no specific solution was provided in the study for how to address these issues, the introduction of other techniques, such as guard dogs, could allow dingoes to remain in an area without posing a threat to economic endeavors.

159. The author is most likely addressing this passage to

(A) animal rights groups.

(B) teachers.

(C) land developers.

(D) policymakers.

(E) zoo owners.

160. The function of the second paragraph is to

(A) highlight the dingo population in Australia.

(B) showcase a fail-proof system of predator management.

(C) provide an example of how ecosystems and animal populations change due to predator activity.

(D) provide an example of how not to manage predatory behavior in Australia.

(E) provide an example of what will happen if other regions do not take the same measures Australia did against the dingoes.

161. The conclusion that can be reached from the discussion about dingo-proof fences is that

(A) the use of dingo-proof fences is inhumane because dingoes no longer have the food they need to survive.

(B) kangaroos are a bigger problem than dingoes in Australia.

(C) dingo-proof fences improved the stability of the sheep-herding industry.

(D) dingoes don't hunt kangaroos.

(E) the dingo-proof fences help to protect the livestock, but they create other subsequent negative consequences.

162. According to the passage, why is it important to protect the world's ecosystems?

(A) Because changes to the Earth's physical environment can lead to changes in the synthesis of environmental processes, leading to climate change and other detrimental effects.

(B) Because the environment is the most important thing to humankind.

(C) Because ecosystems must remain stagnant so all species are able to thrive.

(D) Because changes in ecosystems lead to changes in how humans manage the environment, which could have detrimental effects on animal populations.

(E) Because top predators rely on the ecosystems to find their prey.

Questions 163 through 167 are based on the following passage.

Despite a number of trials along the way, American sprinter and long-jump phenomenon Carl Lewis is one of the most successful Olympic athletes of all time. With nine Olympic gold medals and eight World Championship gold medals, it would seem that Lewis would enjoy a life of accolades and admiration. Yet, much of his career was plagued with negative press and sentiments from sponsors and teammates because of his perceived attitude on and off the track.

Born to middle-class parents in 1961, Lewis was exposed to cultural and artistic pursuits, such as music and theater. He played the cello and piano and took dance lessons as a young man. His talent as an athlete was hidden by his stature, initially being very short for a boy his age. However, when he was 15 years old, Lewis hit a growth spurt that would stretch him almost 3 inches in a month's time. This rapid growth proved to be too much for his small frame, and he was required to walk with crutches until he grew into his new physique.

Peaking at 6'2", the now long-limbed Lewis excelled at track and field, setting the national prep record his senior year of high school at 26'8". One year later, he qualified for the Moscow Olympics as a freshman at the University of Houston. Unfortunately, an American boycott of the 1980 Summer Olympics impeded his ability to compete. Nonetheless, Lewis continued to blaze through the record books, earning the distinction of being the top U.S. amateur athlete in 1981. This title was clearly his after becoming only the second person in U.S. history to win both the long jump and 100-meter dash at the college championships.

Lewis's trouble with his public image started shortly before the 1984 Olympic Games. As a star collegiate athlete, he had received sponsorship from Nike while still in school. His confidence in his natural talent and his rising popularity left a feeling in society that he was an arrogant and self-serving athlete. Despite his protests of the allegations, he was seen as promoting only himself at the 1984 Los Angeles games, rather than behaving like a member of the U.S. team and supporting the sanctity of the Olympics themselves. The backlash from this image was a lack of corporate sponsorship, which anyone else undoubtedly would have received after winning four gold medals. Lewis also became unpopular with his teammates because of his condemnation of those who used performance-enhancing drugs.

However, the issues with the public and his teammates never hindered Lewis's ability to succeed, and he competed in three more Olympic Games, claiming a number of medals in the 100- and 200-meter races and long jump. In fact, he was able to attain the No. 1 ranking in the long jump with his 1996 Olympic performance, reclaiming it 15 years after reaching it for the first time. After 18 years as a track and field star, Lewis finally retired in 1997. His legacy has superseded his perceived arrogance, and he was named both Sportsman of the Century in 1999 and Olympian of the Century in 2001.

163. What role does the third paragraph play in the passage?

(A) It highlights his accomplishments as an athlete.

(B) It describes the main point of the passage.

(C) It shows the reader what his childhood was like.

(D) It proves that he was an Olympic champion.

(E) It shows how his attitude changed with his success.

164. Select the sentence from the fourth paragraph (reproduced below) that explains why Carl Lewis's public image started to wane.

(1) Lewis's trouble with his public image started shortly before the 1984 Olympic Games. (2) As a star collegiate athlete, he had received sponsorship from Nike while still in school. (3) His confidence in his natural talent and his rising popularity left a feeling in society that he was an arrogant and self-serving athlete. (4) Despite his protests of the allegations, he was seen as promoting only himself at the 1984 Los Angeles games, rather than behaving like a member of the U.S. team and supporting the sanctity of the Olympics themselves. (5) The backlash from this image was a lack of corporate sponsorship, which anyone else undoubtedly would have received after winning four gold medals. (6) Lewis also became unpopular with his teammates because of his condemnation of those who used performance-enhancing drugs.

(A) Lewis's trouble with his public image started shortly before the 1984 Olympic Games.

(B) As a star collegiate athlete, he had received sponsorship from Nike while still in school.

(C) His confidence in his natural talent and his rising popularity left a feeling in society that he was an arrogant and self-serving athlete.

(D) The backlash from this image was a lack of corporate sponsorship, which anyone else undoubtedly would have received after winning four gold medals.

(E) Lewis also became unpopular with his teammates because of his condemnation of those who used performance-enhancing drugs.

165. Lewis became less popular in the eyes of his teammates for which reason?

Consider each of the three choices separately and select all that apply.

[A] They felt he was not a team player.

[B] They were jealous of his Olympic success.

[C] They resented his judgments about their drug use.

166. Why did the author discuss Lewis's growth spurt?

(A) Because it caused him to run funny

(B) Because it signifies the adversity he overcame

(C) Because he thought he would never be able to run

(D) Because it caused him to struggle as an athlete

(E) Because it was hard on him and his family

167. The tone of the passage is

(A) supportive.

(B) judgmental.

(C) informative.

(D) harried.

(E) personal.

Questions 168 through 170 are based on the following passage.

Each year, people travel hundreds of miles to catch a glimpse of the ever elusive, yet magical aurora borealis, also called the northern lights. The lights appear as a constantly shifting swirl of colors dancing in the night sky. Although many people have seen the lights, your chances of stumbling across an occurrence are slim unless you live in the northern hemisphere. Residents of Alaska, Canada, and areas surrounding the Antarctic circle see the lights more often due to their positioning near the aurora oval, which is centered on the magnetic pole. Although, even people in these areas can't predict when the lights will appear.

The haphazard nature of the aurora borealis is because of the mechanism behind it. The mystical illusion occurs when highly charged electrons in the solar wind combine with oxygen and nitrogen atoms in the earth's atmosphere. This wind flows away from the sun towards the earth. It follows the magnetic force created by the earth's core and enters the magnetosphere, a small area of magnetic and electrical fields. The combination of the atmospheric elements and the electrons happens anywhere from 20 to 200 miles in altitude. Depending on the altitude and which atom is interacted with, different colors are created. The constant flow of the wind through the atoms causes the dancing sensation of the colors.

168. Based on the passage, how frequently do residents of the northern hemisphere see the aurora borealis?

(A) Whenever the solar winds combine with atoms in the atmosphere

(B) Every hour

(C) When the sun passes over the magnetosphere

(D) Once a month

(E) Only when they are in Canada

169. Which of the following statements about the northern lights can be inferred from the passage?

(A) It is fairly common for people all over the world to see the northern lights.

(B) The northern lights can only be seen in a very remote area that is hard to get to.

(C) The northern lights change color based on the weather in Antarctica.

(D) The popularity of the northern lights has been decreasing in recent years.

(E) The northern lights are seen as a tourist attraction.

170. Different colors are created in the sky depending on

(A) whether there are electrical fields in the atmosphere.

(B) the speed the solar wind is traveling.

(C) the distance from the north pole.

(D) the combination of altitude and atmospheric elements.

(E) the haphazard nature of the aurora borealis.

Questions 171 through 173 are based on the following passage.

Although parasites represent almost 50 percent of all the life forms on the planet, their existence is often regarded as deleterious and with disdain. Scientists at the American Museum of Natural History have discovered that a majority of researchers have portrayed parasites as nothing more than disease spreading, life-killing pests, mainly because of their blight on many useful and popular species. However, a number of parasitic organisms are vital for the continued success of certain biological and ecological processes, and promotion of parasitic conservation is just as important as any other creature.

For instance, parasites serve as a major player in evolution and population by causing the host species to continually adapt and evolve as the parasite continues to adjust and thrive. Furthermore, scientists are exploring many health benefits of parasitic activity in humans, such as that concerning the sickle-cell gene and malaria. The relationship between how the protein make-up of the gene affecting the red blood cells and providing protection from the *Plasmodium falciparum,* the parasite that causes severe forms of malaria, is still unknown, but evidence suggests that the parasite itself is serving as the vehicle transporting the red blood cells into the body. More information is needed to fully understand the varied roles of parasites in the natural world.

171. The author thinks that parasites are

(A) deleterious.

(B) endangered.

(C) complex.

(D) a blight.

(E) diseased.

172. According to the passage, parasite conservation

(A) is important in the natural processes of the animal kingdom.

(B) is vital for the safety of other species.

(C) is necessary for finding a cure for malaria.

(D) should focus on banning scientific experiments using parasites.

(E) is the responsibility of the American Museum of Natural History.

173. What is the central idea of the passage?

(A) Parasites are no longer considered disgusting creatures.

(B) Maintaining a viable parasite population is important for researching their function in biological processes.

(C) Scientists see parasite activity as groundbreaking for the advancement of disease prevention.

(D) Parasites have the ability to cause the breakdown and extinction of certain biological processes.

(E) Conservation is not a realistic option for parasites.

Questions 174 through 178 are based on the following passage.

The slow food movement isn't just about preserving local foods that are fresh, clean, and humanely acquired. It is also about preserving a way of life that is almost obsolete in the heavily

industrialized agribusiness of the 20th and 21st centuries. Whereas the food people ate used to be provided by local farmers and dictated by the seasons, now machines and chemicals are used to create the food feeding more than 95 percent of the world's population. Variety in foods and flavors has been replaced by ease of mass production as the priority of eating, with just approximately 30 types of food making up a majority of the products sold in America's grocery stores.

Although mainstream agribusiness is so entrenched in the marketplace, changing the habits of 6.5 billion people across the globe is unlikely. Still, since 1986, an ever-growing group of people has been promoting the use of food that is grown, raised, and harvested in a safe and clean manner that properly supports the farmers who provide it. This movement also attempts to support endangered foods and chefs cooking under this ideology. Slow food chapters around the world hold events showcasing these chefs and foods to spread awareness and inform the public about the negative cultural and health effects of industrialized food. The movement now boasts more than 100,000 members and continues to grow.

174. For what reason did the author include the information about grocery stores containing only 30 types of food?

(A) To contradict the main point of the passage

(B) To support the first statement of the sentence

(C) To provide evidence against the second sentence

(D) To create a focus in the paragraph

(E) To add a controversial element

175. Select the sentence from the first paragraph (reproduced below) that best portrays the guiding principle that helped establish the slow food movement.

(1) The slow food movement isn't just about preserving local foods that are fresh, clean, and humanely acquired. (2) It is also about preserving a way of life that is almost obsolete in the heavily industrialized agribusiness of the 20th and 21st centuries. (3) Whereas the food people ate used to be provided by local farmers and dictated by the seasons, now machines and chemicals are used to create the food feeding more than 95 percent of the world's population. (4) Variety in foods and flavors has been replaced by ease of mass production as the priority of eating, with just approximately 30 types of food making up a majority of the products sold in America's grocery stores.

(A) The slow food movement isn't just about preserving local foods that are fresh, clean, and humanely acquired.

(B) It is also about preserving a way of life that is almost obsolete in the heavily industrialized agribusiness of the 20th and 21st centuries.

(C) Whereas the food people ate used to be provided by local farmers and dictated by the seasons, now machines and chemicals are used to create the food feeding more than 95% of the world's population.

(D) Variety in foods and flavors has been replaced by ease of mass production as the priority of eating, with just approximately 30 types of food making up a majority of the products sold in America's grocery stores.

176. Which of the following statements are true about the slow food movement?

Consider each of the three choices and select all that apply.

[A] 6.5 billion people can't be wrong.

[B] Abiding by the rules of the movement is more convenient than eating processed foods.

[C] Food prepared using the slow food method is better for the body.

177. You can conclude that because 95 percent of the world's population consumes processed food

(A) the movement is not very successful.

(B) 95 percent of the world's population is unhealthy.

(C) people don't like variety in their food.

(D) the movement is reaching every facet of the world.

(E) the movement needs to grow significantly to make more of an impact.

178. What should this article be titled?

(A) "The War Against Processed Food"

(B) "Why Slow Food Is Out of Fashion"

(C) "The Effort to Grow Better Food"

(D) "The Popularity of the Slow Food Movement"

(E) "Changing the Global Food Paradigm"

Questions 179 through 183 are based on the following passage.

When D.H. Lawrence wrote *Lady Chatterley's Lover* in the late 1920s, the book was received with outrage and was banned for its anti-puritan content and sexually explicit scenes. However, the impact of this book is not in how it challenged a conservative and religious society in the first half of the century, but in how it shaped a nation and subsequent world in the latter half. On October 21, 1960, the trial of the Crown of England against Penguin Books, also referred to as Lady Chatterley's trial, set the stage for a sexual revolution and tolerance that transformed the concepts of decency and whose influence can be seen in today's liberal and open culture.

The Crown prosecuted Penguin for being in breach of the Obscene Publications Act; however, a loophole existed that stated a work deemed to have literary merit was exempt from the laws encompassed in this act. The prosecution attempted to expose the lewd and depraved content of Lawrence's book in support of its ban in England, but few witnesses came forward to testify on that behalf. In fact, many people, including members of the clergy, came forward to defend the book as an important addition to the literary canon.

Without a case, Penguin was acquitted in six days. Following this decision, the book not only became a bestseller, but it also soldiered in an era where morality and behavior were mandated by the government, even in the private sector of society. Censorship became less and less acceptable, and a formerly chaste culture found a new liberalism and openness to sexuality and freedom of expression. With the popularity of books such as *Fifty Shades of Grey* in the mainstream media, society owes a debt of gratitude to the jurors involved in Lady Chatterley's trial for paving the way.

179. The prosecution failed to prove its case against Penguin because

  (A) a new law legalized lewd publications during the trial.

  (B) they could not prove the book did not have literary merit.

  (C) their witnesses lied on the stand.

  (D) the evidence showed the book did not contain lewd content.

  (E) the Crown dropped the charges.

180. Based on the passage, what was the biggest impact the book had on society?

  (A) Penguin became the largest publisher in the world.

  (B) The victory over the Crown of England was the first ever.

  (C) It broke down strict moral codes of conduct in society.

  (D) The Obscene Publications Act was denounced.

  (E) It paved the way for *Fifty Shades of Grey*.

181. Why does the author say that *Lady Chatterley's Lover* "transformed the concepts of decency?"

  (A) The sentiment in society before the book's publication strictly prohibited indecent behavior.

  (B) People were less polite after the book was published.

  (C) The book fell from the bestseller's list.

  (D) Society was boorish and promiscuous before the book was published.

  (E) The Obscene Publications Act was enacted as a result of the publication.

182. According to the passage, for which reasons does society owe a debt of gratitude to the jurors?

Consider each of the three choices and select all that apply.

  [A] For allowing the book to be published

  [B] For helping to overturn censorship laws

  [C] For initiating a movement toward a more liberal view of sexuality

183. The author's attitude toward the trial outcome can best be described as

   (A) amazed at the atrocity of allowing such a book to be read.

   (B) excited about the lack of censorship in the world.

   (C) annoyed that the prosecution didn't make a good case.

   (D) scholarly interest in cases versus the Crown of England.

   (E) intrigued by the trial's impact on society.

Questions 184 through 187 are based on the following passage.

Popular culture has brought the concept of zombies into the norm with a myriad of movies and television shows depicting the undead roaming the streets and forests in search of anything with a breath of life still in it. The zombie craze has developed the concept of a zombie apocalypse, and whether you believe it or not, a number of reputable organizations and publications have gotten on board.

For instance, the *Huffington Post* published an article detailing the essentials needed to survive the zombie apocalypse, and many retailers and private citizens have created survival kits you can purchase online. In fact, the Centers for Disease Control printed an article on their "Public Health Matters Blog" about the best way to prepare your family in the event of the apocalypse. The CDC also noted that these measures were appropriate, in general, for other major epidemic or social crises, which perhaps leads to the underlying nature of these predictions.

That the earth will ever be taken over by zombies has never been suggested. No evidence exists of such an event or even of the existence of one single zombie. But there are many historical cases of disease and consequences of actions of war creating mass destruction and sweeping fatalities in society. It is possible that the fascination with zombies is merely a cover for a deep-rooted fear of an Ebola outbreak or nuclear attack, and painting a brain-eating picture on this fear assuages the intensity and reality of such a

horrific occurrence. Regardless, maybe having an emergency kit and plan is better than nothing.

184. Based on the passage, when will the zombie apocalypse take place?

   (A) Likely soon

   (B) After a nuclear attack

   (C) During a massive disease outbreak

   (D) Never

   (E) When everyone is prepared

185. The author's attitude toward the zombie apocalypse is

   (A) skeptical that it will happen.

   (B) concerned about how to prepare.

   (C) fearful of the idea of zombies.

   (D) mocking of those who believe in it.

   (E) bleak about society's prospects for survival.

186. The third paragraph serves what function in the passage?

   (A) It provides evidence to support the existence of zombies.

   (B) It places blame on the CDC for the apocalypse.

   (C) It provides a theory about the fascination with the zombie apocalypse.

   (D) It synthesizes the research from the CDC and the *Huffington Post.*

   (E) It provides the author's opinion about the CDC.

187. What should this passage be titled?

(A) "Preparing for the Zombie Apocalypse"

(B) "How to Prevent the Zombie Apocalypse"

(C) "When Zombies Come Calling"

(D) "Society's Fear and Fascination with Zombies"

(E) "The Causes of the Zombie Apocalypse"

Questions 188 through 190 are based on the following passage.

Is it a fun form of community building, or is it a detriment to the safety of local citizens and businesses? That is the primary question facing many law enforcement agencies across the country concerning flash mobs. What originally started as a funny trend in the early 2000s, with large groups of people conducting spontaneous dance routines or other disruptive antics, has taken on a new trend of commotion, referred to as *flash robs*. Although not merely involving group vandalism and robberies, these criminal forms of flash mobs, organized and perpetrated mostly by teens, are also turning violent, with assaults on pedestrians and destruction of private property becoming an increasing problem. This trend has become so pervasive in certain areas that police and city officials are scrambling to understand how to handle and avert these threats in their communities.

The challenge of thwarting these flash events exists in the legitimacy of monitoring the forms of communication being used to organize the gatherings. Facebook, texts messages, and Twitter are a few of the forms of social media teens use to spread the word about an upcoming flash incident. Successfully staying abreast of this information would likely require tapping into private social accounts, which many organizations and politicians fear would violate civil rights laws. Also, many agencies don't have the staff in place or the funding to dedicate someone to 24-hour social media surveillance. The conundrum of how to squelch criminal acts in the community without breaching individual rights and whether community-based regulations, such as curfews for adolescents, are enough to protect their citizens are issues that the government will need to look into in the future.

188. According to the passage, why is it difficult for law enforcement to thwart flash robs?

(A) Because no crimes are being committed

(B) Because they do not have the knowledge of how these events are organized

(C) Because the methods needed to catch the perpetrators may be unconstitutional

(D) Because their surveillance is only for part of the day

(E) Because they don't have Facebook accounts

189. What is the main difference between flash mobs and flash robs?

(A) Flash mobs cause the destruction of property.

(B) Flash mobs only aim to entertain or innocently disrupt the peace momentarily.

(C) Flash robs are organized by career criminals.

(D) There is no difference.

(E) Flash robs started before flash mobs.

190. The idea of a community-enforced curfew for minors would be a great solution to the flash rob problem if which of the following statements were true?

(A) The police use secret technologies to track videos of flash robs in action.

(B) Parents are able to override the curfew if they see fit.

(C) Both adults and teens organize flash robs.

(D) The curfew is only for teens with previous records.

(E) Flash robs only occur in the evenings.

Questions 191 through 195 are based on the following passage.

The advent of the Affordable Care Act highlights an important cyclic occurrence in the history of social work. The need for social workers in the health system will increase substantially, and their roles will mirror those of the social work profession's founding members. By examining the etiology of medical social work and the predominant population being served at that time, the increasing importance of social workers in the medical arena today is apparent in the comparable population of uninsured and underserved individuals for whom they will advocate.

Health social work has experienced tremendous growth since its establishment in the early 20th century. An immense migration of more than 35 million Europeans to lower Manhattan Island in New York City between 1820 and 1924 created a health crisis due to overcrowded tenements, unsanitary living conditions, food shortages, and a high rate of infant deaths. Multiple languages and cultural conceptions about how illness is treated complicated the issue and confounded medical providers.

Because of the cultural and demographic disparities, medical professionals began to change their notions about health and the barriers to proper health. With the elucidation of this cultural context, Dr. Richard Cabot, a physician from Massachusetts, hired the first social worker with his own money in 1905. This position became the foundation for the initiation of the health social worker. Cabot believed that the social worker should serve as a liaison between the doctor and patient, scrutinizing all aspects of care and disseminating medicine in a social context. He envisioned that the hospital social worker would communicate with the patients about the social and mental factors involved in their illness and treatment.

Cabot was right. This bidirectional communication led to a decrease of recurring patients and conditions, which drew the attention of the American Medical Association and other prominent organizations in the first quarter of the century. The success of the health social worker was undeniable, and the placement of social workers in the hospital setting became more prevalent. By 1954, the American Association of Medical Social Workers lauded 2,100 members.

Specific actions by the government created a system of increasing costs for healthcare in the 1960s that remains the current trend and hinders the ability of social workers to adequately represent their clients. However, with the Affordable Care Act, vast areas of potential benefit for social workers exist. A staggering 21 million individuals are projected to remain uninsured under the Act by 2015 due to their undocumented status and the barriers involved in purchasing insurance under the new coverage exchanges. Social workers will be vital to integrate and coordinate care to improve patient experiences and liaise with hospitals and physicians.

Although the social work field has weathered multiple challenges, its preliminary focus on client-centeredness is as evident today as in Cabot's time. Similarly, the population of those requiring the most services resembles the immigrant population that filtered into Ellis Island at the turn of the 20th century. The current increasing number of immigrants and refugees, as well as individuals affected by violence and war, is one of the main challenges under the coming healthcare system. Convincing the medical field of the importance of social factors in health and adapting how they treat the sick seem to echo the challenges presented to early health social workers. It is important to look at how the pioneers of social work successfully served their clients toward achieving optimal health outcomes and translate that work to mitigate the challenges to come.

191. Which of the following most accurately states the main idea of the passage?

(A) Social workers are vital to the health-care field to help immigrants sign up for insurance under the Affordable Care Act.

(B) The need for social workers in the health arena is largely due to the diverse demographics of patients requiring services.

(C) The immigrant population in the United States is just as big as it was in the early 20th century.

(D) Social workers should be providing more services to immigrants who are unable to receive health insurance.

(E) The problem with healthcare today is the same as it was in the early 1900s, despite the new Affordable Care Act.

192. Which of the following is the reason that the author mentions the immigrant population filtering into Ellis Island?

Consider each of the choices separately and select all that apply.

[A] To point out how people without health insurance are living in the same circumstances as the immigrants from Ellis Island

[B] To express the similarities between the need for social work in the medical arena then and now

[C] To draw attention to the characteristics of the population still experiencing a lack in health services in the current society

193. Which of the following statements about social work can be inferred from the passage?

(A) Without the Affordable Care Act, there would be no social work.

(B) Despite changes in the healthcare system, social work has stayed true to its founding principles.

(C) Social work has made it possible for immigrants and impoverished individuals to receive the care they need.

(D) The history of social work is more important than what is happening today with best practices.

(E) Social work has not changed since the first social worker was introduced into the hospital setting.

194. Which statement best represents the author's attitude about the Affordable Care Act?

(A) The Affordable Care Act was important for revealing a pattern in the healthcare system.

(B) More jobs will be available to health social workers thanks to the Affordable Care Act.

(C) The Affordable Care Act provides an opportunity for health social workers to get back to their roots.

(D) Because of the Affordable Care Act, health social workers will find themselves needed in ways similar to those of their founding members.

(E) The Affordable Care Act is only worthwhile if health social workers are involved.

195. Select the sentence from the fifth paragraph (reproduced below) that explains why health social workers will be important under the Affordable Care Act.

(1) Specific actions by the government created a system of increasing costs for healthcare in the 1960s that remains the current trend and hinders the ability of social workers to adequately represent their clients. (2) However, with the Affordable Care Act, vast areas of potential benefit for social workers exist. (3) A staggering 21 million individuals are projected to remain uninsured under the Act by 2015 due to their undocumented status and the barriers involved in purchasing insurance under the new coverage exchanges. (4) Social workers will be vital to integrate and coordinate care to improve patient experiences and liaise with hospitals and physicians.

(A) Specific actions by the government created a system of increasing costs for healthcare in the 1960s that remains the current trend and hinders the ability of social workers to adequately represent their clients.

(B) However, with the Affordable Care Act, vast areas of potential benefit for social workers exist.

(C) A staggering 21 million individuals are projected to remain uninsured under the Act by 2015 due to their undocumented status and the barriers involved in purchasing insurance under the new coverage exchanges.

(D) Social workers will be vital to integrate and coordinate care to improve patient experiences and liaise with hospitals and physicians.

Questions 196 through 200 are based on the following passage.

Search Engine Optimization (SEO) has become a popular tactic by individuals hoping to drive visitors to their web pages. The practice involves understanding the mechanisms of search engines, how people use search engines, and which terms or images will most effectively tap into the searches made by their desired audience. Once these factors are understood, page text and design codes can be manipulated to promote a person's page when search results are provided. The usefulness and competitive edge SEO creates for a webmaster is so great, many companies now hire people skilled solely in this task.

However, when first introduced, it was discovered that webmasters were duplicating content from other competing sites or creating false pages stuffed with keywords to tip the scales in their favor. When popular search engines, such as Google and Yahoo, realized the underhandedness of these actions, they changed their ranking algorithms to block the inundation of falsely inflated keywords and linkages from webmasters looking to undermine the system. These algorithms have continuously been revamped as more information and knowledge about SEO has come to the surface. However, the whole point of sites like Google, Bing, and Yahoo is to provide accurate and advantageous search results for their users. Thus, working with SEO practitioners to explain the most optimal strategies creates a symbiotic relationship where each entity can operate fairly and successfully.

196. According to the passage, search engines consistently change their algorithms because

(A) it is standard practice.

(B) the algorithms expire after every few years and must be updated.

(C) viruses cause the linking mechanism of the algorithms to fail.

(D) it blocks webmasters from SEO practices.

(E) webmasters figure out how to manipulate the search engine to inflate their ranking.

197. The author's attitude toward SEO can best be described as

(A) supportive of the practice.

(B) distant from the whole concept.

(C) bitter about the level of competition on the web.

(D) excited about the effectiveness.

(E) uninformed about the latest updates.

198. This passage is primarily concerned with

(A) the pros and cons of search engine optimization.

(B) the efficiency and process involved in search engine optimization.

(C) top search engines and the most searched topics.

(D) how to create the most successful SEO campaign.

(E) unethical practices of webmasters.

199. Which of the following statements about search engine companies can best be inferred from the passage?

(A) They create algorithms that allow webmasters to monopolize most of the Internet traffic.

(B) They are highly competitive with SEO practitioners.

(C) Creating a positive relationship with webmasters supports both entities in positive ways.

(D) There are only three search engines left.

(E) They manipulate the Internet to make it more difficult for SEO to work.

200. Select the phrase that best represents the result of the validity of SEO.

(A) Many companies now hire people skilled solely in this task.

(B) The practice involves understanding the mechanisms of search engines.

(C) Once these factors are understood, page text and design codes can be manipulated.

(D) These algorithms have continuously been revamped as more information and knowledge about SEO have come to the surface.

(E) Working with SEO practitioners to explain the most optimal strategies creates a symbiotic relationship.

Questions 201 through 205 are based on the following passage.

The art of Feng Shui has become synonymous with "new age" and attributed to spiritualists or hippies. The practice is not considered very beneficial on a practical level by most contemporaries, and popular culture all but dismisses its relevance as a means of attaining a peaceful and productive home. Yet, the concepts of Feng Shui are not new at all. In fact, the principles and practice have been around since the Jin Dynasty of the early part of the century.

Any Internet search can give readers tips on where to place the bed and what location is best for the proper placement of certain items, such as electronics and furniture. But when digging deeper into the art, it is revealed that many more elements are considered when designing the perfect Feng Shui residence.

When practicing the true art of Feng Shui, individuals must take into consideration factors such as Qi, or energy, that exists in an environment. What items enhance or detract from this Qi? At what points in the day is the Qi strongest, and when is it most diminished? How does your personal Qi interact with the environmental Qi? Then, how do factors such as natural light, wind, climate, and architecture influence the Qi in the home? Once these questions are answered, purposeful decision making is possible regarding the appropriate colors, fabrics, pieces of furniture, lighting, aromatics, and placement of household items.

For example, certain colors mix with certain levels of Qi to produce an environment that promotes wealth or stability. The way a person uses Feng Shui in their home is based on what they want to manifest in their lives and how they want energy to flow throughout the rooms.

Although it is not likely that the art of Feng Shui will gain pop culture status or become mainstream for interior decorators, learning more about the principles could be of major benefit to modern societies. These benefits are unknown and possibly endless, but those who are deeply familiar with the practice understand the implications if city planners and architects put more thought in how they design public structures. The power of Qi to create reality could serve facilities, such as hospitals or educational institutions, well in promoting the appropriate environments for healing and learning, respectively.

201. Which of the following would be the best title for the passage?

(A) "The Feng Shui Boom"

(B) "The Lost Art of Feng Shui"

(C) "Creating Your Best Space with Feng Shui"

(D) "Dos and Don'ts of Feng Shui"

(E) "How to Create Qi in the Home"

202. The tone of the passage is

(A) aloof.

(B) forceful.

(C) pushy.

(D) promotional.

(E) defeated.

203. The primary function of the third paragraph is to

(A) provide a history of Feng Shui.

(B) determine which fabrics best suit you according to Feng Shui principles.

(C) criticize people who do not believe in the art of Feng Shui.

(D) give advice on finding the most Qi in your home.

(E) describe the factors involved in true Feng Shui.

204. According to the passage, city planners might benefit from Feng Shui principles because

(A) schools would serve students better if they were located closer to hospitals.

(B) everybody should understand Feng Shui.

(C) certain colors should be used for certain types of buildings.

(D) understanding the relationship between space and energy could lead to appropriate design of city structures and grounds.

(E) Qi exists everywhere and can be used for great things.

205. When determining the best Feng Shui for your home, what factors do you need to consider?

Consider each of the three choices separately, and select all that apply.

[A] How your Qi works with the environmental Qi

[B] What colors support your Qi

[C] Where your Qi is strongest

Questions 206 through 210 are based on the following passage.

It is not very common for the public to know specific details about a specialty field like architecture, but one name stands out from the rest: Frank Lloyd Wright. Perhaps the reason is that he was so prolific during his active years, designing more than 1,100 structures and completing 532 of them. Whatever the reason, his mark on classic and contemporary architecture is not only valued by the world, but also visible in many of the world's biggest cities and a few smaller communities.

Wright was a born architect, experiencing his first taste of structural design on his family farm in Wisconsin as a young man. Both a high school and college dropout, Wright left the confines of institutionalized education to pursue his passion in Chicago in 1887. Once he touched down in the Windy City, the world of architecture would never be the same. Rather than focusing on European design concepts and pragmatic functionality, Wright believed that form and function were a single entity and space was something to be honored, not partitioned. His early homes turned away from conventional room encasements and opted for connecting rooms with free-form structures, such as fireplaces as the centerpieces of the home and differing window placements to cast varying forms of light.

When Wright started designing larger buildings, his sentimentality came through, displaying a disdain for urban sprawl and a love of the natural environment. He often used natural materials and created shapes that mimicked items seen in the natural world. Buildings were created in the shape of trees, and elements allowing natural light to engulf a room were a common feature. The prowess and vision Wright had for creating grand structures was evident early on. Students and practitioners have attempted to emulate his style, and today, his influence can be seen in not only the form of many standing structures, but also in how function is incorporated to better serve the natural tendencies of life.

206. Which of the following is mentioned as a convention used by Wright?

Consider each of the three choices separately, and select all that apply.

[A] He partitioned rooms into separate entities.

[B] He created structures that mimicked the natural world.

[C] He thought natural light distorted open spaces.

207. Which of the following statements about Wright's influence can be inferred from the passage?

(A) His work has influenced how people think about form and function.

(B) More people are now creating more natural light in their homes.

(C) Only students in architect courses feel his influence.

(D) Wright's work is located in select destinations.

(E) Wright's techniques are the only principles taught in architecture courses.

208. The passage is primarily concerned with

(A) showcasing the popular buildings Wright designed.

(B) informing about Wright's past and growth as an architect.

(C) Wright's passion for the environment.

(D) Wright's life on the family farm.

(E) the number of buildings Wright constructed.

209. Based on the passage, how successful was Wright in constructing his designs?

(A) Almost completely successful

(B) Not stated in the passage

(C) Moderately successful

(D) Very successful

(E) Unsuccessful

210. Select the sentence that describes Wright's vision as an architect.

Wright was a born architect, experiencing his first taste of structural design on his family farm in Wisconsin as a young man. Both a high school and college dropout, Wright left the confines of institutionalized education to pursue his passion in Chicago in 1887. Once he touched down in the Windy City, the world of architecture would never be the same. Rather than focusing on European design concepts and pragmatic functionality, Wright believed that form and function were a single entity and space was something to be honored, not partitioned. His early homes turned away from conventional room encasements and opted for connecting rooms with free-form structures, such as fireplaces as the centerpieces of the home and differing window placements to cast varying forms of light.

When Wright started designing larger buildings, his sentimentality came through, displaying a disdain for urban sprawl and a love of the natural environment. He often used natural materials and created shapes that mimicked items seen in the natural world. Buildings were created in the shape of trees, and elements allowing natural light to engulf a room were a common feature. The prowess and vision Wright had for creating grand structures was evident early on. Students and practitioners have attempted to emulate his style, and today, his influence can be seen in not only the form of many standing structures, but also in how function is incorporated to better serve the natural tendencies of life.

(A) The prowess and vision Wright had for creating grand structures was evident early on.

(B) Wright believed that form and function were a single entity and space was something to be honored, not partitioned.

(C) Students and practitioners have attempted to emulate his style.

(D) His sentimentality came through, displaying a disdain for urban sprawl and a love of the natural environment.

(E) Wright was a born architect, experiencing his first taste of structural design on his family farm in Wisconsin as a young man.

Questions 211 through 213 are based on the following passage.

The career of Dr. John exemplifies the creative and persistent fortitude that allows an artist to find success without ever reaching fame. Despite early regard as an eclectic guitarist and keyboardist, his greatest success would come from his unique voice, which was gruff and dripping with New Orleans flare. Lending his voice to television advertisements and voiceovers, he was able to remain visible on the scene.

Dr. John began his career as a promising studio performer for the likes of some of New Orleans's biggest R&B and blues musicians in the 1950s. He quickly learned the trade of producer and helped fellow musicians with their musical arrangements and track productions. However, an injury to his hand caused him to quit the guitar, and in the early 1960s, he began focusing solely on the keyboard. Trouble with local authorities and the underbelly of the Big Easy led to a life change that took him to Los Angeles.

Dr. John is best known for his outlandish dress in traditional Mardi Gras attire and his creation of a mysterious new sound, described as a mix of New Orleans blues with a new voodoo twist.

After the success of his first album, *Gris-Gris*, Dr. John struggled to surpass his creative peak, with his next few albums only reaching moderate sales. The next few decades would lead to a dearth of music production and a reliance on hit singles or popular standards that were sure moneymakers. Despite the stagnancy of his own career, Dr. John continues to collaborate with top names in blues and R&B.

211. According to the passage, Dr. John stopped making albums because

(A) he was in trouble with the law.

(B) he preferred to make television commercials.

(C) he wanted to try producing music for other musicians.

(D) he had hit his creative plateau.

(E) he lost the ability to play the guitar.

212. Why does the author state that Dr. John was able to find success, even with the lack of success of his own albums?

    (A) Because his style was unique from other styles of his time

    (B) Because he found a way to use his talents to remain relevant as an artist

    (C) Because other musicians still asked him to play on their tracks

    (D) Because he made more money doing commercial voiceovers than selling records

    (E) Because his first album was a major success

213. Which of the following would be the best title for this passage?

    (A) "Succeeding in the Face of Adversity"

    (B) "From New Orleans to Los Angeles: A Poet's Tale"

    (C) "Mardi Gras Traditions and Attire"

    (D) "Against All Odds"

    (E) "The Evolution of New Orleans Blues"

Questions 214 through 216 are based on the following passage.

Although a naturally occurring substance in the body, synthetic use of human growth hormone (hGH) by competitive athletes has been a topic of conversation regarding anti-doping policies. In the body, hGH is produced by a pituitary gland in the brain. This biological process helps stimulate bone growth and proper cellular health. Most importantly, hGH activates insulin secretion in the body. Because of these actions, hGH is considered a promoter of efficient cellular functioning.

As a supplement, the use of hGH helps to increase stamina and muscle performance and rehabilitation. For these reasons, athletes often use hGH to enhance their training or improve the effects of steroids. Scientists caught on to this increasing practice and determined that hGH should be considered a performance-enhancing substance and added it to the list of banned substances by the World Anti-Doping Agency. The first test for hGH in competition was implemented in the 2004 Summer Olympic Games in Athens, Greece.

Beyond the improved abilities hGH affords athletes, it has a number of dangerous side effects, including heart complications, organ dysfunction, muscle and bone degeneration, and factors associated with diabetes. It seems that the success gained with the use of hGH is not worth the long-term complications to a person's health.

214. Based on the passage, why do athletes take hGH?

    (A) To heal from injuries

    (B) To improve their insulin production

    (C) Because they want to win a medal

    (D) Because they are addicted to it

    (E) To improve their endurance and strength

215. The tone of the passage is

    (A) accusatory.

    (B) cautionary.

    (C) jovial.

    (D) informative.

    (E) persuasive.

216. The author's attitude about the use of hGH can best be described as

    (A) encouraging, promoting its use for athletic training.

    (B) adverse, believing the risks outweigh the benefits.

    (C) neutral, providing sufficient evidence for both sides of the argument.

    (D) skeptical, desiring more research about the benefits of its use.

    (E) supportive, suggesting the regulations are unnecessary.

Questions 217 through 221 are based on the following passage.

As a new generation began to transition into the influential role of trend-setting young adults, a number of fashion styles and conventions started to emerge that had been dormant for some time. One of these styles was the resurgence of fashionable mustaches and facial hair by young "hipsters," connecting with a lost tradition in gentlemanly appearance. Themed movements, such as Mustache March and the steam punk genre, have increased the number of young men choosing to adorn their faces with a variety of shapes and sizes of facial hair.

Yet, despite the levity with which this movement has resurfaced, the history of facial hair in society stems from a darker, more poignant history that symbolizes a tumultuous period of racial segregation and the lengths society would go to in establishing white male dominance.

In the pre-Revolutionary War era of America, men were deemed respectable as clean-shaven gentlemen. The smooth appearance of these men's faces represented elitism, a trait most men aspired to. Their clean shaves showed they were able to afford the luxury of a skilled barber trained in the use of the straight-blade razor. Men who couldn't afford proper grooming appeared haggard and boorish in comparison.

Another possible trait that clean-shaven men represented was that of slaveholder. Many white slaveholders utilized their black male servants as barbers, ensuring a perfect shave every time, for the consequences of a mishap were severe. Because of this habit, after the war, when slaves were freed, many men had attained the skills necessary to move into barber posts, a position white men found inferior.

For many decades, black men found success in crafting a casual and upscale environment to please their rich white patrons. Despite their status as a less-than race, white society approved the patronage of black barbers, and this position was viewed as an outlet of hope for men desiring an independent and respectable life beyond menial labor and service. However, dreams of prosperity were dashed as increasing racial tensions caused white society to turn against black barbers and promote an ideology of fear against what was seen as a dangerous position of power: black men with razors against the throats of white men.

This new perspective led many white men to return to personal grooming routines. Unfortunately, because of the skill required to use a straight blade and the delicate care the tool required, men were injuring themselves with the sharp razor, becoming afflicted with tetanus and other infections, and growing distasteful of the laborious maintenance. Enter the era of facial hair. This new trend, which started from this need for an alternative to shaving, took the form of a superior characteristic that white society saw as a representation of their dominance as a race and sex. Facial hair on white men differentiated them from other races seen as being unable to achieve the same features, as well as from women, who were gaining power in other arenas of society. If the young trendsetters of today understood the legacy they were celebrating, the movement would likely be less popular.

217. The primary function of the fourth paragraph is to

(A) expose the hidden agenda of barbers at the time.

(B) summarize the success of the anti-slave movement.

(C) explain the dangers involved with barbering.

(D) describe the advent of mustaches in high society.

(E) highlight the rise and fall of a prosperous avenue for distinction in the black community.

218. Why were black men seen as better suited for barbering than white men?

Consider each of the three choices separately, and select all that apply.

[A] They surpassed their white counterparts in their skills with straight blades.

[B] Many were already skilled in the trade from having practiced on their owners as slaves.

[C] White society felt it was above this type of service position.

219. Which of the following statements is NOT a reason white men began opting for facial hair?

(A) They became intolerant of the daily upkeep of self-barbering.

(B) The skills required to use the straight blades were beyond their abilities.

(C) Facial hair became a symbol of racial dominance.

(D) Fears of retaliation from black men drove them away from barbershops.

(E) They were tired of looking like women.

220. The conclusion the author reached about the modern day popularity of facial hair is that

(A) today's trend serves the same purpose as it did in the past.

(B) Mustache March is celebrated in honor of the black men who struggled for independence.

(C) the history of the trend is a much different reality than the fashionable homage suggests.

(D) facial hair is no more significant today than it was during the Revolutionary War.

(E) the resurgence of facial hair is a symbol of changing tides in today's race relations.

221. Which paragraph represents the main idea of the passage?

(A) Paragraph 2

(B) Paragraph 1

(C) Paragraph 4

(D) Paragraph 5

(E) Paragraph 3

Questions 222 through 225 are based on the following passage.

Imagine you are diagnosed with a disease that has no cure or you suffer a heart attack that permanently damages your cardiovascular system. In the face of certain death, would you find peace with your mortality or would you seek a solution that would allow you to come back in another time when medical advances were capable of healing you? For some in today's culture, the latter option is a viable one, despite the sci-fi nature of the concept. Affluent men and women all over the world are choosing to hire companies that claim the ability to freeze their bodies in the event of heart failure so that they can be brought back in the future to live a healthy life.

This act is called cryonics, and it encompasses the idea of salvaging a minimal amount of brain functioning from a person deemed "legally dead" by suspending his body in a frozen state. A company providing cryonic services has a contract with the client to take immediate action in the event of sudden cardiovascular death. After retrieving the client's body, the client is stored on ice and given drugs to help protect the blood cells and vessels from damage during the freezing process. Once the freezing is completed, the body is stored in a vessel filled with liquid nitrogen until the client is ready to be revived.

Although the cryonic craze has not swept the globe, many individuals are handing over hundreds of thousands of dollars to preserve their bodies. Yet, no one has ever been revived because the technology is not available as of yet. Thus, there is no guarantee that those frozen will gain any benefit from their extreme efforts to remain alive.

222. The author is most likely addressing this passage to

(A) the general public.

(B) wealthy citizens.

(C) scientists.

(D) family of the deceased.

(E) cryonic physicians.

223. According to the passage, how common is the practice of cryonics?

(A) About as frequent as death

(B) Very common

(C) Uncommon

(D) Common in certain groups

(E) Nonexistent

224. The author most likely feels that the practice of cryonics is

(A) untested and far-fetched.

(B) viable and a good alternative.

(C) worth the money.

(D) dangerous and illegal.

(E) suspicious and immoral.

225. Which of the following states the central idea of the passage?

(A) Scientists are working to make cryonics more affordable.

(B) The success of cryonics is indisputable.

(C) Cryonics is gaining interest as an alternative to death.

(D) Cryonics is a realistic alternative to death.

(E) Cryonics helps keep important people around longer.

Questions 226 through 229 are based on the following passage.

Technological innovation has led to many advances in the sciences, creating new treatments, theories, and tools that enhance human life. One field of science that has developed and is, perhaps, outside of the box regarding innovation is that of molecular gastronomy. Molecular gastronomy is the science of food and cooking, with chefs using the chemical and physical makeup of foods to manipulate their flavors and appearance. For instance, a chef who is a skilled gastronome may look at the cellular structure of an onion and recognize ways to break it down and create a different texture or structure. There are a number of techniques that the skilled chef has at his or her disposal to accomplish this task, such as using quick-freezing agents or varying levels of heat to change the physical format of food.

Other techniques are popular in molecular gastronomy, including the use of different agents to create certain textures. Gelling, foaming, emulsifying, and thickening agents may all be incorporated to find innovative presentations of a certain food item. The study of molecular gastronomy has increased, and competition among chefs for the next big innovation or food trend is fierce. Beyond traditional talents as gourmet chefs, molecular gastronomy has become an avenue for aspiring chefs to make a name for themselves. Before long, as technology continues to advance, the way we eat and what we eat may be completely unidentifiable from traditional standards of cuisine.

226. Molecular gastronomy would not be possible without which of the following?

(A) Gourmet chefs

(B) Gelling agents

(C) Technology

(D) Better culinary schools

(E) Competition

227. According to the passage, why is molecular gastronomy an advantageous avenue for aspiring chefs?

(A) There are too many traditional chefs already.

(B) They can become pioneers of innovative techniques rather than part of the pool of talented traditional chefs.

(C) The public is beginning to demand innovative dishes.

(D) Traditional styles of cooking are falling out of favor.

(E) The practice is relatively uncommon with older chefs, leaving the door open for them.

228. The author most likely included the last sentence to

(A) prophesize how this form of cooking could affect our culture.

(B) dissuade people from trying new foods.

(C) showcase the technology used by gastronomes.

(D) prepare people for the future.

(E) warn against a movement away from traditional standards.

229. The best title for this passage is

(A) "The Outdated Profession of Gourmet Chefs"

(B) "Out With the Old and In With Gastronomy"

(C) "How to Turn an Onion into Foam"

(D) "The Different Techniques of Molecular Gastronomy"

(E) "The Influence of Science in the Culinary World"

Questions 230 through 234 are based on the following passage.

Beginning at the end of the 20th century, illegal music sharing, or piracy, became a popular pastime for music lovers around the world. Fans were becoming more familiar with digital platforms purported by the growing Internet era. Music was being illegally passed from person to person, including complete strangers, in an attempt to reduce the dependence on music industry conglomerates that marked up album prices to amounts beyond the economic ability of the core fan base: youth. However, this seemingly liberating move may have done more to destroy the art fans so eagerly celebrated than enhance it.

Today, because of illegal music file sharing, revenue generated by music labels has decreased substantially. In fact, losses have totaled almost half of what the revenue had been at the turn of the century. Although the belief these dedicated fans have is that the rich labels can handle a loss here or there, what is actually occurring is a gross accumulation of small losses adding up to major economic pitfalls. The lasting effects of these losses are layoffs of the subordinate employees working in production or marketing and a lack of new musical talent.

Without money to spend, labels are not putting forth efforts to discover new talent. The relationship between future success and sales of new artists and the investment made in their promotion is compromised when those sales do not happen. Looking at music sharing in this light — that of job loss and economic hardships, both within the industry and at the national level — exposes the hypocritical nature of supporting an artist by sharing their music while destroying their ability to create due to budget constraints.

230. The tone of the passage is

(A) critical.

(B) argumentative.

(C) passive.

(D) harsh.

(E) unaffected.

231. The passage is primarily concerned with

(A) ways to stop music piracy.

(B) exposing the problems associated with music piracy.

(C) defining what music piracy is.

(D) forming a relationship between record labels and fans.

(E) explaining how to share music files.

232. The author most likely mentions job losses of subordinate employees for which reason?

(A) To increase negative attitudes toward record labels

(B) To point out who is really suffering because of music piracy

(C) To gain sympathy for music executives

(D) To shame people into buying their own music

(E) To complain about the lack of new music

233. Which of the following explains why the author calls the actions of those who illegally share music hypocritical?

Consider each of the three choices separately, and select all that apply.

[A] They are destroying the jobs they want to attain.

[B] Their fickle musical tastes are causing certain genres to fall out of favor.

[C] Their love for music is actually decreasing the ability of musicians to make more.

234. Which sentence most accurately describes the main consequence of music piracy?

Beginning at the end of the 20th century, illegal music sharing, or piracy, became a popular pastime for music lovers around the world. Fans were becoming more familiar with digital platforms purported

by the growing Internet era. Music was being illegally passed from person to person, including complete strangers, in an attempt to reduce the dependence on music industry conglomerates that marked up album prices to amounts beyond the economic ability of the core fan base: youth. However, this seemingly liberating move may have done more to destroy the art fans so eagerly celebrated than enhance it.

Today, because of illegal music file sharing, revenue generated by music labels has decreased substantially. In fact, losses have totaled almost half of what the revenue had been at the turn of the century. Although the belief these dedicated fans have is that the rich labels can handle a loss here or there, what is actually occurring is a gross accumulation of small losses adding up to major economic pitfalls. The lasting effects of these losses are layoffs of the subordinate employees working in production or marketing and a lack of new musical talent.

(A) The people feeling the sting of this loss are the subordinates working in production or marketing and the artists.

(B) The lasting effects of these losses are layoffs of the subordinate employees working in production or marketing and a lack of new musical talent.

(C) However, this seemingly liberating move may have done more to destroy the art fans so eagerly celebrated than enhance it.

(D) Although the belief these dedicated fans have is that the rich labels can handle a loss here or there, what is actually occurring is a gross accumulation of small losses adding up to major economic pitfalls.

(E) Fans were becoming more familiar with digital platforms purported by the growing Internet era.

Questions 235 through 239 are based on the following passage.

Bill Cosby may be famous for his elaborate facial expressions and comedic timing, but more than a comedian, he was a scholar who used his talent for making people laugh to promote racial equality and family values. Most of the projects Cosby was famous for were geared toward positive images of African Americans and creating a commonality among families of all races. He also made educating children a major endeavor of his work. Although goofy and lighthearted in character, his savvy business sense and creative vision made him an important player and leader in the social and entertainment spheres.

Cosby's beginnings in the entertainment industry were no different from any other budding comedian at the time except for one difference: He was black. During the volatile sixties, when the Civil Rights Movement was gaining momentum, fame for a black comedian was unheard of. However, when Cosby hit the club circuit in all the major cities across the country, his tow-the-line comedy, which differed greatly from some of the more lewd comics on the scene at the time, hit home with traditional audiences. His comedy was accessible to everyone.

This ease of entertaining people landed him a spot on the *Tonight Show* in the first part of the 1960s. Shortly after, Cosby would receive a record deal and a co-starring role on the popular TV drama *I Spy*. His casting to the show was controversial, with certain southern states refusing to run the program because it starred a black character. Yet, the rest of the nation became loyal fans, and Cosby set the precedent for other black comedians to find the same success in the future.

Over the next 20 years, Cosby would make a name for himself, not as one of the most famous black comedians, but as one of the leading comics of his generation. Despite recording a number of comedic albums, making frequent appearances on television programs, and starring in his own show for a few years, Cosby found time to return to school and attain his master's and doctorate degrees in education. He would use this knowledge to create programming aimed at educating the youth in America. His educational cartoon series *Fat Albert and the Cosby Kids* was one such program and was extremely popular in the Saturday morning lineup.

Even with all of this success, Cosby is best known for the television show *The Cosby Show,* which shattered network ratings records and broke open the ideology of the perfect American family in television. The upper-class, educated Huxtable family portrayed an image of black society that was different from other shows centered on black families. With each episode, Cosby was able to highlight an important aspect of family life and moral values, which reached into the hearts of all Americans and created unity among races. His efforts to bridge the racial gap would continue throughout his life, making Cosby an important activist as well as a star.

235. Based on the passage, a motivating factor for Cosby's work was

(A) to improve how society related to black culture.

(B) to replace education with entertainment for America's youth.

(C) to push the envelope on race relations.

(D) to portray comedy as a way to make a substantial income.

(E) to be the most famous black comedian.

236. The primary function of the last paragraph is to

(A) express the popularity of The Cosby Show.

(B) introduce Cosby's most notable achievement.

(C) showcase how Cosby changed racial ideologies about black families.

(D) attack his obsession with mainstream society.

(E) exemplify his comedic genius.

237. The author most likely sees Cosby as a

(A) goof.

(B) pioneer.

(C) elitist.

(D) actor.

(E) scholar.

238. Which sentence most accurately describes why Cosby was able to find success in a time when racial tensions were high?

Bill Cosby may be famous for his elaborate facial expressions and comedic timing, but more than a comedian, he was a scholar who used his talent for making people laugh to promote racial equality and family values. Most of the projects Cosby was famous for were geared toward positive images of African Americans and creating a commonality among families of all races. He also made educating children a major endeavor of his work. Although goofy and lighthearted in character, his savvy business sense and creative vision made him an important player and leader in the social and entertainment spheres.

Cosby's beginnings in the entertainment industry were no different from any other budding comedian at the time except for one difference: He was black. During the volatile sixties, when the Civil Rights Movement was gaining momentum, fame for a black comedian was unheard of. However, when Cosby hit the club circuit in all the major cities across the country, his tow-the-line comedy, which differed greatly from some of the more lewd comics on the scene at the time, hit home with traditional audiences. His comedy was accessible to everyone.

This ease of entertaining people landed him a spot on the *Tonight Show* in the first part of the 1960s. Shortly after, Cosby would receive a record deal and a co-starring role on the popular TV drama *I Spy*. His casting to the show was controversial, with certain southern states refusing to run the program because it starred a black character. Yet, the rest of the nation became loyal fans, and Cosby set the precedent for other black comedians to find the same success in the future.

(A) Most of the projects Cosby was famous for were geared toward positive images of African Americans and creating a commonality among families of all races.

(B) His casting to the show was controversial, with certain southern states refusing to run the program because it starred a black character.

(C) Although goofy and lighthearted in character, his savvy business sense and creative vision made him an important player and leader in the social and entertainment spheres.

(D) Yet, the rest of the nation became loyal fans, and Cosby set the precedent for other black comedians to find the same success in the future.

(E) His comedy was accessible to everyone.

239. Which of the following statements about Bill Cosby's career can best be inferred from the passage?

(A) His career suffered because of his fascination with education.

(B) He was a typical star who sought fame and fortune.

(C) He would have experienced greater success if he had catered to black audiences more.

(D) He used his multiple skills and talents to help influence social change.

(E) He was a better actor than comedian.

Questions 240 through 242 are based on the following passage.

It is not a new trend for holidays to serve as more than just a celebration of the intended meaning of the day. Thanksgiving is seen as not only a time to give thanks, but also as the beginning of the biggest shopping day of the year. Likewise, Easter has changed from a strictly religious holiday to one steeped in commercialism, with chocolate bunnies and Easter egg hunts often serving as the most anticipated aspects of the day. Thus, it should come as no surprise that the national holiday of Labor Day has taken on several meanings beyond its founding significance.

Started in 1887 as a way to honor the dedication and achievements of the American workforce, Labor Day was marked with neighborhood celebrations and orations by renowned leaders in the labor arena. However, as commercialism grew in America, so grew the opportunities for retailers to target a population of people all idle on the same day. This recognition created a trend in market advertising, which led to Labor Day becoming one of the biggest shopping days of the year.

The holiday has also come to represent the end of summer for many families, and members of upper-class America see it as a marker of appropriate fashion styles, stating it is not acceptable to wear white after Labor Day. Although the origin of the holiday is still celebrated by certain factions, the importance of honoring those who support and promote the American economy has faded. The fact that those employed at retailers must continue to work long hours on their day of recognition is a testament to this reality.

240. Which of the following is the reason the author mentions Easter in the passage?

(A) To explain how holidays have changed in popular culture

(B) Because Easter is the holiday that precedes Labor Day

(C) To provide an example of a holiday still steeped in tradition

(D) Because Easter is almost as popular as Labor Day in the magnitude of celebration

(E) Because Labor Day and Easter celebrate the same thing

241. The author's attitude toward the Labor Day celebration can be best described as

(A) indifferent.

(B) excited.

(C) cynical.

(D) hateful.

(E) supportive.

242. The author most likely wrote this passage to

(A) convince retail owners to allow their employees to have time off on Labor Day.

(B) criticize society for placing more importance on shopping than honoring the workforce.

(C) provide information about how Labor Day has evolved over time.

(D) show disdain for all holidays.

(E) persuade Americans to participate more in parades.

Questions 243 through 246 are based on the following passage.

The issue of medical uses of cannabis, or marijuana, has been and continues to be a hot topic of debate in the medical and political sectors. Researchers have conducted several studies outlining the benefits of marijuana use for patients suffering from terminal illnesses and to alleviate symptoms of chronic pain. Still, according to the federal government, marijuana is considered to have no legitimate medical use and a high abuse rate. Critics of medicinal marijuana suggest that the side effects of continued use and the drug's popular recreational use make it inappropriate as a form of treatment. Yet, proponents point to the addictive nature and detrimental side effects of abusing FDA-approved prescription and over-the-counter medication, such as oxycodone and NSAIDs.

The argument wavers between the service of providing relief and comfort to people in perilous health and the abuse of prescription marijuana recreationally. On one side, the need for marijuana is seen as superfluous with so many other legal drugs available to patients. On the other side, the negative attributes of legal prescription drugs are seen as just as concerning, if not more so, than those of marijuana use. Critics want to ensure that the wool isn't pulled over the government's eyes by opportunists who seek to use medicinal marijuana for financial gain. Proponents want to ensure that patients who are debilitated by illness have access to every possible form of assistance they can get. In the end, the issue likely comes down to user responsibility, as it does with other addictive prescription substances.

243. The tone of the passage is

    (A) convincing.

    (B) forceful.

    (C) subjective.

    (D) encouraging.

    (E) balanced.

244. The conclusion that the author reaches from the analysis of the debate is that

    (A) the FDA has the best interest of the American people in mind.

    (B) marijuana should remain an illegal substance.

    (C) individuals are accountable for their own drug use.

    (D) there is no solution to this problem.

    (E) other drugs are just as beneficial as marijuana for pain relief.

245. The passage is most likely concerned with

    (A) supporting the use of medical marijuana.

    (B) forming a conclusion based on evidence.

    (C) presenting the dangers of prescription drugs.

    (D) discussing both sides of the argument.

    (E) persuading the reader against the use of marijuana medicinally.

246. Which of the following best highlights the case made in the passage against the use of medical marijuana?

Consider each of the three choices separately, and select all that apply.

    (A) Medical marijuana can be used as a front for drug dealing.

    (B) The use of marijuana is only necessary in patients who are terminal.

    (C) The side effects of marijuana are too dangerous for commercial use.

Questions 247 through 250 are based on the following passage.

More than 30 years after the theatrical release of Stanley Kubrick's *The Shining,* fans of the cult classic are still enthralled by its eerie undertones and dynamic chill factor. The movie is considered by many film critics and directors to be one of the top horror films of all time. Yet, the fascination with *The Shining* is far from being about the ruthlessly visceral portrayal of Jack Torrance, the caretaker of the Overlook Hotel, where the film is set, or the grotesquely graphic events that unfold in the rooms of the hotel. What keeps fans buzzing are the theories surrounding secret messages or alternative meanings found in Kubrick's retelling of the famous Stephen King novel.

Wild interpretations point to conspiracies involving the moon landing, observations about the Holocaust, or commentary on society's complacence with the loss of American ideals. Although Kubrick never admitted to any secret implications in the content, a number of articles and documentaries have tackled the problem of disseminating his vision. The answers to the questions about hidden messages may never be found, but perhaps the point is not to find definitive answers. Perhaps the point is simply to keep this cinematic tour-de-force relevant as a standard of American horror films.

247. The author is most likely addressing this passage to

- (A) conspiracy theorists.
- (B) students.
- (C) cinematic historians.
- (D) horror novelists.
- (E) journalists.

248. Which of the following statements most accurately represents certain fans' responses to Kubrick's film?

- (A) *The Shining* is only as relevant as its theories.
- (B) *The Shining* was too scary and graphic.
- (C) It is clear that Kubrick is not the best director of horror films.
- (D) *The Shining* is just another movie without any special meaning.
- (E) It is clear that Kubrick was trying to make a statement with the movie.

249. The primary function of the first paragraph is to

- (A) share the results of investigations into the movie's meaning.
- (B) explain the respect and significance of a popular horror film.
- (C) diminish the validity of conspiracy theories.
- (D) support the different theories about *The Shining*.
- (E) discuss the plot of *The Shining*.

250. Which of the following would be the best title for this passage?

- (A) "The Evolution of a Cult Classic"
- (B) "Why Kubrick is Better Than King"
- (C) "The Best Horror Movie Ever Made"
- (D) "Intrigue and Speculation Surrounding *The Shining*"
- (E) "The Real Meaning of *The Shining*"

Questions 251 through 255 are based on the following passage.

The music industry witnessed a groundbreaking suit in the mid-1990s when internationally renowned rock band Pearl Jam sued Ticketmaster, the most popular ticket outlet service, claiming antitrust activity in an attempt to attain a monopoly in ticket sales. This was the first time a band had taken such a drastic action in an attempt to support their fans by keeping ticket prices low.

Because Ticketmaster was the only successfully operating ticket agency at the time, the band opted to stop touring, rather than play ball with what they saw as illegal price gouging. However, the question was raised as to how much the band's actions were actually serving their fan base if their fans were not able to attend their performances. In order to answer this question, as well as determine if their claims were legitimate, it is necessary to consider the specifics of the band's accusation.

The issue at hand was the anti-competitive practices Pearl Jam accused Ticketmaster of performing. According to a 1994 *Rolling Stone* article by Neil Strauss and Tom Dunkel, the anti-competitive claim surrounded the actions taken by Ticketmaster to ensure concerts were held and tickets were needed. One such action was payouts to venues, distributed as loans, so the fees related to holding a performance could be met. As a result of this money exchange, Ticketmaster added a service fee of up to 30 to 40 percent to the cost of each individual ticket to recoup those expenses and turn a profit.

This surcharge, Pearl Jam claimed, took advantage of the fans because there was no competition to keep the level of service fees stable. However, critics of the suit believed that in a roundabout fashion, the organization of Ticketmaster's operations actually benefited fans more than it hurt them. For instance, if Ticketmaster did not provide the funds to support the performance, many venues would not be able to meet the required show budget. Thus, the venue would either increase their portion of the prices or cancel the show. In both scenarios, the fans lose.

The fact that smaller ticketing agencies do not have the revenue to support venues in this way was where the anti-competitive claim took shape. Yet, these companies could still conduct business with smaller venues that did not require the same financial investment. Thus, if Pearl Jam wanted to support their fans, they always had the option of performing at less grandiose locales than large arenas and concert halls. In the end, the smaller companies were not able to operate successfully and went out of business, and the suit was eventually dropped.

251. The author's attitude toward Pearl Jam's suit could best be described as

(A) comparable.

(B) admiring.

(C) unsympathetic.

(D) irritable.

(E) skeptical.

252. According to the passage, although inadvertent, the monopoly enjoyed by Ticketmaster stems from

(A) its ability to forge agreements for performances that smaller companies can't compete with.

(B) its saturation of the market with cheap tickets to multiple shows.

(C) the agreement made with event venues to work only with its company.

(D) its underhanded actions to force its competitors out of business.

(E) its ability to keep ticket prices at a reasonable rate for the general population.

253. Which sentence best supports the idea that Pearl Jam did not have the best interest of its fans in mind?

This surcharge, Pearl Jam claimed, took advantage of the fans because there was no competition to keep the level of service fees stable. However, critics of the suit believed that in a roundabout fashion, the organization of Ticketmaster's operations

actually benefited fans more than it hurt them. For instance, if Ticketmaster did not provide the funds to support the performance, many venues would not be able to meet the required show budget. Thus, the venue would either increase their portion of the prices or cancel the show. In both scenarios, the fans lose.

The fact that smaller ticketing agencies do not have the revenue to support venues in this way was where the anti-competitive claim took shape. Yet, these companies could still conduct business with smaller venues that did not require the same financial investment. Thus, if Pearl Jam wanted to support their fans, they always had the option of performing at less grandiose locales than large arenas and concert halls. In the end, the smaller companies were not able to operate successfully and went out of business, and the suit was eventually dropped.

(A) This surcharge, Pearl Jam claimed, took advantage of the fans because there was no competition to keep the level of service fees stable.

(B) However, critics of the suit believed that in a roundabout fashion, the organization of Ticketmaster's operations actually benefited fans more than it hurt them.

(C) The fact that smaller ticketing agencies do not have the revenue to support venues in this way was where the anti-competitive claim took shape.

(D) Thus, if Pearl Jam wanted to support their fans, they always had the option of performing at less grandiose locales than large arenas and concert halls.

254. Which of the following statements best summarizes the critics' viewpoint of the allegations against Ticketmaster?

(A) Ticketmaster has a right to charge service fees because they are the best at what they do.

(B) Paying a service fee is a small price to pay for convenience.

(C) The fans are indebted to Ticketmaster, without which no performances would ever happen.

(D) Ticketmaster procures big-name concerts that would likely not be possible otherwise.

(E) If the fans bought more records, concert tickets wouldn't have to be so expensive.

255. It can be inferred from the passage that the underlying problem for Pearl Jam is that

(A) the fans can't afford to attend shows.

(B) the band wants part of Ticketmaster's profits.

(C) the band is not able to perform at major venues while keeping ticket prices low.

(D) the band is too popular for small venues.

(E) the band is not able to form productive relationships with smaller ticketing agencies.

Questions 256 through 260 are based on the following passage.

A lot has happened in the world of animation since the flipbook was introduced in 1868. Animation moguls, such as Disney and Pixar, have made a major impact in the motion picture industry with their famed animated movies. Films such as *The Little Mermaid, Finding Nemo,* and *Toy Story* would set precedents in animation technique and technologies, but these films could never have been made without some path-setting advances along the way.

In the early part of the 20th century, inventions like the cinematograph made it possible for a series of pictures to be shown consecutively on a large screen using light to enhance the images. This action led to perceived movement when the pictures were shown at a quick pace. Animators took this invention a step further when they began drawing images directly on the film. In this way, the quickly paced drawings also created the sense of movement, only with two-dimensional objects rather than real life.

Stop-motion animation also created the sense of movement with inanimate objects, taking a picture of a set scene, changing the position of the objects, and taking another picture. When the pictures were linked together, the objects were set in motion. Artists became interested in this new phenomenon in motion pictures, and the animation boom took off. From the first cartoon to use voice and sound features, *Steamboat Willie,* made in 1928 by Disney and which introduced America to Mickey Mouse, to Saturday morning cartoons, animation found its niche in the entertainment industry.

The field was transformed again in the last decade of the century with the development of computer-generated imagery (CGI). These days, animation is not simply used for cartoons. Movies with living persons now incorporate CGI animation to create historic or difficult locales, fictitious characters, and special effects. Box office blockbusters such as the *Lord of the Rings* trilogy and the *X-Men* franchise would not be the same today without the help of animation.

256. Which of the following represents an action that led to the boom in the animation industry?

Consider each of the choices separately, and select all that apply.

[A] The cinematograph was invented.

[B] Mickey Mouse became a household name.

[C] Computers improved certain aspects of animation.

257. What function does the last paragraph serve in this passage?

(A) It forms an opinion about the quality of today's films.

(B) It provides a history of animation.

(C) It promotes films that use CGI animation.

(D) It gives an account of contemporary animation practices.

(E) It compares old technology to new technology.

258. It can be inferred that the author agrees with which of the following statements?

(A) Motion pictures are better when animation is used.

(B) Stop-motion animation is antiquated and ineffective.

(C) Motion pictures have been improved through the use of animation.

(D) Animation is the best thing to happen to the cinema.

(E) The animation industry has taken over Hollywood.

259. The author most likely mentions the flip-book at the beginning of the passage to

(A) provide an example of CGI.

(B) set the tone of the passage.

(C) show how far animation has come.

(D) exhibit early forms of technology.

(E) describe a popular animation technique.

260. Based on the passage, the cinematograph changed animation by

(A) using light to create movement in pictures.

(B) creating sound to accompany movement from pictures.

(C) producing the X-Men series.

(D) making inanimate objects appear to move.

(E) allowing pictures to seemingly move on the big screen.

Chapter 3

Argument Analysis

• •

An Argument Analysis question challenges your ability to identify whether the author has done a sufficient job of presenting and supporting his position. Graduate schools expect you not only to read with understanding but also to scrutinize the information and argument presented and sort logic that is reasonable from logic that is not.

Each question consists of a short argument followed by one question and five answer choices. You may strengthen the argument, weaken the argument, or discern the roles of highlighted sentences within the argument.

The Problems You'll Work On

When working through the questions in this chapter, be prepared to

- ✔ Identify the premise and conclusion of an argument.
- ✔ Find the hidden assumption.
- ✔ Spot weaknesses in supporting details.
- ✔ Explore common logical fallacies.
- ✔ Leverage the process of elimination.

What to Watch Out For

These passages use a lot of flawed logic, so watch out for arguments that

- ✔ Rely on circular reasoning, in which a premise supports itself
- ✔ Assume erroneous cause-and-effect arguments, where two independent events are described as one having caused the other
- ✔ Use sweeping generalizations, in which something that has an effect in one context will have the same effect in another

261. The parkway project is an organization started by Mary Jennings, a local farmer in the community of Vernal, Utah. As part of the project, local homeless living along the parkway are compensated with food and small stipends for picking up the litter strewn along the path. **Not only has this project helped reduce the amount of visible waste on the streets, but it has also provided the homeless population with a sense of community and pride.** This change in perception has led to many improvements in their quality of life.

In the above passage, the boldfaced sentence plays which of the following roles?

(A) It discusses the negative aspects of the parkway project.

(B) It provides evidence to support the effectiveness of the parkway project.

(C) It explains what the parkway project is about.

(D) It highlights the struggles faced by the homeless population.

(E) It shows the environmental impact of the parkway project.

262. Although the American Medical Association does not consider acupuncture to be a legitimate medical procedure, the benefits and effectiveness of this kind of therapy are clear. In China, where acupuncture is common practice, the average person is 10 years younger in health than he is in age, whereas in the United States, the average health age is 5 years older than actual age. If acupuncture were deemed worthy by the A.M.A., more Americans would live healthier lives.

The argument that more Americans would live healthier lives if acupuncture were deemed worthy relies on which of the following assumptions?

(A) People do not consider acupuncture to be a suitable mode of healing.

(B) Acupuncture is a new therapy gaining ground in many countries around the world.

(C) The only cause for longevity in China is acupuncture.

(D) The Chinese are more progressive than Americans.

(E) The AMA supports alternative therapy for certain illnesses.

263. Launching a direct-mail campaign is the smartest move a business can make. Billboards are typically overlooked or blend into the surrounding environment. Television commercials are often muted or abandoned while the viewer flips to a different channel or walks away for a moment. Everyone checks his or her mail once a day and looks at every piece before deciding what to throw away. More prospective consumers will be exposed to the product through direct-mail marketing. This exposure will cause businesses to flourish.

Select the sentence which best states the assumption.

(A) Billboards are typically overlooked or blend into the surrounding environment.

(B) Everyone checks their mail once a day and looks at every piece before deciding what to throw away.

(C) Launching a direct-mail campaign is the smartest move a business can make.

(D) Television commercials are often muted or abandoned while the viewer flips to a different channel or walks away for a moment.

(E) This exposure will cause businesses to flourish.

264. Are toll roads a more effective strategy for raising road maintenance funds, or would a flat tax increase solve the problem just as well, if not better? In places where tourism is heavy, toll roads may be more beneficial because the roads are being used by more than the taxpaying citizens in the area. However, for rural areas, a flat tax may be more beneficial because not enough money is able to be generated from the infrequent use. Either way, the roads must be maintained in good condition.

Which of the following statements, if true, most supports the argument that a toll is best for high-traffic roads?

(A) Local taxpayers use the roads just as much as tourists use them.

(B) Rural roads require more maintenance than urban roads.

(C) Local citizens should not be responsible for the wear and tear caused by visitors.

(D) The state is responsible for maintaining the condition of all roads.

(E) Tolls only contribute a small portion of the funds required for maintenance.

265. The organic food movement was designed to provide healthier food options without the use of pesticides or unnatural substances, such as growth hormones. The high prices of organic foods deter many people from being able to experience these positive attributes of food. Manufacturers say the cost of certifying their produce as organic is high. Part of this financial burden must fall to the consumers. If the government provided financial assistance to these producers, more people could lead healthier lives.

Select the sentence that best supports the assumption of the argument.

(A) If the government provided financial assistance to these producers, more people could lead healthier lives.

(B) The organic food movement was designed to provide healthier food options without the use of pesticides or unnatural substances, such as growth hormones.

(C) Part of this financial burden must fall to the consumers.

(D) The high prices of organic foods deter many people from being able to experience these positive attributes of food.

(E) Manufacturers say the cost of certifying their produce as organic is high.

266. Schools that provide afterschool programs have higher graduation rates than schools that do not. Students benefit from these programs because they keep them involved in the educational environment rather than being idle or getting into trouble. Schools with high dropout rates should implement more afterschool programs.

Which of the following, if true, would most strengthen the above argument?

Choose all that apply.

[A] Afterschool programs have been criticized for a lack of proper supervision.

[B] Studies have proven that afterschool programs increase the decision-making abilities of students.

[C] Afterschool programs provide structure and stability for students.

267. Animal rescue shelters present contradictory policies to their seeming mission of providing good homes for abandoned animals. A good example of this is their foster home policy. A person or family is allowed to foster an animal during the period it is up for adoption, but that same person or family is not allowed to adopt the animal if it becomes attached to the pet. Only persons unaffiliated with the shelter are allowed to adopt pets. This is why so many pets remain in limbo without permanent homes.

The author's assumption presupposes which of the following?

(A) The level of care needed for permanent placement is more than foster parents can provide.

(B) Foster parents are not good permanent parents.

(C) Rescue shelters know what is best for each animal.

(D) Rescue shelters frequently turn down adoption offers from foster parents.

(E) Rescue shelters avidly reach out to foster parents for adoption.

268. LinkedIn has become a major arena for professional networking and job seeking. People with professionally created profiles generate more activity on their pages than those without quality profiles. It is worth it to spend the money on a professional profile if you want to make yourself marketable to head hunters and talent scouts.

Which one of the following, if true, would most support the author's argument?

(A) LinkedIn is only used for networking.

(B) People who create their own profiles do not create quality profiles.

(C) LinkedIn is predominantly used to post photos.

(D) Professional profiles are not worth the money required to create them.

(E) Job providers do not consider LinkedIn a legitimate website.

269. The admissions policies for entrance into Harvard University have changed, beginning with the class of 2016. Along with the current requirements of high school GPA, standardized test scores, and letters of recommendation, each prospective incoming freshman will be required to submit a five-year plan describing his or her academic pursuits and career development post-graduation. Although this information will only be used to get a sense of each student's ambitions, students are encouraged to set high goals. The office of admissions believes these goals demonstrate the seriousness with which students view their lives. Students without this plan will not be taken into consideration.

Which statement from the passage most accurately supports the resulting assumption?

(A) These goals demonstrate the seriousness with which they view their lives.

(B) Along with the current requirements of high school GPA, standardized test scores, and letters of recommendation, each prospective incoming freshman will be required to submit a five-year plan describing their academic pursuits and career development post-graduation.

(C) The admissions policies for entrance into Harvard University have changed, beginning with the class of 2016.

(D) Students without this plan will not be taken into consideration.

(E) Although this information will only be used to get a sense of each student's ambitions, students are encouraged to set high goals.

270. Child labor laws are put into place in the entertainment industry to safeguard minors who work as actors for television and movies. These regulations ensure that minors are not exploited or worked beyond a reasonable level. These laws, however, do not apply to children in reality television series because those children are viewed as participants, not actors. Unless these laws are changed, children on reality television programs will continue to be vulnerable.

Which of the following statements most accurately identifies the assumption that must be true for the conclusion to be true?

(A) Child labor laws are antiquated.

(B) Chaperones are always present during the filming of reality shows using children.

(C) Producers of reality television look for ways to exploit child labor.

(D) Reality television does not use child actors.

(E) The government is not responsible for the care of child actors.

271. Critics of the video-gaming industry have pointed to a 33% decrease in activity levels of today's adolescents because of America's obsession with video games. The convenience that new technologies, such as tablets and smartphones, have created allows children to play games wherever they are, further reducing the need for physical activities and increasing their health risks. Researchers note, however, that the introduction of games that actually promote movement, such as Wii Sports and Dance Dance Revolution, has reduced this percentage in the last few years.

The argument is structured to lead to which of the following conclusions?

(A) All video games are detrimental to children's health.

(B) Video games are more educational than active.

(C) Games that promote activity are not as popular as other games.

(D) Technology has caused a health crisis in today's youth.

(E) Games that require physical movement help keep children in shape.

272. People enjoy eating out more when the person they are with is not on the phone. For instance, one restaurant in China put up a firewall screen blocking all communication signals within the restaurant. Since this action, their revenue has increased by 15%. Other restaurants would be more successful if they took the same measure.

Which of the following must be true in order for the assumption to be true?

(A) A new chef created a better menu at the restaurant in China.

(B) No other factors beyond the firewall screen can be attributed to the restaurant's success.

(C) Studies show that people do not use their cellphones during meals.

(D) A peaceful environment is not the ideal for a night out.

(E) Cellphone use has decreased over the past decade.

273. Tensions were high at the Paloma County Chili Cook-off this year. The winner, Lucy Butterfield, took the prize with her Texas Green Machine Chili, made from Serrano peppers grown in her backyard. **Lucy's cousin was one of the four judges of the event.** A call for a revote with an impartial judge was made by the other contestants to avoid favoritism.

Which of the following best describes the function of the boldfaced statement in the argument above?

(A) It shows that the cousin cheated.

(B) It gives the reason for the revote request.

(C) It supports the outcome of the contest.

(D) It highlights the level of competition.

(E) It describes the solution to the problem.

274. The Super Bowl is the biggest event of the year for sports fans. More than 100,000 people tuned in for the big game last year. An advertising slot during this game is a high-priced ticket due to the extreme exposure to the public. Companies lucky enough to get one of these slots see immediate increases in sales. Only the largest companies are able to purchase these ad slots. Thus, smaller companies do not benefit from this tremendous audience, which perpetuates their status as a small company. The network should reduce the cost of these ad slots so the companies who really need the exposure can get it.

Select the sentence which most supports the assumption in this argument.

(A) More than 100,000 people tuned in for the big game last year.

(B) Companies lucky enough to get one of these slots see immediate increases in sales.

(C) The Super Bowl is the biggest event of the year for sports fans.

(D) Advertising slots during the game are a high-priced ticket due to the extreme exposure to the public.

(E) Thus, smaller companies do not benefit from this tremendous audience, which perpetuates their status as a small company.

275. **Aluminum has been identified as a contributor to worsening symptoms of Alzheimer's disease.** Aluminum is one of the main ingredients in most major brands of deodorant. Alternative brands of deodorant provide aluminum-free options. Consumers of the alternative deodorants are not likely to suffer from Alzheimer's disease later in life.

In the argument given, the boldfaced sentence plays which of the following roles?

(A) It supports the assumption.

(B) It weakens the argument.

(C) It presents the conclusion.

(D) It presents the assumption.

(E) It has no role.

276. Although green tea does not have the same energy-lifting properties as coffee, its antioxidants help promote natural energy. Coffee is full of toxins. Also, the process of making coffee actually creates carcinogens, which can lead to cancer. Contrarily, antioxidants reduce the risk of cancer and provide essential vitamins and minerals. It is clear that green tea is the better option than coffee in the morning.

Select the sentence in the argument which best states the conclusion.

(A) It is clear that green tea is the better option than coffee in the morning.

(B) Contrarily, antioxidants reduce the risk of cancer and provide essential vitamins and minerals.

(C) Also, the process of making coffee actually creates carcinogens, which can lead to cancer.

(D) Although green tea does not have the same energy-lifting properties as coffee, its antioxidants help promote natural energy.

(E) Coffee is full of toxins.

277. The current minimum wage in the United States is $7.25. However, with inflation and a growing national debt, this amount barely equals a living wage for many Americans, who are forced to work multiple jobs to afford to live. Members of congress state the wage is fair for both employees and employers, finding the balance to allow both to thrive. However, new information from the International Monetary Fund, an organization aimed at creating a stable and flourishing global economy, cautioned against this low wage, predicting the U.S. economy will crash if its citizens are not able to put money back into it. Some major cities, such as Seattle, Washington, have now taken the matter into local hands, increasing the minimum wage in city boundaries to almost twice that of the national amount. This action by one of America's most popular cities could start a trend across the country.

Select the sentence which most accurately weakens the assumption that there is a need to increase the minimum wage amount.

(A) Members of congress state the wage is fair for both employees and employers, finding the balance to allow both to thrive.

(B) Some major cities, such as Seattle, Washington, have now taken the matter into local hands, increasing the minimum wage in city boundaries to almost twice that of the national amount.

(C) . . . the U.S. economy will crash if its citizens are not able to put money back into it.

(D) This action by one of America's most popular cities could start a trend across the country.

(E) However, with inflation and a growing national debt, this amount barely equals a living wage for many Americans.

278. A new study, published in the American Journal of Clinical Nutrition, reveals that college students have poor health and are overweight due to unclear nutritional labels on food in campus dining facilities. The FDA is proposing a change to the nutritional content labels to place more emphasis on percent values of fat, carbohydrates, and protein, as well as highlighting the number of calories and more accurate portion size. With this new labeling system, college students will now be able to be healthier.

Which of the following statements, if true, does not support the assumption made in the passage?

(A) College students never read the nutritional labels on their food.

(B) Nutritional labeling is the only factor affecting food choices for college students.

(C) College students are more likely to abide by suggested portion size than by what their friends are eating.

(D) College dining facilities provide only healthy food.

(E) College students will not eat food they know is bad for them.

279. According to recent statistics, cars equipped with compressed natural gas (CNG) make up only 4 percent of the vehicles currently on the road, but they cause 90 percent less damage to the environment. With CNG costing almost two-thirds less than regular fuel and acquiring almost 200 miles more per gallon over the duration of a full tank, more Americans should be choosing this alternative. The answer for why they are not lies in economics, with CNG-ready vehicles from the manufacturers costing up to $8,000 more than a standard vehicle, and upgrading your current vehicle is approximately $10,000. Americans need to prioritize the environment over their pocketbooks.

The argument above assumes which of the following?

(A) Converting a car to run on CNG is not worth the savings in gas.

(B) If the price of acquiring a CNG car were lower, more Americans would be driving them.

(C) If regular cars were more fuel efficient, there would be no need for CNG cars.

(D) Americans are attached to their old cars.

(E) The upfront cost of CNG vehicles is less than what an average person spends on gas.

280. The University of Missouri has been criticized for its poor graduation rate of student athletes, predominantly in the sports of football and basketball. To address the issue, the athletic director hired a new academic advisor to keep close tabs on the educational advancement of the school's players. **However, after some investigation, it was discovered that the new advisor had been kicked out of the first college she attended for plagiarism;** thus, she was no longer the best candidate for the position.

Which of the following best describes the function of the boldfaced statement in the argument above?

(A) It supports the hiring of the new advisor.

(B) It structures the argument so there is only one outcome.

(C) It provides the reasoning behind the assumption made about the new advisor.

(D) It shows that the candidate was not worthy to work as an advisor.

(E) It states the eligibility requirements for student athletes.

281. To boost the national economy, the Obama administration has introduced a number of incentives to encourage small business entrepreneurs to start their own companies. Studies show that small businesses provide 25 percent lower salaries and 50 percent fewer benefits to their employees than corporations do. Therefore, encouraging the growth of small businesses is not the appropriate way to boost the national economy.

The argument above is structured to lead to which of the following conclusions?

(A) Small business owners are not held to the same level of employee support as larger corporations.

(B) The Obama administration believes in free enterprise.

(C) The national economy is thriving.

(D) The small business incentives are solely motivated by a desire to boost the national economy.

(E) People work harder for small businesses than for larger corporations.

282. School uniforms are not considered cool by adolescents and teens, but for administrators, uniforms represent more than a desired aesthetic effect. They are tools used to curb violence stemming from subtle intended meanings hidden in apparel choices. Public schools, where uniforms are not required, relate a 15 percent higher rate of student violence and gang activity than private and denomination-affiliated schools, showing that teens are not responsible enough to choose the appropriate attire for school.

Which of the following statements, if true, would most weaken the argument that teens are not responsible enough to choose the appropriate attire for school?

(A) School uniforms provide a sense of unity among the students.

(B) The federal government is considering a bill to require school uniforms in all schools.

(C) The study providing the statistic was conducted in a school district located in a high-crime neighborhood.

(D) Public schools have placed a ban on wearing labels on your clothing.

(E) The most recent incident in the public school in question involved a pair of basketball shoes.

283. The 2005 *Lawrence vs. the State of California* case caught national attention and created outrage in the American public. Lawrence, a former finance manager for the state, claimed he was wrongfully terminated after it was discovered that he participated in a clean-air protest in 1982 that forced a dramatic shift in industrial waste and fossil fuel emission regulations. Thousands of people signed their names to an online petition in support of Lawrence, arguing that freedom of speech and expression were protected by the U.S. Constitution. Unfortunately, the signatures were not enough to persuade the state's Supreme Court to rule in favor of the plaintiff. Instead, they ruled there was lack of sufficient support for the case.

The argument above assumes which of the following?

(A) Lawrence lost the case because he did not attain enough signatures on the petition.

(B) The courts don't consider petitions when hearing testimony.

(C) The petition was only part of the dossier of evidence gathered by the plaintiff.

(D) Participating in a protest makes a person ineligible for fair treatment.

(E) The Constitution has strict rules about unlawful termination.

284. Identity fraud is likely to happen to one of three Americans during their lifetimes. For this reason, online shopping merchandisers have amped up the security settings for customer purchases, attempting to safeguard personal information. Hackers, however, were able to crack the firewall protection for one of the nation's largest department stores, taking a few hundred credit card numbers out of the database. Therefore, despite the convenience, it is still wiser to shop in person than enter personal information online.

Which of the following, if true, supports the position that it is wiser to shop in person than enter personal information online?

Choose all that apply.

[A] The department store that was breached used poor security software to firewall their website.

[B] The firewall protection used in the breached department store is representative of all firewall security on the Internet.

[C] Most retailers' in-store transaction networks are more secure than online shopping networks.

285. Is it any wonder that gender inequality in America remains a point of contention when so many marketing strategies are aimed at the homemaker, more often than not portrayed by a woman? A recent commercial shows a man in a state of panic because his wife was running late and wouldn't have time to fix dinner for their family. What message does this send to our youth, and how is this affecting the way young girls dream of their futures? If equal rights are to become reality, the media needs to rethink the way it represents gender roles in its ads.

Which of the following statements, if false, most weakens the argument?

Choose all that apply.

[A] Gender roles are not clearly distinguished in modern society.

[B] It is the responsibility of the media to shape the cultural values of society.

[C] Gender roles are clearly distinguished in modern society.

286. The city of Mount Claire is accepting applications for volunteer firefighters. Join the ranks of men and women giving their time and energy to a worthy cause. **Training is provided to ensure the safety of all volunteers.** Interested parties must have health insurance in order to participate. Mount Claire assumes no responsibility for incidents or injuries that occur during the course of duty.

In the argument given, the boldfaced sentence plays which of the following roles?

(A) It highlights the training provided.

(B) It provides evidence to support the lack of responsibility by Mount Claire.

(C) It supports the need for health insurance.

(D) It represents a contradiction.

(E) It advocates against volunteering.

287. Back of Beyond Books is having another blowout sale on all new and used books Labor Day weekend. Barry Simmons, the store's owner, hopes the sale will increase readership and provide a foundation to carry the business through the next quarter. Book sales have decreased substantially with the advent of electronic reading devices and e-books. The last few sales have allowed the store to break even despite this new trend in reading. **Simmons does not believe that reading an e-book provides the same level of enjoyment as reading a bound book. He will have to continue holding as many sales as it takes to keep his doors open.**

Which of the following best describes the function of the boldfaced sentences in the argument above?

(A) The first provides the evidence to support the assumption; the second provides part of the assumption.

(B) The first provides the assumption; the second provides the evidence to support it.

(C) The first is the conclusion; the second weakens the conclusion.

(D) The first states the problem; the second weakens the argument.

(E) The first weakens the assumption; the second is the assumption.

288. One of the biggest challenges facing Roosevelt High School is generating enough funding to support its traveling choir program. Thirty students comprise the school's choir, making attendance at competitions and events an expensive endeavor. However, these competitions and events raise awareness and sometimes garner cash prizes for the winning schools. That money can be used for travel costs and the purchase of new choir robes, which the group has not had for many years. Without the robes, success in competitions is unlikely. Therefore, for the betterment of the student body, the student council should support the choir and its endeavor for new choir robes.

Which statement, if true, most weakens the assumption in the argument?

(A) The school has a policy against fundraising.

(B) All of the students enjoy singing in the choir.

(C) The betterment of the choir has no effect on the rest of the student body.

(D) The choir is the school's most successful club.

(E) Success at choir competitions is a priority of the administration.

289. The new ride service in Seattle is causing a buzz in the state legislature. Formal taxi companies, such as Yellow Cab, are lobbying for laws that would hinder the ability of informal independent ride companies to grab a portion of the ride service market by providing a lower cost alternative. The reduced rates provided by the independent services are drawing the attention of urban dwellers, and Yellow Cab has seen its profits decrease since these companies hit the scene. Legislation requiring these independent services to pay higher tax rates would force them to raise their prices, making the competition fair.

Which of the following statements, if true, most weakens the assumption that higher tax rates make the competition fair?

(A) Yellow Cab pays more taxes than the other companies.

(B) The burden to improve Yellow Cab's business is on the state.

(C) Higher tax rates will force the other companies out of business.

(D) Yellow Cab could lower its rates to remain competitive.

(E) Taxi service use is at an all-time low.

290. Media is an integral and essential part of national elections in that it allows the public to stay informed and follow the candidates throughout their campaigns to get a solid feel for their character. When used the right way, the media supports the democratic process by promoting transparency. Yet, the public is often skeptical about media sources, assuming that some sort of corruption is taking place. That's why the most important role the media plays in the democratic process is in broadcasting the candidate debates. More than 67 million people tuned in to the first presidential debate in 2012, according to the Nielson ratings, which accounts for more than half of the number of votes during the election. Thus, most voters were able to make an informed decision at the polls.

Which of the following statements must be true for the assumption that the most important role the media plays in the democratic process is in broadcasting the candidate debates to be false?

(A) The debates are the only source of coverage elections get.

(B) The media provides informed coverage of the debates.

(C) Newspapers and magazines are more widely viewed by voters than other news outlets.

(D) Voters consider the media to be a trustworthy source of information.

(E) Voters always vote according to the outcomes of the debates.

291. The popularity of social media, such as Instagram and Facebook, allows people to post anything to anyone. Recent trends in tweets, posts, and links include reposting professional photos, sharing music, and using quoted material to convey a particular message. Copyright infringement laws dictate that these forms of work, outside of the public domain, require permission and licensing to use for personal reasons. The federal government cracked down on music piracy in the 2000s, but no such action has been implemented thus far concerning Internet copyright infringement and social media. This issue is clearly not as important as music piracy.

Which of the following best represents the assumption of the above argument?

(A) Music is easier to copy than photos and quoted material.

(B) In the new age of the Internet, copyright no longer applies.

(C) As long as the material is attributed to the originator, it is not copyright infringement.

(D) The federal government does not consider social media as a legitimate publishing venue.

(E) The federal government views everything on the Internet as public domain.

292. More than $2 million is spent each year by anxious parents who want their children to get into good colleges. What is this money spent on? It's not tuition or bribes. Rather, this money goes to college entrance exams, test preparation courses, and tutors, with the hope of increasing their child's score and landing that elusive place on the accepted list. **However, just having a good score on the entrance exam will not get a child into a good school.** Admissions officers also look at the type of high school courses taken by students and their level of success in those courses. Schools are also interested in extracurricular activities and anything that shows a student is well rounded. Therefore, as much attention needs to be paid to other factors in a child's education as that given to entrance exams.

What is the function of the boldfaced sentence in the above argument?

(A) It states the assumption.

(B) It weakens the assumption.

(C) It states the main problem.

(D) It provides the cause of the problem.

(E) It provides support for the assumption.

293. Most of the world's population outside of English-speaking countries are fairly fluent in English or can at least be conversational. This bilingualism stems from the recognition of the advantages of knowing English in modern society. Children in Germany, China, France, and Italy, to name a few, all learn English as part of the academic requirements in the K-12 curriculum. Despite the fact that, according to the U.S. Census, there are 50 million Hispanics living in the United States, Spanish is still considered a foreign language and is just one of the many languages students can choose to learn. Yet, as the population of non-native English speakers increases, the need for bilingual communicators will also increase. It is time for the U.S. education system to start making Spanish a mandatory language to learn.

The author's argument suggests which of the following?

(A) There is no indication that learning Spanish will increase a student's chances for future success.

(B) Spanish is declining in popularity.

(C) Students who do not know Spanish will be at a disadvantage.

(D) There are just as many opportunities for non-Spanish speakers as there are for Spanish speakers.

(E) English is the most important language in the world.

294. Animal rights activists believe that the activity of hunting is cruel and unnecessary. The argument is that animal lives are just as valuable as human lives and should be protected as such, not proffered up for murder. Whereas there may be truth in these ideas, many people around the world live in poverty and are malnourished. Government regulations and policies do not provide the appropriate resources to help these individuals in need, so many, especially in rural communities, turn to hunting to procure nourishment for them and their families. If the activists had their way, these families would not be able to survive.

Which of the following statements strengthens the assumption that families would not be able to survive if the activists had their way?

(A) Hunting is not the only way needy families can get food.

(B) Animal activists understand the need for families to be independent of government subsidies.

(C) Many families rely on hunting to survive during difficult times.

(D) Federal subsidies effectively provide support for impoverished families.

(E) Hunting is mostly done recreationally.

295. States should revise their traffic laws to remove the "no fault" clause regarding rear-end accidents. **Currently, the law says that the person in the last car is responsible for the accident.** This assumption is based on the premise that the person in the back should have been traveling at a safe enough distance to stop in the event of an emergency. This law is unfair and often punishes the wrong person.

What role does the boldfaced sentence play in supporting the assumption?

(A) It provides a solution to the assumption.

(B) It does not support the assumption.

(C) It weakens the assumption.

(D) It states the problem leading to the assumption.

(E) It supports the problem.

296. *Avatar* grossed more sales than any other movie in history. The special effects used in the movie were a new development by the director. Graphics and other animation techniques created mind-blowing visual effects that stunned audiences. Other movies released at the same time did not contain visual effects and did not do as well at the box office. It is clear that moviegoers are not interested in standard film production anymore.

Select the sentence from the passage which best supports the reasoning behind *Avatar*'s success at the box office.

(A) Graphics and other animation techniques created mind-blowing visual effects that stunned audiences.

(B) Other movies released at the same time did not contain visual effects and did not do as well at the box office.

(C) The special effects used in the movie were a new development by the director.

(D) *Avatar* grossed more sales than any other movie in history.

(E) It is clear that moviegoers are not interested in standard film production anymore.

297. Public health is a major concern for the Centers for Disease Control in Atlanta, Georgia. One of the projects the scientists are always working on is the impact of environmental factors on human beings. What they found was that the hormones used in raising cattle for slaughter are transferred to the human body during ingestion. These hormones increase the availability of enzyme receptors that attach to cancerous cells in the body. With information such as this, it is no wonder cancer rates have skyrocketed in the last 15 years.

Which of the following, if true, would most strengthen the argument?

(A) The beef industry is in peril due to the advent of cancer in cows.

(B) More Americans are eating white meat instead of beef.

(C) Hormones provide the body with cancer-fighting agents.

(D) The CDC has determined that there is no connection between beef consumption and cancer.

(E) The consumption of beef has increased over the last 15 years.

298. Scientists believe if the rate of human use of fossil fuels and methane gas continues into the future, the greenhouse gas effect will increase, causing detriment to the natural environment and human health. It would be wise for people living near the polar caps and the ocean to invest in flood insurance.

The argument above presupposes which of the following?

(A) Worsening environmental conditions will lead to increased sea levels.

(B) Humans are incapable of stopping the negative effects to the environment.

(C) Fossil fuels cause floods.

(D) The polar caps are not affected by greenhouse gases.

(E) Fossil fuels and methane gases are the only factors affecting the environment.

299. Forty people showed up to contest the new dog park regulations at Wednesday's city council meeting. Opponents to the rules, which state all dog waste must be picked up and discarded in the provided receptacles, argue that the nature of the park makes it impossible to always know what your dog is doing. They claim it would require them to follow their dogs around the whole park. "It ruins the whole experience," said James Warren, an avid park attendant. A petition was given to the council stating a boycott of the park would take effect immediately with the passing of the regulations.

Which sentence most accurately supports the assumption made by dog park users in the argument?

(A) Opponents to the rules, which state all dog waste must be picked up and discarded in the provided receptacles, argue that the nature of the park makes it impossible to always know what your dog is doing.

(B) It ruins the whole experience.

(C) Forty people showed up to contest the new dog park regulations at Wednesday's city council meeting.

(D) They claim it would require them to follow their dogs around the whole park.

(E) A petition was given to the council stating a boycott of the park would take effect immediately with the passing of the regulations.

300. In response to a lawsuit regarding the lack of maternity leave, furniture mogul Genie Phillips and Co. has implemented a new policy that addresses not only the court's concerns, but the company's as well. Affective March 3, 2012, all pregnant employees will be provided two months paid leave, after which they have the choice to return to work or work remotely for a portion of their salary for a duration of two additional months. There are no options for unpaid leave.

Which of the following, if true, casts the most doubt about the fairness of the maternity policy?

(A) Most companies only allow two months of leave before requiring unpaid time for an extended leave.

(B) Maternity policies are not required by law.

(C) The amount of work required during the additional two months of remote work is proportional to the reduced salary.

(D) The amount of work required during the additional two months of remote work is the same load as someone working full-time onsite.

(E) Employees wishing to return to work after two months can use vacation days to take additional time off.

301. **Lactose intolerance is a growing health concern for many families.** Fortunately, soy milk is a suitable alternative. **This non-dairy option allows those unable to digest milk proteins and enzymes to still enjoy like products without the problems.** In fact, one in five consumers said they couldn't tell the difference between regular yogurt and soy yogurt. If this trend continues, America's dairy farmers may find themselves out of business.

In the argument given, the boldfaced statements play which of the following roles?

(A) The first statement presents the problem, and the second statement expresses a solution.

(B) The first statement sets up the conclusion, and the second statement supports it.

(C) The second statement is the assumption made, and the first statement weakens this assumption.

(D) The first statement sets up the assumption, and the second statement weakens this assumption.

(E) The second statement provides support for the solution made in the first statement.

302. In a worldwide survey, 500 adults ages 18 to 25 were asked the number one reason they purchased their cars. A majority (72 percent) said they bought their cars to get to and from work. Other top motives included convenience (15 percent), status (8 percent), and social pursuits (5 percent). The type of vehicle purchased showed a correlative trend with the motivation behind the purchase. **Stable and economically sound vehicles were the top choices for those using their cars for professional reasons, and flashy, more expensive cars were the most popular choices for those with more personal and social interests.**

The boldfaced statement helps structure the argument around which assumption?

(A) Focusing car promotions on the more expensive, flashy vehicles will increase sales the most.

(B) Car manufacturers can increase sales by catering certain vehicles to a certain audience.

(C) Although the motivations are different, the types of cars chosen are similar.

(D) People use their emotions when deciding what car to purchase.

(E) Young drivers are less responsible than older drivers.

303. The following memo was distributed to company employees.

Dear employees of Burgden and Associates:

Effective July 1, you will have the option of either receiving a modest increase in your pay rate or purchasing shares in the company. Shares will be sold at a reduced rate of 92% of the cost to the public per share. Over the course of 5 years, you have the opportunity to recoup a 215% return on your investment. However, this figure depends on the market. If the market drops, the price of the shares will decrease, which could result in a financial loss for the shareholders. Regardless, it is in the best interest of all employees to invest in the company in this way. Decisions must be made no later than June 28. Please see your HR representative for more information.

Which of the following statements, if true, best supports the company's position that it is in the best interest of employees to invest in the company?

(A) Employees should prioritize their financial interests over those of the company.

(B) The salary earned from incremental raises during the five year period is equal to the return on shares.

(C) The stock market is at its lowest point in history.

(D) The shares will increase in value at the end of 10 years.

(E) The return from the investment will be matched by the company to equal what would have been earned through a raise at the end of 5 years.

304. Annie May was forced to close the doors of her bakery after a Krispy Donuts opened across the street. She was unable to compete with the conglomerate's low prices. She would have had to reduce her prices by 25 percent to remain in line with her competition. A reduction of that proportion would have caused her to lose money, which would have run the business into the ground. Banking on customer loyalty was the best option for Annie May.

Which of the following sentences most successfully strengthens the assumption of the argument?

(A) A reduction of that proportion would have caused her to lose money.

(B) Annie May was forced to close the doors of her bakery after a Krispy Donuts opened across the street.

(C) She would have had to reduce her prices by 25 percent to remain in line with her competition.

(D) That sort of loss would have run the business into the ground.

(E) She was unable to compete with the conglomerate's low prices.

305. A recent study revealed that former beauty pageant contestants are four times more likely to suffer from severe clinical depression than are average women in the same age group. Other complications such as eating disorders and chemical dependency are also more prevalent in this population of women. It is clear that the pressure for these women, often very young at the time, to constantly appear beautiful while competing has detrimental effects on their self-esteem in later life.

The argument above relies on which of the following assumptions?

(A) Pageant judges are harsh toward the contestants.

(B) Being judged by one's appearance leads to psychological trauma.

(C) The desire to be beautiful is the only motivation for women.

(D) Depression is a serious disease with many causes.

(E) Many young women gain confidence from competing in beauty pageants.

306. **Many causes of poor health in the world stem from food production. The ingredients in the food and the methods used to produce it often lead to disturbances in the digestive system that affect all facets of physical health.** For instance, the methods used to create iodized salt strip the product of all essential minerals, but these minerals are required for proper functioning in the body. If these elements are not present, the body must deplete its mineral stores to make up for it. Contrarily, Himalayan salt, as well as sea salt and other mineral-rich salts, maintains the natural integrity of the mineral and support proper bodily functioning.

Which of the following best describes the function of the boldfaced sentences in the argument?

(A) They both represent the assumption.

(B) They contradict each other in supporting the assumption.

(C) The first weakens the argument; the second supports it.

(D) The first presents the problem; the second weakens it.

(E) The first strengthens the assumption; the second weakens it.

307. The American Civil Liberties Union launched a complaint against a Mississippi middle school in 2008 in defense of a student expelled, because of an unconstitutional search of his cellphone after it was taken by a teacher. According to the complaint, the act of searching the phone without permission or probable cause is in violation of the student's privacy and civil rights. However, school officials state it is their responsibility to protect the student body by exposing all forms of suspicious activity. If the state's supreme court agrees with the school, it could mean a major shift in how privacy laws are managed within school districts.

Which of the following statements, if true, would most weaken the student's argument?

(A) A rash of bullying has occurred at the school.

(B) Only school-affiliated materials are the property of the school.

(C) The principal has a history of overstepping his bounds.

(D) School policies do not state any regulations regarding cellphones.

(E) Anything brought onto school property is subject to searches.

308. The flash of dollar signs can be hard to ignore for a budding athlete with dreams of professional stardom. Yet, an athlete who plays at the college level is not eligible to receive income from sponsorships, public appearances, interviews, or the use of his name and likeness in advertisements and on merchandise. Many college athletes are not able to meet their financial needs with the stipends. Rather, the universities recoup this income and use it for infrastructure and other financial needs of the school. This inability to make a living off their status is the reason that many athletes choose to turn pro right out of high school or after one year. If professional athletes didn't make so much money, the amateur athletes would not be enticed in the same way.

Select the sentence which strengthens the assumption of the above argument.

(A) Yet, an athlete who plays at the college level is not eligible to receive income from sponsorships, public appearances, interviews, or the use of his name and likeness in advertisements and on merchandise.

(B) If professional athletes didn't make so much money, the amateur athletes would not be enticed in the same way.

(C) The flash of dollar signs can be a hard thing to ignore for a budding athlete with dreams of professional stardom.

(D) Many college athletes are not able to meet their financial needs with the stipends.

(E) This inability to make a living off their status is the reason that many athletes choose to turn pro right out of high school or after one year.

309. Smoking, including the use of e-cigarettes, on airplanes is not allowed in the United States. This law has many passengers up in arms, claiming that long flights create anxiety for smokers unable to calm their nerves except by smoking. The FAA needs to address this new crisis in passenger comfort to avoid problems stemming from unruly passenger behavior.

Which statement must be false in order for the assumption to be true?

(A) Smoking on planes is common in other countries.

(B) Smoking was not allowed on flights even before the advent of e-cigarettes.

(C) Reports of stressful flight experiences have never been attributed to a lack of smoking.

(D) The FAA does not support smoking anywhere in the airport.

(E) E-cigarettes do not produce harmful second-hand smoke like cigarettes do.

310. Social work researchers have determined that cognitive development begins within the first five years of life. A study of 100 children followed from birth to 13 years old shows a surprising trend in high test scores for children who attended preschool. These preschools, though pricey, give these children an advantage in elementary school over children who haven't attended preschool. This report has prompted more parents to shell out thousands of dollars to enroll their kids in private preschools. This phenomenon has created a difficult predicament for families in lower socioeconomic classes.

Select the sentence which best supports the assumption of the above argument.

(A)   This phenomenon has created a difficult predicament for families in lower socioeconomic classes.

(B)   A study of 100 children followed from birth to 13 years old shows a surprising trend in high test scores for children who attended preschool.

(C)   These preschools, though pricey, give these children an advantage in elementary school over children who haven't attended preschool.

(D)   Social work researchers have determined that cognitive development begins within the first five years of life.

(E)   This report has prompted more parents to shell out thousands of dollars to enroll their kids in private preschools.

Chapter 4

Problem Solving

• •

*T*he math problems in the GRE cover the same topics that you covered in high school. If you're fresh out of math class, you'll probably be fine going through these quickly. However, if it's been a few years since you've added fractions, you may want to work these carefully and pay close attention to the solutions.

The Problems You'll Work On

When working through the questions in this chapter, be prepared to answer questions on

- ✔ Basic math, including fractions, decimals, percentages, and ratios
- ✔ Algebra, including linear equations, coordinate geometry, and quadratic equations
- ✔ Geometry, which covers both basic shapes and 3-dimensional shapes
- ✔ Word problems, including weighted averagers, rate/time/distance, and permutations and combinations
- ✔ Tables and graphs, including arithmetic mean, standard deviation, and data analysis

What to Watch Out For

Shortfalls in math are in three basic categories. See whether you're prone to one of these in particular:

- ✔ Mistakes in simple math, such as not placing the decimal point correctly
- ✔ Mistakes in working the problem, such as multiplying exponents when you should be adding them
- ✔ Not knowing how to work a certain math problem, such as setting up a probability

All numbers used in this exam are real numbers.

All figures lie in a plane.

Angle measures are positive; points and angles are in the position shown.

311. 10, 5, 0, –5, –10

Which of these numbers is the farthest from the number 1 on a number line?

(A)   10

(B)   5

(C)   0

(D)   –5

(E)   –10

312. Tabitha is the 32nd person in line counting from one end and the 12th person in line counting from the other. How many total people are in line?

313. What is the sum of all the positive integer factors of 12?

314. Which of the following integers are multiples of both 2 and 3?

Select all the correct answers.

[A]   8

[B]   9

[C]   12

[D]   18

[E]   21

[F]   36

315. Which of the following numbers have a product between –1 and 0?

Select the two choices that meet the criteria when multiplied together.

(A)   –20

(B)   –10

(C) 2^{-4}

(D) 3^{-2}

316. If $n \neq 0$, which of the following expressions could have a value less than n?

Select all the correct answers.

[A] $2n$

[B] n^2

[C] $2 - n$

317. n and p are integers > 1. $5n$ is the square of a number and $75np$ is the cube of a number. What is the smallest value for $n + p$?

(A)   14

(B)   18

(C)   20

(D)   22

(E)   38

318. Two sets of four consecutive positive integers have exactly one integer in common. How much greater is the sum of the integers in the set with the greater numbers than the sum of the integers in the other set?

(A)   4

(B)   7

(C)   8

(D)   10

(E)   12

319. A straight fence is to be constructed from 6-inch-wide posts and separated by 5-foot-long chains. If the fence begins and ends with a post, which of the following could be the length of the fence in feet?

Select all the correct answers.

[A] 17

[B] 28

[C] 35

[D] 39

[E] 50

320. The sum of the odd integers from 1 to 99, inclusive, is 2,500. What is the sum of the even integers from 2 to 100, inclusive?

321. Three children share the same birthday. John is more than twice as old as Sean and Sean is more than four years older than Randy. If John is less than 16 years old, which of the following are possible values for Sean's age in years?

Select all the correct answers.

[A] 5

[B] 6

[C] 7

[D] 8

[E] 9

322. The sum of four consecutive integers is 410. What is the value of the least of these integers?

323. If $81 is to be divided among n people, where $n > 1$, so that each person gets $$x$, where x is a whole number > 1, how many different values could there be for n?

324. In a game of 50 questions, the final score is calculated by subtracting twice the number of wrong answers from the total number of correct answers. If a player answered all questions and received a final score of 35, how many wrong answers did he give?

325. 45, 300, 610, 1,230

In the preceding sequence, every term after the first is formed by multiplying by x and then adding y, where x and y are positive integers. What is the value of $x + y$?

326. a, b, and c are integers, and a and b are not equivalent. If $ax + bx = c$, where c is a prime integer, which of the following is the value of x?

(A) 1

(B) 2

(C) 3

(D) 4

(E) 5

327. If x is a prime number, which of the following *could* be used to describe $3x$?

Select all the correct answers.

[A] Even

[B] Odd

[C] Prime number

[D] Divisible by 4

328. Evaluate $\dfrac{3x}{y}$, where x is the smallest prime number and y is the least common multiple of 5 and 10.

(A) 2

(B) 3

(C) 5

(D) $\dfrac{2}{5}$

(E) $\dfrac{3}{5}$

329. Evaluate $\dfrac{2x}{y}$, where x is the smallest odd prime number and y is the second smallest odd prime number.

(A) $\dfrac{1}{5}$

(B) $\dfrac{2}{5}$

(C) $\dfrac{3}{5}$

(D) $\dfrac{4}{5}$

(E) $1\dfrac{1}{5}$

330. Evaluate $\dfrac{1}{2}x(y)$, where x is the third smallest prime number and y is the smallest two-digit prime number.

(A) 21

(B) 25

(C) 27.5

(D) 30

(E) 31.5

331. Evaluate $\left| x^3 + 5 \right|$ where $x = -3$.

(A) 46

(B) 32

(C) 22

(D) −22

(E) −32

332. What is the smallest possible value of $\left| 2x^2 - 7 \right|$, when x is a whole number greater than 1?

(A) 0

(B) 1

(C) −1

(D) 11

(E) −11

333. Evaluate $\left| \dfrac{3}{4}x - 2 \right|$ where $x = -4$.

(A) 5

(B) 3

(C) 2

(D) −2

(E) −3

334. What values for x make $\left| x + 2 \right| = 7$ true?

Select all the correct answers.

[A] 9

[B] 5

[C] 4

[D] −5

[E] −9

335. Which values of x make $\left| 2x - 3 \right| - 4 = 3$ true?

Select all the correct answers.

[A] 9

[B] 5

[C] 2

[D] −2

[E] −5

336. Which values of x make $\left(\dfrac{|2x-3|}{4}\right)^2 = 9$ true?

Select all the correct answers.

[A] 7.5

[B] 4.5

[C] −4.5

[D] −7.5

[E] −9

337. Which values of x make $|x-4| < 3$ true?

Select all the correct answers.

[A] 1

[B] 2

[C] 3

[D] 4

[E] 5

[F] 6

[G] 7

338. Which values of x make $|2x+3| < 6$ true?

Select all the correct answers.

[A] 1

[B] 0.5

[C] 0

[D] −1

[E] −2

[F] −3.5

339. Which of these absolute value inequalities results in $-2 < x < 4$?

(A) $|x+1| < 3$

(B) $|x-1| < 3$

(C) $|x+1| < 2$

(D) $|x-1| < 2$

(E) $|x-2| < 3$

340. Which values of x make $|x-2| > -3$ true?

Select all the correct answers.

[A] 7

[B] 5

[C] 2

[D] 0

[E] −1

[F] −2

[G] −3

341. A store sells pencils for $0.25 each and erasers for $0.35 each. What is the total cost of 18 pencils and 100 erasers?

342. Box A is 20 inches long and 3 inches wide. Box B is 9 inches long and 10 inches wide. What number can be multiplied by the area of Box A in order for it to equal the area of Box B?

(A) 1

(B) 1.5

(C) 2

(D) 3.5

(E) 5

343. On a number line, the values 0.312 and 0.326 are separated by seven evenly spaced intervals. Point P is three intervals to the right of 0.312 and four intervals to the left of 0.326. What is the value of P?

344. If a car gets 33 miles per gallon using gasoline that costs $2.95 per gallon, what is the approximate cost, in dollars, of the gasoline used to drive the car 350 miles?

(A) $10

(B) $20

(C) $30

(D) $40

(E) $50

345. What is the average of $\frac{4}{10}$ and $\frac{5}{1,000}$?

(A) 25,002

(B) 2,502

(C) 0.225

(D) 0.2025

(E) 0.02025

346. Write 8.206×10^{-3} as a decimal.

(A) 0.008206

(B) 0.8206

(C) 82.06

(D) 820.6

(E) 8,206

347. Write 5.85×10^{-5} as a decimal.

(A) 585,000

(B) 5,850

(C) 5.85

(D) 0.00585

(E) 0.0000585

348. Write 1.27562×10^4 as a decimal.

(A) 1.27562

(B) 127.562

(C) 12,756.2

(D) 0.127562

(E) 0.000127562

349. Which of these expressions will give a value $0.5 < x < 1$?

Select all the correct answers.

[A] $1 + 0.04$

[B] $(1 - 0.04)2$

[C] $1 - (0.04)^{\frac{1}{2}}$

[D] $1 + 0.042$

[E] $1 - 0.043$

[F] $\dfrac{(1 - 0.043)}{2}$

[G] $(1 - 0.043)^2$

350. A gallon of water weighs approximately 8.3 pounds. How many gallons of water are there in 614.2 pounds?

(A) 74,000

(B) 7,400

(C) 740

(D) 74

(E) 7.4

351. Find the difference between four and ninety nine one-hundredths and three and five one-hundredths.

(A) 1.94

(B) 8.04

(C) 1.64

(D) 0.61

(E) 1.41

352. Lauren bought 4 pounds of steak at $3.89 per pound, 4 dozen eggs at $1.05 per dozen, 2 gallons of milk at $1.99 each, and three loaves of bread at $1.79 each. Calculate the total cost of these items.

(A) $23.74

(B) $25.13

(C) $29.11

(D) $24.91

(E) $8.72

353. Shipment of packages costs $0.65 for the first 250 grams and $0.10 for each additional 100 grams. Which could be the weight, in grams, of a package for which the charge is $1.55?

(A) 1,155

(B) 1,145

(C) 1,040

(D) 950

(E) 259

354. The total weight of a tin and the cookies it contains is 2 pounds. After $\frac{3}{4}$ of the cookies are eaten, the tin and the remaining cookies weigh 0.8 pounds. What is the weight of the empty tin in pounds?

(A) 0.2

(B) 0.3

(C) 0.4

(D) 0.5

(E) 0.6

355. Which values of x make $\frac{1}{3} < x < 0.76$ true? Select all the correct answers.

[A] $\frac{2}{5}$

[B] $\frac{1}{4}$

[C] $\frac{5}{16}$

[D] $\frac{1}{3}$

[E] $\frac{2}{3}$

356. A machine puts *a* labels on boxes in *m* minutes. What fraction represents the number of hours it will take to put labels on *b* boxes?

(A) $60\frac{bm}{a}$

(B) $\frac{bm}{60a}$

(C) $\frac{ba}{60m}$

(D) $\frac{60b}{am}$

(E) $\frac{b}{60am}$

357. *S* is the sum of 8, 6, 4, 2 and *x*. What is the value of *x* if $x = \frac{1}{5}S$?

358. Of the following, which is greater than $\frac{1}{2}$?

Select all the correct answers.

[A] $\frac{2}{5}$

[B] $\frac{4}{7}$

[C] $\frac{4}{9}$

[D] $\frac{5}{11}$

[E] $\frac{6}{13}$

[F] $\frac{8}{15}$

[G] $\frac{9}{17}$

359. A 6-inch ruler is marked in $\frac{1}{10}$-inch units. How many marks will there be on the ruler, including the 0 and 6-inch marks?

360. How much greater is the number 0.127 than $\frac{1}{8}$?

(A) $\frac{1}{2}$

(B) $\frac{1}{5}$

(C) $\frac{1}{50}$

(D) $\frac{1}{500}$

(E) $\frac{1}{250}$

361. If Kristen earned \$$x$ and spent \$$y$ in a week, what part of her weekly salary did she save?

(A) $\frac{x-y}{y}$

(B) $\frac{x}{y}$

(C) $\frac{y}{x}$

(D) $\frac{y-x}{x}$

(E) $\frac{x-y}{x}$

362. What must $2\frac{1}{7}$ be divided by to give $1\frac{3}{7}$?

(A) $\frac{2}{3}$

(B) $\frac{1}{4}$

(C) $1\frac{1}{2}$

(D) $\frac{1}{3}$

(E) $1\frac{3}{4}$

363. What must $3\frac{4}{5}$ be multiplied by to give $10\frac{2}{5}$?

(A) $2\frac{2}{9}$

(B) $\frac{9}{20}$

(C) $39\frac{13}{20}$

(D) $2\frac{14}{19}$

(E) $\frac{19}{52}$

364. John wanted to share his candy with his friends. He gave half of his candy plus an additional piece to Jerry. He gave half of the remaining candy plus an additional piece to Bruce. By this time, John had one candy left. How many candy pieces did he start with?

(A) 8

(B) 9

(C) 10

(D) 11

(E) 12

365. A fisherman sold half of his catch and then ate one fish for lunch. He had 22 fish remaining. How many fish did he catch?

(A) 43

(B) 44

(C) 45

(D) 46

(E) 47

366. One pipe can fill a tank in 1 hour, while another pipe can fill the same tank in 2 hours. How long will it take to fill the tank if both pipes are used together?

(A) $\frac{2}{3}$ hour

(B) $\frac{1}{3}$ hour

(C) 1 hour

(D) $\frac{4}{5}$ hour

(E) $\frac{3}{4}$ hour

367. There remains one third as much time as has gone. Given the day starts at 12 a.m. (midnight), what is the current time?

(A) 12 p.m.

(B) 6 p.m.

(C) 4 p.m.

(D) 8 p.m.

(E) 6 a.m.

368. Jill walked to her neighbor's house at 2:32 p.m. and returned home at 5:13 p.m. How long was Jill out of her house?

(A) 2 hours 81 minutes

(B) 1 hour 41 minutes

(C) 1 hour 36 minutes

(D) 2 hours 41 minutes

(E) 3 hours 19 minutes

369. Considering the positions on the number line, which of the following could be a value for x?

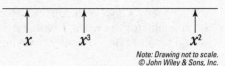

Note: Drawing not to scale.
© John Wiley & Sons, Inc.

Select all the correct answers.

[A] $\frac{5}{3}$

[B] $\frac{3}{5}$

[C] $\frac{-2}{5}$

[D] $\frac{-3}{4}$

[E] $\frac{-5}{2}$

370. The sum of the numerator and the denominator of a certain fraction is 104, and the value of the fraction reduces to $\frac{9}{17}$. What is the fraction?

(A) $\frac{36}{68}$

(B) $\frac{36}{104}$

(C) $\frac{42}{62}$

(D) $\frac{48}{56}$

(E) $\frac{68}{36}$

371. A recycling company collected $6\frac{2}{3}$ tons of scrap metal on Monday, $7\frac{3}{4}$ tons on Tuesday, and $4\frac{1}{2}$ tons on Wednesday. If the company's goal is to collect 25 tons of scrap metal for the week, what amount would result in the company reaching its goal?

Select all the correct answers.

[A] $6\frac{1}{12}$ tons

[B] $6\frac{1}{2}$ tons

[C] $5\frac{1}{2}$ tons

[D] $6\frac{1}{4}$ tons

[E] $6\frac{1}{13}$ tons

[F] 7 tons

[G] $6\frac{1}{3}$ tons

[H] $5\frac{3}{5}$ tons

372. If two adults can do the amount of yard work in $3\frac{1}{2}$ days that takes a child six days to do, what fraction of the work would remain unfinished after two adults and two children had been working in the yard for just one day?

(A) $\frac{19}{21}$

(B) $\frac{1}{3}$

(C) $\frac{1}{7}$

(D) $\frac{2}{19}$

(E) $\frac{2}{21}$

373. There are small hoses and large hoses filling a swimming pool. Each of the three small hoses works at $\frac{2}{3}$ the rate of the one large hose. If all four hoses work at the same time, in what fraction of the time should the pool be filled than if the large hose worked alone?

(A) $\frac{1}{3}$

(B) $\frac{2}{3}$

(C) $\frac{3}{4}$

(D) $\frac{4}{5}$

(E) $\frac{4}{7}$

374. A bag contains red, green, and blue candies. One-fifth of the candies are red. There are $\frac{1}{3}$ as many blue candies as green candies, and there are ten fewer red candies than green candies. How many candies are in the bag?

(A) 20

(B) 25

(C) 15

(D) 12

(E) 10

375. The numerator of a certain fraction is a positive integer that is two less than the denominator, and the sum of the fraction and its reciprocal is equal to $\frac{25}{12}$. What is the fraction?

(A) $\frac{6}{8}$

(B) $-\frac{6}{8}$

(C) $\frac{8}{10}$

(D) $\frac{10}{12}$

(E) $-\frac{16}{18}$

376. In a school election, there were two candidates for class president. The candidate who got 40% of the votes polled was defeated by 16,000 votes. Calculate the total number of votes polled.

(A) 24,000

(B) 28,000

(C) 30,000

(D) 35,000

(E) 40,000

377. Twenty-five percent of 600 is equal to 15% of what number?

378. A soccer team has won ten games and has lost five games. If the team wins the remaining games of the season, it will have won 80% of its games. How many games in total will have been played?

379. A store made a profit of $5 on the sale of a shirt that cost the store $15. What is the profit expressed as a percent of the store's cost? Give your answer to the nearest whole percent.

380. A circular label is enlarged to fit the lid of a jar. The new label diameter is 50% larger than the original. By what percentage has the area of the label increased?

(A) 50

(B) 80

(C) 100

(D) 125

(E) 250

381. A typist can type 45 words per minute. He increases his speed by 20%. How many words can he now type per hour?

382. A number x is eight times another number y. What percentage is y less than x?

(A) 1%

(B) 11%

(C) 12.5%

(D) 80%

(E) 87.5%

383. If S is 150% of T, what percent is T of $S + T$?

(A) 33.33%

(B) 40%

(C) 60%

(D) 75%

(E) 80%

384. The price of a TV is reduced by 25%. The new price is reduced by an additional 20%. What is the total discount after the two price reductions?

(A) 45%

(B) 40%

(C) 35%

(D) 32.5%

(E) 30%

385. A church was able to raise 75% of the total amount it needs for a new building by receiving an average donation of $600 from each parishioner. The people already solicited represent 60% of all parishioners. If the church is to raise exactly the amount it needs for the new building, what should be the average donation from the remaining people to be solicited?

(A) $150

(B) $250

(C) $300

(D) $400

(E) $500

386. What is $\sqrt{5}\%$ of $5\sqrt{5}$?

(A) 0.05

(B) 0.25

(C) 0.5

(D) 2.5

(E) 25

387. A discounted shirt is marked at $D, which is 15% less than the original price. Store employees are allowed an additional 10% reduction on the discounted price. If an employee buys the shirt, what will she have to pay in terms of D?

(A) 0.75D

(B) 0.76D

(C) 0.765D

(D) 0.775D

(E) 0.805D

388. What number is 150% greater than 6?

(A) 3

(B) 9

(C) 15

(D) 18

(E) 90

389. An ice cream shop received two types of cones (sugar cones and waffle cones). The box of sugar cones contained 10% broken cones and the box of waffle cones contained 4% broken cones. If the total number of broken cones is 66 and the total number of waffle cones is three times the total number of sugar cones, find the total number of all cones the shop received.

(A) 300

(B) 600

(C) 900

(D) 1,200

(E) 1,500

390. If the selling price of a product is increased by $162, the company will make a profit of 17% instead of having a loss of 19%. What is the cost price of this product for the company?

(A) $200

(B) $360

(C) $450

(D) $540

(E) $600

391. Participation in team sports was up 25% at the end of last year, but participation in individual sports was down 25%. How many times greater was the ratio of participation in team sports to individual sports at the end of the year, than the ratio at the beginning of the year? Round your answer to two decimal places.

392. A four-serving recipe uses 3 cups of flour and 2 cups of milk. How much flour and milk are needed for a 16-serving recipe?

(A) 3 cups of flour and 2 cups of milk

(B) 2 cups of flour and 3 cups of milk

(C) 9 cups of flour and 6 cups of milk

(D) 8 cups of flour and 12 cups of milk

(E) 12 cups of flour and 8 cups of milk

393. Karen can run a mile in 5 minutes and 50 seconds. Cameron can run a mile in 6 minutes and 40 seconds. Find the ratio of Karen's time to Cameron's time.

(A) 5.5 : 6.4

(B) 55 : 64

(C) 7 : 8

(D) 8 : 7

(E) 5 : 6

394. ∠ *AOC* is a right angle. Find the measurement of ∠ *BOC*.

$$\angle AOB : \angle BOC = 2 : 3$$

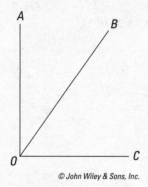

© John Wiley & Sons, Inc.

(A) 36°

(B) 45°

(C) 54°

(D) 60°

(E) 90°

395. A live horse is 1.8 meters high. A statue of the horse is 3 meters high. Find the ratio of the height of the horse to the height of the statue.

(A) 3 : 5

(B) 2 : 3

(C) 5 : 3

(D) 6 : 1

(E) 1 : 3

396. If three painters, painting at the same rate, take five days to paint a wall, how many days longer will it take with only two painters working?

397. The distance between two towns is 25 kilometers. Find the scale of the map if the distance between the towns on the map is 5 centimeters.

(A) 1 : 5,000,000

(B) 1 : 500,000

(C) 1 : 50,000

(D) 1 : 5,000

(E) 1 : 500

398. *AOC* is a straight line. Find the size of ∠ *AOB*.

$$\angle AOB : \angle BOC = 4 : 11$$

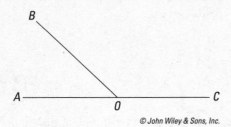

© John Wiley & Sons, Inc.

(A)   40°

(B)   48°

(C)   60°

(D)   132°

(E)   180°

399. A recipe for pastry has flour, butter, and water mixed in a $24 : 8 : 3$ ratio. If only 3 cups of flour are used, how many cups of butter should be used?

(A)   1/3 cup

(B)   3/8 cup

(C)   2/3 cup

(D)   3/4 cup

(E)   1 cup

400. The tallest building in the world, the Burj Khalifa in Dubai, is 828 meters tall. A model of the building is made using the ratio $1 : 5,000$.

Find the height of the model in centimeters (cm).

(A)   1,656 cm

(B)   165.6 cm

(C)   16.56 cm

(D)   1.656 cm

(E)   0.1656 cm

401. Point *B* lies on segment *AC*. *AB* = 7 and *BC* = 5. Find *AC*.

(A)   2

(B)   5

(C)   7

(D)   12

(E)   35

402. *AB* = 16. Point *M* is the midpoint of segment *AB*. Find *AM*.

(A)   2

(B)   4

(C)   8

(D)   16

(E)   32

403. What is the maximum number of points of intersection of four distinct lines in a single plane?

404. In this figure, AD = AC = CB. If *y* = 28, what is the value of *x*?

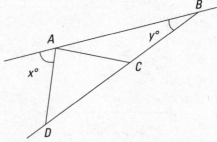

© John Wiley & Sons, Inc.

405. Lines *l* and *m* lie in the same plane, but have no points in common. They are both tangent to a circle with an area of 9π. What is the shortest distance between any point on line *l* and any point on line *m*?

406. Ray *YW* bisects angle *XYZ*. The measure of angle *XYZ* = 70 degrees. Find the measure of angle *XYW*.

(A) 35°

(B) 45°

(C) 70°

(D) 90°

(E) 180°

407. Lines *AB* and *CD* are parallel. Angles *1* and *4* are same-side interior angles. If the measure of angle *1* = 66 degrees, find the measure of angle *4*.

(A) 66°

(B) 90°

(C) 114°

(D) 180°

(E) 360°

408. Point *C* does not lie on line *AB*. How many lines can be drawn through point *C* that are parallel to line *AB*?

A ———————————————— B

. *C*

(A) 0

(B) 1

(C) 2

(D) 3

(E) 4

409. If two lines intersect at a point to form four angles, and one angle is twice as large as its adjacent angle, what is the degree measure of the smallest angle?

410. What positive value for *n* would make the following equations a pair of parallel lines on the same coordinate axes?

$$y = nx - 2$$
$$ny = 9x - 7$$

411. Find the area.

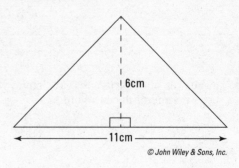

(A) 17 cm

(B) 23 cm

(C) 33 cm

(D) 60 cm

(E) 66 cm

412. Find the area.

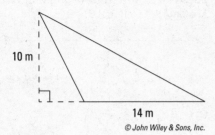

© John Wiley & Sons, Inc.

   (A)   4 m

   (B)   24 m

   (C)   30 m

   (D)   50 m

   (E)   70 m

413. The length of a rectangle is $\frac{2}{7}$ of the perimeter. What is the value of the diagonal of the rectangle, if the perimeter is 14 units?

414. How many times greater is the area of a rectangle with sides x and $3x$ than the area of a right angled isosceles triangle with side x?

415. If the area of this triangle is 108 cm², what is its perimeter in centimeters?

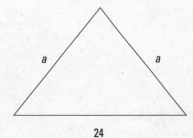

© John Wiley & Sons, Inc.

416. Find the length of c.

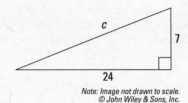

Note: Image not drawn to scale.
© John Wiley & Sons, Inc.

   (A)   5

   (B) $\sqrt{527}$

   (C)   25

   (D)   30

   (E)   31

417. Find the length of a.

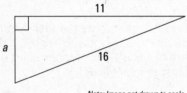

Note: Image not drawn to scale.
© John Wiley & Sons, Inc.

   (A)   5

   (B) $\sqrt{35}$

   (C) $\sqrt{135}$

   (D) $\sqrt{176}$

   (E) $\sqrt{377}$

418. Find the second leg of a right triangle with one leg of 3 centimeters (cm) and a hypotenuse of 5 centimeters.

   (A)   1 cm

   (B)   2 cm

   (C)   3 cm

   (D)   4 cm

   (E)   5 cm

419. Town B is 8 miles north and 17 miles east of Town A. How many miles apart are the two towns?

(A)   15 miles

(B)   18.5 miles

(C)   18.8 miles

(D)   20 miles

(E)   25 miles

420. Find the second leg of a right triangle with a first leg of 6 centimeters (cm) and a hypotenuse of 4 centimeters longer than the first leg.

(A)   2 cm

(B)   4 cm

(C)   6 cm

(D)   8 cm

(E)   10 cm

421. Find the area.

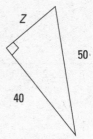

© John Wiley & Sons, Inc.

(A)   30

(B)   60

(C)   120

(D)   600

(E)   1,200

422. Triangle *ABC* is a right triangle. *AC* = 5, *CB* = 3, and angle *ADB* is a right angle. What is the length of *DB*?

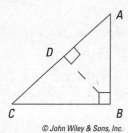

© John Wiley & Sons, Inc.

423. Find the perimeter of a right triangle with one leg of 12 centimeters (cm) and a hypotenuse of 15 centimeters.

(A)   21 cm

(B)   24 cm

(C)   27 cm

(D)   36 cm

(E)   40 cm

424. Find the perimeter of a right triangle with one leg of 6 centimeters (cm) and a hypotenuse of 4 centimeters longer than this leg.

(A)   8 cm

(B)   10 cm

(C)   20 cm

(D)   24 cm

(E)   25 cm

425. Find the length of the diagonal of a rectangle with a length of 3 and a width of 2.

(A) $\sqrt{5}$

(B) $\sqrt{6}$

(C) $\sqrt{13}$

(D)   5

(E)   6

426. Find the width of a rectangular field with a length of 100 yards and a diagonal length of 125 yards.

(A) 75 yards

(B) 100 yards

(C) 125 yards

(D) 150 yards

(E) 200 yards

427. Find the diagonal length across a square that has a side of 1 centimeter.

(A) 1

(B) $\sqrt{2}$

(C) 2

(D) $\sqrt{5}$

(E) 4

428. Find the area.

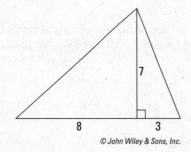

© John Wiley & Sons, Inc.

(A) 37.5

(B) 38.5

(C) 45

(D) 49

(E) 84

429. Find the area.

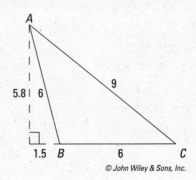

© John Wiley & Sons, Inc.

(A) 17.4

(B) 18

(C) 21.75

(D) 27

(E) 30

430. The area of the triangle is 42 units². Find the height of the triangle.

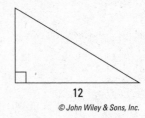

© John Wiley & Sons, Inc.

(A) 5

(B) 6

(C) 7

(D) 8

(E) 9

431. The area of the triangle is 22.5 units². Find the base of the triangle.

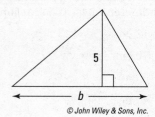

© John Wiley & Sons, Inc.

(A)   5

(B)   7

(C)   8

(D)   9

(E)   10

432. Find the perimeter.

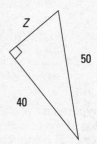

© John Wiley & Sons, Inc.

(A)   60

(B)   90

(C)   120

(D)   150

(E)   180

433. Find the perimeter of a right triangle with one leg of 12 centimeters (cm) and a hypotenuse of 1 centimeter longer than this leg.

(A)   1 cm

(B)   5 cm

(C)   12 cm

(D)   25 cm

(E)   30 cm

434. Find the perimeter of a right triangle with one leg of 3 centimeters (cm) and a hypotenuse of 5 centimeters.

(A)   7 cm

(B)   8 cm

(C)   9 cm

(D)   10 cm

(E)   12 cm

435. Find the area of this right triangle.

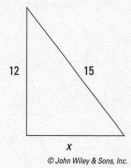

© John Wiley & Sons, Inc.

(A)   27

(B)   54

(C)   108

(D)   180

(E)   729

436. Find the length of the diagonal *AC*.

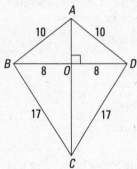

Note: Image not drawn to scale.
© John Wiley & Sons, Inc.

(A)   16

(B)   19

(C) $\sqrt{389}$

(D)   21

(E)   24

437. Find the length of *x*.

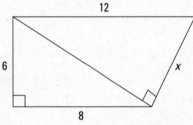

Note: Image not drawn to scale.
© John Wiley & Sons, Inc.

(A)   5

(B) $\sqrt{34}$

(C) $2\sqrt{11}$

(D)   8

(E) $2\sqrt{61}$

438. Find the perimeter of a right triangle if one leg is 1 centimeter (cm) longer than the second leg and the hypotenuse is 1 centimeter longer than the longest leg.

(A)   12 cm

(B)   10 cm

(C)   5 cm

(D)   4 cm

(E)   3 cm

439. If the area of the right triangle is 72, what is the value of *x*?

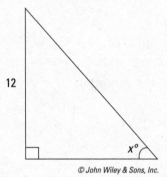

© John Wiley & Sons, Inc.

440. Find the hypotenuse of a right triangle with one leg of 8 centimeters (cm) and a perimeter of 24 centimeters.

(A)   6 cm

(B)   8 cm

(C)   10 cm

(D)   12 cm

(E)   18 cm

441. Rectangle *R* has a length of 30 inches and a width of 10 inches. Square *S* has a length of 5 inches. The perimeter of *S* is what fraction of the perimeter of *R*?

442. *ABCD* is a quadrilateral. Find the measure of angle *D*.

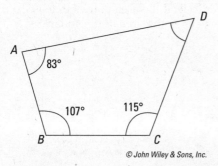

© John Wiley & Sons, Inc.

(A) 35°

(B) 45°

(C) 55°

(D) 65°

(E) 75°

443. *ABCD* is a parallelogram. Find the measure of angle *A*.

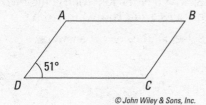

© John Wiley & Sons, Inc.

(A) 39°

(B) 51°

(C) 102°

(D) 119°

(E) 129°

444. The sides of a rectangular piece of cardboard are each 10% too long for a particular project. By what percentage is the area too large?

445. *ABCD* is an isosceles trapezoid. Find the measure of angle *A*.

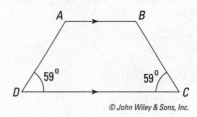

© John Wiley & Sons, Inc.

(A) 59°

(B) 91°

(C) 111°

(D) 121°

(E) 129°

446. What is the approximate circumference of a circular rug having a radius of 10 feet?

(A) 20 feet

(B) 31.4 feet

(C) 62.8 feet

(D) 157 feet

(E) 314 feet

447. Find the circumference of a circle that has a diameter of 14 inches. (Use $\frac{22}{7}$ as an approximate for π.)

(A) 22 inches

(B) 44 inches

(C) 50 inches

(D) 88 inches

(E) 154 inches

448. Find the area of a circle that has a radius of 7 centimeters (cm). (Use $\frac{22}{7}$ as an approximate for π.)

(A) 77 cm²

(B) 154 cm²

(C) 231 cm²

(D) 408 cm²

(E) 485 cm²

449. Find the approximate area of a circle that has a radius of 1.2 meters (m).

(A) 4.52 m²

(B) 2.26 m²

(C) 7.54 m²

(D) 3.77 m²

(E) 3.14 m²

450. Find the approximate radius of a circle having a circumference of 62.8 millimeters.

(A) 1

(B) 5

(C) 10

(D) 20

(E) 100

451. Find the circumference of a circle that has a radius of 21 centimeters (cm). (Use $\frac{22}{7}$ as an approximate for π.)

(A) 66 cm

(B) 132 cm

(C) 198 cm

(D) 346.5 cm

(E) 693 cm

452. In the accompanying figure, the square has two sides that are tangent to the circle. If the area of the circle is $4a^2\pi$, what is the area of the square?

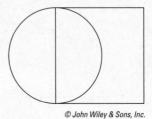

© John Wiley & Sons, Inc.

(A) $2a^2$

(B) $4a$

(C) $4a^2$

(D) $16a^2$

(E) $64a^2$

453. The distance from Town A to Town B is five miles. Town C is six miles from Town B. Which of the following could be the distance from Town A to Town C?

Select all the correct answers.

[A] 1

[B] 3

[C] 4

[D] 7

[E] 10

[F] 11

454. Find the combined area of the two circles.

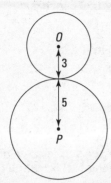

© John Wiley & Sons, Inc.

(A) 9π

(B) 13π

(C) 16π

(D) 25π

(E) 34π

455. Find the area of a circle that has a diameter of 14 inches (in). (Use $\frac{22}{7}$ as an approximate for π.)

(A) 22 in^2

(B) 44 in^2

(C) 154 in^2

(D) 484 in^2

(E) 516 in^2

456. *ASB* is a quarter circle. *PQRS* is a rectangle with sides *PQ* = 8 and *PS* = 6. What is the length of the arc *AQB*?

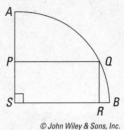

© John Wiley & Sons, Inc.

(A) 5π

(B) 10π

(C) 28

(D) 25

(E) 14

457. A 3 by 4 rectangle is inscribed inside of a circle. What is the circumference of the circle?

(A) 2.5π

(B) 3π

(C) 4π

(D) 5π

(E) 10π

458. Find the area of a semicircle that has a diameter of 14 centimeters (cm). (Use $\frac{22}{7}$ as an approximate for π.)

(A) 21 cm^2

(B) 42 cm^2

(C) 77 cm^2

(D) 124 cm^2

(E) 154 cm^2

459. Find the area of the shaded ring.

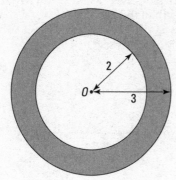

© John Wiley & Sons, Inc.

(A) 4π

(B) 5π

(C) 9π

(D) 10π

(E) 13π

460. The line through *AB* is tangent to two circles with centers *D* and *C* and whose areas are in the ratio of 4:1.

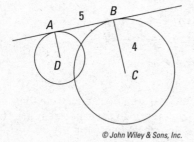

© John Wiley & Sons, Inc.

If *AB* = 5 and *BC* = 4, what is the length of line segment *DC* (not shown)? Give your answer to two decimal places.

461. Calculate the volume of a cube with an edge length of 5 inches.

(A) 25 in³

(B) 100 in³

(C) 125 in³

(D) 150 in³

(E) 250 in³

462. Calculate the surface area of a cube with an edge length of 5 centimeters (cm).

(A) 125 cm²

(B) 150 cm²

(C) 250 cm²

(D) 550 cm²

(E) 900 cm²

463. What is the total surface area of two identical cubes which together have a volume of 54 units?

464. Three cubes, each with a side of 6 inches, are glued together to make a rectangular box. How much less is the surface area of the rectangular box than the total surface area of the three separate cubes?

465. Calculate the total surface area of the cylinder.

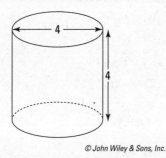

© John Wiley & Sons, Inc.

(A) 24π

(B) 28π

(C) 32π

(D) 50π

(E) 64π

466. Twelve liters of water are poured into an aquarium with dimensions of 50 centimeters (cm) in length, 30 cm in width, and 40 cm in height. How high (in cm) will the water rise? (1 liter = 1,000 cm³)

(A) 6

(B) 8

(C) 10

(D) 20

(E) 40

467. Each of the individual cubes in this structure has a side of one unit. How many units larger is the total combined surface area of all the individual cubes than the surface area of the larger structure?

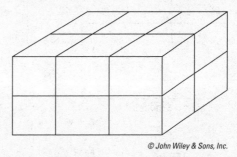

© John Wiley & Sons, Inc.

(A) 32

(B) 40

(C) 60

(D) 72

(E) 80

468. A large ice cube is formed by melting three smaller ice cubes of sides 3, 4, and 5 centimeters. What is the ratio of the total surface areas of the three smaller cubes to the larger cube?

(A) 2:1

(B) 3:2

(C) 5:4

(D) 25:18

(E) 27:20

469. Calculate the surface area of the rectangular solid.

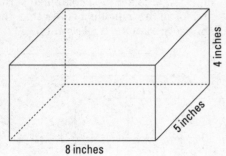

8 inches

© John Wiley & Sons, Inc.

(A) 150 in²

(B) 152 in²

(C) 160 in²

(D) 164 in²

(E) 184 in²

470. Calculate the volume of the rectangular solid.

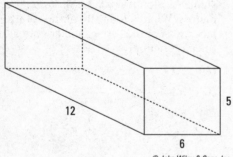

© John Wiley & Sons, Inc.

(A) 240

(B) 260

(C) 300

(D) 324

(E) 360

471. Simplify $9a^2 - 6a + 1$.

(A) $(6a-1)^2$

(B) $3a-1$

(C) $(3a-1)^2$

(D) $9a^2+1$

(E) $-6a^2$

472. Simplify $\dfrac{a^0 b^{-5}}{a^{-3} b}$.

(A) $\dfrac{a^6}{b^3}$

(B) $\dfrac{a^{-3}}{b^6}$

(C) $\dfrac{a^3}{b^6}$

(D) $\dfrac{a^3}{b^{-6}}$

(E) $\dfrac{a^6}{b^{-3}}$

473. Simplify $3x^2 y^3 (15x^3 y^2) \times 5x^2 y$.

(A) $x^3 y^2$

(B) xy^3

(C) xy^2

(D) $x^2 y^2$

(E) $x^2 y^3$

474. Simplify $x^2 + 2xy + y^2 - xz - yz$.

(A) $(x+y)(x+y-z)$

(B) $(x+y-z)$

(C) $(x+y)$

(D) $(x+y)(x-y-z)$

(E) $(x-y)(x+y-z)$

475. Find the value of $(-1)^{-5}$.

(A) 1

(B) −1

(C) 10

(D) −5

(E) 5

476. Find the value of $(-10)^0$.

(A) -10

(B) -1

(C) 0.1

(D) 1

(E) 10

477. Find the value of $2^2 - 2^{-2}$.

(A) 0

(B) 3.75

(C) 4

(D) 4.25

(E) 5

478. Simplify $\dfrac{x-y+z}{yz} + \dfrac{y+z-x}{zx} + \dfrac{z+x-y}{xy}$.

(A) $\dfrac{-2xy+z^2}{xyz}$

(B) $\dfrac{x^2+2xz+y^2+z^2}{xyz}$

(C) $\dfrac{x^2-2xy+2xz+y^2+z^2}{xyz}$

(D) $\dfrac{x^2-2xy+y^2+z^2}{xyz}$

(E) $x^2-2xy+2xz+y^2+z^2$

479. Find the value of $(-2)^{-3}5^2$.

(A) $\dfrac{25}{8}$

(B) $\dfrac{-8}{25}$

(C) $\dfrac{5}{8}$

(D) $\dfrac{-25}{8}$

(E) $\dfrac{-5}{8}$

480. Solve $8 = 16^{x+1}$.

(A) $-\dfrac{1}{6}$

(B) $-\dfrac{1}{4}$

(C) $-\dfrac{1}{8}$

(D) -4

(E) -2

481. Simplify $(-x^{2a})^{3b}$.

(A) $-x^{6ab}$

(B) $-x^{3ab}$

(C) x^{6ab}

(D) x^{2ab}

(E) $-x^{2ab}$

482. What is the greatest value of $\dfrac{1}{2^n}$, where n is a nonnegative integer?

(A) 0.5

(B) 1

(C) 2

(D) 5

(E) 10

483. Evaluate $\left(\sqrt{2}-\sqrt{3}\right)^2$.

(A) $5-2\sqrt{6}$

(B) $5-\sqrt{6}$

(C) $1-2\sqrt{6}$

(D) $1-\sqrt{2}$

(E) 1

484. Evaluate $2^{30} + 2^{30} + 2^{30} + 2^{30}$.

(A) 8^{120}

(B) 8^{30}

(C) 2^{32}

(D) 2^{30}

(E) 2^{26}

485. Evaluate $\dfrac{6^5 - 6^4}{5}$.

(A) $\dfrac{1}{5}$

(B) $\dfrac{6}{5}$

(C) 6^3

(D) $\dfrac{6^4}{5}$

(E) 6^4

486. Which of the following values could be the units digit of 57^n where n is a positive integer?

Select all the correct answers.

(A) 1

(B) 3

(C) 5

(D) 7

(E) 9

487. Solve $0.1^x = 100$.

488. If $2^{n+1} = 8$, what is the value of n?

489. $f(x) = x - 1$
What is the value of y if y is a positive integer such that $\dfrac{1}{3} f(y^2) = 5$?

490. If n is a prime number, how many different integer values for n will make the equation
$n < \dfrac{1}{(-2)^{-n}} < 135$ true?

(A) 0

(B) 1

(C) 2

(D) 4

(E) 5

491. Given $x * y = (3x)(2y)$
Evaluate $3 * 5$

(A) 10

(B) 90

(C) 9

(D) 15

(E) 19

492. Given $x \odot y = x + 2y$
Evaluate $3 \odot 4$

(A) 3

(B) 4

(C) 7

(D) 8

(E) 11

493. Given $x \cup y = x - 2y$
Evaluate $4 \cup 2$

(A) 6

(B) 4

(C) 2

(D) 1

(E) 0

494. Given $x \otimes y = 3x + 2y$
Evaluate $1 \otimes 3$

(A)   1
(B)   7
(C)   4
(D)   9
(E)   6

495. Given $x \oplus y = \frac{1}{2}xy$
Evaluate $8 \oplus 7$

(A)   28
(B)   11
(C)   56
(D)   15
(E)   112

496. Given $x \oslash y = \left(\sqrt{x}\right)(2y)$
Evaluate $16 \oslash 5$

(A)   100
(B)   80
(C)   160
(D)   40
(E)   20

497. Given $x \mp y = 3y\left(\frac{1}{2x}\right)$
Evaluate 3 ∓ 27

(A)   9
(B)   13.5
(C)   20
(D)   27
(E)   35.5

498. Given $x \therefore y = \frac{1}{y}x + \frac{1}{x}y$
Evaluate $10 \therefore 5$

(A)   2.5
(B)   10
(C)   1
(D)   2
(E)   5

499. Given $x \odot y = 2xy$
Evaluate $4 \odot 5$

(A)   20
(B)   0.8
(C)   10
(D)   40
(E)   1.25

500. If $x \spadesuit y = \left(x + y\right)^2$ for all positive integers
Evaluate $(1 \spadesuit 2) \spadesuit 3$

501. $\left(\frac{3}{x+1}\right) + \left(\frac{x+1}{3}\right) = \frac{3}{8} + \frac{8}{3}$

If x is an integer, what is the value of x?

502. If $5x + 32 = 4 - 2x$, what is the value of x?

(A)   −4
(B)   −3
(C)   4
(D)   7
(E)   12

503. Roberto worked eight hours each day on Monday, Wednesday, and Friday, and six hours each day on Tuesday and Thursday. He did not work on Saturday or Sunday. He earned $324 for the week. How much did Roberto earn in dollars per hour?

(A) $7 per hour

(B) $8 per hour

(C) $9 per hour

(D) $10 per hour

(E) $11 per hour

504. If $V = \dfrac{12R}{(r+R)}$, what is the value of R?

(A) $\dfrac{Vr}{12-V}$

(B) $\dfrac{V(r+1)}{12}$

(C) $Vr - 12$

(D) $Vr + \dfrac{V}{12}$

(E) $\dfrac{V(r+R)}{12}$

505. If $\dfrac{x-3}{3} = \dfrac{x-5}{2}$, what is the value of x?

(A) -9

(B) 9

(C) 5

(D) -5

(E) 12

506. If $\dfrac{2x-3}{9} + \dfrac{x+1}{2} = x - 4$, what is the value of x?

(A) 15

(B) -15

(C) 10

(D) -10

(E) 9

507. If $\dfrac{x-3}{x-1} = \dfrac{x+1}{x+2}$, what is the value of x?

(A) 5

(B) -5

(C) 2

(D) -2

(E) 3

508. If $5 - \dfrac{(x+1)}{3} = 2x$, what is the value of x?

(A) 1

(B) -4

(C) -2

(D) 4

(E) 2

509. If $\dfrac{ab}{c} = \dfrac{st}{u(v+w)x}$, what is the value of x?

(A) $\dfrac{cst}{abu(v+w)}$

(B) $\dfrac{cstabu}{(v+w)}$

(C) $\dfrac{abu}{cst(v+w)}$

(D) $\dfrac{cst(v+w)}{abu}$

(E) $\dfrac{cst}{abu}$

510. A store sells greetings cards in packs for $10 or individually for $2.50 each. In one day, the store had 75 greeting card transactions for a sales total of $375. How many of the $2.50 cards were sold that day?

511. Given $x^2 - x + 6 = 0$, what are the possible values of x?

Select all that apply.

(A) -2

(B) -1

(C) 0

(D) 1

(E) 2

(F) 3

512. Given $x - 5\sqrt{x} + 4 = 0$, which of the following are possible values of x?

Select all that apply.

(A) -2

(B) -1

(C) 0

(D) 1

(E) 2

(F) 3

513. $(3x + 2)(2x - 5) = ax^2 + kx + n$

What is the value of $a - n + k$?

(A) 5

(B) 8

(C) 9

(D) 0

(E) 11

514. Given $3x^2 - 3x + 0 = 0$, which of the following are possible values of x?

Select all the correct answers.

[A] -2

[B] -1

[C] 0

[D] 1

[E] 2

515. Given $x^2 - 3x - 4 = 0$, which of the following are possible values of x?

Select all the correct answers.

[A] -4

[B] -3

[C] -1

[D] 0

[E] 1

[F] 2

[G] 4

516. If $a^2 = 12$, calculate a^4.

(A) 16

(B) 24

(C) 36

(D) 72

(E) 144

517. Factor $5y^2 + 15y$.

(A) $5(y^2 + 3y)$

(B) $y(5y + 15)$

(C) $5y(y + 3)$

(D) $20y^3$

(E) $5y(y - 3)$

518. Factor $3y^2 + 12y$.

(A) $3(y^2 + 4y)$

(B) $3y(y + 4)$

(C) $y(3y + 12)$

(D) $12y^3$

(E) $3y(y - 4)$

519. Factor $4x^2 - 9$.

   (A) $(2x+3)(2x-3)$

   (B) $(2x-3)(2x-3)$

   (C) $(2x-3)^2(2x-3)$

   (D) $2(x+3)^2(x-3)$

   (E) $x(x+3)(x-3)(x-3)$

520. Simplify $\dfrac{-(a^2-b^2)}{a-b}$.

   (A) $-(a-b)$

   (B) $-(a+b)$

   (C) $(a+b)$

   (D) $(a-b)$

   (E) $\dfrac{1}{-(a+b)}$

521. Factor $x^2 + 2xy + y^2 - 25$.

   (A) $(x+y-5)(x+y+5)$

   (B) $(x-y-5)(x+y+5)$

   (C) $(x+y+5)(x+y+5)$

   (D) $(x+y-5)(x-y+5)$

   (E) $(x+y-5)(x+y-5)$

522. Factor $x^2 + 4x + 3$.

   (A) $(x+1)$

   (B) $(x+3)$

   (C) $(x+3)(x-1)$

   (D) $(x+3)(x+1)$

   (E) $(x-3)(x+1)$

523. Factor $2y + 6$.

   (A) $(y+3)$

   (B) $2(y-3)$

   (C) $2(y+3)$

   (D) $2y$

   (E) $(y-3)$

524. Factor $y^{2m} - 36x^2$.

   (A) $(y^m+6x)(x^m+6y)$

   (B) $(y^m+6x)(y^m-6x)$

   (C) $(y^m+6x)(y+6x)$

   (D) $(y^m-6x)(y-6x)$

   (E) $-(y+6x)(y^m-6x)$

525. Factor $x^2 - x - 30$.

   (A) $-(x-6)(x+5)$

   (B) $(x+6)(x+5)$

   (C) $6x(x+5)$

   (D) $(x-6)(x-5)$

   (E) $(x-6)(x+5)$

526. Find the value of $\sqrt{40}$.

   (A) $4\sqrt{10}$

   (B) $2\sqrt{5}$

   (C) $4\sqrt{5}$

   (D) $2\sqrt{10}$

   (E) $4\sqrt{2}$

527. Find the value of $\sqrt{98}$.

   (A) $7\sqrt{2}$

   (B) $2\sqrt{7}$

   (C) $3\sqrt{2}$

   (D) $2\sqrt{49}$

   (E) $2\sqrt{24}$

528. Find the value of $\sqrt{108}$.

   (A) $3\sqrt{3}$

   (B) $3\sqrt{2}$

   (C) $6\sqrt{3}$

   (D) $2\sqrt{3}$

   (E) $3\sqrt{6}$

529. Find the value of $\sqrt{72}$.

    (A) $2\sqrt{12}$

    (B) $2\sqrt{6}$

    (C) $2\sqrt{3}$

    (D) $6\sqrt{2}$

    (E) $3\sqrt{2}$

530. Find the value of $\sqrt{4,500}$.

    (A) $30\sqrt{5}$

    (B) $18\sqrt{50}$

    (C) $3\sqrt{50}$

    (D) $5\sqrt{30}$

    (E) $15\sqrt{10}$

531. Simplify $2\sqrt{3}+3\sqrt{3}$.

    (A) 15

    (B) $23\sqrt{6}$

    (C) $5\sqrt{6}$

    (D) $3\sqrt{5}$

    (E) $5\sqrt{3}$

532. Simplify $3\sqrt{3}+2\sqrt{5}+\sqrt{3}$.

    (A) $6\sqrt{8}$

    (B) $2\sqrt{3}+4\sqrt{5}$

    (C) $4\sqrt{3}+2\sqrt{5}$

    (D) $8\sqrt{15}$

    (E) $3\sqrt{4}+5\sqrt{2}$

533. Simplify $3\sqrt{50}-2\sqrt{8}-5\sqrt{32}$.

    (A) $-9\sqrt{2}$

    (B) $-3\sqrt{2}$

    (C) $9\sqrt{2}$

    (D) $15\sqrt{2}$

    (E) $-5\sqrt{2}$

534. Simplify $\sqrt{18}-2\sqrt{27}-3\sqrt{3}-6\sqrt{8}$.

    (A) $-9\sqrt{2}-39$

    (B) $9\sqrt{2}+39$

    (C) $3\sqrt{3}-12$

    (D) $-9\sqrt{2}-3\sqrt{3}$

    (E) $-2\sqrt{9}-3\sqrt{3}$

535. Simplify $8\sqrt{8}+2\sqrt{24}-2\sqrt{18}$.

    (A) $5\sqrt{2}+4\sqrt{6}$

    (B) $10\sqrt{2}-2\sqrt{6}$

    (C) $14\sqrt{2}+\sqrt{6}$

    (D) $22\sqrt{2}+4\sqrt{6}$

    (E) $10\sqrt{2}+4\sqrt{6}$

536. Simplify $\left(\sqrt{25}\right)\left(\sqrt{9}\right)$.

    (A) 3

    (B) 5

    (C) 15

    (D) 8

    (E) $\sqrt{15}$

537. Simplify $\left(\sqrt{16}\right)\left(\sqrt{16}\right)$.

    (A) 1

    (B) 4

    (C) 16

    (D) $\sqrt{16}$

    (E) 0

538. Simplify $\sqrt{\left(\frac{8}{2}\right)}$.

    (A) $\sqrt{6}$

    (B) 16

    (C) 4

    (D) 2

    (E) -2

539. Simplify $\sqrt{\left(\dfrac{3}{25}\right)}$.

(A) $\dfrac{3}{5}$

(B) $\dfrac{-3}{5}$

(C) $\dfrac{5}{\sqrt{3}}$

(D) $\sqrt{15}$

(E) $\dfrac{\sqrt{3}}{5}$

540. Simplify $\dfrac{10}{\sqrt{5}}$.

(A) $2\sqrt{5}$

(B) $10\sqrt{5}$

(C) $10\sqrt{2}$

(D) $\sqrt{2}$

(E) $\dfrac{1}{\sqrt{2}}$

541. Simplify $\left(\sqrt{3}+\sqrt{5}\right)\left(\sqrt{3}-\sqrt{6}\right)$.

(A) $3+\sqrt{15}+3\sqrt{2}+\sqrt{30}$

(B) $\sqrt{9}-\sqrt{30}$

(C) $\sqrt{8}-\sqrt{3}$

(D) $-\sqrt{24}$

(E) $3+\sqrt{15}-3\sqrt{2}-\sqrt{30}$

542. Simplify $\left(\sqrt{3}+\sqrt{5}\right)\left(\sqrt{3}-\sqrt{5}\right)$.

(A) -2

(B) 2

(C) $\sqrt{8}-\sqrt{2}$

(D) $\sqrt{6}$

(E) $\sqrt{16}$

543. Simplify $\sqrt{2x}\left(\sqrt{3xy}\right)$.

(A) $\dfrac{x}{\sqrt{6y}}$

(B) $y\sqrt{6x}$

(C) $\dfrac{\sqrt{6y}}{x}$

(D) $x\sqrt{6y}$

(E) $x+\sqrt{6y}$

544. Simplify $\dfrac{14\sqrt{27}}{7\sqrt{9}}$.

(A) 6

(B) $7\sqrt{3}$

(C) $2\sqrt{6}$

(D) $2\sqrt{3}$

(E) $\sqrt{3}$

545. Simplify $\dfrac{18\sqrt{60}}{2\sqrt{30}}$.

(A) $\sqrt{2}$

(B) $9\sqrt{2}$

(C) $9\sqrt{20}$

(D) $9\sqrt{30}$

(E) $\dfrac{9}{\sqrt{2}}$

546. Evaluate $\left(\sqrt{4}+\sqrt{5}\right)\left(\sqrt{4}-\sqrt{5}\right)$.

(A) -1

(B) 1

(C) -2

(D) 2

(E) 0

547. Evaluate $\sqrt{3}\left(2\sqrt{3}+\sqrt{5}\right)$.

(A) $6-\sqrt{15}$

(B) 6

(C) 4

(D) $6+\sqrt{15}$

(E) $4+\sqrt{15}$

548. Evaluate $\left(1+\sqrt{2}\right)\left(3-\sqrt{2}\right)$.

(A) 1

(B) $2\sqrt{2}$

(C) $\sqrt{2}$

(D) $1+\sqrt{2}$

(E) $1+2\sqrt{2}$

549. Evaluate $\left(\sqrt{12}-2\right)^2$.

(A) $-4\sqrt{3}$

(B) $16+8\sqrt{3}$

(C) $16-8\sqrt{3}$

(D) $2+2\sqrt{3}$

(E) $4-4\sqrt{3}$

550. Evaluate $\left(\sqrt{2}+\sqrt{2}\right)\left(\sqrt{5}-\sqrt{2}\right)$.

(A) $2\sqrt{10}+4$

(B) $2\sqrt{10}-4$

(C) $4\sqrt{10}+4$

(D) $-\sqrt{10}+\sqrt{4}$

(E) $-\sqrt{10}-\sqrt{4}$

551. For the line represented by $y=-2x+3$, what is the slope?

(A) 1

(B) 2

(C) -2

(D) 3

(E) -3

552. For the line represented by $y=-2x+3$, what is the y-intercept?

(A) 1

(B) 2

(C) -2

(D) 3

(E) -3

553. For the line represented by $x=2y-3$, what is the slope?

(A) 1

(B) 2

(C) $\dfrac{1}{2}$

(D) $-\dfrac{1}{2}$

(E) $1\dfrac{1}{2}$

554. For the line represented by $x=2y-3$, what is the y-intercept?

(A) 1

(B) 2

(C) $\dfrac{1}{2}$

(D) $-\dfrac{1}{2}$

(E) $1\dfrac{1}{2}$

555. Find the equation of the line in this diagram.

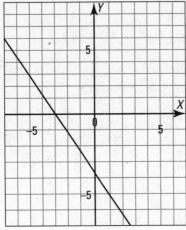

© John Wiley & Sons, Inc.

(A) $y = -\dfrac{4}{3}x - 3$

(B) $y = \dfrac{4}{3}x - 4$

(C) $y = -\dfrac{4}{3}x - 4$

(D) $y = -\dfrac{3}{4}x - 3$

(E) $y = -\dfrac{3}{4}x - 4$

556. Find the equation of the line in this diagram.

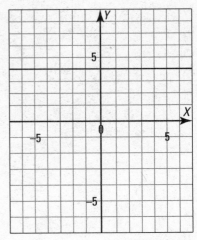

© John Wiley & Sons, Inc.

(A) $y = 4$

(B) $x = 4$

(C) $y = -4x + 4$

(D) $y = 4x + 4$

(E) $y = -4x - 4$

557. Find the equation of the line in this diagram.

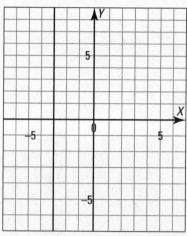

(A) $y = -3x - 3$

(B) $y = -3x + 3$

(C) $y = 3x - 3$

(D) $x = -3$

(E) $y = -3$

558. Find the equation of the line in this diagram.

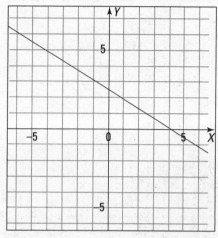

(A) $y = -1.2x + 2.5$

(B) $y = -0.6x + 2.5$

(C) $y = 1.2x + 2.5$

(D) $y = 0.6x + 2.5$

(E) $y = 0.6x - 2.5$

559. Find the equation of the line in this diagram.

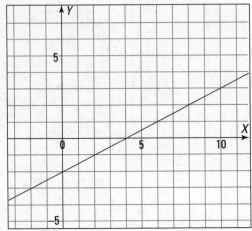

(A) $y = 2x - 2$

(B) $y = -2x + \dfrac{1}{2}$

(C) $y = -\dfrac{1}{2}x + 2$

(D) $y = \dfrac{1}{2}x - 2$

(E) $y = \dfrac{1}{2}x + 2$

560. Find the equation of the line in this diagram.

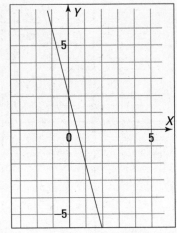

(A) $y = -0.25x + 2$

(B) $y = 4x + 2$

(C) $y = 0.25x + 2$

(D) $y = -4x + 2$

(E) $y = 4x - 2$

561. Solve for x and y.

$4x + 5y = 12$

$3x - 5y = 9$

(A) $x = 0, y = 3$

(B) $x = 1, y = 0$

(C) $x = 7, y = 0$

(D) $x = 3, y = 0$

(E) $x = 7, y = 1$

562. Solve for x and y.

$y = x + 2$

$x + y = 4$

(A) $x = 2, y = 1$

(B) $x = 1, y = 4$

(C) $x = 2, y = 4$

(D) $x = 3, y = 1$

(E) $x = 1, y = 3$

563. Solve for x and y.

$x + y = -12$

$x - y = 2$

(A) $x = -5, y = -7$

(B) $x = -7, y = -5$

(C) $x = 5, y = 7$

(D) $x = 7, y = 5$

(E) $x = -12, y = 2$

564. Solve for x and y.

$x + 8y = -15$

$7x + 8y = 39$

(A) $x = -9, y = 3$

(B) $x = 9, y = 3$

(C) $x = -9, y = -3$

(D) $x = 9, y = -3$

(E) $x = -3, y = 9$

565. Solve for x and y.

$-0.1x + 0.6y = 1.3$

$0.8x + 0.6y = -5$

(A) $x = 7, y = 1$

(B) $x = -7, y = 1$

(C) $x = -7, y = -1$

(D) $x = 7, y = -1$

(E) $x = -1, y = 7$

566. Solve for x and y.

$2x + y = 5$

$x + 2y = 1$

(A) $x = 3, y = 1$

(B) $x = -3, y = -1$

(C) $x = 3, y = -1$

(D) $x = -3, y = 1$

(E) $x = -1, y = 3$

567. Solve for x and y.

$x + 2y = 7$

$2x + 3y = 5$

(A) $x = -9, y = 11$

(B) $x = 11, y = 9$

(C) $x = -11, y = 9$

(D) $x = -11, y = -9$

(E) $x = 11, y = -9$

568. Solve for x and y.

$x - 6y = -18$

$2x - 7y = -16$

(A) $x = 6, y = -11$

(B) $x = -12, y = -11$

(C) $x = 4, y = 6$

(D) $x = -12, y = 4$

(E) $x = 6, y = 4$

569. Solve for x and y.

$x + 5y = 6$

$-2x + 6y = -12$

(A) $x = 6, y = 0$

(B) $x = 6, y = 4$

(C) $x = 0, y = 6$

(D) $x = 0, y = 4$

(E) $x = -6, y = 4$

570. Solve for x and y.

$4x + 5y = -4$

$x - y = 8$

(A) $x = 4, y = 4$

(B) $x = -4, y = -4$

(C) $x = -4, y = 4$

(D) $x = 4, y = -4$

(E) $x = -1, y = 4$

571. {. . . –20, –16, –12, –8, . . .}

Which of the following could be a term in the preceding sequence?

Select all the correct answers.

[A]   –250

[B]   –192

[C]   0

[D]   34

[E]   200

[F]   440

[G]   668

[H]   762

[I]   816

[J]   902

572. Find the sixth term of the sequence given by $x_n = 3 \times (2)^n$.

(A)   128

(B)   192

(C)   24

(D)   1

(E)   64

573. Find the 21st term of the sequence given by $x_n = 4n - 3$.

(A)   6

(B)   61

(C)   72

(D)   81

(E)   87

574. Find the third term of the sequence $\{a_n\} = \left\{ \left(\dfrac{1}{n} \right)^{n-1} \right\}$.

(A) $\dfrac{1}{2}$

(B) $\dfrac{1}{5}$

(C) $\dfrac{1}{625}$

(D) $\dfrac{1}{25}$

(E) $\dfrac{1}{125}$

575. If n is a positive integer less than 5, what is the sum of the squares of all the possible values of n?

(A)   16

(B)   21

(C)   31

(D)   50

(E)   75

576. The nth hexagonal number is given by $h_n = n(2n - 1)$. Find the sixth hexagonal number.

(A)   17

(B)   22

(C)   50

(D)   66

(E)   150

577. The nth term of a sequence is given by $x_n = 3n^2 - 1$. Find the value of n when $x_n = 26$.

(A)   1

(B)   2

(C)   3

(D)   4

(E)   5

578. If the number of bacteria in a Petri dish doubles every 20 minutes, the population after 1 hour and 20 minutes will be how many times the population at the start?

579. The nth term of a sequence is given by $x_n = \dfrac{n^2 - 1}{n + 5}$. Find the term of the sequence that is equal to 4.

(A) The third term

(B) The fifth term

(C) The seventh term

(D) The eighth term

(E) The tenth term

580. For the sequence defined by $a_n = n^2 - 5n + 2$, find the smallest value of n for which a_n is positive.

(A) 2

(B) 3

(C) 4

(D) 5

(E) 6

581. Calculate the number of miles a car travelling 30 miles per hour would go in 120 minutes.

(A) 30 miles

(B) 60 miles

(C) 90 miles

(D) 100 miles

(E) 120 miles

582. A boat has a speed of 36 kilometers per hour. What is its speed in meters per second? (1 kilometer = 1,000 meters)

(A) $10 \dfrac{m}{s}$

(B) $12.96 \dfrac{m}{s}$

(C) $100 \dfrac{m}{s}$

(D) $129.6 \dfrac{m}{s}$

(E) $1,000 \dfrac{m}{s}$

583. Two cars start from the same location and travel in opposite directions. Car 1 travels at 40 miles per hour and Car 2 travels at 50 miles per hour. If they both leave at 5 a.m., at what time will they be 450 miles apart?

(A) 7 a.m.

(B) 8 a.m.

(C) 9 a.m.

(D) 10 a.m.

(E) 11 a.m.

584. Two cars start from the same location and travel in the same direction. Car 1 leaves at 9 a.m. and travels at 40 miles per hour. Car 2 leaves at 10 a.m. and travels at 60 miles per hour. At what time will Car 2 pass Car 1?

(A) 8 a.m.

(B) 9 a.m.

(C) 10 a.m.

(D) 11 a.m.

(E) 12 p.m.

585. Two cars leave from the same location at 8 a.m. Car 1 travels due east at 30 miles per hour, and Car 2 travels due north at 40 miles per hour. If the cars don't stop or change speed, at what time will they be exactly 500 miles apart?

(A) 2 p.m.

(B) 4 p.m.

(C) 6 p.m.

(D) 8 p.m.

(E) 10 p.m.

586. The following data set has a mean of 8. Find the value of x.

3, 12, 4, x, 12

(A) 5

(B) 8

(C) 9

(D) 10

(E) 11

587. The following data set has a mean of 10. Find the value of x.

$\{7, 12, 7, 12, 7, x\}$

(A) 10

(B) 12

(C) 14

(D) 15

(E) 17

588. The following data set has a mean of 4.2. Find the value of x.

$\{3.4, -2.2, 1, x, 5.2, 6.6\}$

(A) 7

(B) 10.2

(C) 11.2

(D) 12

(E) 14

589. The following data set has a median of 14. Which could be the value of x?

$\{10, 14, 13, 17, x\}$

(A) 5

(B) 8

(C) 10

(D) 13

(E) 17

590. The following data set has a mode of 10. Find the value of x.

$\{10, 20, 3, 5, x, 4\}$

(A) 3

(B) 4

(C) 5

(D) 10

(E) 20

591. The following data set has a range of 4. Find a possible value of x.

$\{5, 9, 8, x\}$

(A) 3

(B) 4

(C) 8

(D) 10

(E) 12

592. The following data set has a range of 3. What could be the value of x?

$\{12, 11, x, 10, 12\}$

Select all possible answers.

[A] 8

[B] 9

[C] 10

[D] 11

[E] 13

593. The following data set has a mean of 10. Find the value of x.

$\{3, 8, x, x, 5\}$

(A) 8

(B) 9

(C) 10

(D) 15

(E) 17

594. The following data set has a mean of 4. Find the value of x.

$\{2, 3, x + 1, x, 2\}$

(A) 6

(B) 6.5

(C) 7

(D) 7.5

(E) 8

595. The following data set has a mean of 5. Find the value of $x + y$.

$\{6, 3, x, 4, 3, 5, y\}$

(A) 10

(B) 12

(C) 14

(D) 15

(E) 17

596. The numbers 1, 2, 3, and 4 have weights 0.1, 0.2, 0.3, and 0.4 respectively. Calculate the weighted mean.

(A) 2.5

(B) 2.8

(C) 3.0

(D) 3.2

(E) 3.5

597. The numbers 1, 2, 3, 4, 5, and 6 have weights 0.5, 0.1, 0.1, 0.1, 0.1, and 0.1 respectively. Calculate the weighted mean.

(A) 2.5

(B) 2.8

(C) 3.0

(D) 3.2

(E) 3.5

598. The numbers 40, 45, 80, 75, and 10 have weights 1, 2, 3, 4, and 5 respectively. Calculate the weighted mean.

(A) 47

(B) 48

(C) 49

(D) 50

(E) 51

599. The numbers 90, 35, 20, 55, 70, and 75 have weights 6, 5, 4, 2, 2, and 1 respectively. Calculate the weighted mean.

(A) 61

(B) 57.5

(C) 56

(D) 55.5

(E) 52

600. Math grades for the year are calculated from assignments, tests, and a final exam, which count for 30%, 20%, and 50%, respectively, of the overall math grade. Calculate the overall grade for an assignment grade of 85, a test grade of 72, and an exam grade of 61.

(A) 70%

(B) 70.4%

(C) 71%

(D) 71.4%

(E) 72.6%

601. A tennis player got her first serve 80% of the time in the first ten matches. In the remaining five matches, she only got her first serve 50% of the time. Calculate the percent of her first serves for the whole season.

(A) 65%

(B) 65.5%

(C) 66.7%

(D) 67.5%

(E) 70%

602. Course grades are calculated using a weighted average. Homework counts 10%, quizzes 20%, and tests 70%. Calculate the course grade if the homework grade is 92, the quiz grade is 68, and the test grade is 81.

(A) 68%

(B) 75.5%

(C) 79.5%

(D) 81%

(E) 82%

603. A pallet holds ten boxes weighing 6 pounds each and five boxes weighing 9 pounds each. Calculate the average box weight.

(A) 6 pounds

(B) 7 pounds

(C) 8 pounds

(D) 9 pounds

(E) 10 pounds

604. A class of 25 students took a test. Ten students had an average score of 80%. The other students had an average score of 60%. What was the entire class average on the test?

(A) 60%

(B) 65%

(C) 65.5%

(D) 68%

(E) 70%

605. The overall score in a competition is calculated with a weighted score of 80% for execution and 20% for difficulty. Determine the score for difficulty with a score of 9.8 for execution and an overall score of 9.5.

(A) 8.1

(B) 8.3

(C) 8.5

(D) 9.2

(E) 9.7

606. Calculate the simple interest paid in one year on a $1,000 loan at an annual interest rate of 10%.

(A) $0.10

(B) $1

(C) $10

(D) $100

(E) $1,000

607. Marco borrowed $5,000 for three years and paid $1,350 in simple interest. Find the annual rate of interest that was paid.

(A) 5%

(B) 6%

(C) 7%

(D) 8%

(E) 9%

608. Chandra borrowed $4,500 for two years and paid $630 in simple interest. Find the annual rate of interest that was paid.

(A) 6%

(B) 6.5%

(C) 7%

(D) 7.5%

(E) 8%

609. Brooks borrowed $7,000 at an annual interest rate of 3% and paid $840 in simple interest. Find the amount of time on the loan.

(A) 2 years

(B) 2.5 years

(C) 3 years

(D) 3.5 years

(E) 4 years

610. Randy borrowed $5,000 for three years and paid $1,350 in simple interest. Find the rate of annual interest that was paid.

(A) 8.5%

(B) 9%

(C) 9.5%

(D) 10%

(E) 10.5%

611. A large container holds a mixture of 10 liters of a 6% saline solution and 5 liters of a 9% saline solution. Calculate the resulting percent of saline solution mixture.

(A) 6%

(B) 6.5%

(C) 7%

(D) 7.5%

(E) 8%

612. A nut mixture is made by adding 2 pounds of cashews that cost $5/pound and 2 pounds of pecans that cost $3/pound. Calculate the price of the nut mixture.

(A) $3/pound

(B) $3.50/pound

(C) $4/pound

(D) $4.50/pound

(E) $5/pound

613. Cheyenne has 25 liters of a 50% soap solution. Calculate the amount of water she needs to make a 25% soap solution.

(A) 20 liters

(B) 23 liters

(C) 25 liters

(D) 29 liters

(E) 30 liters

614. Calculate the number of liters of a 20% alcohol solution needed to be added to 40 liters of a 50% alcohol solution to make a 30% solution.

(A) 70 liters

(B) 72 liters

(C) 75 liters

(D) 80 liters

(E) 83 liters

615. A 20-pound coffee mixture is made up of Coffee A that costs $5/pound and Coffee B that costs $3/pound. The mixture costs $3.50/pound. Calculate the number of pounds of each kind of coffee in the mixture.

(A) 5 pounds Coffee A and 15 pounds Coffee B

(B) 10 pounds Coffee A and 10 pounds Coffee B

(C) 15 pounds Coffee A and 5 pounds Coffee B

(D) 8 pounds Coffee A and 12 pounds Coffee B

(E) 7 pounds Coffee A and 13 pounds Coffee B

616. Calculate the amount of water needed to make a 10% saline solution, if mixed with 100 kilograms (kg) of a 30% saline solution.

(A)   200 kg

(B)   210 kg

(C)   213 kg

(D)   220 kg

(E)   243 kg

617. A ticket booth sold 400 tickets to a show and collected a total of $1,100 in ticket sales. The price of an adult ticket is $5.00 and the price of a child ticket is $2.00. Find the number of each type of ticket that was sold.

(A)   200 adult tickets and 200 child tickets

(B)   100 adult tickets and 300 child tickets

(C)   300 adult tickets and 100 child tickets

(D)   150 adult tickets and 250 child tickets

(E)   250 adult tickets and 150 child tickets

618. A local grocery store sells chocolate candies that cost $3.89/pound and peanuts that cost $2.49/pound. Tyson mixed the chocolate candies and peanuts in the same container, making a 100-pound mixture that now costs $3.19/pound. Find how much of each item is in the mixture.

(A)   20 peanuts and 80 chocolate candies

(B)   40 peanuts and 60 chocolate candies

(C)   50 peanuts and 50 chocolate candies

(D)   60 peanuts and 40 chocolate candies

(E)   55 peanuts and 45 chocolate candies

619. A 100% concentrate cranberry juice is to be mixed with a mixture having a concentration of 20% apple juice to obtain 40 gallons of a juice mixture with a concentration of 50%. Calculate the amount of the 100% concentrate needed.

(A)   5 gallons

(B)   8 gallons

(C)   10 gallons

(D)   12 gallons

(E)   15 gallons

620. Sterling silver is 92.5% pure silver and 7.5% alloy. Calculate the number of grams of sterling silver necessary to obtain 500 grams of a 91% silver alloy, if mixed with a 90% silver alloy.

(A)   170 grams

(B)   175 grams

(C)   190 grams

(D)   200 grams

(E)   225 grams

621. Calculate the chances of rolling a 4 or a 3 with a single, six-sided die.

(A) $\frac{1}{6}$

(B) $\frac{1}{5}$

(C) $\frac{1}{4}$

(D) $\frac{1}{3}$

(E) $\frac{1}{2}$

622. A box contains five chocolates with soft centers, six with nut centers, and eleven with caramel centers. Three people take turns taking a chocolate at random from the box and eating it. If the probability that all three people take soft centers is $\frac{1}{x}$, what is the value of x?

623. A pentagon spinner has five triangles numbered 1 to 5. Calculate the probability of the spinner stopping on an odd number.

(A) $\frac{1}{5}$

(B) $\frac{1}{4}$

(C) $\frac{2}{5}$

(D) $\frac{1}{2}$

(E) $\frac{3}{5}$

624. Each letter of the word MISSISSIPPI is written on a separate piece of paper that is then folded, put in a hat, and mixed thoroughly. One piece of paper is chosen at random from the hat. Calculate the probability that the letter chosen from the hat is an I.

(A) $\frac{4}{11}$

(B) $\frac{2}{5}$

(C) $\frac{1}{3}$

(D) $\frac{1}{4}$

(E) $\frac{1}{5}$

625. A card is chosen at random from a deck of 52 playing cards. There are four queens and four kings in a deck of playing cards. Calculate the probability that the chosen card is a queen or a king.

(A) $\frac{1}{13}$

(B) $\frac{2}{13}$

(C) $\frac{1}{8}$

(D) $\frac{2}{11}$

(E) $\frac{4}{52}$

626. Two square flowerbeds are placed symmetrically in a rectangular garden as shown in the diagram. The distance between the beds is y, as is the width of the border around the beds on each side. A seed blown into the garden by the wind is equally likely to land anywhere in the garden. What is the probability that it actually lands in a flowerbed?

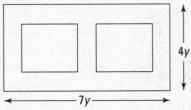

© John Wiley & Sons, Inc.

627. A single, six-sided die is thrown. Calculate the probability that the face shown is a factor of 6.

(A) $\frac{1}{6}$

(B) $\frac{1}{3}$

(C) $\frac{1}{2}$

(D) $\frac{2}{3}$

(E) 1

628. A coin is tossed three times. Calculate the probability of obtaining one "heads up" and two "tails up."

(A) $\frac{1}{4}$

(B) $\frac{1}{3}$

(C) $\frac{3}{8}$

(D) $\frac{1}{2}$

(E) $\frac{5}{8}$

629. $N\{12, 18, 2, 6\}$
$P\{1, 4, 2, 3\}$

If n and p are selected at random from sets N and P respectively, what is the probability that $\frac{n}{2p}$ will be a member of set P?

630. A bag contains three red marbles and four blue marbles. Two marbles are drawn at random without replacement. If the first marble drawn is blue, calculate the probability that the second marble is also blue.

(A) $\frac{3}{7}$

(B) $\frac{1}{2}$

(C) $\frac{4}{7}$

(D) $\frac{2}{3}$

(E) 1

631. In a group of 40 students, 14 are taking English and 29 are taking Chemistry. There are five students in both classes. Calculate the number of students who are *not* taking either of the two classes.

(A) 1

(B) 2

(C) 3

(D) 5

(E) 9

632. In a group of 40 students, 14 are taking English and 29 are taking Chemistry. There are five students in both classes. Calculate the number of students who are taking only one class.

(A) 22

(B) 23

(C) 33

(D) 5

(E) 43

633. A group of 25 children were asked whether they have a pet at home. Twelve children said that they have a dog and 18 children said that they have a cat. Eight children have both a dog and a cat. Calculate the number of children who *do not* have a pet at home.

(A) 1

(B) 2

(C) 3

(D) 8

(E) 11

634. A group of 25 children were surveyed and asked whether they had a pet at home. Twelve children said that they had a dog and 18 children said that they had a cat. Eight children had both a dog and a cat. Calculate the number of children who had only one pet at home.

(A) 8

(B) 9

(C) 10

(D) 12

(E) 14

635. One hundred coffee drinkers were surveyed and asked whether they like cream and/or sugar in their coffee. Fifty-five said that they like sugar, and 36 said that they like cream. Twenty responded that they like both cream and sugar in their coffee. Calculate the number of coffee drinkers who like cream, but not sugar.

(A) 15

(B) 16

(C) 35

(D) 51

(E) 80

636. One hundred coffee drinkers were surveyed and asked whether they like cream and/or sugar in their coffee. Fifty-five said that they like sugar and 36 said that they like cream. Twenty responded that they like both cream and sugar in their coffee. Calculate the number of coffee drinkers who like sugar, but not cream.

(A) 15

(B) 16

(C) 35

(D) 51

(E) 80

637. One hundred coffee drinkers were surveyed and asked whether they like cream and/or sugar in their coffee. Fifty-five said that they like sugar and 36 said that they like cream. Twenty responded that they like both cream and sugar in their coffee. Calculate the number of coffee drinkers who like neither cream nor sugar.

(A) 15

(B) 16

(C) 29

(D) 51

(E) 80

638. One hundred people were surveyed and asked whether they had ever studied a foreign language. The results are as follows:

52 people studied French
63 people studied Spanish
25 people studied Latin
4 people studied French, Spanish, and Latin
9 people studied French and Latin
11 people studied Spanish and Latin
24 people studied French and Spanish

Calculate the number of people who studied Latin, but *not* French or Spanish.

(A) 9

(B) 13

(C) 15

(D) 23

(E) 38

639. One hundred people were surveyed and asked whether they had ever studied a foreign language. The results are as follows:

52 people studied French
63 people studied Spanish
25 people studied Latin
4 people studied French, Spanish, and Latin
9 people studied French and Latin
11 people studied Spanish and Latin
24 people studied French and Spanish

Calculate the number of people who studied French, but *not* Latin or Spanish.

(A) 9

(B) 13

(C) 15

(D) 23

(E) 38

640. One hundred people were surveyed and asked whether they had ever studied a foreign language. The results are as follows:

52 people studied French
63 people studied Spanish
25 people studied Latin
4 people studied French, Spanish, and Latin
9 people studied French and Latin
11 people studied Spanish and Latin
24 people studied French and Spanish

Calculate the number of people who studied Spanish, but *not* Latin or French.

(A) 9

(B) 13

(C) 15

(D) 32

(E) 38

641. Calculate the number of different outfits you can make with three shirts and four pairs of pants.

(A) 3

(B) 4

(C) 7

(D) 8

(E) 12

642. Calculate the number of different ice-cream cone combinations you can make with one scoop of ice cream and one cone, with six flavors of ice cream and three different types of cones.

(A) 6

(B) 9

(C) 12

(D) 18

(E) 21

643. At a local pizza parlor, a customer can choose either a large or a medium pizza. There are seven different toppings and three different choices of crust. Calculate the number of different single-topping pizzas that can be made.

(A) 12

(B) 20

(C) 27

(D) 35

(E) 42

644. Reagan has nine different skirts, seven different tops, ten different pairs of shoes, two different necklaces, and five different bracelets. Calculate the number of different outfits Reagan can make.

(A) 6,300

(B) 7,560

(C) 12,600

(D) 50,000

(E) 63,000

645. A restaurant offers five choices of appetizer, ten choices of entrees, and four choices of dessert. A customer can choose to eat just one course, two different courses, or all three courses. Assuming all choices are available, calculate the number of different possible meals the restaurant offers.

(A) 329

(B) 330

(C) 200

(D) 150

(E) 19

646. Evaluate 5!2!.

(A) 100

(B) 210

(C) 240

(D) 265

(E) 330

647. Evaluate $\frac{8!}{5!}$.

    (A) 3

    (B) 56

    (C) 85

    (D) 336

    (E) 378

648. Evaluate $\frac{9!}{5!4!}$.

    (A) 126

    (B) 136

    (C) 151

    (D) 189

    (E) 216

649. Evaluate $\frac{(x+1)!}{(x+3)!}$.

    (A) $\frac{x+1}{x+3}$

    (B) $\frac{x+1}{x^2+5x+6}$

    (C) $\frac{1}{x^2+5x+6}$

    (D) $\frac{x+3}{x+1}$

    (E) $\frac{1}{x^2+5x+3}$

650. Evaluate $\frac{(n!)^2}{(n-1)!(n+1)!}$.

    (A) $\frac{1}{n+1}$

    (B) $n-1$

    (C) n^2+1

    (D) $\frac{1}{n^2}$

    (E) $\frac{n}{n+1}$

651. A confectioner has 500 mint candies, 500 orange candies, and 500 strawberry candies. He wants to make packets that contain ten mint, five orange, and five strawberry candies. What is the maximum number of packets that can be made with this combination?

652. A = {A, B, C, D, E, F, G}

B = {0, 1, 2}

C = {1, 2, 3, 4, 5, 6, 7, 8, 9}

The filing system in an office requires each file to have an alphanumeric code name of the form *abc*. A, B, and C are the sets from which *a*, *b*, and *c* must be chosen. How many possible code names are there?

653. Calculate the number of ways that five different novels can be placed on a shelf.

    (A) 1

    (B) 8

    (C) 40

    (D) 64

    (E) 120

654. If three different people are to be chosen at random from a group of ten people to win first, second, and third prizes, respectively, how many possible ways can the prizes be distributed?

    (A) 84

    (B) 120

    (C) 240

    (D) 504

    (E) 720

655. Calculate the number of ways to arrange three books that are chosen from a set of seven different books.

(A) 70

(B) 140

(C) 210

(D) 280

(E) 350

656. Calculate the number of different three-digit numerals that can be made from the digits 4, 5, 6, 7, and 8, if each digit can be used just once in each numeral.

(A) 5

(B) 8

(C) 60

(D) 543

(E) 800

657. Four friends are walking down the street. Calculate the number of different ways the friends can arrange themselves in a side-by-side pattern.

(A) 30

(B) 24

(C) 15

(D) 12

(E) 4

658. Calculate the number of ways that 2 of the 26 letters of the alphabet can be arranged, if no letter is used more than once.

(A) 325

(B) 650

(C) 1,300

(D) 1,950

(E) 2,600

659. Calculate the number of ways that all the letters of the word "English" can be arranged, if no letter is used more than once.

(A) 117,649

(B) 5,040

(C) 2,401

(D) 343

(E) 49

660. Calculate the number of ways that the letters of the word "square" can be arranged, if no letter is used more than once.

(A) 82

(B) 720

(C) 1,956

(D) 7,313

(E) 9,331

661. Six people meet at an event. Each person shakes hands once with each other person present. How many handshakes take place?

(A) 10

(B) 15

(C) 18

(D) 21

(E) 30

662. Different four-letter passwords can be constructed using the letters A, B, C, and D only once. How many passwords exist if either B or C must be in second position?

663. John is the chairman of a committee. Calculate the number of ways a committee of five can be chosen from a group of ten people, given that John must be one of them.

(A) 126

(B) 252

(C) 495

(D) 1,005

(E) 3,024

664. Calculate the number of different committees of five people that can be chosen from a group of ten people.

(A) 252

(B) 2,002

(C) 5,150

(D) 30,240

(E) 100,000

665. Calculate the number of ways that a child can take four candies from a bowl containing five.

(A) 1

(B) 4

(C) 5

(D) 9

(E) 20

666. Monique has seven shirts, but she wants to take only four shirts on her trip. Calculate the number of ways she can do this.

(A) 11

(B) 28

(C) 35

(D) 140

(E) 343

667. A teacher wants to select three students from her class of ten. Calculate the number of ways she can do this.

(A) 77,520

(B) 15,504

(C) 1,520

(D) 500

(E) 120

668. In a conference of nine schools, calculate the number of football games that can be played during the season if each team plays each other team exactly one time.

(A) 36

(B) 30

(C) 18

(D) 11

(E) 9

669. Calculate the number of different 2-card hands that can be drawn from a standard deck of 52 cards.

(A) 52

(B) 208

(C) 1,326

(D) 43,264

(E) 270,725

670. Sixteen teams enter a competition. The teams are divided into four pools (A, B, C, and D) of four teams each. Each team plays one match against each other team in its pool. After these matches are completed, the winner of Pool A plays the second-place team of Pool B, the winner of Pool B plays the second-place team of Pool A, the winner of Pool C plays the second-place team of Pool D, and the winner of Pool D plays the second-place team of Pool C. The winners of these four matches then play semi-finals, and the winners of the semi-finals play in the final. Calculate the total number of matches that are played.

(A) 21

(B) 23

(C) 31

(D) 32

(E) 63

671. Find the median of 0.3, 0.33, 0.003, 0.31, and 0.0003.

(A) 0.33

(B) 0.3

(C) 0.0003

(D) 0.31

(E) 0.003

672. Find the median of 3, 11, 6, 5, 4, 7, 12, 3, and 10.

(A) 4

(B) 5

(C) 6

(D) 7

(E) 8

673. Find the median of 75, 83, 69, 56, 71, 80, 65, 67, 77, and 44.

(A) 65

(B) 67

(C) 69

(D) 70

(E) 71

674. The graph shows the sales figures for a certain company in five consecutive years. Find the median sales.

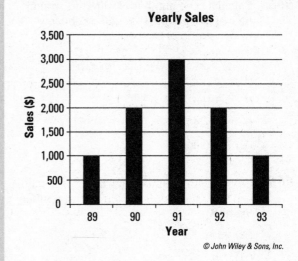

Yearly Sales

© John Wiley & Sons, Inc.

(A) $1,000

(B) $1,500

(C) $1,800

(D) $2,000

(E) $2,500

675. Find the median of 3, 13, 7, 5, 21, 23, 23, 40, 23, 14, 12, 56, 23, and 29.

(A) 21

(B) 22

(C) 23

(D) 24

(E) 25

676. A survey asked drivers how many accidents they have had over the past five years. The table below shows the survey results. What is the median number of accidents per driver?

Number of accidents	0	1	2	3	4	5	6
Number of drivers	17	13	21	4	2	2	1

© John Wiley & Sons, Inc.

(A) 0.5

(B) 1

(C) 1.5

(D) 2

(E) 4

677. Find the median of the squares of the nine lowest positive integers.

(A) 16

(B) 25

(C) 30.5

(D) 36

(E) 49

678. Given the number set {7, 12, 5, 16, 23, 44, 18, 9, Z}, which of the following values could be equal to Z if Z is the median of the set?

Select all the correct answers.

[A] 11

[B] 12

[C] 13

[D] 14

[E] 15

[F] 16

679. Find the median of the first seven prime numbers.

(A) 7

(B) 11

(C) 13

(D) 17

(E) 19

680. Find the extra number that must be included with the following list of numbers in order to increase the current median value by 1:

16, 7, 24, 2, 11

(A) 10

(B) 11

(C) 12

(D) 13

(E) 14

681. Find the mode for the numbers 7, 6, 5, 8, 7, 5, 9, 3, 5, and 4.

(A) 5

(B) 5.5

(C) 5.9

(D) 7

(E) 7.5

682. Find the mode for the numbers 19, 8, 29, 35, 19, 28, and 15.

(A) 15

(B) 16

(C) 17

(D) 18

(E) 19

683. Find the mode for the numbers 1, 3, 3, 3, 4, 4, 6, 6, 6, and 9.

(A) 6 and 9

(B) 3 and 6

(C) 6

(D) 4

(E) 3

684. The numbers 7, 6, 10, 13, 7, 2, 5, 6, and x have only one mode, and the mean, median, and mode are all equal. Find the value of x.

(A) 5

(B) 5.5

(C) 6

(D) 6.5

(E) 7

685. The mean of the numbers 11, 18, 5, 24, 12, 3, and x is 13. Find the mode.

(A) 11

(B) 12

(C) 13

(D) 15

(E) 18

686. Find the range for the values $2.06, $0.98, $1.32, $1.62, $1.97, $1.46, $2.05, $0.99, and $1.99.

(A) $1.09

(B) $0.98

(C) $1.08

(D) $0.73

(E) $1.07

687. Find the range for the numbers 15, 21, 57, 43, 11, 39, 56, 83, 77, 11, 64, 91, 18, and 37.

(A) 80

(B) 91

(C) 64

(D) 77

(E) 78

688. Find the range for the numbers 57, –5, 11, 39, 56, 82, –2, 11, 64, 18, 37, 15, and 68.

(A) 68

(B) 75

(C) 82

(D) 85

(E) 87

689. Find the range of the numbers of books read.

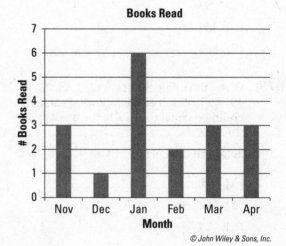

© John Wiley & Sons, Inc.

(A) 1

(B) 2

(C) 3

(D) 5

(E) 7

690. Find the range of the tree heights.

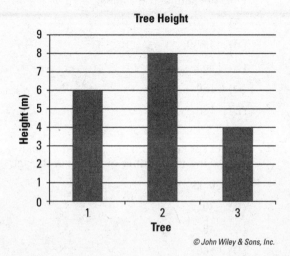

© John Wiley & Sons, Inc.

(A) 1

(B) 2

(C) 3

(D) 4

(E) 6

691. An athlete completed a mile run. His average time was six minutes per mile. If he ran the first and last miles in five minutes, and the other two miles were each run in the same amount of time, what was the average time for the two miles in the middle?

(A) 5 minutes per mile

(B) 6 minutes per mile

(C) 7 minutes per mile

(D) 12 minutes per mile

(E) 14 minutes per mile

692. If the mean of 8, 11, 25, and x is 15, find $8+11+25+x$.

(A) 60

(B) 45

(C) 35

(D) 20

(E) 15

693. Find the mean of the numbers 3, –7, 5, 13, and –2.

(A) 2

(B) 2.4

(C) 5.5

(D) 6

(E) 10.2

694. If the mean of 8, 11, 25, and x is 15, find x.

(A) 10

(B) 12

(C) 15

(D) 16

(E) 20

695. Find the mean number of books read.

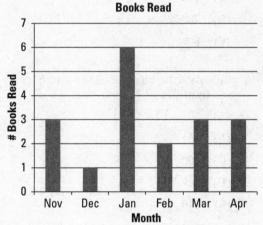

© John Wiley & Sons, Inc.

(A) 1

(B) 2

(C) 3

(D) 4

(E) 5

696. The table shows Juan's test scores for six tests. Calculate his mean test score.

Test	Score
1	86%
2	67%
3	62%
4	72%
5	84%
6	76%

© John Wiley & Sons, Inc.

(A) 74.5%

(B) 75.5%

(C) 76%

(D) 78.5%

(E) 80%

697. Calculate the mean of all the multiples of ten from 10 to 190, inclusive.

(A) 90

(B) 95

(C) 100

(D) 105

(E) 110

698. A data set of 20 values has a sum of 500. Find the mean.

(A) 25

(B) 30

(C) 250

(D) 300

(E) 500

699. A data set of 30 values has a mean of 6. Find the sum of the values.

(A) 0.207

(B) 4.839

(C) 36.2

(D) 150

(E) 180

700. A data set has a sum of 1,200 and a mean of 40. Find the number of values in the set.

(A) 0.03

(B) 30

(C) 40

(D) 860

(E) 23,112

701. The graph shows the sales figures for a certain company for five consecutive years. Calculate the mean sales.

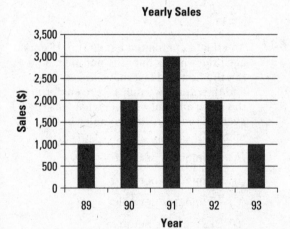

© John Wiley & Sons, Inc.

(A) $1,000

(B) $1,500

(C) $1,800

(D) $2,000

(E) $2,500

702. Find the mean tree height.

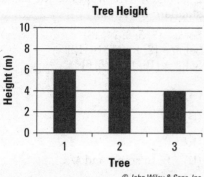

Tree Height

© John Wiley & Sons, Inc.

(A) 1

(B) 2

(C) 3

(D) 4

(E) 6

703. Find the mean number of Italian recipes that each person makes.

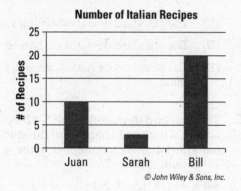

Number of Italian Recipes

© John Wiley & Sons, Inc.

(A) 8

(B) 9

(C) 10

(D) 11

(E) 12

704. The mean of six numbers is 20. One number is removed and the mean changes to 15. What is the number that is removed?

(A) 50

(B) 45

(C) 40

(D) 35

(E) 30

705. Three numbers are written on a piece of paper. The middle number is 8. The mean of the two largest numbers is 9 and the mean of all three numbers is 7. Calculate the mean of the two smallest numbers.

(A) 3

(B) 3.5

(C) 5

(D) 5.5

(E) 7

706. Two numbers are written on a piece of paper. The mean of the numbers is 10 and one number is 6 more than the other. Find the value of the smaller of the two numbers.

(A) 6

(B) 7

(C) 8

(D) 9

(E) 10

707. The mean final exam score from a class of 30 students was 55%. The mean final exam score from a class of 25 students was 44%. Calculate the mean final exam score of all the students.

(A) 48.5%

(B) 49%

(C) 49.5%

(D) 50%

(E) 50.5%

708. If $x = 3y = 6z$, what is the mean of x, y, and z in terms of x?

(A) $\frac{1}{4}x$

(B) $\frac{1}{2}x$

(C) x

(D) $2x$

(E) $\frac{2}{x}$

709. The mean of 15 numbers is 12. An extra number is added and the mean increases to 13. Find the value of the extra number.

(A) 12

(B) 15

(C) 21

(D) 25

(E) 28

710. A data set has values 1, 2, 4, 5, 6, 6, 7, 8, 9, 10, 12, and an unknown value, x. Find the value of x if the mean is 6.

(A) 1

(B) 2

(C) 6

(D) 8

(E) 10

711. Under a normally distributed curve, what is the probability that a member of the population would fall below the mean?

(A) 13.5%

(B) 34%

(C) 50%

(D) 68%

(E) 70%

712. Consider the following three data sets, L, M, and N. Which set has the smallest standard deviation?

Set L = {5, 5, 8, 14, 18}
Set M = {2, 10, 16, 10, 12}
Set N = {16, 14, 8, 6, 6}

(A) L

(B) M

(C) N

(D) Both sets L and M

(E) Both sets M and N

713. The standard deviation of the Set A below is 7.56. What would happen to the standard deviation if each number in the set were increased by 2?

Set A = {3, 8, 12, 17, 25}

(A) The standard deviation is increased by 2.

(B) The standard deviation is decreased by 2.

(C) The standard deviation doubles.

(D) The standard deviation is halved.

(E) The standard deviation stays the same.

714. The standard deviation of the Set B below is 7.56. What would happen to the standard deviation if each number in the set were multiplied by 3?

Set A = {3, 8, 12, 17, 25}

(A) The standard deviation is increased by 3.

(B) The standard deviation is multiplied by 9.

(C) The standard deviation triples.

(D) The standard deviation is increased by 9.

(E) The standard deviation stays the same.

715. Consider the following data set. What value for y would cause Set A to have the smallest standard deviation?

Set $A = \{1, 2, 3, 4, 5, 6, y\}$

(A)   1

(B)   2.5

(C)   3.5

(D)   5.5

(E)   7

716. Consider the following three data sets, A, B, and C. Which set has the largest standard deviation?

Set $A = \{7, 9, 10, 11, 13\}$
Set $B = \{10, 10, 10, 10, 11\}$
Set $C = \{1, 2, 10, 19, 50\}$

(A) A

(B) B

(C) C

(D)   Both sets A and C

(E)   Both sets B and C

717. Consider the following data set:

Set $A = \{2, 4, 6, x, y, z\}$
If the mean of x, y, and z is equal to 4, which of the following statements could be true?

Select all the correct answers.

(A)   The standard deviation of the set is equal to 4.

(B)   The standard deviation of the set is less than 4.

(C)   The standard deviation of the set is greater than 4.

(D)   The standard deviation of the set is the same with or without the inclusion of values of x, y, and z.

718. If the normally distributed mean height for a group of dogs is 65 centimeters and the standard deviation is 5 centimeters, what is the probability that the height of a randomly chosen dog in the group will be less than 60 centimeters?

(A)   50%

(B)   16%

(C)   60%

(D)   34%

(E)   65%

719. If the normally distributed mean height for a group of 200 dogs is 65 centimeters and the standard deviation is 5 centimeters, about how many of the dogs have heights that are between 65 centimeters and 75 centimeters?

(A)   47

(B)   50

(C)   95

(D)   99

(E)   105

720. The normally distributed mean test score was 70%, and the standard deviation was 12 points. If a student scored 95% on the test, approximately what percentage of test-takers scored below this student?

(A)   82%

(B)   85%

(C)   90%

(D)   95%

(E)   98%

721. The reaction time of some children was measured and the average time that it took a child to respond to a stimulus was 0.135 seconds. With a normal distribution and standard deviation of 0.021 seconds, how many standard deviations would a measured reaction time of 0.205 seconds be away from the average?

(A) 0–1 standard deviations

(B) 1–2 standard deviations

(C) 2–3 standard deviations

(D) 3–4 standard deviations

(E) 4–5 standard deviations

722. The mean score for a math test was 60 and the standard deviation was 15. If a student's score was within 2 standard deviations of the mean, what is the lowest possible value of that score?

(A) 25

(B) 30

(C) 50

(D) 60

(E) 90

723. Managers of a bus company were interested in understanding the popularity of one of their tours, so they began monitoring the number of travelers. The numbers of passengers on the trips were 22, 33, 21, 28, 22, 31, 44, 50, and 19. The standard deviation of these nine trips was approximately 10.2. If each trip had had triple the number of passengers, what would have been the standard deviation?

(A) 7.2

(B) 10.2

(C) 13.2

(D) 26.4

(E) 30.6

724. Consider a data set that has a mean of 10 and a standard deviation of 1.5. Which pair of numbers, if added to the data set, would decrease the standard deviation the most?

(A) 2, 10

(B) 7, 13

(C) 9, 11

(D) 10, 18

(E) 16, 16

725. The administrators of a standardized test found that the average score was a 72 with a standard deviation of 8. The administrators consider a test score to be "exceptional" if it is more than 2.5 standard deviations above the average score. What is the lowest possible test score that would be considered "exceptional" by the administrators?

(A) 95%

(B) 93%

(C) 92%

(D) 90%

(E) 88%

726. Rank the following data sets from least standard deviation to greatest standard deviation:

Set A = {3, 4, 5, 5, 6, 7}
Set B = {2, 2, 2, 8, 8, 8}
Set C = {15, 15, 15, 15, 15, 15}

(A) A, B, C

(B) B, C, A

(C) C, A, B

(D) A, C, B

(E) B, A, C

727. Consider a set of numbers with a mean of 10 and a standard deviation of 2. What is the probability that a number selected from the set is equal to 5?

(A) 50%

(B) 34%

(C) 13.5%

(D) 5%

(E) 2%

728. A group of 300 students have a combined weight of 21,600 pounds. If the weight of these students has a normal distribution and the standard deviation equals 12 pounds, approximately what percentage of the students weigh more than 84 pounds?

(A) 12%

(B) 16%

(C) 25%

(D) 36%

(E) 40%

729. Consider a data set with a standard deviation of 6. If 10 is added to each number in the set, which expression represents the change in the standard deviation?

(A) 0

(B) $\dfrac{3}{5}$

(C) $6^{10}\ 7^{10}$

(D) $10^{6}\ 10^{7}$

(E) $\dfrac{5}{3}\ \dfrac{10}{7}$

730. Consider the following data set:

Set A = {5, 8, 13, 21, 34}
Which of the following sets has a standard deviation that is the same as that of Set A?

Set R = {35, 38, 43, 51, 64}
Set S = {10, 16, 26, 42, 68}
Set T = {46, 59, 67, 72, 75}
Select all the correct answers.

(A) Set R

(B) Set S

(C) Set T

For questions 731–733, use the following table showing the results from a used car auction.

Results of a Used-Car Auction		
	Small Cars	Large Cars
Number of cars offered	32	23
Number of cars sold	16	20
Projected sales total for cars offered (in thousands)	$70	$150
Actual sales total (in thousands)	$41	$120

© John Wiley & Sons, Inc.

731. What was the average large-car sale price?

732. What was the ratio of small cars offered to small cars sold?

(A) 5:4

(B) 1:2

(C) 3:2

(D) 3:1

(E) 2:1

733. Approximately what percent of the cars sold were large cars?

(A) 44%

(B) 87%

(C) 56%

(D) 80%

(E) 50%

For questions 734–735, use the following world population pie chart.

World Population by Continent

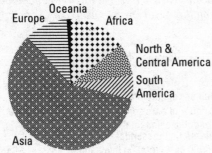

© John Wiley & Sons, Inc.

734. Approximately what percent of the world's population lives in Asia?

(A) 40%

(B) 50%

(C) 60%

(D) 80%

(E) 90%

735. Approximately what percent of the world's population lives in Africa?

(A) 5%

(B) 15%

(C) 25%

(D) 40%

(E) 50%

For questions 736–737, use the following histogram showing the heights of students.

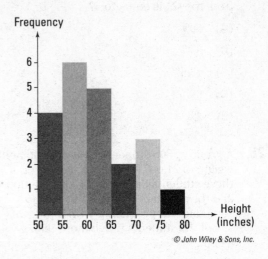

© John Wiley & Sons, Inc.

736. How many students are greater than or equal to 60 inches tall?

(A) 6

(B) 11

(C) 15

(D) 17

(E) 21

737. How many students are greater than or equal to 55 inches tall, but less than 70 inches tall?

(A) 11

(B) 13

(C) 15

(D) 16

(E) 17

For questions 738–739, use the following histogram showing the lengths of bird eggs.

For questions 740–741, use the following bar graph showing Tom's scores in his classes.

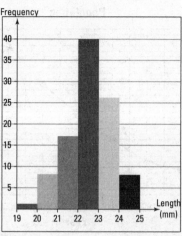

© John Wiley & Sons, Inc.

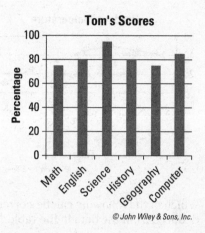

© John Wiley & Sons, Inc.

738. How many eggs are less than 23 millimeters in length?

(A) 26

(B) 40

(C) 66

(D) 92

(E) 100

739. How many eggs are measured altogether in the graph?

(A) 25

(B) 40

(C) 75

(D) 90

(E) 100

740. How many more percentage points did Tom earn in English than in History?

(A) 0

(B) 2

(C) 5

(D) 10

(E) 15

741. How many more percentage points did Tom earn in Science than in History?

(A) 0

(B) 2

(C) 5

(D) 10

(E) 15

For questions 742–743, use this line graph showing the outdoor temperature throughout the day.

For questions 744–746, use this line graph showing the population of a town.

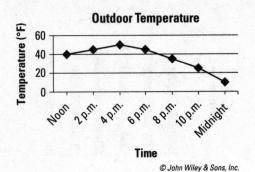

© John Wiley & Sons, Inc.

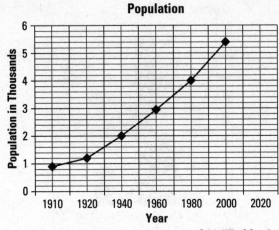

© John Wiley & Sons, Inc.

742. Which of the following can be correctly deduced from the data in the table?

Select all the correct answers.

[A] The temperature is about 30°F at 9 p.m.

[B] The range of temperatures is 40°F.

[C] The average temperature during this time frame is 25°F.

[D] There is a 40% decrease in temperature between 6 p.m. and 8 p.m.

743. What is the percent increase in temperature from noon to 4 p.m.?

(A) 20%

(B) 25%

(C) 35%

(D) 40%

(E) 50%

744. Between which years did the population increase at least 100%?

Select all the correct answers.

[A] 1940–1960

[B] 1940–1980

[C] 1910–1920

[D] 1910–1940

[E] 1980–2000

745. Assuming that the trend in the population growth continues, what will be the approximate population of the town in the year 2020?

(A) 5,000

(B) 5,500

(C) 6,000

(D) 6,400

(E) 7,400

746. Approximately how much did the population increase between 1920 and 1980?

(A) 2,500

(B) 2,800

(C) 3,000

(D) 3,800

(E) 4,000

For questions 747–748, use this line graph showing the scores on a die after rolling.

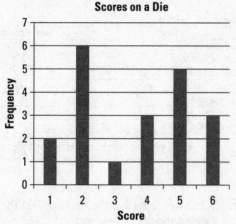

© John Wiley & Sons, Inc.

747. If this information were displayed in a pie chart, what would be the angle of the sector of the pie chart representing the score of 5?

(A) 23°

(B) 84°

(C) 90°

(D) 98°

(E) 108°

748. What is the sum of the percentages of rolls that resulted in the die landing on a 2 or a 6?

(A) 33%

(B) 36%

(C) 40%

(D) 42%

(E) 45%

For questions 749–751, use this pie chart showing the favorite pets of schoolchildren.

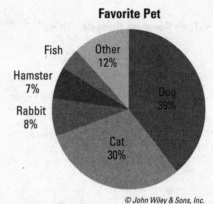

© John Wiley & Sons, Inc.

749. What is the angle for the sector of the pie chart representing fish?

(A) 4°

(B) 9°

(C) 14.4°

(D) 24°

(E) 50.4°

750. If 800 children were surveyed, how many said their favorite pet was a fish?

(A) 4

(B) 9

(C) 14

(D) 20

(E) 32

751. If 312 children said their favorite pet was a dog, how many children said their favorite pet was a rabbit?

(A) 46

(B) 50

(C) 56

(D) 64

(E) 75

For questions 752–754, use this pie chart showing the amount of time that Susan spends on various activities each 24-hour day.

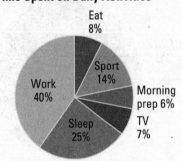

Time Spent on Daily Activities

© John Wiley & Sons, Inc.

752. If this information were displayed using a bar graph with hours on the vertical axis, what would be the height of the bar for work?

(A) 4

(B) 4.9

(C) 5.5

(D) 8

(E) 9.6

753. Approximately how many hours does Susan spend playing sports each day?

(A) 1.5 hours

(B) 2.5 hours

(C) 3.5 hours

(D) 4.5 hours

(E) 5.5 hours

754. How much more time does Susan spend sleeping than morning prep and eating each day?

(A) 1 hour 44 minutes

(B) 2 hours 38 minutes

(C) 2 hours

(D) 2 hours 26 minutes

(E) 3 hours 36 minutes

For questions 755–757, use this table showing the numbers of patients with mental illnesses.

Mental Illness in India

Disease	Total Patients
Schizophrenia	24,651
Psychotic diseases	10,279
Mild and severe mental retardation	2,255
Neuroses	1,122
Drug dependence	996
Alcoholism	692
Personality disorders	627
Others	1,052
Total	41,674

© John Wiley & Sons, Inc.

755. What percent of patients makes up the largest disease category?

(A) 59%

(B) 42%

(C) 69%

(D) 17%

(E) 25%

756. If the number of patients with schizophrenia decreases by 10% and the number with psychotic diseases decreases by 5%, what is the overall reduction of the number of patients suffering from mental illness?

(A) 4%

(B) 5%

(C) 6%

(D) 7%

(E) 8%

757. Which pair of mental illnesses has a combined percent that is at least 5%?

Select all the correct answers.

[A] Neuroses and Drug dependence

[B] Alcoholism and Others

[C] Neuroses and Alcoholism

[D] Neuroses and Others

[E] Drug dependence and Alcoholism

[F] Drug dependence and Others

For questions 758–760, use this graph showing the annual profit for two companies.

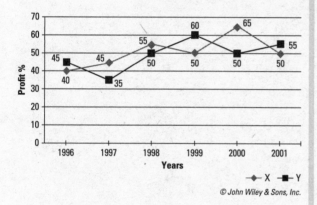

© John Wiley & Sons, Inc.

758. Which of the following can be correctly deduced from the data in the graph?

Select all the correct answers.

[A] The median percent profit for Company X is half the mode percent profit for Company Y.

[B] Both companies have the same mode percent profit.

[C] Both companies have the same median percent profit.

[D] The mode percent profit for Company X is greater than the median percent profit for Company Y.

[E] The mode percent profit for Company X is equal to the median percent profit for Company Y.

759. What percentage describes the increase in profit for Company X from 1996 to 1998?

(A) 27%

(B) 37.5%

(C) 40%

(D) 50%

(E) 55%

760. Which of the following can be correctly inferred from the data in the graph?

Select all the correct answers.

[A] The percent profit for Company X rose uniformly over the 6-year period.

[B] The difference between percent profit for Company X and percent profit for Company Y was less than 15% in more than half the years shown.

[C] The percent profit for Company X was never less than 75% of the percent profit for Company Y.

Chapter 5

Quantitative Comparisons and More Problem Solving

. . . .

Many of the GRE math problems are Quantitative Comparisons. The problem lists Quantity A and Quantity B, and these quantities can be numbers, variables, equations, words, figures, and so on. Your job is to compare these two quantities and determine whether one is greater, they're equal, or the relationship can't be determined.

In this chapter, the first half of the questions are pure Quantitative Comparison for you to practice. The second half of the questions are mixed Quantitative Comparison and Problem Solving to simulate the actual test-taking experience, where the questions are mixed.

The Problems You'll Work On

These questions cover the same topics as the Problem Solving questions:

- ✔ Basic math, including prime numbers, factors, multiples, and absolute values
- ✔ Algebra, including exponents, solving for *x*, functions, and sequences
- ✔ Geometry, including circles, rectangles, triangles, cylinders, and cubes
- ✔ Word problems, including mixtures, Venn diagrams, counting methods, and work problems
- ✔ Tables and graphs, including the median, range, and standard deviation

What to Watch Out For

Quantitative Comparison questions have a lot of tricks and traps. Watch out for questions that

- ✔ Deceive you with equal appearances
- ✔ Distract you with drawings not drawn to scale
- ✔ Deter you with vague pictures that don't include detail

For quantitative comparison questions in this chapter, the answer choices are as follows:

(A) Quantity A is greater.

(B) Quantity B is greater.

(C) The quantities are equal.

(D) It cannot be determined from the information given.

The following notes apply:

All numbers used in the exam are real numbers.

All figures lie in a plane.

Angle measures are positive; points and angles are in the position shown.

761. Which quantity is greater?

A: $-1(-1)$

B: $-1+(-1)$

    (A)   Quantity A is greater.

    (B)   Quantity B is greater.

    (C)   The quantities are equal.

    (D)   It cannot be determined from the information given.

762. Which quantity is greater?

A: 62,210 rounded to the nearest hundredths place

B: 62,210 rounded to the nearest thousandths place

    (A)   Quantity A is greater.

    (B)   Quantity B is greater.

    (C)   The quantities are equal.

    (D)   It cannot be determined from the information given.

763. x is a positive integer. Which quantity is greater?

A: x

B: $2x$

    (A)   Quantity A is greater.

    (B)   Quantity B is greater.

    (C)   The quantities are equal.

    (D)   It cannot be determined from the information given.

764. n is an even integer. Which quantity is greater?

A: The remainder when n is divided by 3

B: The remainder when n is divided by 5

    (A)   Quantity A is greater.

    (B)   Quantity B is greater.

    (C)   The quantities are equal.

    (D)   It cannot be determined from the information given.

765. n is an integer greater than 0. Which quantity is greater?

A: $\frac{1}{n}+n$

B: 2

    (A)   Quantity A is greater.

    (B)   Quantity B is greater.

    (C)   The quantities are equal.

    (D)   It cannot be determined from the information given.

766. Which quantity is greater?

A: The number of integers between 50 and 100 that are multiples of 3

B: The number of integers between 10 and 81 that are multiples of 4

(A)   Quantity A is greater.

(B)   Quantity B is greater.

(C)   The quantities are equal.

(D)   It cannot be determined from the information given.

767. Robbi has more than twice the number of candies that Sara and Tina have together. Which quantity is greater?

A: The number of candies that Robbi has

B: Three times the number of candies that Sara and Tina have together

(A)   Quantity A is greater.

(B)   Quantity B is greater.

(C)   The quantities are equal.

(D)   It cannot be determined from the information given.

768. Which quantity is greater?

A: Twice an odd integer greater than 6

B: Three times an odd integer greater than 2

(A)   Quantity A is greater.

(B)   Quantity B is greater.

(C)   The quantities are equal.

(D)   It cannot be determined from the information given.

769. The rate of a certain chemical reaction doubles for every 10° rise in temperature. Which quantity is greater?

A: Twice the rate at 10°

B: Half the rate at 30°

(A)   Quantity A is greater.

(B)   Quantity B is greater.

(C)   The quantities are equal.

(D)   It cannot be determined from the information given.

770. x, y, and z are consecutive integers and $xyz = 0$. Which quantity is greater?

A: z

B: 0

(A)   Quantity A is greater.

(B)   Quantity B is greater.

(C)   The quantities are equal.

(D)   It cannot be determined from the information given.

771. Which quantity is greater?

A: The greatest prime factor of 36

B: The greatest prime factor of 48

(A)   Quantity A is greater.

(B)   Quantity B is greater.

(C)   The quantities are equal.

(D)   It cannot be determined from the information given.

772. Which quantity is greater?

A: The greatest prime factor of 40

B: The greatest prime factor of 24

(A)   Quantity A is greater.

(B)   Quantity B is greater.

(C)   The quantities are equal.

(D)   It cannot be determined from the information given.

773. Which quantity is greater?

A: The greatest prime factor of 540

B: The greatest prime factor of 90

   (A)   Quantity A is greater.

   (B)   Quantity B is greater.

   (C)   The quantities are equal.

   (D)   It cannot be determined from the information given.

774. Which quantity is greater?

A: The number of different prime factors of 252

B: The number of different prime factors of 3,150

   (A)   Quantity A is greater.

   (B)   Quantity B is greater.

   (C)   The quantities are equal.

   (D)   It cannot be determined from the information given.

775. Which quantity is greater?

A: The number of different prime factors of 2,500

B: The number of different prime factors of 1,215

   (A)   Quantity A is greater.

   (B)   Quantity B is greater.

   (C)   The quantities are equal.

   (D)   It cannot be determined from the information given.

776. Which quantity is greater?

A: $|-5|$

B: $|7|$

   (A)   Quantity A is greater.

   (B)   Quantity B is greater.

   (C)   The quantities are equal.

   (D)   It cannot be determined from the information given.

777. Which quantity is greater?

A: $|-3|$

B: -3

   (A)   Quantity A is greater.

   (B)   Quantity B is greater.

   (C)   The quantities are equal.

   (D)   It cannot be determined from the information given.

778. Which quantity is greater?

A: $|-3|+|-2|$

B: $-3+(-2)$

   (A)   Quantity A is greater.

   (B)   Quantity B is greater.

   (C)   The quantities are equal.

   (D)   It cannot be determined from the information given.

779. Which quantity is greater?

A: $|8-3|$

B: $|3-8|$

   (A)   Quantity A is greater.

   (B)   Quantity B is greater.

   (C)   The quantities are equal.

   (D)   It cannot be determined from the information given.

780. Which quantity is greater?

A: $\left|-3\times6\right|$

B: $-\left|-12\right|$

(A)   Quantity A is greater.

(B)   Quantity B is greater.

(C)   The quantities are equal.

(D)   It cannot be determined from the information given.

781. Which quantity is greater?

A: $\left|2\times7\right|$

B: $\left|\dfrac{3}{1}+7\right|$

(A)   Quantity A is greater.

(B)   Quantity B is greater.

(C)   The quantities are equal.

(D)   It cannot be determined from the information given.

782. Which quantity is greater?

A: $\left|5\times-3\right|$

B: $-\left|5-9\right|$

(A)   Quantity A is greater.

(B)   Quantity B is greater.

(C)   The quantities are equal.

(D)   It cannot be determined from the information given.

783. Which quantity is greater?

A: $-\left|-6\right|\div\left|-2\right|$

B: $\left|-6\right|\times-\left|2\right|$

(A)   Quantity A is greater.

(B)   Quantity B is greater.

(C)   The quantities are equal.

(D)   It cannot be determined from the information given.

784. Which quantity is greater?

A: $\dfrac{-4\times\left|3-8\right|}{\left|1+3\right|}$

B: $\dfrac{4\times\left|8-3\right|}{\left|-2\right|}$

(A)   Quantity A is greater.

(B)   Quantity B is greater.

(C)   The quantities are equal.

(D)   It cannot be determined from the information given.

785. Which quantity is greater?

A: $\left|\dfrac{-4\div2}{6-8}\right|\times\dfrac{-3}{4}$

B: $\left|\dfrac{-4\times2}{8-6}\right|\times\dfrac{3}{4}$

(A)   Quantity A is greater.

(B)   Quantity B is greater.

(C)   The quantities are equal.

(D)   It cannot be determined from the information given.

786. Which quantity is greater?

A: The place value of the digit 2 in the number 35.982

B: The place value of the digit 2 in the number 36.92

(A)   Quantity A is greater.

(B)   Quantity B is greater.

(C)   The quantities are equal.

(D)   It cannot be determined from the information given.

787. Which quantity is greater?

A: 1,000%

B: 10

(A) Quantity A is greater.

(B) Quantity B is greater.

(C) The quantities are equal.

(D) It cannot be determined from the information given.

788. Which quantity is greater?

A: $1.01(-1.01)$

B: $-1.01 + (-1.01)$

(A) Quantity A is greater.

(B) Quantity B is greater.

(C) The quantities are equal.

(D) It cannot be determined from the information given.

789. Which quantity is greater?

A: 2.2740 rounded to the nearest hundredths place

B: 2.2704 rounded to the nearest thousandths place

(A) Quantity A is greater.

(B) Quantity B is greater.

(C) The quantities are equal.

(D) It cannot be determined from the information given.

790. Which quantity is greater?

$4.5 < x < 8.3$ and $3.1 < y < 7.8$

A: $x - y$

B: 5.2

(A) Quantity A is greater.

(B) Quantity B is greater.

(C) The quantities are equal.

(D) It cannot be determined from the information given.

791. Which quantity is greater?

A: $\dfrac{1}{3}$

B: $\dfrac{2}{3}$

(A) Quantity A is greater.

(B) Quantity B is greater.

(C) The quantities are equal.

(D) It cannot be determined from the information given.

792. Which quantity is greater?

A: $\dfrac{5}{6}$

B: $\dfrac{29}{36}$

(A) Quantity A is greater.

(B) Quantity B is greater.

(C) The quantities are equal.

(D) It cannot be determined from the information given.

793. Which quantity is greater?

A: A fraction with a numerator of 5

B: A fraction with a numerator of 3

(A) Quantity A is greater.

(B) Quantity B is greater.

(C) The quantities are equal.

(D) It cannot be determined from the information given.

794. Which quantity is greater?

$\frac{7}{8} > x > \frac{5}{6}$

A: x

B: $\frac{6}{7}$

(A) Quantity A is greater.

(B) Quantity B is greater.

(C) The quantities are equal.

(D) It cannot be determined from the information given.

795. Which quantity is greater?

A: The numerator of an equivalent fraction to $\frac{2}{3}$ with a denominator of 12

B: The denominator of an equivalent fraction to $\frac{1}{2}$ with a numerator of 8

(A) Quantity A is greater.

(B) Quantity B is greater.

(C) The quantities are equal.

(D) It cannot be determined from the information given.

796. Which quantity is greater?

A: The numerator of the sum of $\frac{2}{7} + \frac{3}{7}$

B: The numerator of the sum of $\frac{1}{4} + \frac{3}{8}$

(A) Quantity A is greater.

(B) Quantity B is greater.

(C) The quantities are equal.

(D) It cannot be determined from the information given.

797. Which quantity is greater?

A: The least common denominator of $\frac{2}{9}, \frac{5}{12}$, and $\frac{1}{36}$

B: The least common denominator of $\frac{1}{3}, \frac{7}{12}$, and $\frac{5}{8}$

(A) Quantity A is greater.

(B) Quantity B is greater.

(C) The quantities are equal.

(D) It cannot be determined from the information given.

798. Which quantity is greater?

A: The least common denominator of $\frac{5}{12}$ and $\frac{8}{9}$

B: 24

(A) Quantity A is greater.

(B) Quantity B is greater.

(C) The quantities are equal.

(D) It cannot be determined from the information given.

799. Which quantity is greater?

A: The numerator in the product of $\frac{5}{8} \times \frac{4}{5}$

B: The numerator in the product of $\frac{2}{7} \times \frac{4}{3}$

(A) Quantity A is greater.

(B) Quantity B is greater.

(C) The quantities are equal.

(D) It cannot be determined from the information given.

800. $\frac{1}{3}, \frac{4}{5}, \frac{3}{11}, \frac{1}{2}$

Considering these fractions, which quantity is greater?

A: The smallest fraction shown

B: The product of the greatest fraction shown and $\frac{2}{3}$

(A)   Quantity A is greater.

(B)   Quantity B is greater.

(C)   The quantities are equal.

(D)   It cannot be determined from the information given.

801. The price of a laptop is p dollars. Which quantity is greater?

A: The price of the laptop after a 15% discount

B: 0.85p dollars

(A)   Quantity A is greater.

(B)   Quantity B is greater.

(C)   The quantities are equal.

(D)   It cannot be determined from the information given.

802. Which quantity is greater?

A: 75% of 60

B: 55% of 55

(A)   Quantity A is greater.

(B)   Quantity B is greater.

(C)   The quantities are equal.

(D)   It cannot be determined from the information given.

803. Which quantity is greater?

A: The percentage that equals 16 out of 20

B: The percentage that equals 27 out of 50

(A)   Quantity A is greater.

(B)   Quantity B is greater.

(C)   The quantities are equal.

(D)   It cannot be determined from the information given.

804. Which quantity is greater?

A: The percentage difference between 14 and 26

B: The percentage difference between 26 and 38

(A)   Quantity A is greater.

(B)   Quantity B is greater.

(C)   The quantities are equal.

(D)   It cannot be determined from the information given.

805. If 45% of m = 54 and 90% of n = 108, which quantity is greater?

A: m

B: n

(A)   Quantity A is greater.

(B)   Quantity B is greater.

(C)   The quantities are equal.

(D)   It cannot be determined from the information given.

806. Which quantity is greater?

A: The percentage of the multiples of 2 that are also multiples of 5

B: The percentage of the multiples of 5 that are also multiples of 2

(A)   Quantity A is greater.

(B)   Quantity B is greater.

(C)   The quantities are equal.

(D)   It cannot be determined from the information given.

807. The graph shows the sales figures for a certain company in five consecutive years. Which quantity is greater?

Year Sales

© John Wiley & Sons, Inc.

A: The percentage increase in sales from 1989 to 1991

B: The percentage fall in sales from 1991 to 1993

(A) Quantity A is greater.

(B) Quantity B is greater.

(C) The quantities are equal.

(D) It cannot be determined from the information given.

808. Which quantity is greater?

A: Total savings on 40 gallons of fuel bought at $1.152 per gallon instead of $1.245

B: $3.70

(A) Quantity A is greater.

(B) Quantity B is greater.

(C) The quantities are equal.

(D) It cannot be determined from the information given.

809. In a school, 28% of the students in Class A pack their lunches and 14% in Class B pack their lunches. Which quantity is greater?

A: The percentage of students in Class A and Class B combined who pack their lunches

B: 20%

(A) Quantity A is greater.

(B) Quantity B is greater.

(C) The quantities are equal.

(D) It cannot be determined from the information given.

810. In a class of 32 students, 75% of the students are girls and 50% of the students study Spanish. Which quantity is greater?

A: The number of girls who study Spanish

B: 7

(A) Quantity A is greater.

(B) Quantity B is greater.

(C) The quantities are equal.

(D) It cannot be determined from the information given.

811. A class of 32 students has 12 girls. Which quantity is greater?

A: The ratio of girls to boys

B: 3 : 5

(A) Quantity A is greater.

(B) Quantity B is greater.

(C) The quantities are equal.

(D) It cannot be determined from the information given.

812. Which quantity is greater?

A: 4 : 5

B: 8 : 10

(A)   Quantity A is greater.

(B)   Quantity B is greater.

(C)   The quantities are equal.

(D)   It cannot be determined from the information given.

813. There are 10 cars parked in a lot. Three of the cars in the lot are red. Which quantity is greater?

A: The ratio of red cars to other-colored cars

B: 3 : 7

(A)   Quantity A is greater.

(B)   Quantity B is greater.

(C)   The quantities are equal.

(D)   It cannot be determined from the information given.

814. A 10-foot plank of wood is cut into four pieces, with three having equal lengths and one having a shorter length. Which quantity is greater?

A: The length of one of the equal pieces

B: 3 feet

(A)   Quantity A is greater.

(B)   Quantity B is greater.

(C)   The quantities are equal.

(D)   It cannot be determined from the information given.

815. The profit from a business is to be divided in the ratio 4 to 5 between X and Y respectively. Which quantity is greater?

A: The money X receives when the profit is $153.00

B: $70.00

(A)   Quantity A is greater.

(B)   Quantity B is greater.

(C)   The quantities are equal.

(D)   It cannot be determined from the information given.

816. Which quantity is greater?

A: The distance between the tips of the hour hand and the minute hand of a clock at 10:05

B: The distance between the tips of the hour hand and the minute hand of a clock at 10:30

(A)   Quantity A is greater.

(B)   Quantity B is greater.

(C)   The quantities are equal.

(D)   It cannot be determined from the information given.

817. C is the midpoint of segment AE and AB < DE. Which quantity is greater?

A: BC

B: CD

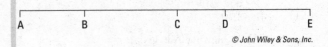

© John Wiley & Sons, Inc.

(A)   Quantity A is greater.

(B)   Quantity B is greater.

(C)   The quantities are equal.

(D)   It cannot be determined from the information given.

818. Lines *l, m,* and *n* are parallel. $\angle ABC = 90°$.

Which quantity is greater?

A: $x + y$

B: 90°

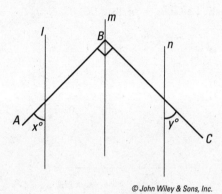

© John Wiley & Sons, Inc.

(A)   Quantity A is greater.

(B)   Quantity B is greater.

(C)   The quantities are equal.

(D)   It cannot be determined from the information given.

819. Which quantity is greater?

A: The perimeter of a triangle with sides of 4, 5, and 6

B: 20

(A)   Quantity A is greater.

(B)   Quantity B is greater.

(C)   The quantities are equal.

(D)   It cannot be determined from the information given.

820. Which quantity is greater?

A: The perimeter of an equilateral triangle with a side of 6

B: 18

(A)   Quantity A is greater.

(B)   Quantity B is greater.

(C)   The quantities are equal.

(D)   It cannot be determined from the information given.

821. Which quantity is greater?

A: The area of a triangle with a base of 3

B: The area of a triangle with a base of 5

(A)   Quantity A is greater.

(B)   Quantity B is greater.

(C)   The quantities are equal.

(D)   It cannot be determined from the information given.

822. Which quantity is greater?

A: The perimeter of a scalene triangle with sides of 1 and 2

B: 5

(A)   Quantity A is greater.

(B)   Quantity B is greater.

(C)   The quantities are equal.

(D)   It cannot be determined from the information given.

823. $AC > CB > AB$. Which quantity is greater?

A: b

B: a

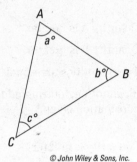

© John Wiley & Sons, Inc.

(A)   Quantity A is greater.

(B)   Quantity B is greater.

(C)   The quantities are equal.

(D)   It cannot be determined from the information given.

824. Which quantity is greater?

A: Angle 4

B: Angle 2

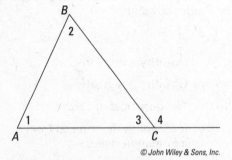

© John Wiley & Sons, Inc.

(A)   Quantity A is greater.

(B)   Quantity B is greater.

(C)   The quantities are equal.

(D)   It cannot be determined from the information given.

825.   Angle $ABC = 59$

Angle $ACB = 61$

Which quantity is greater?

A: The length of side AB

B: The length of side BC

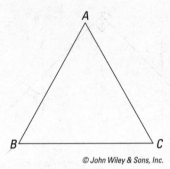

© John Wiley & Sons, Inc.

(A)   Quantity A is greater.

(B)   Quantity B is greater.

(C)   The quantities are equal.

(D)   It cannot be determined from the information given.

826. The lengths of two sides of a triangle are 4 and 6. Which quantity is greater?

A: The length of the third side

B: 10

(A)   Quantity A is greater.

(B)   Quantity B is greater.

(C)   The quantities are equal.

(D)   It cannot be determined from the information given.

827. *AB* is a diameter of the circle. All triangles above the diameter in the diagram are equal in area. All triangles below the diameter are equal in area. Which quantity is greater?

A: Total area of the triangles above *AB*

B: Total area of the triangles below *AB*

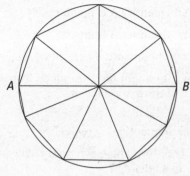

Note: Drawing is not to scale.
© John Wiley & Sons, Inc.

(A)   Quantity A is greater.

(B)   Quantity B is greater.

(C)   The quantities are equal.

(D)   It cannot be determined from the information given.

828. Which quantity is greater?

A: The area of a rectangle with a perimeter of 10

B: The area of a triangle with a base of 6 and a height of 3

(A)   Quantity A is greater.

(B)   Quantity B is greater.

(C)   The quantities are equal.

(D)   It cannot be determined from the information given.

829. *ABCD* is a rectangle. Which quantity is greater?

A: The length of the curved path from *A* to *C*

B: 5

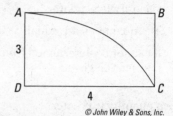

© John Wiley & Sons, Inc.

(A)   Quantity A is greater.

(B)   Quantity B is greater.

(C)   The quantities are equal.

(D)   It cannot be determined from the information given.

830. *O* is the center of the circle, and angle *POQ* is a right angle. Which quantity is greater?

A: *MN* : *PQ*

B: 2 : 1

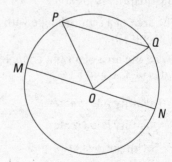

© John Wiley & Sons, Inc.

(A)   Quantity A is greater.

(B)   Quantity B is greater.

(C)   The quantities are equal.

(D)   It cannot be determined from the information given.

831. Which quantity is greater?

A: The largest angle in a right triangle.

B: 105°

(A)   Quantity A is greater.

(B)   Quantity B is greater.

(C)   The quantities are equal.

(D)   It cannot be determined from the information given.

832. Which quantity is greater?

A: The smallest angle of an isosceles right triangle

B: The smallest angle of a scalene right triangle

(A)   Quantity A is greater.

(B)   Quantity B is greater.

(C)   The quantities are equal.

(D)   It cannot be determined from the information given.

833. Which quantity is greater?

A: The area of a right triangle with sides of 6, 8, and 10

B: Twice the area of a right triangle with sides of 3, 4, and 5

(A)   Quantity A is greater.

(B)   Quantity B is greater.

(C)   The quantities are equal.

(D)   It cannot be determined from the information given.

834. Which quantity is greater?

A: The diagonal created by cutting a rectangle with a side of 4 into two equal triangles

B: The diagonal created by cutting a square with a side of 4 into two equal triangles

(A)   Quantity A is greater.

(B)   Quantity B is greater.

(C)   The quantities are equal.

(D)   It cannot be determined from the information given.

835. Which quantity is greater?

A: The third angle of a right triangle with an angle of 67°

B: 33°

(A)   Quantity A is greater.

(B)   Quantity B is greater.

(C)   The quantities are equal.

(D)   It cannot be determined from the information given.

836. *ABCD* is a quadrilateral. Which quantity is greater?

A: Angle *D*

B: 55°

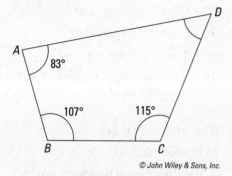

© John Wiley & Sons, Inc.

(A) Quantity A is greater.

(B) Quantity B is greater.

(C) The quantities are equal.

(D) It cannot be determined from the information given.

837. Which quantity is greater?

A: The sum of the interior angles of a quadrilateral

B: 360°

(A) Quantity A is greater.

(B) Quantity B is greater.

(C) The quantities are equal.

(D) It cannot be determined from the information given.

838. 10 millimeters = 1 centimeter. Which quantity is greater?

A: The area of a square with sides of 1 centimeter

B: 10 times the area of a square with sides of 1 millimeter

(A) Quantity A is greater.

(B) Quantity B is greater.

(C) The quantities are equal.

(D) It cannot be determined from the information given.

839. Which quantity is greater?

A: The diagonal of a rectangle

B: Half the perimeter of the same rectangle

(A) Quantity A is greater.

(B) Quantity B is greater.

(C) The quantities are equal.

(D) It cannot be determined from the information given.

840. Angles *QPS* and *QRS* are right angles. *QR* = 3, *RS* = 4, and *PS* = 2. Which quantity is greater?

A: Side *PQ*

B: 5

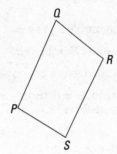

Note: Figure not drawn to scale.
© John Wiley & Sons, Inc.

(A)   Quantity A is greater.

(B)   Quantity B is greater.

(C)   The quantities are equal.

(D)   It cannot be determined from the information given.

841. Which quantity is greater?

A: The circumference of a circle with a radius of 5

B: 10π

(A)   Quantity A is greater.

(B)   Quantity B is greater.

(C)   The quantities are equal.

(D)   It cannot be determined from the information given.

842. *r* is the radius of circle *C*. *s* is the circumference of circle *C*. Which quantity is greater?

A: 6*r*

B: *s*

(A)   Quantity A is greater.

(B)   Quantity B is greater.

(C)   The quantities are equal.

(D)   It cannot be determined from the information given.

843. Which quantity is greater?

A: The radius of a circle

B: The diameter of that same circle

(A)   Quantity A is greater.

(B)   Quantity B is greater.

(C)   The quantities are equal.

(D)   It cannot be determined from the information given.

844. A circle and a line lie in the same plane. Which quantity is greater?

A: The greatest possible number of points that are on both the circle and the line

B: 2

(A)   Quantity A is greater.

(B)   Quantity B is greater.

(C)   The quantities are equal.

(D)   It cannot be determined from the information given.

845. Each of six sectors of a circle is assigned a number such that the numbers in any two adjacent sectors add up to 15. Which quantity is greater?

A: *x*

B: 8

© John Wiley & Sons, Inc.

(A)   Quantity A is greater.

(B)   Quantity B is greater.

(C)   The quantities are equal.

(D)   It cannot be determined from the information given.

846. *A* is a point on the circle and *BC* is a chord, but not a diameter of the circle. Which quantity is greater?

A: *x*

B: 90°

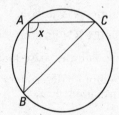

Note: Figure not drawn to scale.

© John Wiley & Sons, Inc.

(A)   Quantity A is greater.

(B)   Quantity B is greater.

(C)   The quantities are equal.

(D)   It cannot be determined from the information given.

847. A beach resort is 2 kilometers from the city, and a sports complex is 10 kilometers from the city. The city, resort, and sports complex all lie at sea level. Which quantity is greater?

A: The distance from the beach resort to the sports complex

B: 7 kilometers

(A)   Quantity A is greater.

(B)   Quantity B is greater.

(C)   The quantities are equal.

(D)   It cannot be determined from the information given.

848. Which quantity is greater?

A: The number of edges on a cube

B: The number of edges on a triangular prism

(A)   Quantity A is greater.

(B)   Quantity B is greater.

(C)   The quantities are equal.

(D)   It cannot be determined from the information given.

849. Which quantity is greater?

A: Twice the volume of a cube with a side of 1

B: The volume of a cube with a side of 2

(A)   Quantity A is greater.

(B)   Quantity B is greater.

(C)   The quantities are equal.

(D)   It cannot be determined from the information given.

850. The area of one face of a rectangular block is 16, and the area of an adjacent face is 20. Which quantity is greater?

A: The volume of the block

B: 100

(A) Quantity A is greater.

(B) Quantity B is greater.

(C) The quantities are equal.

(D) It cannot be determined from the information given.

In the actual GRE, questions in the Math section are mixed Quantitative Comparison and Problem Solving. The following questions are likewise mixed to give you practice switching mental gears in midstream.

851. What is the value of 247^0?

(A) 247

(B) $\dfrac{1}{247}$

(C) 0

(D) 1

(E) −1

852. If you expand 3.0×10^7, how many zeroes follow the 3?

(A) 7

(B) 6

(C) 5

(D) 8

(E) 4

853. Express x^{-6} with a positive exponent.

(A) x^6

(B) $\dfrac{1}{x^6}$

(C) $-6x$

(D) $\dfrac{1}{-6x}$

(E) $1x^6$

854. Which quantity is greater?

A: $3^5 \times 3^2$

B: 3^7

(A) Quantity A is greater.

(B) Quantity B is greater.

(C) The quantities are equal.

(D) It cannot be determined from the information given.

855. Which quantity is greater?

A: $5^9 \div 5^3$

B: 5^3

(A) Quantity A is greater.

(B) Quantity B is greater.

(C) The quantities are equal.

(D) It cannot be determined from the information given.

856. Which quantity is greater?

A: $\left(4^3\right)^4$

B: $4^4 \times 3^4$

(A) Quantity A is greater.

(B) Quantity B is greater.

(C) The quantities are equal.

(D) It cannot be determined from the information given.

857. Simplify $21x^3 - 17x^3 + 14y^2 + 12x^3 - 6y^2$.

(A) $24x^3y^2$

(B) $24xy^5$

(C) $16x^3 + 8y^2$

(D) $16x^3 + 8y^0$

(E) $12x^3 + 12$

858. Which quantity is greater?

A: $16^5 \times 16^2$

B: x^{16}

(A) Quantity A is greater.

(B) Quantity B is greater.

(C) The quantities are equal.

(D) It cannot be determined from the information given.

859. Which quantity is greater?
A: $2,126^0$ B: x^2

(A) Quantity A is greater.

(B) Quantity B is greater.

(C) The quantities are equal.

(D) It cannot be determined from the information given.

860. Which quantity is greater?

A: x^{14}

B: x^{-2}

(A) Quantity A is greater.

(B) Quantity B is greater.

(C) The quantities are equal.

(D) It cannot be determined from the information given.

861. $f(x) = 2x + 5$. Solve for $f(3)$.

(A) 3

(B) 11

(C) 10

(D) 28

(E) Cannot be determined

862. If $x \otimes 3 = 3x + 1$, what is the value of $5 \otimes 3$?

(A) 8

(B) 2

(C) $\frac{5}{3}$

(D) $\frac{3}{5}$

(E) 16

863. $f(x) = \frac{x}{3} + 2$. Solve for $f(6)$.

(A) 4

(B) 6

(C) 0

(D) 30

(E) Cannot be determined

864. If $x \odot y = \frac{x+y}{xy}$, what is the value of $7 \odot 3$?

(A) 21

(B) 10

(C) 2.1

(D) $\frac{10}{21}$

(E) $\frac{21}{10}$

865. If $x \oplus y = x^2 + y^2$, what is the value of $6 \oplus 8$?

(A) 48

(B) 14

(C) 2

(D) 100

(E) 196

866. Solve for x where $7x + 5 = 3x$.

(A) $x = 1.5$

(B) $x = 4$

(C) $x = \frac{4}{5}$

(D) $x = \frac{5}{4}$

(E) $x = -\frac{5}{4}$

867. Solve for x where $15 = 13x - 2x$.

(A) $x = 15.11$

(B) $x = 1$

(C) $x = -1$

(D) $x = \dfrac{15}{11}$

(E) $x = \dfrac{17}{13}$

868. Solve for x where $3x + 5 = 5x - 7$.

(A) $x = 1.5$

(B) $x = -6$

(C) $x = 6$

(D) $x = -1$

(E) $x = 1$

869. Solve for x where $\dfrac{(x-5)}{11} = \dfrac{(3x+2)}{4}$.

(A) $x = 11$

(B) $x = 4$

(C) $x = -44$

(D) $x = 29$

(E) $x = -\dfrac{42}{29}$

870. Solve for x where $5(2x - 11) = \dfrac{(x+3)}{7}$.

(A) $x = 543$

(B) $x = 388$

(C) $x = \dfrac{388}{69}$

(D) $x = \dfrac{55}{7}$

(E) $x = 11.7$

871. Multiply the binomials:

$(a - 5)(b + 3)$

(A) $-5a + 3b - 15$

(B) $ab + 3a - 5b - 15$

(C) $ab - 5b + 3a - 15$

(D) $a^2 - b^2 + 15$

(E) $a^2 + b^2 - 15$

872. Multiply the binomials: $(2x - 5)(3x + 6)$

(A) $6x^2 + 8x - 14$

(B) $8x^2 + 6x - 14$

(C) $14x^2 + 6x - 8$

(D) $6x^2 - 14x + 8$

(E) $6x^2 + 20x - 14$

873. Multiply the binomials: $(3x - y)(x + 3y)$

(A) $3x^2 + 8xy - 3y$

(B) $9x^2y - x - 3y$

(C) $9x^2 - xy - 9y$

(D) $15x^2 - x - 4y^2$

(E) $3x^2 + 12x - 4$

874. Multiply the binomials: $\left(\dfrac{1}{2}x - 3\right)(4x + 6)$

(A) $\dfrac{1}{2}x^2 - 15x - 18$

(B) $2x^2 - 9x - 18$

(C) $2x^2 - 18x - 9$

(D) $2x^2 - 15x - 18$

(E) $2x^2 + 15x - 18$

875. Multiply the binomials: $(3x + 2y)(5x - 7y)$

(A) $15x^2 + 10xy - 14y^2$

(B) $8x^2 - 3xy - 5y^2$

(C) $15x^2 - 31xy - 14y^2$

(D) $15x^2 - 11xy - 14y^2$

(E) $x^3 + 9x^2 - 4xy - 91y^2$

876. Factor $x^2 - 3x - 18$.

(A) $(x + 3)(x - 6)$

(B) $(x - 3)(x - 18)$

(C) $(x^2 - 3)(x - 18)$

(D) $(x - 3)(x + 6)$

(E) $(x^2 - 18)(x + 3)$

877. Factor $2x^2 + 3x - 20$.

    (A) $(2x+3)(x-20)$

    (B) $(2x-3)(x+20)$

    (C) $(x^2-2)(3x-20)$

    (D) $(2x-5)(x+4)$

    (E) $(3x^2-6)(4x+5)$

878. Solve for x: $x^2 - 2x - 24 = 0$

    (A) $x = \{-4, 6\}$

    (B) $x = \{-6, 4\}$

    (C) $x = \{2, 12\}$

    (D) $x = \{-12, 2\}$

    (E) $x = \{-12, -2\}$

879. Solve for x : $2x^2 + 15x + 44 = 0$

    (A) $x = \{-11, 2\}$

    (B) $x = \{11, -2\}$

    (C) $x = \{15, 44\}$

    (D) $x = \{-15, 44\}$

    (E) $x = \{-2, 22\}$

880. Solve for x : $x^2 + 4x - 45 = 0$

    (A) $x = \{5, -9\}$

    (B) $x = \{-9, 5\}$

    (C) $x = \{3, 15\}$

    (D) $x = \{-4, 45\}$

    (E) $x = \{-45, 4\}$

881. Estimate the value of the radical $\sqrt{7}$.

    (A) 7

    (B) 4

    (C) 3.2

    (D) 2.6

    (E) 1.9

882. Estimate the value of the radical $\sqrt{21}$.

    (A) 4

    (B) 5

    (C) 4.6

    (D) 5.1

    (E) 3.9

883. Estimate the value of the radical $\sqrt{125}$.

    (A) 5

    (B) 15.1

    (C) 25.2

    (D) 11.2

    (E) 12.3

884. Estimate the value of the radical $\sqrt{27}$.

    (A) 4.8

    (B) 5.2

    (C) 5.8

    (D) 3

    (E) 9

885. Estimate the value of the radical $\sqrt{63}$.

    (A) 7.1

    (B) 7.9

    (C) 8.1

    (D) 8.9

    (E) 9.2

886. Add the radicals $4\sqrt{17} + 7\sqrt{17}$.

    (A) $11\sqrt{17}$

    (B) $28\sqrt{17}$

    (C) $3\sqrt{17}$

    (D) $21\sqrt{24}$

    (E) Not possible

887. Subtract the radicals $13\sqrt{2} - 6\sqrt{2}$.

(A) $19\sqrt{2}$

(B) $7\sqrt{2}$

(C) $19\sqrt{4}$

(D) $7\sqrt{4}$

(E) 7

888. Combine the radicals $4\sqrt{7} + 7\sqrt{7} - 6\sqrt{7}$.

(A) $5\sqrt{21}$

(B) $17\sqrt{21}$

(C) $5\sqrt{7}$

(D) $17\sqrt{21}$

(E) $5 - \sqrt{7}$

889. Simplify and combine the radicals $\sqrt{125} + 3\sqrt{5} - \sqrt{45}$.

(A) $3\sqrt{85}$

(B) $3\sqrt{175}$

(C) $19\sqrt{5}$

(D) $5\sqrt{5}$

(E) $19\sqrt{5}$

890. Simplify and combine the radicals $4\sqrt{11} - \sqrt{128} + \sqrt{77} - \sqrt{98}$.

(A) $-5\sqrt{22}$

(B) $5\sqrt{22}$

(C) $11\sqrt{11} + 15\sqrt{2}$

(D) $-4\sqrt{13}$

(E) $11\sqrt{11} - 15\sqrt{2}$

891. Multiply the radicals $(\sqrt{7})(\sqrt{2})$.

(A) $\sqrt{14}$

(B) 14

(C) $2\sqrt{7}$

(D) $7\sqrt{2}$

(E) $(49)(4)$

892. Multiply the radicals $(2\sqrt{3})(4\sqrt{5})(\sqrt{2})$.

(A) $8\sqrt{30}$

(B) $6\sqrt{10}$

(C) $8\sqrt{10}$

(D) $6\sqrt{30}$

(E) $\sqrt{240}$

893. Divide the radicals $(9\sqrt{14}) \div (3\sqrt{2})$.

(A) 21

(B) $3\sqrt{7}$

(C) $27\sqrt{28}$

(D) $54\sqrt{7}$

(E) $6\sqrt{12}$

894. Multiply the radicals and simplify $(2\sqrt{18})(5\sqrt{32})$.

(A) $30\sqrt{48}$

(B) $10\sqrt{96}$

(C) $10\sqrt{50}$

(D) $7\sqrt{576}$

(E) $120\sqrt{2}$

895. Divide and simplify the radicals $(10\sqrt{128}) \div (3\sqrt{64})$.

(A) $\dfrac{10\sqrt{2}}{3}$

(B) $\dfrac{20}{3}$

(C) $3.3\overline{3}$

(D) 30

(E) $30\sqrt{96}$

896. Simplify $\sqrt{2 + \dfrac{3}{8} + \dfrac{13}{8}}$.

(A) $\sqrt{2 + \dfrac{16}{16}}$

(B) $2\sqrt{\dfrac{16}{8}}$

(C) 2

(D) $\sqrt{\dfrac{36}{8}}$

(E) 6

897. Simplify $\sqrt{2(3+5)-7}$.

(A) 8

(B) 16

(C) 9

(D) 3

(E) $2\sqrt{1}$

898. Simplify $4\sqrt{\frac{2}{3}+\frac{5}{9}}$.

(A) $4\frac{2}{3}$

(B) $4\sqrt{\frac{2}{3}}$

(C) $\frac{44}{3}$

(D) $\frac{4\sqrt{11}}{3}$

(E) $4\sqrt{\frac{7}{12}}$

899. Simplify $\frac{\sqrt{4(5+3)}}{\sqrt{2}}$.

(A) 32

(B) 16

(C) $\sqrt{2}$

(D) 4

(E) $\sqrt{4}$

900. Simplify $\frac{\sqrt{4(2+2)}}{\sqrt{50}}$.

(A) $\sqrt{\frac{4}{25}}$

(B) $\frac{2}{5}$

(C) $5\frac{29}{60}$

(D) $5\sqrt{\frac{29}{60}}$

(E) $\frac{4}{5\sqrt{2}}$

901. Which of the following coordinate pairs make the equation $3x-7y=24$ true?

(A) (5, 2)

(B) (3, –7)

(C) (–3, 7)

(D) (–3, 1)

(E) (1, –3)

902. Which of the following pairs makes the equation $-2x+3y=2$ true?

(A) (5, 4)

(B) (–2, 3)

(C) (3, –2)

(D) (4, –5)

(E) (–3, 2)

903. What are the x and y intercepts of the equation $2x+4y=12$?

(A) (3, 0) and (0, 6)

(B) (6, 0) and (0, 3)

(C) (2, 0) and (0, 4)

(D) (0, 2) and (4, 0)

(E) (10, 0) and (0, 8)

904. Which equation includes the point (5, –2)?

(A) $-2y=x+14$

(B) $5x-y=0$

(C) $-2y=-2x+14$

(D) $-2x+5y=20$

(E) $2x-7y=20$

905. Which equation includes the point (–2, 7)?

(A) $3x+9y=-8$

(B) $6x+3y=9$

(C) $2x-4y=36$

(D) $-2x+5y=20$

(E) $8x-7y=20$

906. What are the respective values of x and y?

$x - 3y = -1$

$-3x + 3y = -9$

(A) $(5, 2)$

(B) $(2, 5)$

(C) $(3, 9)$

(D) $(9, 3)$

(E) $(3, -3)$

907. What are the respective values of x and y?

$-3x + y = 13$

$y = -x - 3$

(A) $(4, -1)$

(B) $(3, 13)$

(C) $(13, -3)$

(D) $(-4, 1)$

(E) $(3, -3)$

908. What are the respective values of x and y?

$-2x + 3y = 0$

$4x + y = 14$

(A) $(2, -3)$

(B) $(3, 2)$

(C) $(-3, 2)$

(D) $(-2, -3)$

(E) $(2, 3)$

909. What are the respective values of x and y?

$6x + 2y = -14$

$y - 2 = 3(x + 3)$

(A) $(2, -3)$

(B) $(3, 2)$

(C) $(-3, 2)$

(D) $(-2, -3)$

(E) $(2, 3)$

910. Brian bought some movies and games on sale. The movies were $5 each, and the games were $11 each. Brian spent $215 and purchased 25 items. How many movies and how many games did he purchase?

(A) 10 movies and 15 games

(B) 15 movies and 10 games

(C) 5 movies and 11 games

(D) 11 movies and 5 games

(E) 16 movies and 25 games

911. The mean of a set of data is 15, and the values include 14, 14, 14, 15, 15, 15, 16, 16, and x. What is the value of x?

(A) 13

(B) 14

(C) 15

(D) 16

(E) 17

912. The mean of a set of data is 16, and the values include 6, 8, 12, 19, 19, 20, 21, 24, and x. What is the value of x?

(A) 13

(B) 14

(C) 15

(D) 16

(E) 17

913. A certain set of data contains 13 values. The average of the first 12 values is 24. If the overall average is 26, what is the 13th value?

(A) 50

(B) 55.8

(C) 29

(D) 42.5

(E) 68

914. Jennifer's math course grade is an average of her five major exam scores. The average of her first four exams is 75%. What is the best grade she can get for the course without extra credit?

(A) 75.4%

(B) 80%

(C) 86.5%

(D) 100%

(E) 86%

915. Sayber and Tuscany are taking the same humanities course. Sayber's test scores so far are 76%, 82%, 88%, 91%, and 94%. Tuscany's are 72%, 85%, 86%, 94%, and 97%. If Tuscany bombs her final and gets only a 58%, what is the minimum Sayber needs to score on the final to have a better overall grade than Tuscany?

(A) 58%

(B) 61%

(C) 73%

(D) 76%

(E) 92%

916. A phone company sells subsidized smart-phones at three price points. Twenty-five percent of the phones sell for $99 each, 25% sell for $149 each, and 50% sell for $199 each. What is the weighted average price of a cellphone from the company?

(A) $142.50

(B) $128.50

(C) $155.33

(D) $161.50

(E) $149.00

917. Soup and Sandwich sells four different lunch-to-go packages. On Monday, they sold 16 orders of Package #1 for $4.00 each, 21 orders of Package #2 for $5.00 each, 13 orders of Package #3 for $5.00 each, and 8 orders of Package #4 for $7.00 each. What is the weighted average sales price for lunch at Soup and Sandwich?

(A) $5.00

(B) $5.70

(C) $3.25

(D) $5.25

(E) $4.55

918. Use the information given in the table to find the weighted average.

Frequency	Value
4	8
7	7
2	9
7	3

(A) 2

(B) 4

(C) 6

(D) 20

(E) 120

919. Use the information given in the table to find the weighted average.

Frequency	Value
4	12
6	10
1	14
5	14

(A) 11

(B) 12

(C) 16

(D) 70

(E) 192

920. Use the information given in the table to find the weighted average.

Frequency	Value
1	26
12	7
9	16
2	9

(A) $11\frac{1}{3}$

(B) 12.5

(C) $15\frac{2}{3}$

(D) 272

(E) 24

921. Use the information given in the table to find the weighted average, rounded to the nearest tenth.

Percent	Value
10%	12
25%	16
30%	20
35%	10

(A) 1.2

(B) 2.6

(C) 2.0

(D) 3.7

(E) 2.9

922. Use the information given in the table to find the weighted average.

Percent	Value
75%	32
15%	10
6%	50
4%	25

(A) 15.5

(B) 17.25

(C) 25

(D) 29.5

(E) 34.5

923. A group of friends went to the cinema together. Half of them spent $5.50 each on snacks, one-quarter spent $4.00 each, three-sixteenths spent $3.00 each, and one-sixteenth spent $8.00 each. What was the weighted average cost of snacks for the friends?

(A) $4.33

(B) $4.45

(C) $7.50

(D) $5.25

(E) $7.56

924. Bananas are available at three local supermarkets. At Food-2-Go, they are $0.60 per pound, at SuperSaver they are $2.70 for three pounds, and at Speedy Mart they are $3.60 for six pounds. What is the weighted average price per pound for bananas in town?

(A) $0.59

(B) $0.60

(C) $0.70

(D) $2.21

(E) $3.80

925. Students in four different grades were asked how many daily hours they spent playing on a computer. The results were as follows:

15 seniors averaged 2 hours each.

15 juniors averaged 1 hour each.

20 sophomores averaged 3 hours each.

25 freshmen averaged 3 hours each.

What is the weighted average number of hours spent on a computer daily for the students?

(A) 60.2

(B) 3.5

(C) 3.0

(D) 2.4

(E) 1.5

926. Abbi invested $1,250 for one year and earned $100 in simple interest. What was the interest rate?

(A) 6%

(B) 7%

(C) 8%

(D) 9%

(E) 10%

927. Ryan invested some money at 4% simple interest for one year and earned $600. How much money did he invest?

(A) $9,000

(B) $9,500

(C) $12,500

(D) $14,000

(E) $15,000

928. Cameron borrowed $20,000 from the bank at 5% annual simple interest and paid $8,000 in interest. How long was the loan term?

(A) 1 year

(B) 2 years

(C) 3 years

(D) 5 years

(E) 8 years

929. Savannah borrowed $15,000 from the bank for six years at 3.00% simple annual interest on the principal. How much did she pay in interest?

(A) $2,700

(B) $3,200

(C) $2,875

(D) $4,250

(E) $10,350

930. Maia borrowed $250,000 from the bank for 11 years at 2% simple annual interest on the principal. How much did she pay in interest?

(A) $37,881.25

(B) $52,500.00

(C) $55,000.00

(D) $72,250.25

(E) $75,235.00

931. Chocolate chips cost $2.25 per pound, and peanuts cost $1.25 per pound. How many pounds of chocolate chips should be added to 4 pounds of peanuts to make a snack mix costing $2.00 per pound?

(A) 1.25 pounds

(B) 2.50 pounds

(C) 5 pounds

(D) 7.25 pounds

(E) 12.5 pounds

932. A small, private school has a limited sports budget and wants to spend $5.00 per ball on new equipment. If soccer balls are $4.00 each and footballs are $6.00 each, and the school wants 25 soccer balls, how many footballs should they buy to bring the average cost per ball to $5.00?

(A)   15

(B)   16

(C)   20

(D)   25

(E)   30

933. How many liters of a saltwater solution that is 20% salt must be added to a saltwater solution that is 50% salt in order to make 20 liters of a 40% salt solution?

(A)   3 liters

(B)   5 liters

(C) $6\frac{2}{3}$ liters

(D) $7\frac{3}{4}$ liters

(E)   8 liters

934. How many gallons of a sugar-water mixture containing 25% sugar must be added to 100 gallons of a 10% sugar-water mixture to create a mixture with 15% sugar?

(A)   6 gallons

(B)   27 gallons

(C)   44 gallons

(D)   50 gallons

(E)   65 gallons

935. Paul stays on task at work 25% of the time, and Mary stays on task 75% of the time. How many hours does Mary have to work if Paul works 12 hours and they need to have 50% time-on-task as a team?

(A)   3 hours

(B)   6 hours

(C)   12 hours

(D)   18 hours

(E)   24 hours

936. What is the probability of pulling a yellow marble at random from an opaque bag containing 11 green, 3 blue, 4 yellow, and 7 red marbles?

(A) $\frac{4}{25}$

(B) $\frac{4}{21}$

(C) $\frac{1}{16}$

(D) $\frac{21}{25}$

(E) $\frac{16}{25}$

937. A spinner is split into equal sections for each of the colors: red, orange, yellow, green, blue, and violet. What is the probability of a single, random spin landing on either red or violet?

(A) $\frac{1}{6}$

(B) $\frac{1}{3}$

(C) $3\frac{1}{3}$

(D) $\frac{1}{4}$

(E) $\frac{2}{5}$

938. What is the probability of a spinner with an equal number of red, green, blue, and yellow spaces landing on green three times in a row?

(A) $\frac{1}{4}$

(B) $\frac{1}{8}$

(C) $\frac{1}{64}$

(D) $\frac{1}{16}$

(E) $\frac{1}{32}$

939. What is the probability of pulling and keeping cards 1, 2, 3, and 4, one at a time and in any order, from a deck of 10 cards?

(A) $\frac{4}{10}$

(B) $\frac{1}{3}$

(C) $\frac{1}{420}$

(D) $\frac{4}{48}$

(E) $\frac{1}{210}$

940. What is the probability of pulling either a 4 or a 5 from a standard 52-card deck and then rolling either a three or a four on a standard 6-sided die?

(A) $\frac{2}{52}$

(B) $\frac{2}{39}$

(C) $\frac{1}{78}$

(D) $\frac{3}{16}$

(E) $\frac{1}{13}$

941. If 28 vehicles are red, 40 are trucks, and 14 are red trucks, how many vehicles are there total?

(A) 28

(B) 68

(C) 54

(D) 42

(E) 56

942. If 28 vehicles are red, 40 are trucks, and 14 are red trucks, how many trucks are not red?

(A) 14

(B) 40

(C) 54

(D) 26

(E) 12

943. If 28 vehicles are red, 40 are trucks, and 14 are red trucks, how many red vehicles are not trucks?

(A) 14

(B) 40

(C) 54

(D) 26

(E) 12

944. According to the distribution table, what is the probability that a randomly chosen student from the classroom will be wearing a red shirt?

Shirt Color	*Number of Students*
Red	12
White	8
Yellow	6
Striped	10

(A) $\frac{1}{5}$

(B) 25%

(C) 48%

(D) 33.3%

(E) 32.4%

945. According to the distribution table, what is the probability that a randomly chosen student from the classroom will not be wearing a yellow shirt?

Shirt Color	Number of Students
Red	10
White	6
Yellow	6
Striped	8

(A) $\frac{1}{3}$

(B) 20%

(C) 48%

(D) 66%

(E) 80%

946. The corner ice-cream shop carries nine flavors of ice cream and offers three flavors of cones and five different ice-cream toppings. How many different desserts are there?

(A) 9

(B) 27

(C) 17

(D) 125

(E) 135

947. How many possible number combinations are there when three standard dice are rolled together? Assume that the order matters.

(A) 18

(B) 6

(C) 216

(D) 36

(E) 120

948. How many different outfits are possible from a closet containing two pairs of jeans, four shirts, and five pairs of shoes?

(A) 11

(B) 40

(C) 60

(D) 45

(E) 21

949. Larame wears a suit to work every day. He owns 2 suit jackets, 5 pairs of slacks, 14 ties, and 2 pairs of dress shoes. How many five-day work weeks can he go without repeating an outfit?

(A) 280

(B) 52

(C) 56

(D) 29

(E) 1,040

950. Suppose you flip a coin twice and roll a standard 6-sided die three times. How many different possible combinations are there?

(A) 57

(B) 312

(C) 864

(D) 2,198

(E) 5,616

951. You start with a stack of ten different, randomly shuffled cards. If you pull and discard one card at a time, how many possible outcomes are there?

(A) 100

(B) 9^{10}

(C) 10^9

(D) 9!

(E) 10!

952. Which quantity is greater?

A: 8!

B: 8^8

(A) Quantity A is greater.

(B) Quantity B is greater.

(C) The quantities are equal.

(D) It cannot be determined from the information given.

953. Which quantity is greater?

A: $\dfrac{7!}{5!}$

B: 2!

(A) Quantity A is greater.

(B) Quantity B is greater.

(C) The quantities are equal.

(D) It cannot be determined from the information given.

954. Which quantity is greater?

A: $(7!)(5!)$

B: 12!

(A) Quantity A is greater.

(B) Quantity B is greater.

(C) The quantities are equal.

(D) It cannot be determined from the information given.

955. Which quantity is greater?

A: The number of handshakes if nine people each shake everyone else's hand exactly once

B: 81

(A) Quantity A is greater.

(B) Quantity B is greater.

(C) The quantities are equal.

(D) It cannot be determined from the information given.

956. The latest casual tablet game ranks the top ten players by high score. How many ways could these same top ten players be ranked?

(A) 100

(B) 9^{10}

(C) 10^9

(D) 9!

(E) 10!

957. A large stock brokerage firm is conducting a competitive internship for three new positions, with starting bonuses that reduce by final ranking. If five people compete, how many first-, second-, and third-place outcomes are possible?

(A) 5

(B) 12

(C) 30

(D) 60

(E) 120

958. Baskin-Robbins has 31 flavors of ice cream. How many two-scoop cones are possible, assuming the order of the scoops matters?

(A) 31

(B) 62

(C) 899

(D) 930

(E) 961

959. If there are 33 racers in the Indianapolis 500, how many possibilities are there for first and second place?

(A) 32

(B) 33

(C) 500

(D) 1,056

(E) 33,031

960. If there are 13 students in an advanced statistics class, how many possibilities are there for the top first, second, and third students?

(A) 36

(B) 155

(C) 1,716

(D) 20,389,320

(E) 5^{31}

961. A large stock brokerage firm is conducting a competitive internship for three new positions. If five people compete, how many groups of three people are possible?

(A) 3

(B) 5

(C) 20

(D) 40

(E) 60

962. A student has 12 pencils of different lengths. How many different-sized triangles can she make by laying the pencils out on the desk, three at a time?

(A) 12

(B) 36

(C) 220

(D) 1,320

(E) 1,728

963. How many different two-card hands are possible from a deck of 20 cards?

(A) 20

(B) 40

(C) 190

(D) 380

(E) 2.2×10^{36}

964. How many different 3-coin sets are possible from a pile of 15 coins?

(A) 15

(B) 35

(C) 210

(D) 455

(E) 3.1×10^{10}

965. The parking lot at the theatre has 25 spaces, including 2 in the row closest to the entrance. If the lot will be full, how many different groups of two can park in the two closest to the entrance?

(A) 25

(B) 24

(C) 300

(D) 600

(E) 1,200

966. What is the median salary at a company with salary tiers of $71,000, $34,000, $52,000, $64,000, and $27,000?

(A) $49,000

(B) $49,600

(C) $52,000

(D) $52,500

(E) $60,000

967. What is the median of the following numbers?

{71, 13, 66, 31, 25, 66, 70, 12}

(A) 28

(B) 31

(C) 44.25

(D) 48.5

(E) 66

968. According to the data in the following chart from *Forbes* magazine, what is the median price of a Galaxy S-Series (either S4 or S3) phone from a major U.S. carrier?

	AT&T	Verizon	Sprint	T-mobile
iPhone 5S	$200	$200	$100	$99
iPhone 5C	$100	$100	$0	$0
iPhone 4S	$0	$50	$0	$0
Galaxy S4	$200	$200	$100	$100
Galaxy S3	$100	$100	$0	$20
Galaxy Note II	$200	$250	$150	$100
HTC One	$200	$200	$100	$100
HTC 8x	$1	$50	$0	N/A
Lumia	$100	$0	N/A	$30
Q10	$200	$200	$100	$100
Z10	$100	$0	N/A	$100

© John Wiley & Sons, Inc.

(A) $102.50

(B) $100.00

(C) $150.00

(D) $200.00

(E) $820.00

969. What would happen to the median if 256 were added to the following data set?

{138, 145, 147, 143, 145, 149, 147, 144, 144, 148, 140, 256}

(A) It would decrease slightly.

(B) It would decrease significantly.

(C) It would increase slightly.

(D) It would increase significantly.

(E) It would not change at all.

970. The population of a particular virus starts at 1 and doubles each hour. What is the median hourly population at the start of the 16th hour?

(A) 8.5

(B) 9

(C) 16

(D) 512

(E) 4,096

971. What is the mode of the salaries at a company with salary tiers of $71,000, $34,000, $52,000, $64,000, and $27,000?

(A) $49,000

(B) $49,600

(C) $52,000

(D) $52,500

(E) There is no mode.

972. What is the mode of the following numbers?

{71, 13, 66, 31, 25, 66, 70, 12}

(A) 28

(B) 31

(C) 44.25

(D) 48.5

(E) 66

973. According to the data in the following chart from *Forbes* magazine, what is the modal price of an HTC phone (either the One or the 8x) from a major U.S. carrier?

	AT&T	Verizon	Sprint	T-mobile
iPhone 5S	$200	$200	$100	$99
iPhone 5C	$100	$100	$0	$0
iPhone 4S	$0	$50	$0	$0
Galaxy S4	$200	$200	$100	$100
Galaxy S3	$100	$100	$0	$20
Galaxy Note II	$200	$250	$150	$100
HTC One	$200	$200	$100	$100
HTC 8x	$1	$50	$0	N/A
Lumia	$100	$0	N/A	$30
Q10	$200	$200	$100	$100
Z10	$100	$0	N/A	$100

© John Wiley & Sons, Inc.

(A) $0

(B) $50.00

(C) $100.00 and $200.00

(D) $200.00

(E) There is no mode.

974. According to the data in the following chart from *Forbes* magazine, what is the modal price of an iPhone (4S, 5C, or 5S) from a major U.S. carrier?

	AT&T	Verizon	Sprint	T-mobile
iPhone 5S	$200	$200	$100	$99
iPhone 5C	$100	$100	$0	$0
iPhone 4S	$0	$50	$0	$0
Galaxy S4	$200	$200	$100	$100
Galaxy S3	$100	$100	$0	$20
Galaxy Note II	$200	$250	$150	$100
HTC One	$200	$200	$100	$100
HTC 8x	$1	$50	$0	N/A
Lumia	$100	$0	N/A	$30
Q10	$200	$200	$100	$100
Z10	$100	$0	N/A	$100

© John Wiley & Sons, Inc.

(A) $0.00

(B) $50.00

(C) $74.50

(D) $100.00

(E) $200.00

975. What is the range of the salaries at a company with salary tiers of $71,000, $34,000, $52,000, $64,000, and $27,000?

(A) $44,000

(B) $49,600

(C) $52,000

(D) $52,500

(E) $60,000

976. What happens to the range of the following data if 129 is added to the original set?

{42, 49, 56, 61, 61, 79, 83, 85, 87}

(A) It decreases slightly.

(B) It decreases significantly.

(C) It increases slightly.

(D) It increases significantly.

(E) There is no change.

977. Which quantity is greater?

A: The range of {888, 891, 905, 909, 914, 921}

B: The range of {14, 18, 23, 29, 35, 42, 49}

(A) Quantity A is greater.

(B) Quantity B is greater.

(C) The quantities are equal.

(D) It cannot be determined from the information given.

978. Which quantity is greater?

A: The range of {128, 212, 43, 56, 198, 187, 243}

B: The range of {402, 391, 488, 451, 527, 591, 520}

(A) Quantity A is greater.

(B) Quantity B is greater.

(C) The quantities are equal.

(D) It cannot be determined from the information given.

979. A block of ice at 32°F is placed into a pot on a hot stove on the beach and heated at a constant rate of 8 degrees per minute until it melts and then boils at 212°F.

What is the range of the temperatures it undergoes during the process?

(A) 0°F

(B) 212°F

(C) 32°F

(D) 106°F

(E) 180°F

980. What is the mean salary at a company with salary tiers of $71,000, $34,000, $52,000, $66,000, and $27,000?

(A) $49,000

(B) $50,000

(C) $52,000

(D) $54,000

(E) $60,000

981. What is the mean of these numbers?

71, 13, 66, 31, 25, 66, 76, 12

(A) 28

(B) 31

(C) 45

(D) 48

(E) 50

982. According to the data in the following chart from *Forbes* magazine, what is the mean price of any Galaxy phone (S4, S3, or Note II) from a major U.S. carrier?

	AT&T	Verizon	Sprint	T-mobile
iPhone 5S	$200	$200	$100	$99
iPhone 5C	$100	$100	$0	$0
iPhone 4S	$0	$50	$0	$0
Galaxy S4	$200	$200	$100	$100
Galaxy S3	$100	$100	$0	$20
Galaxy Note II	$200	$250	$150	$100
HTC One	$200	$200	$100	$100
HTC 8x	$1	$50	$0	N/A
Lumia	$100	$0	N/A	$30
Q10	$200	$200	$100	$100
Z10	$100	$0	N/A	$100

© John Wiley & Sons, Inc.

(A) $102.50

(B) $100.00

(C) $126.67

(D) $150.00

(E) $166.33

983. According to the data in the following chart from *Forbes* magazine, what is the mean price of a Lumia phone from a major U.S. carrier?

	AT&T	Verizon	Sprint	T-mobile
iPhone 5S	$200	$200	$100	$99
iPhone 5C	$100	$100	$0	$0
iPhone 4S	$0	$50	$0	$0
Galaxy S4	$200	$200	$100	$100
Galaxy S3	$100	$100	$0	$20
Galaxy Note II	$200	$250	$150	$100
HTC One	$200	$200	$100	$100
HTC 8x	$1	$50	$0	N/A
Lumia	$100	$0	N/A	$30
Q10	$200	$200	$100	$100
Z10	$100	$0	N/A	$100

© John Wiley & Sons, Inc.

(A) $32.50

(B) $43.33

(C) $50.00

(D) $100.00

(E) There is no mean.

984. The population of a particular virus starts at 10 and doubles each hour. What is the mean hourly population at the start of the 11th hour?

(A) 8.5

(B) 9

(C) 16

(D) 512

(E) 1,861

985. Which quantity is greater?

A: The standard deviation of {7, 14, 25, 29, 34, 35}

B: The standard deviation of {14, 23, 23, 25, 26, 33}

(A) Quantity A is greater.

(B) Quantity B is greater.

(C) The quantities are equal.

(D) It cannot be determined from the information given.

986. Which quantity is greater?

A: The standard deviation of {2, 4, 6, 8, 10, 12}

B: The standard deviation of {1, 3, 5, 7, 9, 11}

(A) Quantity A is greater.

(B) Quantity B is greater.

(C) The quantities are equal.

(D) It cannot be determined from the information given.

987. How would the standard deviation of these numbers be affected by adding the number 15?

{5, 10, 15, 20, 25}

(A) Increase less than 2.0

(B) Increase more than 2.0

(C) Decrease less than 2.0

(D) Decrease more than 2.0

(E) Remain unchanged

988. According to the following table from *Forbes* magazine, which quantity is greater?

	AT&T	Verizon	Sprint	T-mobile
iPhone 5S	$200	$200	$100	$99
iPhone 5C	$100	$100	$0	$0
iPhone 4S	$0	$50	$0	$0
Galaxy S4	$200	$200	$100	$100
Galaxy S3	$100	$100	$0	$20
Galaxy Note II	$200	$250	$150	$100
HTC One	$200	$200	$100	$100
HTC 8x	$1	$50	$0	N/A
Lumia	$100	$0	N/A	$30
Q10	$200	$200	$100	$100
Z10	$100	$0	N/A	$100

© John Wiley & Sons, Inc.

A: The mean price of an iPhone 5S

B: The standard deviation of the price of an iPhone 5S

(A) Quantity A is greater.

(B) Quantity B is greater.

(C) The quantities are equal.

(D) It cannot be determined from the information given.

989. S is the set of numbers {4, 8, 12, 16, 20, 24}. Which quantity is greater?

A: The mean of set S

B: The standard deviation of set S

(A) Quantity A is greater.

(B) Quantity B is greater.

(C) The quantities are equal.

(D) It cannot be determined from the information given.

Chapter 6

Writing

• •

The GRE begins with two writing assignments: one Issue essay and one Argument essay. These essays are 30 minutes each, for a total of 60 minutes of intense writing before you even encounter any of the other test questions.

The Problems You'll Work On

When working through the practice essays based on the sample topics in this chapter, be prepared to

- ✔ Declare your position and support it with sound reasoning and examples.

- ✔ Communicate clearly, so that your point can be understood by someone who doesn't know the topic.

- ✔ Critically think about how a topic fits in the big picture.

- ✔ Analyze an argument that hinges on flawed assumptions or missing information.

- ✔ Clearly describe how the flawed assumption and missing information affect the validity of the argument.

What to Watch Out For

Your challenge is to complete two quality essays with 30 minutes each. Avoid these common pitfalls:

- ✔ Not clearly describing your point of view (as if assuming the essay grader can also read your mind)

- ✔ Taking too long to think about your topic, then rushing through the writing process and making all kinds of grammatical and spelling errors

- ✔ Getting stuck on the essays and panicking, thus using up all of the energy that you need for the rest of the GRE

Analysis of an Issue

990. Write an essay in response to the following statement. Discuss the extent to which you agree or disagree with the statement. Explain your reasoning in a clear, well-organized essay that supports your position. Consider both sides of the issue when developing your response.

Today's teens are not developing the same level of analytical reasoning skills as their predecessor generations because information is too easily attained through search engines, like Google and Yahoo!. Because information is readily available at any moment, working through a problem logically is no longer needed.

991. Write an essay in response to the following statement. Discuss the extent to which you agree or disagree with the statement. Explain your reasoning in a clear, well-organized essay that supports your position. Consider both sides of the issue when developing your response.

The way that a culture deals with its elderly population dictates the way that the youth of that culture understands relationships.

992. Write an essay in response to the following statement. Discuss the extent to which you agree or disagree with the statement. Explain your reasoning in a clear, well-organized essay that supports your position. Consider both sides of the issue when developing your response.

Some people believe that social programs, such as welfare and unemployment, help support underserved or struggling members of society, whereas others who note that people abuse the systems feel they are a waste of taxpayers' money and believe people use the programs to avoid being responsible for themselves.

993. Write an essay in response to the following statement. Discuss the extent to which you agree or disagree with the statement. Explain your reasoning in a clear, well-organized essay that supports your position. Consider both sides of the issue when developing your response.

It is more advantageous for a small community to allow development of their surrounding wilderness land for economic gain, rather than preserve it for recreational purposes.

994. Write an essay in response to the following statement. Discuss the extent to which you agree or disagree with the statement. Explain your reasoning in a clear, well-organized essay that supports your position. Consider both sides of the issue when developing your response.

Regardless of the known benefits of playing a musical instrument for brain development, administrators facing a budget crisis should first cut music programs from the curriculum.

995. Write an essay in response to the following statement. Discuss the extent to which you agree or disagree with the statement. Explain your reasoning in a clear, well-organized essay that supports your position. Consider both sides of the issue when developing your response.

A petition to change the way people vote has started circulating in preparation for the 2016 presidential elections. The current national voting system is intrinsically flawed and badly due for an overhaul.

Analysis of an Argument

996. Write a response to the following argument that analyzes its stated or implied assumptions, reveals how the argument's position depends on the assumptions, and explains the effect of any flawed assumptions on the argument's validity.

The increase in skiing accidents at the country's top ski resorts has many executives scratching their heads about the best solution. A study was conducted to find the causes of the increase, and a number of skiers were interviewed as part of the data collection process. The results showed that between the years 1995 and 2010, the number of injuries resulting from ski accidents jumped 33 percent from the results found in pre-1995 data. Interestingly, this result coincides with the advent of snowboarding and the opening of most of the mountains to snowboarders. Snowboards cut the snow differently than skis do, creating deep grooves that skiers get stuck in and making moguls more challenging. Thus, ski resorts should ban snowboarding on their mountains to reduce the number of ski injuries.

997. Write a response to the following argument that analyzes its stated or implied assumptions, reveals how the argument's position depends on the assumptions, and explains the effect of any flawed assumptions on the argument's validity.

The following appeared in a letter from a supervisor to an employee.

"Your inability to turn in your timesheet correctly is unacceptable. Two times in the last six months you have asked to update your timesheet after the submission deadline. It is clear you do not respect the policies of this company. It has been determined that you are not responsible enough to manage your time correctly; thus, beginning with the next pay period, you will only be paid for a certain set number of hours, regardless of what you actually work."

998. Write a response to the following argument that analyzes its stated or implied assumptions, reveals how the argument's position depends on the assumptions, and explains the effect of any flawed assumptions on the argument's validity.

A ban on cigarette smoking on all public beaches in Hawaii is up for review by the state legislature. At a clean-up event last year on the Big Island, volunteers picked up more than 10,000 butts in only a few hours. Smoking in public not only is harmful due to second-hand smoke, but creates a significant amount of waste that litters the beaches and threatens tourism in the area. Tourism makes up a majority of the revenue generated in the state. To preserve the beauty and enjoyment of the state's beaches, as well as maintain tourism revenue, smoking should be banned.

999. Write a response to the following argument that analyzes its stated or implied assumptions, reveals how the argument's position depends on the assumptions, and explains the effect of any flawed assumptions on the argument's validity.

A rally in front of the proposed site for the new Virgin Records coming to Lawrence, Kansas, will be held at 12 p.m. Tuesday afternoon. The rally will attempt to dissuade the city from allowing the mega-store to set up shop downtown. Area residents do not want to see their local music stores go out of business because of the competition, and local musicians fear a decrease in their popularity if the local stores are not able to support them. To preserve the town's small businesses and provide an outlet for local music, the city council should vote to deny Virgin's license application.

1000. Write a response to the following argument that analyzes its stated or implied assumptions, reveals how the argument's position depends on the assumptions, and explains the effect of any flawed assumptions on the argument's validity.

Housing First is a program that places homeless individuals into independent-living situations. The concept is based on the idea that having a home provides an individual with a sense of stability and pride, which translates into better habits, such as reduced alcohol or substance use and better physical and mental health outcomes. Great success has been achieved in cities such as Portland and Salt Lake City, with homeless individuals showing a decrease of 15 percent in their use of public resources annually and a reduced rate of alcohol consumption of 9 percent per year since the beginning of the program 5 years ago. Every major city should implement a Housing First model to support its homeless population.

1,001 Write a response to the following argument that analyzes its stated or implied assumptions, reveals how the argument's position depends on the assumptions, and explains the effect of any flawed assumptions on the argument's validity.

A major downside of McCarther University is the surrounding neighborhood in which it lies. When McCarther was built, the town was only just being developed, and the proximity of the neighborhood to the school brought in teachers and administrators. However, as the city grew, the neighborhood moved farther away from the school. What was left was an unkempt area that now boasts one of the highest crime rates in the city. Because it is a private school, its students are prime targets for theft and harm. The university should relocate to a better neighborhood to safeguard its students and increase enrollment.

Part II
The Answers

 Head to www.dummies.com/cheatsheet/1001GRE
to access the free Cheat Sheet created specifically for this book.

In this part . . .

Here's where you can find the answers and explanations for all the problems in this book. As you read through the explanations, if you find that you need a little more help with certain concepts, *For Dummies* has your back. Check out this title if you need more help with the concepts and material covered on the GRE:

✔ *GRE For Dummies*, 8th Edition (Ron Woldoff and Joe Kraynak)

Visit www.dummies.com for more information.

Chapter 7

Answers

1.

B. anomaly; C. irregularity

If the dancer has odd ways, her movements likely differ from those of other dancers. You can dismiss Choices (A) and (E), *offensiveness* and *grotesquery,* because they're too strong and are opposites of brilliant. *Mastery,* Choice (D), seems logical because the dancer would have likely mastered her steps if she were performing. However, no other answer choice has an equivalent meaning, so this cannot be the correct answer. *Banality,* Choice (F), means common. *Anomaly,* Choice (B), and *irregularity,* Choice (C), both refer to something outside of what's typical and are interchangeable in this context, so they're the correct answers.

2.

C. garner; F. accumulate

Before an interview, you want to be prepared with as much information as possible. You can predict that the blank refers to answer choices that mean to acquire as many facts as possible to be prepared. The only terms that represent the idea of attaining something are *garner,* Choice (C), and *accumulate,* Choice (F). *Accrete,* Choice (A), means to make something bigger, which doesn't fit the sentence, nor does the meaning of *comprise,* Choice (E), which means to be made up of something. Choices (B) and (D), *eradicate* and *jettison,* are the opposite of what the sentence requires.

3.

A. zenith; B. apex

The clues of "highlighted" and "honor" let us know the distinction is a big deal. You can start eliminating choices on that information alone. *Plateau,* Choice (C), means the flattened part of something or the absence of growth, and *median,* Choice (D), is the middle. Neither would be a big deal. *Pedestal* and *foundation,* Choices (E) and (F), are the low or bottom parts of things. *Zenith* and *apex,* Choices (A) and (B), both represent the top point of something, which fits the desired meaning for the blanks.

4.

C. eclectic; E. diverse

If her palette was not adventurous and the mismatch of his with hers was a problem, then you can assume the blanks are words that represent James's adventurous or daring tastes in food. *Humdrum* and *lackluster,* Choices (A) and (D), are clearly opposite of that description. Nothing in the sentence suggests that his tastes are *dazzling* or *inspired,* Choices (B) and (F), just more open to different foods. *Diverse,* Choice (E), works well, and *eclectic,* Choice (C), also suggests varied interest or items.

5.   E. decorum; F. tact

Mr. Horton's changing color suggests he was mad that Ricky's antics were the opposite of what was expected, which is what you need to look for from the choices. *Unruliness* and *violence,* Choices (A) and (D), are not likely what Mr. Horton would want. The other four choices — *tranquility,* Choice (B); *majesty,* Choice (C); *decorum,* Choice (E); and *tact,* Choice (F) —are all possibilities, so you need to determine which of the four share a meaning. *Decorum* (dignity of good taste) and *tact* (understanding what is appropriate) are the only words that are close and create the same meaning in the sentence.

6.   B. banal; E. conventional

The transition "Considering" tells you that her outfit at the awards was the opposite of her usual outlandish attire. Thus, the missing words mean "common" or "usual." Choices (A) and (F), *extraordinary* and *unique,* would describe a gown more in line with her outlandish wardrobe. Choice (C), *predictable,* would also suggest something more outlandish, and there is nothing to suggest that her gown was copied or taken from something else as Choice (D), *derivative,* would indicate. Only *banal* and *conventional,* Choices (B) and (E), describe an ordinary and unexceptional gown.

7.   C. pragmatic; F. rational

The transition "as much as" tells you that Carl's feelings countered his longing for the mountain bike. For whatever reason, the purchase would be a bad idea. The blanks ask for what the decision *wasn't,* so you can rule out *risky* and *precarious,* Choices (B) and (E). *Trustworthy* and *corrupt,* Choices (A) and (D), are out of scope. *Pragmatic* and *rational,* Choices (C) and (F), both refer to sensible mindsets, which this decision was.

8.   B. plucky; E. fearless

Although the skiers may be *egotistical* and *haughty,* Choices (D) and (F), about their abilities to ski 80 miles per hour, these characteristics don't determine their willingness to do it. They clearly aren't *tentative,* Choice (C), and whether or not they are coy (bashful), Choice (A), is out of scope. It could be said that they are *fearless,* Choice (B), for competing in such a dangerous sport, as well as *plucky* (courageous), Choice (E).

9.   B. glower; E. scowl

If John and Kim haven't actually made amends, she wouldn't *beam* at him, Choice (A). Kim could *smirk* at him, Choice (D), but no other choice means to give a leering smile. *Contort* and *mope,* Choices (C) and (F), don't make sense in this context. That leaves *glower* and *scowl,* Choices (B) and (E), which both represent negative expressions directed at someone.

10.   D. enigmatic; F. mysterious

If Nichelle had a low GPA, it would be very surprising for her to get into a top school like Harvard. The fact that Nichelle was able to get in may be *enlightening,* Choice (A), with regard to Harvard's admission standards, but this is unrelated to her actually getting in. There is nothing to suggest that her acceptance was *furtive* (secretive), Choice (B), or *incoherent,* Choice (C). *Explicable,* Choice (E), is the opposite of what it is. *Mysterious,* Choice (F), fits perfectly with the sentence, and *enigmatic,* Choice (D), means something that is puzzling.

11. **B. placate; F. appease**

The diners were angry that they weren't going to get any lobster bisque, so the best the cooks could do was find something else to satisfy them and calm them down. The cooks wouldn't want to *annoy* or *provoke* the angry diners, as Choices (A) and (D) suggest. *Remedy* and *improve*, Choices (C) and (E), are similar in meaning, as are *placate* and *appease*, Choices (B) and (F). The cooks could *improve* or *remedy* the situation, but you wouldn't say, "improve the angry diners." *Placate* and *appease* mean to soothe a person. Thus, Choices (B) and (F) are the best answers.

12. **C. sully; E. tarnish**

A scandal doesn't typically *extol, heighten,* or *boost* a reputation, which eliminates Choices (A), (B), and (F). On the contrary, a scandal can ruin a reputation, even if only for a brief moment. *Sully,* Choice (C), means to discredit or dirty; *belittle,* Choice (D), means to put down; and *tarnish,* Choice (E), means to stain or blemish. Of these three choices, *sully* and *tarnish* match in meaning.

13. **A. explosive; D. volatile**

If the crowd is growing angrier, things could get out of hand quickly. *Explosive,* Choice (A), rightly describes the rising tensions in the stadium. The stadium could be becoming *vulnerable,* Choice (B), but to what? *Tenuous,* Choice (C), describes the opposite of explosive, as do *weak* and *steady,* Choices (E) and (F). *Volatile,* Choice (D), also means explosive or unstable.

14. **B. plebeian; F. coarse**

Sarah's high-class parents obviously considered Tommy's manners to be low-class, not *polished,* Choice (A), or *refined,* Choice (E). Nothing suggests that Tommy was *naughty* in any way, and *abrasive* is too severe, ruling out Choices (D) and (C). They could have considered his manners *coarse,* Choice (F), and the *plebeians,* Choice (B), were the commoners in ancient Rome.

15. **D. grovel; F. plead**

Though one is usually willing to ask for a raise, one usually refuses to *beg* for a raise. What choices are similar in meaning to *beg*? She could *crave* a raise, as Choice (A) suggests, but that's a personal feeling. One doesn't typically *pray* for a raise, so you can eliminate Choice (B). *Inquire* about and *request,* Choices (C) and (E), are similar to *ask,* which one is usually willing to do. That only leaves *grovel* and *plead,* Choices (D) and (F), which both signify the humbling of oneself in a desperate appeal.

16. **B. salient; D. prominent**

The beginning of the sentence tells you that despite the charade of not wanting attention, the family does something to get it. Mrs. Jones makes her wealth conspicuous by wearing an expensive fur coat to a little league game. *Modest, trivial,* and *unobtrusive,* Choices (A), (C), and (E), don't fit "conspicuous," and *palpable,* Choice (F), is out of scope. Both *salient* and *prominent,* Choices (B) and (D), signify something obvious and noticeable.

17. **D. whimsical; E. capricious**

The teacher's style kept the students guessing about what the day would bring. The missing words emulate a sense of impulse. Thus, *humdrum, knowable,* and *trite,* Choices (A), (B), and (C), would be the opposite of the teacher's style. *Whimsical,* Choice (D), means imaginative and unpredictable. That works. *Capricious,* Choice (E), also lends to the idea of unexpectedness. *Innovative,* Choice (F), means new or advanced. An argument could be made that the teacher is *innovative,* but there is no matching term for it. Choices (D) and (E) are the best answers.

18. **C. palatial; E. lavish**

If there is a chandelier in the bathroom of a room that is fit for a king, this must be one very fancy hotel room. Nothing suggests the room is *unique* or *unparalleled* in its extravagance, eliminating Choices (A) and (F), and no room with a chandelier would be considered *moderate* or *pedestrian,* ruling out Choices (B) and (D). *Palatial* and *lavish,* Choices (C) and (E), characterize the proper level of luxury.

19. **B. efficacy; E. effectiveness**

If the results were beyond what the researchers had thought, the intervention must have been very successful or effective. You can see quickly that Choices (B) and (E) begin the sentence in the same manner. None of the other words — *ineptitude,* Choice (A); *shortcoming,* Choice (C); *tolerability,* Choice (D), or *acceptability,* Choice (F) — describes the usefulness of the intervention.

20. **B. caustic; C. sarcastic**

If the father's comments made Karen feel he didn't respect what she did, then he must have made disparaging remarks or made fun of her. *Encouraging* and *supportive,* Choices (D) and (F), are opposites of this concept. *Blasphemous,* Choice (E), means speaking out against God, and *profane,* Choice (A), means foul language, so they don't fit. *Caustic* and *sarcastic,* Choices (B) and (C), both describe comments that mock or deride someone.

21. **B. opined; D. preached**

It sounds as if the speaker is opinionated and forceful with his opinions. The only answer choices that carry the weight necessary to describe his actions are *opined* and *preached,* Choices (B) and (D). The other choices — *pondered,* Choice (A); *consulted,* Choice (C); *deliberated,* Choice (E); and *reflected,* Choice (F) — all encompass a level of communication not suggested by this sentence.

22. **E. prosaic; F. pedestrian**

The sentence doesn't suggest that the date was *tasteless* or *dreary,* as Choices (A) and (C) suggest, just ordinary. Carol wouldn't have thought it was *imaginative,* Choice (B), or *thrilling,* Choice (D). Rather she thought the date was *prosaic,* Choice (E), and *pedestrian,* Choice (F), or lacking in imagination.

23. **D. acme; E. pinnacle**

From the last part of the sentence, you can guess that the play was the only positive experience Charlotte had in college, which would make it the highlight. Thus, it wouldn't be the *standard,* Choice (A), or the typical *makeup,* Choice (B), of her experience. The *quality,* Choice (C), of the college experience is not in question. The play could be considered a *peculiarity,* Choice (F), but there's no match for this term. *Acme* and *pinnacle,* Choices (D) and (E), are the only words that fit the sentence.

24. **A. droll; B. witty**

The missing words represent the description of "clever" and "humorous." *Droll* and *witty,* Choices (A) and (B), both describe this trait. None of the other choices — *obvious,* Choice (C); *dense,* Choice (D); *obtuse,* Choice (E); or *classic,* Choice (F) — encompasses the appropriate meaning.

25. **C. condoning; F. pardoning**

The speaker thinks that society overlooks these crimes or allows them based on the celebrity status of athletes. Society is not said to be *punishing* or *rebuking* the crimes, as Choices (A) and (E) indicate, nor is it *praising* or *lauding* them, per Choices (B) and (D). *Condoning* and *pardoning,* Choices (C) and (F), mean to overlook misdoings, which fits.

26. **A. erratic; D. intermittent**

If the travel patterns make photography tricky, then the patterns are sporadic. *Transparent, obvious,* and *foreseeable* — Choices (B), (C), and (E) — are the opposite of sporadic. *Unimagined,* Choice (F), is a bit out of scope. *Erratic* and *intermittent,* Choices (A) and (D), both mean irregular in occurrence.

27. **B. gregarious; D. extroverted**

Mr. Depp ventures into towns and communes with the townspeople rather than sequestering himself in his trailer; therefore, he is sociable. *Introverted* and *pompous,* Choices (C) and (E), do not fit this personality, nor does *reluctant,* Choice (F). He may be *confident,* Choice (A), in his ability to socialize, but that doesn't describe the act. *Gregarious* and *extroverted,* Choices (B) and (D), both describe the act of being sociable.

28. **D. intrepid; E. gallant**

Soldiers who place themselves in terrifying situations to help others are very brave. Which words share that meaning? The soldiers may be *proficient* in what they do, Choice (A), but that's outside the scope of their character; likewise, *resolute* (determined), Choice (B), may be true but is out of scope. *Established* and *clever,* Choices (C) and (F), don't fit the context, leaving *intrepid* and *gallant,* Choices (D) and (E), which both mean brave or courageous.

29.

B. doctrinaire; C. dogmatic

If your attitude hinders your ability to learn from others and improve, you are likely closing yourself off to other ideas. Which words describe this behavior? *Lenient*, Choice (A), is the opposite. *Doctrinaire* and *dogmatic*, Choices (B) and (C), fit the meaning and match each other. Peruse the other words to make sure these are the best choices. *Prejudiced*, Choice (D), is close, but it doesn't have a match, and *generous* and *partisan*, Choices (E) and (F), are out of scope.

30.

A. engendered; F. stimulated

This sentence states that what the president did led to economic growth and reduced unemployment. *Obstructed* and *inhibited*, Choices (B) and (D), imply the opposite. *Allowed*, Choice (C), could work, but to say that the president allowed or did not allow for the growth goes beyond the action suggested in the sentence. *Certified*, Choice (E), is out of scope. *Engendered* (caused something), Choice (A), and *stimulated* (encouraged the development of), Choice (F), both create the same sentence and are therefore correct.

31.

C. paragon; D. exemplar

By providing ample benefits for its employees, Google can be assumed to be treating them well. Thus, the terms needed for the blanks should represent their success in creating a positive workplace. *Deficiency* and *shortcoming*, Choices (A) and (E), are opposites of that description. *Surplus* and *intemperance*, Choices (B) and (F), don't make sense. Google wouldn't be considered as having too much of a positive workplace. Both *paragon* and *exemplar*, Choices (C) and (D), mean an ideal or model of something, which fits the sentence.

32.

B. nominal; F. negligible

Fortunately, Jordan's quick notice of his missing wallet minimized the damage to his bank account. Which word choices represent the meaning of something that is minimal? Although *microscopic*, Choice (A), describes something that is small, it takes the meaning a little too far in regard to the context of the sentence. *Petite*, Choice (E), also represents something small, but it's used to describe an object rather than an outcome. If most of his money was untouched, the damage wasn't *immense* or *significant*, ruling out Choices (C) and (D). *Nominal* and *negligible*, Choices (B) and (F), both represent the concept of something that is minimal in effect.

33.

B. maudlin; C. mawkish

Clearly, the students were negatively affected by the professor's teary state or else they would still be coming to class. The missing words describe the negative, weepy state the professor is often in. He is not *composed*, Choice (A), if he's crying in class, nor is he *impassive* (unemotional), Choice (E). He is quite the opposite *(mawkish)*, Choice (C). He may be *neurotic*, Choice (F), but that term describes different behavior. He is not showing *affection* with his tears as Choice (D) suggests, but he is overly sentimental or *maudlin*, Choice (B).

34. B. mores; E. norms

The clues "act accordingly" and "starts and ends the same way" let you know you are looking for words that represent habitual standards that are geared toward proper behavior. *Agendas* and *authority,* Choices (A) and (C), relate to structure, but they don't go far enough in describing the implied routine. *Formulas,* Choice (F), is out of scope, and *strategies,* Choice (D), doesn't seem to fit either. *Mores,* Choice (B), are habitual customs of a particular group, and *norms,* Choice (E), describe a standard pattern of behavior. Both complete the sentence toward the same idea.

35. D. parley; F. confer

The referees couldn't decide on how to end the game, so the coaches decided to discuss the decision. It would seem this would be a contentious conversation because both coaches would likely want to win. The word "agreed" lets you know that despite the contentiousness, it was a mutually accepted action. Therefore, *dispute* and *squabble,* Choices (B) and (E), would be too severe. Likewise, *analyze* and *concur,* Choices (A) and (C), would be too amicable. *Parley* and *confer,* Choices (D) and (F), represent the appropriate level of discussion from opposing sides.

36. A. endemic; F. rife

The poor grades are caused by the missed classes. If all the players are missing classes, it is likely they all have poor grades, which would make them prevalent. *Measly* and *sparse,* Choices (C) and (D), are the opposite of prevalent. Nothing in the sentence suggests that poor grades are an *exclusive* problem of the basketball team, eliminating Choice (E), and *native,* Choice (B), doesn't make sense in this context. *Endemic* and *rife,* Choices (A) and (F), both suggest something that is extensive.

37. A. prudence; C. providence

If it hadn't been for the hiker's foresight, he would have run out of water on the long hike. It may have been *destiny,* Choice (B), or good *fortune,* Choice (E), but it was his decision, not something that happened to him. If he had shown *retrospection* and *hindsight,* per Choices (D) and (F), his decision would have been after the fact. He did show *prudence* (careful management), Choice (A), and *providence* (good judgment), Choice (C).

38. B. symbiosis; E. mutualism

The example of the cat and the farmer is a mutually cooperative interaction. Each helps the other and gets something in return. The cat has *sovereignty* (independence), Choice (A), in the barn, but that doesn't describe his relationship with the farmer. The same could be said about *freedom,* Choice (D). *Addiction,* Choice (F), is too severe in meaning, as is *enslavement,* Choice (C). *Symbiosis,* Choice (B), means a mutually beneficial relationship, as does *mutualism,* Choice (E), with the added meaning of "between two species." These fit the sentence perfectly.

39. **A. hermetic; F. reclusive**

You can use the clues "remote cabin" and "few accounts of his personal life" to piece together that the missing words mean sheltered. *Forsaken* and *derelict*, Choices (B) and (D), are too extreme, meaning abandoned and neglected, respectively. *Lonely*, Choice (C), is a judgment call that only Mr. Salinger could determine, and *deserted*, Choice (E), is a bit out of scope. It is clear he was living a *reclusive* and *hermetic* life alone in his cabin, making Choices (A) and (F) correct.

40. **B. credulous; C. gullible**

Henry must have told a good tale to pass class without doing his assignments. Either that, or the professor was quick to believe everything. A *seasoned* professor likely would have seen through these excuses, as would a *cunning* professor, ruling out Choices (A) and (F). The professor may be *gullible*, Choice (C), but not necessarily *immature* or *inept*, as Choices (D) and (E) suggest. *Credulous*, Choice (B), means too easily convinced, which matches *gullible*, Choice (C).

41. **C. wily; F. crafty**

If Ms. Miller was in a con when they met, the expected change would be away from that behavior. Despite the callous and insensitive nature of her actions, there is nothing to suggest that she has no feelings, as *stony* and *unemotional*, Choices (A) and (E), suggest. She is most certainly not *honorable* or *sincere* if she is conning people, which eliminates Choices (B) and (D). *Wily* and *crafty*, Choices (C) and (F), both represent people who are sneaky and cunning, which fits Ms. Miller perfectly.

42. **A. craven; F. pusillanimous**

The officer showed a real lack of courage when he ran from the building instead of securing the area, as he was trained to do. Although people may view him as weak or *feeble* and *pitiable*, Choices (B) and (E), these meanings don't match the context. He is not going to be commended for his bravery or for being *valiant* and *heroic*, ruling out Choices (C) and (D). Thus, he was *craven* (gutless), Choice (A), and *pusillanimous* (cowardly), Choices (A) and (F), in his actions.

43. **D. propriety; F. etiquette**

If Ms. Post is teaching young women to be ladies, she is probably teaching them manners and appropriate behavior, which is what her name would be synonymous with. *Insolence* and *audacity*, Choices (A) and (C), both encompass disrespect in their meaning, which is the opposite of what you're looking for. A respectable woman may be *sympathetic* and *sensitive*, as Choices (B) and (E) suggest, but those are subtraits of her disposition. The main traits would involve *propriety* and *etiquette*, Choices (D) and (F), or courteous and polite behavior.

44. **B. puerile; C. infantile**

His roles in the comedies are likely funny, but they are also going to be in contrast to his serious or dramatic roles, which would be light and goofy. These roles wouldn't be *mature* or *wise*, eliminating Choices (D) and (F), and *irresponsible* and *petty*, Choices (A) and (E), are too severe for the context. *Puerile* and *infantile*, Choices (B) and (C), represent something childish or silly, which fits the goofiness of Steve Martin's comedic roles.

45. **D. sardonic; F. mordant**

If his jokes offended people, they most likely would not be considered *heartfelt,* Choice (A). Although the audience really didn't like him, it would be a stretch to assume they found his jokes to be *duplicitous* (deceitful), Choice (B), and *dishonest,* Choice (C), unless he were telling lies, which the sentence doesn't suggest. There is also nothing to suggest that his jokes were *hypocritical,* Choice (E). That leaves you with *sardonic* and *mordant,* Choices (D) and (F), which both represent some form of mockery and sarcasm, which could be viewed as offensive if taken the wrong way.

46. **B. redress; E. remedy**

The father was making up for Bill's mistake by making it right with money. He wasn't trying to *exacerbate* the situation, Choice (A). And although *alleviate* and *recuperate,* Choices (C) and (D), are close in meaning to one definition of *remedy,* they don't fit the context of this sentence. In this sentence, *remedy,* Choice (E), would mean to make up for, which is also the meaning of *redress,* Choice (B). *Enrich,* Choice (F), is out of scope. Thus, Choices (B) and (E) are correct.

47. **B. sanguine; F. optimistic**

If their candidate was ahead in the polls, then they had reason to hope for a positive outcome. They would be *optimistic,* Choice (F), which means they would not be *cynical,* Choice (A). Nothing suggests that they would be *suspicious,* Choice (C), and they could be *insistent* or *adamant,* per Choices (D) and (E), that their candidate was the best, but these terms are too severe for the context of this sentence. *Sanguine,* Choice (B), means cheerfully confident, which would also complete the sentence in a way that's similar to *optimistic.*

48. **D. implacable; E. unappeasable**

Consuming 500 pounds a day is a big feat that necessitates a great appetite that's difficult to satisfy. The missing words thus mean hard to satisfy. *Replete, temperate,* and *satiated,* Choices (A), (B), and (C), all represent an appetite that is moderate or satisfied. *Implacable* and *unappeasable,* Choices (D) and (E), both mean voracious or difficult to appease. *Abounding,* Choice (F), signifies a large amount, but that would describe the amount of food, not the level of appetite.

49. **A. pariah; B. offscouring**

Punk and preppy are about as opposite as you can get, so the popular kids are excluding Jenny because she is different, or like an outsider. Don't let the word *counter* in *counterpart,* Choice (E), fool you. In this instance, it means a partner or ally, as does *colleague,* Choice (C). Jenny would not be an *interloper,* Choice (D), because nothing suggests she is trying to be part of the popular group. *Expatriate,* Choice (F), is out of scope, but *pariah* and *offscouring,* Choices (A) and (B), both represent someone seen as outside of society.

50. **D. dilettante; F. amateur**

The art dealer was not an expert in art like everyone thought he was. The missing words mean the opposite of an expert. A *proletarian,* Choice (A), represents a group of people, which is out of scope. Given his lack of training, the dealer is not an *authority* or *specialist,* which rules out Choices (B) and (C). Nothing suggests that he was a *curmudgeon* (rude), Choice (E). Both *dilettante* and *amateur,* Choices (D) and (F), represent the casual manner in which the dealer was knowledgeable about art.

51. **E. supplant; F. displace**

Whereas Lisa was *promoted,* the supervisor was clearly fired, which eliminates Choice (A). Lisa was chosen to replace her supervisor, not *invite, terminate,* or *coordinate,* as Choices (B), (C), and (D) indicate. The directors took the action toward the supervisor; Lisa is secondary to that.

52. **A. surly; B. churlish**

Monty doesn't know when enough is enough, which causes him to act in a crass manner that offends people to the point that they no longer want him around. He is clearly not acting *civil,* Choice (D), or *polished,* Choice (E). *Insubordinate* and *defiant,* Choices (C) and (F), are too severe. There are no rules that he is disobeying. He is simply being *surly* and *churlish,* Choices (A) and (B).

53. **B. unconscionable; E. scandalous**

If impeachment was the likely consequence of Nixon's actions, they must have been very unacceptable. There is nothing to suggest his actions caused fear, eliminating Choice (A), and they were certainly not *bravura* (magnificent), Choice (D), or *brilliant,* Choice (F). There was nothing *obscure,* Choice (C), about his actions, but they were *scandalous* and *unconscionable,* Choices (B) and (E).

54. **C. veracity; F. authenticity**

If some jurors thought the defendant was lying, then the others must have believed the defendant was telling the truth. *Fraudulence, equivocation,* and *duplicity,* Choices (A), (B), and (D), are the opposite of the intended meaning. *Directness,* Choice (E), could be a correct answer, but there is no match for it. Thus, *veracity* and *authenticity,* Choices (C) and (F), which both refer to honesty, are the best choices.

55. **A. prodigal; F. extravagant**

It is clear that Tim spent too much on the credit cards. Nothing suggests that this spending was done without thought or awareness, so *oblivious* and *heedless,* Choices (B) and (C), are out. There is nothing *selfless* or *philanthropic* about spending someone else's money, as Choices (D) and (E) suggest. *Prodigal* and *extravagant* spending quickly lead to debt, making Choices (A) and (F) correct.

56. **C. abeyance; D. suspension**

If the banks were concerned with their balances and bankruptcy, they probably weren't handing out money; thus, activities would have ceased. There would not have been an *upsurge, improvement,* or *escalation,* ruling out Choices (A), (E), and (F).

Diminution, Choice (B), means to decrease, which may seem like a good choice, but there is no match for it. *Abeyance* and *suspension,* Choices (C) and (D), better represent the idea of ceasing banking activities.

---

57. **D. fallow; F. dormant**

The volcano has erupted in the past despite its usual nonerupting status. Which terms are suitable for that meaning? *Functional* and *lively,* Choices (A) and (C), indicate the opposite. Nothing suggests the volcano has been *destroyed,* Choice (B), and mountains are not typically mobile, which eliminates Choice (E). *Fallow* and *dormant,* Choices (D) and (F), signify inactivity, which fits the context.

---

58. **B. insurrection; E. uprising**

Nothing in the sentence suggests that the staff started *riots* or protests *(unrest)* during this event, so Choices (A) and (D) are out. It's possible that *complaints* were made, as Choice (C) suggests, but there was clearly no *reconciliation,* Choice (F), of the matter. Thus, there was an *uprising,* Choice (B), or *insurrection,* Choice (E) of the staff.

---

59. **C. lampoon; E. satire**

The playwright exaggerated his mom's annoying traits into something much worse for a greater effect. This created a parody of her. A *tribute,* Choice (B), or *homage,* Choice (D), would be a positive representation, and an *analysis,* Choice (F), is out of scope. The sentence states that it is a play, so *cartoon,* Choice (A), is out of scope as well. A *lampoon* and *satire,* Choices (C) and (E), are both synonymous with a parody.

---

60. **B. enervated; D. languid**

Marathon training while working long hours can make a person tired. *Frenzied* and *reinvigorated,* Choices (A) and (C), match each other in meaning, but they are the opposite of tired. *Supported* and *prohibited,* Choices (E) and (F), don't make sense in this context. Both *enervated* and *languid,* Choices (B) and (D), mean weakened or exhausted, which match each other and the sentence.

---

61. **D. vituperation; F. opprobrium**

The term "vicious" lets you know you are searching for two negatively charged words. *Docility* (meekness), and *commendation* (praise), Choices (A) and (B), are the opposite, and there is nothing vicious about *reticence* (reserve), Choice (C). The judge could have shown *condescension,* Choice (E). Does either *vituperation,* Choice (D), or *opprobrium,* Choice (F), match *condescension?* No, but they both mean severe criticism, which works.

---

62. **A. oblique; D. circuitous**

She wished she had said something simple and succinct, which means she actually said the opposite. You are looking for two words that mean complex or roundabout. *Oblique,* Choice (A), means indirect or not straightforward, which seems to fit. *Persnickety, earnest,* and *punctilious,* Choices (B), (C), and (E), all represent meticulousness or precision, which are opposites of "simple." Between *frivolous,* Choice (F), and *circuitous,* Choice (D), only the latter matches *oblique.*

63.

A. monastic; E. austere

The missing words describe a type of life that results from getting back to nature in a remote cabin without indulgences, or the simple life, in other words. *Monastic,* Choice (A), describes this state of being well, meaning to live reclusively without luxuries. *Zealous, equitable,* and *clement,* Choices (B), (C), and (D), all refer to different characteristics not related to the context. *Altruistic,* Choice (F), is a good trait that probably goes along with a monastic life, but it is inherently different in meaning. *Austere,* Choice (E), also means living a life without luxuries.

64.

E. ingenuous; F. candid

If Cherry's remarks were *sincere* or *amicable,* Choices (A) and (B), people would not be taken aback. *Hypocritical* and *deceitful* remarks would definitely have a negative effect, but you know that Cherry tells the truth, so you can rule out Choices (C) and (D). Therefore, the only answers that match the context of the sentence are *ingenuous* and *candid,* Choices (E) and (F), which both imply direct honesty.

65.

E. nadir; F. depth

It's a low blow to embarrass someone in the way that Carrie was. It certainly wouldn't be considered the *crest* or *peak,* Choices (B) and (D), nor would it be considered an act of *distinction,* Choice (C). Although *infamy,* Choice (A), could seemingly work, there is no match to make a similar sentence so this can't be the correct choice. *Nadir* and *depth,* Choices (E) and (F), both refer to something that is low or the bottom, which fits the context of the sentence.

66.

B. deference; D. regard

More than 4,500 people do not attend the funeral of a man who is held in *revulsion* or *disdain,* Choices (A) and (C). *Infatuation,* Choice (E), is too strong for the context, and *allure,* Choice (F), isn't strong enough. *Deference* and *regard,* Choices (B) and (D), both mean to respect or admire.

67.

C. onerous; E. arduous

If the due date was pushed up, causing Jane duress, it's not likely that the book would be *facile,* Choice (B), to finish or *paltry,* Choice (F). *Convoluted,* Choice (A), is a bit out of scope for the context, and there is nothing *extraneous* (irrelevant), Choice (D), about Jane's work. The book could easily have been *onerous* (troublesome) and *arduous* (difficult), Choices (C) and (E), and both words complete the sentence in a similar fashion.

68.

B. phlegmatic; D. apathetic

It sounds like Dale no longer has any interest in anything or verve for life. Whereas Dale may be a target of ridicule *(derisory),* Choice (A), and be seemingly *pathetic,* Choice (F), these terms don't explain his attitude. He is certainly acting *slothful,* Choice (E), but this term describes more of a physical condition than a mental one. You can rule out *vigorous,* Choice (C), so you're left with *phlegmatic* and *apathetic,* Choices (B) and (D). Both terms relate to a loss of spirit or desire to experience life.

69. **B. perspicacious; C. sagacious**

If the problem is being responsible for every problem, then the teacher's abilities likely make him very perceptive. Which words from the choices relate to that meaning? All the choices relate to some form of knowledge or prowess in thought, but only *perspicacious* and *sagacious,* Choices (B) and (C), encompass the essence of insight or knowledge gained by internal qualities of judgment. *Assiduous, pensive, erudite,* and *introspective,* Choices (A), (D), (E), and (F), don't quite fit the bill.

70. **A. pedant; E. hair-splitter**

The professor uses small details to judge the whole. This behavior would not make him a *connoisseur,* Choice (B), or *specialist,* Choice (F), of information. He is certainly making the situation more complicated as an *obfuscator,* Choice (C), but nothing suggests he is making the whole argument complicated. He is a *contender,* Choice (D), but this is not the best choice because there isn't an equivalent answer option. His focus on the smallest detail makes him a *hair-splitter,* Choice (E), and also a *pedant,* Choice (A), focusing only on unimportant details. Choices (A) and (E) are correct.

71. **D. a peccadillo; E. a misdemeanor**

The crowd clearly thought the crime was more severe than what the jury found it to be. Thus, the missing terms represent the jury's verdict of a less severe crime. No crime would be found to be *reputable,* Choice (A), by a jury. *Wicked* and *nefarious,* Choices (B) and (C), are fairly synonymous, but both words suggest a crime more in line with how the crowd perceived it. Likewise, the crowd wanted the offenders to be found *culpable,* Choice (F). *A peccadillo* and *a misdemeanor,* Choices (D) and (E), represent the minor significance of the jury's decision and are correct.

72. **A. quotidian; B. unexceptional**

Obviously, those who turned in applications described by the missing words were not remarkable. You can quickly guess that *prestigious* and *phenomenal,* Choices (C) and (E), are incorrect. Choice (B), *unexceptional,* seems to fit well. Is there another word with a similar meaning? *Outlandish,* Choice (D), goes a bit too far in the other direction, and *inconsequential,* Choice (F), makes a judgment about the importance of the application, which is probably the same for each applicant. Even if you didn't know that *quotidian,* Choice (A), means commonplace, you could safely choose it after eliminating the other choices.

73. **C. pithy; E. sententious**

It sounds like Vera's date didn't know what hit him with the quick and forceful way she left him in the restaurant. It is possible that Vera's actions could be considered *loutish* (crude and ill-behaved), Choice (B), so now you must find a similar word from the choices. *Straggling,* Choice (A), is out of scope, and no one would mistake her actions as *urbane* (suave) or *chivalrous,* Choices (D) and (F). *Pithy,* Choice (C), means brief and forceful, and *sententious,* Choice (E), is synonymous with *pithy.* Therefore, *loutish* has no match, but Choices (C) and (E) match, making them the correct answers.

74. B. abdicate; E. renounce

King Henry basically forced the clergy to hand over their power and then took it as his own. Which words fit this idea the best? *Congregate*, Choice (A), is beyond the scope of the context, as is *assent*, Choice (C). The king's actions certainly *diverge* from the norms, but that doesn't describe the actions of the clergy, so Choice (D) is also out. Perhaps the clergy *dispersed* after they lost their power, as Choice (F) suggests, but that is also out of scope. They were forced to *abdicate* and *renounce* (both meaning relinquish) their power, making Choices (B) and (E) correct.

75. A. polyglot; C. linguist

Matt has issues with showing off his multi-language skills. The missing words describe what someone with these skills is called. *Genius*, Choice (B), is too extreme, as are *leader* and *mastermind*, Choices (E) and (F). It's possible languages are the only things that Matt has a knack for. A *linguist*, Choice (C), is someone who is skilled with different languages, which sounds like Matt. Don't be tricked by *bilingual*, Choice (D). The sentence states that Matt speaks French and Portuguese, but it also says he is American, which means he speaks English, too. That's three languages, not two. Even if you didn't know that *polyglot*, Choice (A), meant competent in languages, you could choose it through the process of elimination.

76. D. tangential; E. peripheral

The planners were obsessed with details and missed the big picture. *Wooly* and *ambiguous*, Choices (A) and (B), both mean vague or unclear. However, the planners weren't vague about the big picture; they were avoiding it altogether. Nothing in the sentence suggests that the planners were *incongruous* (inappropriate), Choice (C), and *divergent*, Choice (F), seems a bit out of scope. Both *tangential* and *peripheral*, Choices (D) and (E), describe speaking on the fringe of a topic or focusing on incidental details.

77. A. politic; B. astute

Whatever Mr. Wentworth did helped him make a lot of money. The choices for this sentence are a bit tricky. They all relate to finances in some way. Your task is to take the information given and find the best choices that match. *Politic* and *astute*, Choices (A) and (B), both signify a level of shrewdness, or discernment for personal gain. *Parsimonious* and *miserly*, Choices (C) and (E), both represent a personality that is frugal or stingy, which don't seem like the grandfather. He clearly is good with money, but he's also there when someone is in need. However, his help comes for a share in the profits, so it can't be considered *charitable*, Choice (F), or wholly *munificent* (generous), Choice (D). Choices (A) and (B) are the best answers.

78. B. vestige; E. trace

The clue "slightest" lets you know that the family is searching for any part of something left after the tornado. There is a *paucity* (scarcity), Choice (A), of items, but the family is not looking for a scarcity, nor is it looking for an *indication*, Choice (C). They would be thrilled with a *plethora* or *glut* of items, per Choices (D) and (F); they would settle for a *vestige* (small amount), Choice (B), or *trace*, Choice (E), of anything from the past.

79. **B. quixotic; C. idealistic**

The reality she held in her head was that all her dreams would come true, causing her to ignore the practical side of things. Nothing in the sentence suggests that Shelly is *recalcitrant* (stubborn), Choice (A). *Obliging* and *emphatic*, Choices (D) and (E), don't make sense in this context, and *malleable*, Choice (F), means flexible, which it doesn't sound like Shelly is. That leaves *quixotic* and *idealistic*, Choices (B) and (C), which both represent romanticism or impracticality.

80. **E. probity; F. integrity**

The text after the blank describes the missing words. There is a difference between having respect for others and showing mercy, which makes *clemency*, Choice (A), out of scope. Similarly, *commiseration*, Choice (C), suggests sympathy, which is also out of scope. *Impiety* and *malevolence*, Choices (B) and (D), are the opposite of what is right and respectful. However, *probity*, Choice (E), means moral correctness, and *integrity*, Choice (F), carries a similar meaning.

81. **B. narcissism; F. conceit**

To talk about oneself prolifically in a personal blog implies the writer is full of self-love or is at least self-centered. Choices (A) and (D), *ambivalence* and *moderation*, do not fit the context of being prolific or self-centered. A personal blog can be prolific without being eloquent, so Choice (C), *eloquence*, doesn't fit either. Choices (B) and (F), *narcissism* and *conceit*, both mean self-loving, so these are the best descriptions of someone who writes prolifically in a personal blog.

82. **B. prescience; C. foresight**

If Apple stock was really cheap, the company was likely not doing very well. It would have taken a vision that the company would improve to purchase those stocks. The missing words represent that vision. *Circumspection*, Choice (A), is close, but taking into consideration the consequences before acting seems too cautious for this leap of faith. *Negligence* and *imprudence*, Choices (D) and (F), both suggest careless or ignorant behavior, and *gumption*, Choice (E), may be what is needed to take the leap, but doesn't express the action. Only *prescience* and *foresight*, Choices (B) and (C), describe the vision of the future represented in the sentence.

83. **A. sacrosanct; C. inviolable**

For the tombs to protect the dead, they must be impenetrable, or else the thieves and vandals would be able to harm the bodies. A *spindly* and *meager* structure wouldn't do much to keep people out, so you can eliminate Choices (B) and (E), and although many of the tombs in history are *resplendent* (stunning), Choice (F), this aspect doesn't imply protection. *Bounteous* (relating to the number of tombs), Choice (D), is out of scope. *Sacrosanct* and *inviolable*, Choices (A) and (C), refer to something that is secure and sacred.

84. **C. inexorable; E. relentless**

Frodo's mission continued despite every attempt to stop it. Which words represent the idea of being unstoppable? Frodo chose to go on the mission, so it was not *obligatory*, Choice (F), or *unavoidable*, Choice (B). His mission was *preventable*, Choice (A), but he chose not to prevent it. Nothing suggests that his mission was *superfluous* (not essential), Choice (D). Thus, *inexorable* and *relentless*, Choices (C) and (E), must be the correct answers. Both represent the predicted meaning of unstoppable.

85. **C. soporific; F. monotonous**

Despite the interest in the topic, the speaker droned in such a way that it put the audience to sleep. *Invigorating* and *restorative*, Choices (A) and (E), are opposites of droning speech, as is *charismatic*, Choice (D). Nothing suggests that the speaker was *repellant*, Choice (B), just boring. *Soporific* and *monotonous*, Choices (C) and (F), both represent a dull or sleep-inducing manner of speaking.

86. **B. multifarious; E. disparate**

The jobs that are appearing on resumes these days are diverse and varied in scope because of the inconsistent job market. *Analogous*, *uniform*, and *synchronized* resumes, per Choices (A), (C), and (D), would include jobs that were similar in nature. The resumes could be considered *atypical*, Choice (F), but the two remaining choices, *multifarious* and *disparate*, Choices (B) and (E), both represent the concepts of diversity and divergence rather than something unusual.

87. **A. sedative; F. palliative**

The music had a calming effect on the speaker, so the missing words mean calming or soothing. It sounds like the speaker listens to the music when she feels *anguished*, Choice (B), so the music wouldn't have this effect. *Analgesic*, Choice (C), does mean to relieve, but the term is used for pain relief. Nothing suggests the music makes the speaker more *heartening* (cheerful), Choice (D), or *sorrowful*, Choice (E). *Sedative* and *palliative*, Choices (A) and (F), both represent something soothing.

88. **E. fecund; F. prolific**

If writing under his own name would flood the market with his books, King is a very productive writer. He may also be a *learned* and *cultivated* writer, as indicated by Choices (A) and (C), but his intelligence and sophistication do not necessarily lead to productivity. *Infertile*, Choice (B), is out of scope, and he wouldn't be publishing anything if he were a *fruitless* writer, Choice (D). As a *fecund* and *prolific* writer, he is capable of producing at a very fast rate, making Choices (E) and (F) correct.

89. **D. transitory; F. ephemeral**

If they happen so infrequently, celestial eclipses would be considered fleeting events. If they are *colossal* events, as Choice (A) indicates, that explains the magnitude of the event, not the rate. They can't be *infinite* or *eternal* if they are so infrequent, so you can rule out Choices (B) and (C). *Ordained*, Choice (E), is out of scope. *Transitory* and *ephemeral*, Choices (D) and (F), both refer to a temporary event.

90. **D. proliferate; F. burgeon**

If people are responding well, Howard's fan base would be growing, not *diminishing,* as Choice (B) would suggest. The fan base isn't *supplementing* anything, and the fans aren't attempting to *convoy* (group up), so you can eliminate Choices (A) and (E). *Engorge,* Choice (C), is a different connotation for growing. *Proliferate* and *burgeon,* Choices (D) and (F), both mean to increase in number or expand.

91. **B. bevy**

A number of bodyguards wouldn't be necessary for a *deficiency* (lack) of fans, so Choice (A) doesn't apply. A *tribe* or *clique* of fans, each describing a group of people, doesn't make sense in this context, so you can rule out Choices (C) and (E). A *remainder* of fans, Choice (D), doesn't make sense either. A *bevy,* or large group, of fans, Choice (B), makes sense in the context of the sentence.

92. **E. inquest**

An accusation against a police officer is a very serious issue. Thus, the chief would likely take a severe action. Simply making an *observation,* Choice (D), is too mild in this context. Neither *experiment* nor *application,* Choices (A) and (C), fit the context despite their inquisitive natures. An *analysis,* Choice (B), will likely be made, but there must first be evidence to analyze, which can be collected through an investigation, or an *inquest,* Choice (E).

93. **B. repose**

Running a marathon is a lot of activity; therefore, she would likely want to rest and be inactive afterward. Both *recreation* and *agitation,* Choices (C) and (D), mean the opposite of restful. *Support,* Choice (E), could be needed for the body and is a possible answer. A *breather,* Choice (A), does mean to take a rest, but it's often for a short period of time, not a full day. A *repose,* Choice (B), is a condition of rest and tranquility. Choosing between the two plausible answers, simply taking the day off can lead to a *repose,* whereas something more is needed to *support* the body after the day off is taken.

94. **B. panache**

The director wants something that is beyond mere charm, or attractiveness. *Meekness* and *humility,* Choices (A) and (E), would be less expressive than charm, and *charisma,* Choice (C), represents the same level of delightfulness. Nothing in the sentence suggests the director wants a more *complex* personality, so you can rule out Choice (D). On the other hand, *panache,* Choice (B), signifies someone with a spirited or dashing style, which would be more than an attractive style.

95. **D. timorous**

If the singer still requires meditation to calm down before she can go on stage, she is likely dealing with stage fright. *Relaxed* and *tranquil,* Choices (B) and (E), describe how she would feel after meditating, not her normal state of being. Although she may be *exhausted,* Choice (A), from ten performances, she wouldn't want to relax more if that were the case. Nothing suggests that she was agitated or upset, so *overwrought,* Choice (C), is too strong for the blank. *Timorous,* Choice (D), means to be fearful or apprehensive, which fits the context of the sentence and is the correct choice.

96. **B. colluding**

The manager overheard them hatching a plan to steal money from the bank, so the word that fits the blank fits this description. Only *colluding* and *fabricating*, Choices (B) and (E), represent the actions of creating something. However, *colluding* means to specifically work with another person in secret, whereas *fabricating* is simply the construction or creation of something, either alone or with another person. In the context of this sentence, *colluding* fits the blank more accurately. Choices (A), (C), and (D) — *professing, improvising,* and *adjoining* — are out of scope.

97. **A. inter**

You can assume based on the description in the sentence that Jessica buried her dog. *Harvest, unearth,* and *banish* — Choices (B), (C), and (D) — are out of scope. The dog was likely *enclosed,* Choice (E), but in the box, not the ground. The only term that represents the burying of something is *inter,* Choice (A).

98. **C. ameliorate**

Factory workers had to improve the conditions, but *revolutionized,* Choice (A), is too extreme. The sentence also states that changes were made, not new *developments,* so the working conditions already existed, making Choice (B) also out of scope. The restrictions could have forced the owners to improve their working conditions, or *ameliorate* them, Choice (C), but it's unlikely that the restrictions would have suggested a *depreciation* (worsening) of conditions, ruling out Choice (D). Furthermore, nothing suggests that the working conditions were primitive and required *modernizing,* Choice (E). Choice (C) is the best choice.

99. **A. cabal**

If the CEO and his executives wanted to approve a merger despite the disapproval of those with vested interests, the meeting would likely be held in secret. Starting with Choice (A), a *cabal* is a secret or exclusive group of plotters or schemers, which fits in the sentence. A *subordinate,* Choice (B), works under someone, so this is not a top executive. A *clique,* Choice (C), is a group, but this term doesn't signify wrongdoing by nature and isn't typically used in business, nor is *sect,* Choice (D), which refers to religious groups or those with tightly held similar beliefs. *Class,* Choice (E), could represent a higher-ranked group, but this term is used for ranks of society or grades. *Cabal* is the only choice that fits.

100. **C. machination**

The insecure team captain wouldn't want to be outshone, so what would her reputation be that leads to the best players becoming injured? You can check *seniority, prowess,* and *athleticism* — Choices (B), (D), and (E) — off the list. These words could describe a team captain but don't allude to consequences for the other players. That leaves Choices (A) and (C), *trickery* and *machination. Machination* is a plot or scheme toward a negative outcome. Trickery also leads to a dishonest end, but there's no indication that the team captain deceived anyone. Therefore, Choice (C) is the correct answer.

101. **D. pejorative**

Whatever the mother-in-law is saying makes Tracy feel bad about herself. A *discordant* remark would simply be disagreeable or harsh in tone, which wouldn't necessarily cause this reaction, so you can eliminate Choice (A). A *defamatory* remark would slander a person's character or ruin her reputation, which seems to fit the tone of the sentence, but there's no evidence that the remarks led to those outcomes, so you can rule out Choice (B). The remarks wouldn't be *amicable* (friendly) or *congruous* (appropriate for the occasion), so Choices (C) and (E) are out, too. However, a *pejorative* statement is critical and shows displeasure, which would likely create negative feelings in Tracy, making Choice (D) correct.

102. **E. vacillating**

The actions by the marketing department caused a delay in the release of the book. If they were a *resolute* or *remarkable* department, per Choices (A) and (C), they likely would have had the book out in time for the buzz. They could have been *cowardly*, Choice (D), but nothing suggests they were afraid of releasing the book. *Dithering* and *vacillating*, Choices (B) and (E), both describe an indecisiveness that could have led to a delay, but *dithering* adds a nervous element, which is out of the scope of the sentence. Thus, *vacillating* is the best choice.

103. **D. bombastic**

The farmers would have liked the candidate if he were *diplomatic* and *affectionate*, Choices (A) and (B), because both terms are positive personality traits. Nothing suggests he was *vicious* in his speech, ruling out Choice (C), and although speaking in a *circuitous* or indirect way might cause the farmers to distrust him, it wouldn't inherently lead to a sense of snobbery, so you can eliminate Choice (E) as well. A *bombastic* manner of speech, Choice (D), is full of pretentious and overly difficult words to try to impress others, which could create the negative feelings described in the sentence.

104. **A. lassitude**

From the term "fatigue," you can guess that her symptom has something to do with severe exhaustion. *Lassitude*, Choice (A), is a state of weariness or exhaustion, so that fits the context well. *Dexterity*, Choice (B), describes a high level of physical skill, and *ineptitude*, Choice (E), describes the opposite. *Ingenuity*, Choice (C), describes a high level of mental skill; thus, all three choices are out of scope. *Apathy*, Choice (D), tends to create the same lack of activity as exhaustion, but it is an emotional condition rather than a physical one. Therefore, Choice (A) works best.

105. **D. frenetic**

If the crowds were *serene* or *listless*, Choice (A) or (E), the shoppers wouldn't be in any danger or being rushed past. *Distracted*, Choice (B), doesn't make sense regarding the safety of the shoppers either, despite the validity that sales can cause crowds to be distracted. Whereas *fervent* crowds could be rushing around past each other, nothing in the sentence suggests that the crowd is passionate, so Choice (C) is out of scope. A *frenetic* crowd is harried, erratic, and unpredictable, which fits the blank well, making Choice (D) the correct answer.

106. C. blight

Something that is killing more than a million acres of forest would be considered more than a *misfortune,* Choice (A), and it isn't related to a physical or mental human condition; therefore, *affliction,* Choice (E), can be eliminated. *Defacement,* Choice (B), is less severe than what the sentence describes. *Blight* and *infirmity,* Choices (C) and (D), both involve unhealthy conditions, but only *blight* specifically refers to a disease affecting plants or species.

107. E. deride

The blank describes an action by the mayor's critics; thus, the action is critical. *Commend* and *sanction,* Choices (A) and (B), are the opposite of critical, and the sentence doesn't suggest that malicious or *slanderous* statements were made by the critics, excluding Choices (C) *(vilify)* and (D) *(slander).* However, it would be accurate to say the critics showed contempt for the mayor's plan, or *derided* it. Thus, Choice (E) is correct.

108. C. hegemony

If the younger students had no power in the school, then the term in the blank must equate to power. *Inferiority,* Choice (A), is the opposite of power, and *constraint* and *expertise,* Choices (B) and (E), are characteristics outside of the dispersion of power. *Evaluations,* Choice (D), aren't related to the context of the sentence. *Hegemony,* Choice (C), describes the authority or control held by one group, making it the best answer.

109. D. castigated

The action taken by the coach was worse to Joe than his team's anger; therefore, you know the missing term means something negative and hurtful. *Congratulated,* Choice (C), is a positive action and can be eliminated. The term *branded,* Choice (A), is negative, but there's no indication that the coach marked or labeled Joe in any way. *Violated* and *desecrated,* Choices (B) and (E), refer to damage caused to someone or something sacred and are out of scope. *Castigated,* Choice (D), means to harshly criticize someone, which is in line with the meaning of the sentence.

110. A. misanthrope

The term that fits the blank describes the type of person that Kelly is, which is someone who thinks harshly of others and confines herself from the public. Kelly has negative feelings toward others because she is a *skeptic,* someone who is full of doubt, Choice (B), or a *pessimist,* someone who expects the worst, Choice (C), but those characteristics don't explain her extreme avoidance. *Curmudgeon* and *idealist,* Choices (D) and (E), also entail personality traits that she could possess, but they don't lend to her negative feelings toward others. A *misanthrope,* Choice (A), describes a person who distrusts and strongly dislikes people to the point of isolating herself, which fits the context of the sentence.

111. B. obstinate

If the results of the lawmakers' attitudes could be equal rights movements by the masses, then those attitudes would not be *malleable,* Choice (A), which means easily swayed, or *amenable,* Choice (D), which means open to cooperation. *Desultory,* Choice (C), also does not fit the blank because a random attitude is not for one side or the other. Whereas the lawmakers could be *methodical,* Choice (E), in their actions, their refusal to act in the name of the masses would be driven by an *obstinate* attitude, Choice (B), or an unwillingness to change or give up control.

112.   **B. polemic**

All five choices represent bodies of work; however, *opus, proposal,* and *masterpiece* — Choices (C), (D), and (E) — are out of scope. An *opus* describes an artistic piece of work, and nothing indicates that the document *proposed* anything or was well written and worthy of being deemed a *masterpiece.* A *homily,* Choice (A), suggests a moral critique or message, which is a bit strong and presumptuous. Nothing indicates that what the president said was more or less moral than the actions he criticized. A *polemic,* Choice (B), is simply a strongly worded or controversial argument, which would be enough to anger his supporters.

113.   **C. phalanx**

Although *legion, cohort,* and *throng* — Choices (A), (B), and (D) — create the sense of a group of bees, none of them inherently represents a group that stands or binds together physically, whereas a *phalanx,* Choice (C), is a tight group that's difficult to penetrate. A *consortium,* Choice (E), is a group of organizations with a common purpose and doesn't fit this context.

114.   **E. malinger**

Marie's behavior disrupted her work enough that none of her former employers will recommend her. *Hesitate* and *meander,* Choices (A) and (B), may represent poor qualities in an employee, but they aren't egregious. To *tarry,* Choice (C), is to linger, which is also out of scope. An employer would be happy to have a worker who *acquiesces* (complies), Choice (D). Thus, *malinger,* Choice (E), is the only term that describes behavior geared toward avoiding work responsibilities.

115.   **D. lionized**

The terms "downfall" and "juxtapose" let you know that the previous state was great in magnitude. Therefore, the term in the blank describes a high level in which society saw the man. *Decried* and *spurned,* Choices (B) and (C), describe low opinions. *Praised* and *eulogized,* Choices (A) and (E), both describe positive opinions, as does *lionized,* Choice (D); however, *lionize* describes a treatment of someone as a celebrity or exceptional, which would create a stronger pitying effect than mere *praise.* Thus, Choice (D) is the best answer.

116.   **B. criticism; F. created**

The word "adverse" lets you know that Holtorf's statement wasn't liked. Therefore, he probably didn't receive *acclaim,* Choice (C), for it. *Contempt* (a powerful negative emotion), Choice (A), is too strong for this context. *Criticism,* Choice (B), makes sense.

The missing word in the second blank needs to be somewhat synonymous with "renewable." *Buried* and *wasted,* Choices (D) and (E), are the opposite of renewable in this context. Thus, *created,* Choice (F), is the only logical option.

117.

B. sportive; D. ardent

If Juniper is chosen first, it means she has skills in sports, which suggests a level of practice or involvement. *Idle,* Choice (A), doesn't make sense in this context. Juniper could be *eccentric,* Choice (C), but it doesn't explain her prowess at sporting activities. Only *sportive,* Choice (B), which indicates active participation in sports, fits the first blank.

The term in the second blank is another attribute of Juniper's and likely positive because it leads to her being chosen. *Dispassionate* and *furtive,* Choices (E) and (F), have negative connotations and would not likely lead to her being chosen. Only *ardent,* Choice (D), which means showing enthusiasm and passion, fits.

118.

C. ingrates; F. reciprocate

If his friends never showed any appreciation, then they were ungrateful for his kindness. They would not be considered *allies* or *champions,* Choices (A) and (B), if they didn't support Manuel as he did them, so they must be *ingrates,* Choice (C), which means those who are ungrateful.

If Manuel's friends never perform the same acts for him, then they do not *reciprocate* his actions toward them, Choice (F). They clearly do *ignore* his kindness, Choice (D). You can't determine whether they *perceive* his kindness or not, Choice (E), just that they do not return the favor.

119.

C. eloquent; E. sordid

The first blank would be the opposite of "rudimentary babble." A *garbled* statement would be close to babble, and nothing indicates whether the statement was *confidently* made, so you can eliminate Choices (A) and (B). However, an *eloquent* statement, which is articulate and expressive, could be reduced to babble, so Choice (C) fits.

Furthermore, the disc jockey has already been described as bawdy, so you can look for a similar term that also represents his antics and lack of appreciation for the eloquent things. *Hostile,* Choice (F), is out of scope, and *congenial,* Choice (D), would mean he was well mannered, which is the opposite of bawdy. To be *sordid,* Choice (E), is to be lowly and distasteful, which sounds like the disc jockey in this sentence.

120.

B. judicious; E. gratitude

Margaret made a frugal choice that was recognized by her uncle as a good deed. Her nature wouldn't be *hasty* (impetuous), Choice (A), and because her uncle recognized her actions, her nature wouldn't be *discreet,* Choice (C). If she were *judicious,* Choice (B), she would be sensible and prudent, which would lead to less expensive choices.

Her uncle clearly appreciated this behavior if he paid for her meal, so the second blank is synonymous with appreciation. Neither *obligation* nor *vulgarity* fit this meaning, ruling out Choices (D) and (F). *Gratitude,* Choice (E), is the essence of being appreciative and thankful.

121.

C. dogma; F. disdain

The animal activists promote the belief of no harm to animals as a moral ideal they hold to be true. Although they have *dedication,* Choice (A), to that belief, *dedication* doesn't describe the belief itself. This belief could have started as a product of a decision, or a *verdict,* Choice (B), but the longevity of their promotion as a group makes it more of a *dogma,* Choice (C), that is widely held by everyone.

The hunters would clearly be resentful of this denouncement of their sport, so they would hold *disdain,* Choice (F), for the activists. *Esteem,* Choice (D), is opposite of what the hunters would feel, and *mockery,* Choice (E), is out of scope.

122. **C. dilated; D. vain**

If the mirror made June's reflection appear ten times her normal size, it would have enlarged it. The word in the first blank matches this meaning. *Constricted,* Choice (A), means smaller, which is the opposite of the desired meaning. *Exposed,* Choice (B), is out of scope. *Dilated,* Choice (C), signifies the growth or enlargement of something, which fits.

June didn't like looking bigger because she is *vain,* Choice (D), or conceited about her looks. If she were *humble,* Choice (F), she would be unpretentious and wouldn't care about her looks. *Futile,* or pointless, Choice (E), is out of scope.

123. **B. axioms; E. charlatan**

Because the speaker didn't know what he was talking about, he had to rely on commonly accepted and widely known terms. A *mantra,* Choice (A), may fit this description, but nothing suggests that the speaker was repeating the information continuously. *Expertise,* Choice (C), is obviously what he was lacking. An *axiom,* Choice (B), is a generally accepted idea, which fits the meaning for the first blank.

A *maverick,* Choice (D), is someone who refuses to abide by conventions, which would be the opposite of who the speaker is. A *conformist,* Choice (F), is a bit out of scope. But a *charlatan,* Choice (E), is also known as an imposter, which Paula would likely see the speaker as due to his façade of a knowledgeable person.

124. **A. boor; E. audacious**

No one would think that Chad is noble, or a *patrician,* Choice (B), if he is insulting everyone he meets. They may pity him as a *wretch,* Choice (C), but the sentence requires a word that describes his negative actions. Only *boor,* Choice (A), describes his crass and ill-mannered behavior.

Despite his boorish behavior, employers seem to be drawn to Chad. The second blank requires a word that is similar to bold and describes a quality employers are drawn toward. *Audacious,* Choice (E), is closely related to bold and is the only positive attribute of the choices. *Foolhardy,* Choice (D), and *impudent,* Choice (F), are clearly negative characteristics.

125. **C. florid; E. pallid**

The brother who always shows artistry in his gestures and speech is *florid,* Choice (C), or ornate and fanciful. *Ostentatious* and *diffident,* Choices (A) and (B), refer to character traits outside the scope of this description.

The other brother shows little energy and is nothing like his florid brother; thus, you know you are looking for a word that expresses these ideas. *Exultant,* Choice (F), is the opposite of little energy, and *despondent,* Choice (D), is too emotionally severe. However, one meaning for *pallid,* Choice (E), is a lack of intensity or spirit, which is the description you are looking for.

126.   A. paradox; D. dissemble

It would seem that if you moved to a big city, you would be surrounded by more people, so the idea that you could be more alone, although possible, seems incorrect. Thus, this idea is a *paradox,* Choice (A). *Farcicality* and *enigma,* Choices (B) and (C), are beyond the meaning expressed in the sentence.

The word in the second blank explains why the paradox is possible. If she were *secreting* or *articulating* her nature, as in Choices (E) and (F), she would be putting it out for others to see, and she would likely feel more involved in society. However, if she *dissembles* her nature, Choice (D), she is able to conceal part of herself, allowing her to maintain privacy or isolate herself emotionally.

127.   C. itinerant; E. fashion

What sort of life involves making and leaving friends? An *orthodox* life, Choice (A), is traditional, which deters from the leaving part of this life. A *rousing* life, Choice (B), is full of energy and vigor and could be an aspect of this sort of life, but it's not an inherent aspect. An *itinerant* life, Choice (C), is a wandering or nomadic life, which would inherently include leaving locales frequently.

The phrase "new version" lets you know the speaker has choices as to who she will be in each new place. *Simulate* and *parody,* Choices (D) and (F), both lend to a copying or acceptance of a version that is already in existence. Only *fashion,* Choice (E), dictates the ability to create a different version.

128.   B. cacophony; E. gesticulation

If the voices are from the opposing side, they would likely not be described as *melodious,* Choice (A). And a *scarcity* of voices could not drown out the referee, ruling out Choice (C). Thus, a *cacophony,* Choice (B), or loud and harsh tones, fits the sentence best.

The term in the second blank signifies that the referee's ruling could still be understood despite the harsh voices because of his actions. Both *demeanor* and *carriage,* Choices (D) and (F), refer to states of the body or behavior, but *gesticulation,* Choice (E), specifically refers to gestures or signals, which is what this sentence is seeking for the second blank.

129.   A. laconic; D. dearth

The professor only states the information once, so he does not elaborate. The first blank is a term that means the opposite of elaborate. *Interminable,* Choice (C), is synonymous with talkative, which is related to elaboration. Whereas he may be *predictable,* Choice (B), he is only predictably *laconic,* Choice (A), or concise in speech.

Without proper explanation, the students feel their knowledge will be lacking. Thus, there would not be *precision* or a *surfeit* (surplus) in their knowledge, as Choices (E) and (F) suggest. Instead, they would have a *dearth,* or a shortage, in their knowledge, Choice (D).

130. **C. ebullient; F. abominates**

A diplomat must represent his country's interests well; thus, he needs to be polite to visiting leaders. *Doleful,* Choice (A), is the opposite of polite or upbeat, and the sentence doesn't suggest a diplomat needs to be forceful, or *robust,* Choice (B), in his actions. *Ebullient,* Choice (C), is the best choice.

The term "regardless" lets you know that the second blank refers to a word that is not positive like *ebullient* is. To *revere* or *espouse* the agendas would be to support and promote them, which are both positive actions. Thus, you can eliminate Choices (D) and (E). To *abominate* the agenda, Choice (F), is to detest it, which works well.

131. **A. fetid; E. rancorous**

Would a rotten orange give off an *affable,* or pleasant, smell? Not likely, so you can rule out Choice (C). The action of putting the orange in the couch is *despicable,* Choice (B), but the smell itself is *fetid* (foul), Choice (A).

And if this act was intentional, what kind of person would do such a thing? A *benevolent* person would be kind and forgiving, not spiteful, so Choice (F) is out. *Nefarious,* Choice (D), is too strong of a word, describing someone full of evil. This act could have simply been caused by a resentment, so the person would be *rancorous,* Choice (E).

132. **A. diatribe; F. derision**

The receptionist is not speaking to a religious congregation, so she would not deliver a *sermon,* Choice (C). *Diatribe* and *dissertation,* Choices (A) and (B), both describe a lengthy document, but only *diatribe* contains the intention to attack someone with the words, which you can assume the email did if it caused the manager embarrassment.

Based on the information in the first sentence, you can also gather that the manager's coworkers would not approve of his negative treatment of his receptionist and would look at him negatively, which excludes *approbation* (approval), Choice (E). Nothing indicates that violence or cruelty were involved, so *savagery,* Choice (D), is too severe. Only *derision,* Choice (F), describes this negative opinion.

133. **A. dictum; E. incommodious**

The Dalai Lama is considered an authority on the Buddhist principles of life; therefore, what he professes would not be considered a *cliché,* Choice (B). His teachings are philosophies; they are never required or forced on people and, thus, are not *mandates,* Choice (C). A *dictum,* Choice (A), is simply an authoritative statement, which fits the meaning of the first blank well.

If the simple life doesn't fit in with many people's cushy lives, then simplicity must be inconvenient considering everything they are accustomed to having. *Opportune,* Choice (D), would suggest it was the right time to simplify life, and nothing suggests that the decision to simplify is made in haste, or *imprudent,* Choice (F). *Incommodious* (inconvenient), Choice (E), fits well.

134. **A. licentious; D. iconoclasts**

The word missing from the sentence signifies a lack of regard for rules or order. *Scrupulous,* Choice (B), is the opposite, and *depraved,* Choice (C), is too severe. There is no evidence in the sentence that Jeff is wicked or corrupt. Thus, *licentious,* Choice (A), is the only logical answer.

The second missing word describes Jeff's parents, who reject the town's customs. There is no reference to religion or politics, so *fundamentalists,* Choice (F), is out of scope. *Mutineers,* Choice (E), is too severe for a mere rejection, but *iconoclasts,* Choice (D), are people who challenge traditions or customs, which fits the sentence well.

135. **B. mollify; F. durable**

Wood is not bendable by nature, so it would need to be softened to be able to bend. *Congeal* describes an action unrelated to this meaning. Whereas *pacify* does mean to soften in one respect, it is geared toward human emotions. *Mollify* does mean to make an object less rigid and fits the sentence.

Birch is exceptionally hard if it has to pass through the machine multiple times, so the term in the second blank relates to that aspect of birch. *Permeable* would be more fitting for the first blank, and *unequivocal* is out of scope. *Durable* means strong and fits the sentence. Choices (B) and (F) are correct.

136. **B. levity; D. garrulous**

The first description is of someone who is frivolous or light in manner. *Facetiousness,* Choice (A), describes an act of presenting humor without intending it to be funny and doesn't fit the sentence, nor does *intransience,* Choice (C), which refers to a state of stability. *Levity,* Choice (B), is the only term that makes sense.

The second characteristic of someone driven by levity is that he speaks in a way that is unrestrained. A *taciturn,* or reserved, way of speaking, Choice (E), doesn't work. Nothing suggests that the person is *forthcoming* in what he is saying, so Choice (F) doesn't fit either. Thus, *garrulous,* or rambling and talkative speech, Choice (D), is the best choice.

137. **B. nascent; D. industrious**

The word "than" lets you know the missing word is the opposite of a long history of wealth. *Entrenched* wealth, Choice (A), would be the same as a long history of wealth. *Moribund* wealth, Choice (C), would be a loss of money, which doesn't fit either. *Nascent,* or new, wealth, Choice (B), makes sense and is the best choice.

The second blank requires a term that relates to the level of studying the student must do to be able to meet the standards of an Ivy League school. *Languid,* Choice (F), means lazy so that cannot be true of an Ivy League student. Although students who are *vehement* in their studies, Choice (E), will likely attain good grades, nothing suggests this level of intensity, especially when an *industrious* student, Choice (D), will achieve the same grades without the extra emotional charge. *Industrious* is the best choice.

138. **B. bifurcated; F. pugnacious**

To find the correct answers, look at the sentence as a whole. Starting with the last part, you know that the second word must be different from the unified peaceful movement it was before. *Purposive* and *tractable,* Choices (D) and (E), are positive attributes, which would likely be in line with the previous state of things. However, *pugnacious,* or aggressive, Choice (F), is the antithesis of peaceful.

You also know that the word in the first blank led to the two different factions. *Disseminate,* Choice (A), refers to breaking down information for distribution, and *amassed,* Choice (C), would indicate making the resistance larger. Neither term fits the meaning. Only *bifurcate,* Choice (B), means to separate, which is what the organization did to create two distinct groups.

139.   **A. desiccate; E. injurious**

Kindling is a bunch of small, dry twigs people use to start campfires. If the Christmas tree is now good kindling, it must be dry. The tree was allowed to dry out, which is the meaning of the word needed for the first blank. Both *evanesce* and *wane,* Choices (B) and (C), describe a state of diminishing; only *desiccate,* Choice (A), points to dehydration.

The incidents mentioned are the 200 home fires, so they would be neither *innocuous* nor *harmless,* Choices (D) and (F). They do cause damage and potential injury, so *injurious,* Choice (E), makes sense.

140.   **B. obsequious; D. nobility**

The term "nauseatingly" suggests that these assistants behave in a manner that is unflattering to their characters. *Tentative,* Choice (A), does not fit the scope. Both *obsequious* and *unctuous,* Choices (B) and (C), describe unsavory behavior, but *unctuous,* or groveling, is a bit stronger than the information suggests. *Obsequious,* which means fawning, is more in line with the sentence.

If they fawn over the pop star, then there isn't much dignity, or *nobility,* Choice (D), in their positions. The assistants are not humiliated, so their position doesn't provoke *ignominy,* Choice (E), or they would not look down on others. Their positions don't entail much *rectitude* (morality), Choice (F), either.

141.   **C. menaces; D. decimation; I. imperiled**

Try to fill in the blanks with your own words first. You can predict that the word for the first blank is something harmful because the word "although" at the beginning of the sentence signifies something opposite of "vital." Both *delinquents* and *traitors,* Choices (A) and (B), are negative characteristics, but neither is harmful by nature. Only *menaces,* Choice (C), carries the intention to inflict harm.

The second and third blanks are related by the "because of" preposition linking the two words. You can guess that both blanks are also negatively charged based on the conjunction "yet." Despite the vital support of bees in farming, the food supply isn't being helped. Looking at the choices for the third blank, *abolished,* Choice (G), means destroyed or gone, which is too strong for this context. *Preserved,* Choice (H), is positive, so only *imperiled* (placed into danger), Choice (I), serves the context.

The second blank is the cause of the third blank; thus, *phylogeny* (the history of a species), Choice (E), doesn't make sense. *Reversion,* Choice (F), is a change in a population, but *decimation,* Choice (D), meaning a drastic reduction in number, has the desired effect.

142. **B. coalesce; D. burden; G. impeded**

The remaining schools were still functional, so the closed schools didn't *separate* from them, as Choice (C) suggests, but rather joined them. *Coalesce*, Choice (B), signifies the union of two things, which fits. *Secede*, Choice (A), is out of scope.

The overcrowding of students at the remaining schools caused them to use more resources, so the joining of the schools wasn't a *benefit*, Choice (F). Nothing suggests the schools were *obstructed* from the resources, as Choice (E) would indicate, but an overusage would be a *burden*, Choice (D).

Because the students lived so far from their new schools, they couldn't afford to miss the bus, which meant they couldn't participate in after-school activities. Choice (H), *improved*, does not fit this context. There is no indication that these students participated in after-school activities later, so Choice (I), *postponed*, doesn't fit. Thus, the distance hindered, or *impeded*, their ability, Choice (G).

143. **C. arbitrary; D. teeming; H. preference**

If each team had the same chance, then the assignment of players would not be *imbalanced*, Choice (B). It would be without intention, or random. *Irrational*, Choice (A), is out of scope, but *arbitrary*, Choice (C), means random.

However, despite this arbitrary assignment, one team always ended up with the best players. That team would not be *vacant* of the best players, and having those players wouldn't likely be a burden, so you wouldn't say the team was *laden* (bogged down) with the best players. Thus, you can rule out Choices (E) and (F), respectively. *Teeming* (containing a large quantity), Choice (D), fits.

Finally, the parents didn't believe that the best players could accidentally end up on the same team, so they suspected foul play. They would not assume that *neutrality* or *justice*, Choice (G) or (I), was at play, so *preference*, Choice (H), must have been shown.

144. **C. stasis; E. impetuous; I. prejudiced**

What would make Stacy impatient? The wait, or *stasis* (lack of action), Choice (C). *Headway*, Choice (B), would mean developments were happening, and *inertia* (unwillingness to act), Choice (A), is out of scope.

Because of her impatience, she rashly called the manager, which infuriated him and biased him against choosing her. These are the meanings necessary for the other two blanks. The discussion on the phone could have been *adlibbed*, Choice (D), but this term does not fit the action of making the call, and *premeditated*, Choice (F), is an opposite of what you're looking for. *Impetuous* (impulsive), Choice (E), fits.

Predisposed, Choice (G), doesn't fit the third blank because the manager was likely still considering Stacy until the phone call. He could have changed his mind, so he was not *confined*, Choice (H), against her. *Prejudiced*, Choice (I), fits.

145. **A. evanescent; E. perpetual; I. quell**

Cuts and bruises, by nature, are temporary, so you know the term needed in the first blank means temporary. The use of "but" tells you the second blank means the opposite of temporary. *Succinct*, Choice (B), does mean brief, but it doesn't fit the context. *Everlasting*, Choice (C), is the opposite of temporary, but *evanescent*, Choice (A), is synonymous, and therefore fits.

Contrarily, *relenting,* Choice (D), is the opposite of continual. *Procuring,* Choice (F), is out of scope, but *perpetual,* Choice (E), means lasting, which fits.

The term needed in the last blank signifies Justin's parents' desire for him to overcome his fear. *Annihilate,* Choice (G), is too severe, and *motivate,* Choice (H), is the opposite of what is wanted. *Quell,* Choice (I), means to allay fears, which fits.

146.   **C. bemoaned; E. astounding; I. amplified**

The loss would make Thom feel negative, so he wouldn't *rejoice,* Choice (B). He probably wouldn't *gloat* about a loss, either, so Choice (A) is also out. *Bemoaned,* Choice (C), is another way of saying mourned, which one would do after a significant loss.

The grief was so severe because of the shock of the loss, having never lost before this game. The loss would not be considered *sensational,* Choice (F), and nothing suggests there was anything *debauched* (unsavory) about the loss, so Choice (D) doesn't work either. It was simply *astounding* (surprising), Choice (E).

The victory decorations would be a hurtful reminder of the loss after the game. *Defended* and *disregarded,* Choices (G) and (H), don't make sense in this context, but *amplified,* Choice (I), signifies an increase of Thom's anguish.

147.   **A. impervious; F. subdued; H. credence**

The word "despite" tells you that Millie was not affected by John's advances toward her. *Compliant,* Choice (B), is the opposite of this, and nothing about her inaction suggests that she was *disloyal,* Choice (C). *Impervious,* Choice (A), signifies a state of being unmoved by another's sentiments or opinions. The only reason she acted this way was that she didn't feel as strongly for him as he did for her (second blank) and didn't want to give him hope (third blank).

Her feelings were not *unreceptive,* because she did like John, but not in a *considerable* way, so you can rule out Choices (D) and (E), respectively. Her feelings were more *subdued* than his were, Choice (F).

Skepticism, Choice (G), is out of scope in this context, and although John may have shown *tenacity* (persistence) in his feelings, Choice (I), Millie couldn't give that to him. However, if she gave his feelings *credence* (validity), Choice (H), he might develop hope.

148.   **A. venerate; D. invectives; G. wield their power**

The clue in this passage is "turn popular opinion away," which tells you that the second blank is a negative term. If the second blank is negative, the first blank must be positive. *Spurn,* Choice (C), means to reject, which is negative and opposite. *Summon,* Choice (B), is out of scope. *Venerate,* Choice (A), means to show profound respect, which is positive.

Invectives, Choice (D), are violent words used to attack, which fits. *Panegyrics,* Choice (E), means praises, which is an opposite of the meaning you want. *Liabilities,* Choice (F), is out of scope for the context.

The third blank follows the sentence logically. There is no mention of *weapons,* and the paparazzi are not acting with *benevolence* (kindness), so Choices (H) and (I) don't work. The paparazzi *wield their power,* Choice (G), which relates back to the phrase "make or break a celebrity's career."

149. **B. precipitated; E. pervasive; H. abated**

Before the attack, the U.S. "only" gave aid, which means the attack led to its full participation. *Encumbered,* Choice (A), is the opposite of causation, and *abridged,* Choice (C), doesn't fit the scope. *Precipitated,* Choice (B), means initiated something quickly, which fits.

The opinions of the people kept the government from intervening, so they must have been widespread and strong. *Inescapable,* Choice (D), is too severe, and nothing suggests the sentiment was *gratuitous* (unnecessary), Choice (F). *Pervasive,* Choice (E), means present throughout, which fits the meaning.

So, if the initial sentiment was not to intervene, then the "however" signifies that the sentiment now supports intervening. *Besmirched,* Choice (G), is out of scope. Nothing suggests the initial sentiment was the correct one, so *warped,* Choice (I), is too severe. *Abated,* Choice (H), means to lessen, which fits.

150. **A. Spartan; D. stalwart; H. philanthropy**

If Gandhi practiced nonviolent protests, it doesn't follow that he was a *brute* or a *warrior,* as Choices (B) and (C) suggest. A *Spartan,* Choice (A), is someone who shows discipline and frugality in his actions, which is further expressed by "modest living."

Gandhi's *Spartan* nature lent him strength when faced with adversity. Both *biddable* and *pusillanimous,* Choices (E) and (F), describe characters that are easily broken or weakened. *Stalwart,* Choice (D), represents determination, which fits.

All of these admirable attributes toward the betterment of humanity have made Gandhi a symbol of social consciousness, not *belligerence* (hostility), Choice (G). Gandhi may have been *affable,* Choice (I), but that word doesn't efficiently describe his character or contribution to history. *Philanthropy,* Choice (H), refers to the betterment of humanity, which fits.

151. **D. "The Motivating Factors of Whale Migration Activities"**

Although many of the answer choices provide titles that match part of the passage, the passage discusses more than the courting rituals and the breeding grounds, as suggested by Choice (A), "*Courting Rituals of the Humpback Whale,*" and Choice (B), "*Popular Breeding Grounds for Different Whale Species.*" The passage never states that the journey is treacherous, just competitive and enduring, which rules out Choice (C), "*To Alaska and Back: The Treacherous Journey of the Whale.*" Choice (E), "*Great Place to Whale Watch,*" is out of scope; thus, Choice (D), "*The Motivating Factors of Whale Migration Activities,*" is the only title that encompasses all the factors of the humpback whale discussed in the passage.

152. **A. To attract the attention of female whales; C. To make a stand against other whales in the pod**

In the last sentence of the first paragraph, the passage provides three possible reasons behind the breaching action of male whales: assertions of dominance, warnings to other whales in the pod, or as a form of courting. Choices (A) and (C) both paraphrase one of these reasons. The passage never states breathing as a motivating factor, so you can rule out Choice (B), *to take a breath of air.*

153. **B. To express the intense nature of competition between male whales**

Looking at the line preceding the description of the birthing process gives a clue to this answer. The author discusses the race to track a female whale and breed with her. Stating the frequency and gestation cycle of the female directly after this information serves to provide a frame of reference for the urgency the male whales may be feeling during their migration. Only Choice (B) exemplifies this idea.

154. **B. Theodor Adorno was a progressive philosopher whose ideas challenged the fabric of global society and economic policies.**

The main idea of the passage includes the intention of the author and the various topics discussed regarding the main subject, Adorno. Music and Marxism are only parts of Adorno's life presented in the passage. The author points to both as driving forces behind Adorno's actions, but neither is the main focus. The author uses the elements of music and Marxism as motivators for Adorno's main theory, that social phenomena, such as media and the division of equities, is based on the economic motivations of the dominant class. Choice (B) describes that theory nicely, so that is one option. Choice (E), *even famous members of the Jewish faith were persecuted by the Nazis in Germany,* is only briefly mentioned in the passage. Thus, Choice B is the best answer.

155. **E. signifying individual thought beyond the collective ideals of society.**

The last sentence in the third paragraph states that Adorno began to purport art as an embodiment of the subjective and divergent characteristics that challenge the dominance of society. Looking at the choices, the concept of *individual thought transpiring beyond the collective ideals of society* represents that idea well, so Choice (E) is a possible option. Choice (A), *not being significant in the context of social action,* is the opposite of this idea, as is Choice (C), *a hindrance to the growth of social capital.* The *civil rights movement,* Choice (D), was only a small part of the passage and is unrelated to the previously mentioned idea. Whereas Choice (B), *the only logical connection between a free society and governmental law,* may seem tempting, that idea is not outwardly stated in the passage, just inferred, and the question is not asking for an inference. Choice (E) is the best answer.

156. **B. He argued that popular media is shaped by cultural industry to sustain the dominance of the capitalism and social inequality.**

What you are looking for is the statement that serves as evidence for Adorno's idea about the relationship between media and class structure. Choice (A), *the basis for much of Adorno's argument stemmed from this concept of standardization of society through the delineation of thought through economic growth and uniform conceptualization of mass media,* discusses the uniform conceptualization of the media, but it doesn't specifically relate it to class structure. Choice (C), *in keeping the population passive, social media is able to conjure the false sensation of needs in a culture, diverting any free thought of what exists outside of those needs,* discusses the media, but it does so in relation to free-thinking, not class structure. Choice (D), *in this way, socialist theories are expunged, and economic production is able to continue its reign as the predominant effort of the culture,* explains the aftermath of using media to maintain class structure, so it is one step beyond what you are looking for. Only Choice (B) provides an explanation of his theory regarding media as a tool of the dominating class.

157.

A. They saw his lack of actions against the oppressive laws of segregation as a symbol of his concession.

The passage states that Adorno's lack of action regarding political protests is what turned his students against him. Choices (B), (C), (D), and (E) — *they felt supported by his philosophies and actions toward equality, they thought his philosophies further supported the segregation of races, they were pleased with the manner in which Adorno spoke out and rallied against segregation,* and *they were finally able to generate enough support to expose Adorno's negative policies,* respectively — all describe a positive attitude of the students, which is clearly not indicated by the passage. Only Choice (A) supports the negative opinion of Adorno the students developed after what they perceived to be *a lack of action.*

158.

D. Because his appreciation for creative works was a contributing factor in many of his academic theories.

The author discusses Adorno's early academic endeavors in musical composition and how his love and prowess with musical theory "expanded to all forms of art later." The author provides his interests in music as a framework for his later theories regarding the challenging notion of art in society. Choices (A) and (E) — *because it was the driving force in his life to compose the music of his country* and *because philosophy was only a small part of his contributions to the world* — are out of scope of the passage. Choices (B) and (C) — *because he used music to help convince the world of the validity of his theories* and *because he used musical theory to explain his social theories* — both seem to represent this idea, but after a closer look, you can see that both statements focus only on music, not art forms in general. Choice (D) discusses his *appreciation for creative works* in relation to his theories, which encompasses the desired intention of the author well.

159.

D. policymakers.

The article provides information that would be interesting to all of these audiences, but only one group could use the information in the passage in an active way. Choice (C), *land developers,* is tempting, for it would seem that any changes to habitats would involve land; however, in order for land development to happen, policies for why and how to develop the land would first need to be in place. Choice (D) is the logical answer.

160.

C. provide an example of how ecosystems and animal populations change due to predator activity.

The first paragraph discusses the problem with predator populations and the effect their actions have on the ecosystem. The second paragraph uses the circumstances surrounding dingo control in Australia as an example of the possible consequences of disturbing the natural predatory process. The passage never states that the system developed in Australia was fail-proof; in fact, it states the opposite, so Choice (B) — *showcase a fail-proof system of predator management* — is not an option. Nor does it pass judgment on whether the system is flawed or successful, so Choice (D) — *provide an example of how not to manage predatory behavior in Australia* — is incorrect. The passage also never mentions other regions in this paragraph, so Choice (E) — *provide an example of what will happen if other regions do not take the same measures Australia did against the dingoes* — is out of scope. Choice (A) — *highlight the dingo population in Australia* — is clearly wrong, so Choice (C) is the only option that shares the idea of exemplary information.

161.

E. the dingo-proof fences help to protect the livestock, but they create other subsequent negative consequences.

Choices (A) and (C) — *the use of dingo-proof fences is inhumane because dingoes no longer have the food they need to survive* and *dingo-proof fences improved the stability of the sheep-herding industry* — both provide conclusions about the fences made by the author, which is not the case in the passage. The passage also does not provide information that supports the ideas in Choices (B) and (D) — *kangaroos are a bigger problem than dingoes in Australia* and *dingoes don't hunt kangaroos.* Thus, Choice (E) is the only answer that describes the entire discussion of the use of dingo-proof fences in Australia.

162.

A. Because changes to the Earth's physical environment can lead to changes in the synthesis of environmental processes, leading to climate change and other detrimental effects.

The passage states that learning to cohabit with predators could save the ecosystems from *detrimental effects,* such as climate change and environmental instability. Choices (B) and (C) — *because the environment is the most important thing to humankind* and *because ecosystems must remain stagnant so all species are able to thrive* — make assumptions about the environment and ecosystems that the passage does not state outright. Only information in the passage is relevant, unless the question asks for an inference. Choice (D), *because changes in ecosystems lead to changes in how humans manage the environment, which could have detrimental effects on animal populations,* goes too far to include the actions of humans, which were not mentioned in the text. Choice (E), *because top predators rely on the ecosystems to find their prey,* is out of scope. Only Choice (A) discusses the changes to ecosystems in relation to environmental processes.

163.

A. It highlights his accomplishments as an athlete.

If the main point of the passage was only that Lewis was a star athlete, then Choice (B), *it describes the main point of the passage,* would be correct. But the passage is about his attitude and standing in popular opinion, as well as his athletic accomplishments. Choice (C), *it shows the reader what his childhood was like,* would be a good answer if the question was regarding the second paragraph. Choices (D) and (E), *it proves that he was an Olympic champion* and *it shows how his attitude changed with his success,* are not mentioned in the third paragraph. Thus, Choice (A) is the only answer that represents the information about his success as a collegiate athlete.

164.

C. His confidence in his natural talent and his rising popularity left a feeling in society that he was an arrogant and self-serving athlete.

This question is asking for the motivation behind why the public turned against Lewis. Choice (A), *Lewis's trouble with his public image started shortly before the 1984 Olympic Games,* simply states that his public image was in trouble, but it does not provide a reason. Choice (B), *as a star collegiate athlete, he had received sponsorship from Nike while still in school,* sets the stage for what his image was before the trouble. Choice (D), *the backlash from this image was a lack of corporate sponsorship, which anyone else undoubtedly would have received after winning four gold medals,* describes the backlash of his negative public image. Choice (E), *Lewis also became unpopular with his teammates because of his condemnation of those who used performance-enhancing drugs,* is a tempting choice, but this sentence discusses his image with his team, not the public. Only Choice (C) shows how his confidence led the public to deem him arrogant, which is a good representation of a motivation.

165.

A. They felt he was not a team player; C. They resented his judgments about their drug use.

The passage states that Lewis was viewed as only being out for himself in the 1984 Olympic Games and that he condemned his teammates who used performance-enhancing drugs. The passage never states whether his teammates resented his success, Choice (B), but Choices (A) and (C) both represent the preceding facts from the passage. Both choices are correct.

166.

B. Because it signifies the adversity he overcame

The author mentions Lewis's growth spurt as a way to introduce the idea that he was moderately disabled for a period as a child. This reality surely was a difficult situation for Lewis, and the fact that he became such an accomplished athlete despite his adolescent physical development signifies his ability to overcome his early adverse circumstances. Whereas Choice (E), *because it was hard on him and his family,* is likely correct in reality, it is not the reason the author mentions the growth spurt. Choices (A), (C), and (D) — *because it caused him to run funny, because he thought he would never be able to run,* and *because it caused him to struggle as an athlete,* respectively — make assumptions about the nature of his disability, but these ideas are not expressed in the passage. Only Choice (B) encompasses the intention of the author.

167.

C. informative.

The author doesn't discuss his feelings about Carl Lewis or provide an opinion one way or another about his public image or accomplishments. Thus, you can rule out Choices (A), (B), (D), and (E) — *supportive, judgmental, harried,* and *personal,* respectively. The passage is written in an objective manner, simply providing information. Thus, Choice (C) is the only answer that is supported.

168.

A. Whenever the solar winds combine with atoms in the atmosphere

Choice (B), *every hour,* is clearly wrong. The information in the passage makes it clear that this is not an hourly or even daily event. Choices (C) and (E), *when the sun passes over the magnetosphere* and *only when they are in Canada,* use part of the information given in the passage, but the answers use the information in different contexts than what is provided. Choice (D), *once a month,* is not mentioned at all. The passage does state that the lights appear when solar wind combines with oxygen and nitrogen atoms in the atmosphere. Thus, it can be understood that in order for the lights to appear, this interaction must take place. Choice (A) represents that idea.

169.

E. The northern lights are seen as a tourist attraction.

An inference question asks you to make assumptions based on the information provided. All of the answer choices are false assumptions except for Choice (E). There is no evidence in the passage to support the remoteness of viewing areas, Choice (B), or the influence of weather in Antarctica, Choice (C). Choices (A) and (D) — *it is fairly common for people all over the world to see the northern lights* and *the popularity of the northern lights has been decreasing in recent years* — contradict the information in the passage. But the passage begins by stating that people travel from all over the world, in other words, tourists, to see the lights, which makes it a *tourist attraction.* Choice (E) is correct.

170. **D. the combination of altitude and atmospheric elements**

The passage doesn't mention the speed, the wind, or the haphazard nature of the aurora borealis as reasons why the colors appear, eliminating Choices (B) and (E). Choice (A), *whether there are electrical fields in the atmosphere,* describes a constant occurrence, so this aspect is always true when the lights appear, regardless of color. Choice (C), *the distance from the north pole,* is out of scope. The passage states that the colors change as a result of the altitude and element combination in the atmosphere. Choice (D) is correct.

171. **C. complex.**

Parasites may be thought of in all the terms, but Choices (A), (B), (D), and (E) — *deleterious, endangered, a blight,* and *diseased,* respectively — are not the focus of the passage. The author discusses these characteristics of parasites but also puts forth the idea that they may be beneficial to other organisms. This logic creates a complexity in the function of parasites. Choice (C) is correct.

172. **A. is important in the natural processes of the animal kingdom.**

To answer this question, determine which choice is closest to the information provided. Looking at the adjectives used to describe some of the choices can help you remove them as options. For instance, Choices (A) and (C) describe the actions of parasites as both *vital* and *necessary*, respectively, which are not positions the passage takes. Both Choices (D) and (E) — stating that conservation *should focus on banning scientific experiments using parasites* and *is the responsibility of the American Museum of Natural History,* respectively — are out of scope. Choice (A) describes the importance observed in parasitic involvement in the natural processes of living organisms without asserting it as a requirement. Choice (A) is correct.

173. **B. Maintaining a viable parasite population is important for researching their function in biological processes.**

Choices (A) and (E) introduce ideas about parasite conservation that are not presented in the passage, namely that *parasites are no longer considered disgusting creatures* and *conservation is not a realistic option for parasites.* Choices (C) and (D) twist the information provided into conclusions about parasitic activity *(scientists see parasite activity as groundbreaking for the advancement of disease prevention* and *parasites have the ability to cause the breakdown and extinction of certain biological processes),* but these conclusions are not presented by the author. Only Choice (B) represents the theoretical nature of the discussion of parasitic activity and the possible need for conservation.

174. **B. To support the first statement of the sentence**

The use of "with" after the comma in the sentence containing the information about the 30 types of food lets you know this is additional information pertaining to the discrepancy between the ease of mass producing food and variety in foods. The main point of the passage is beyond simple variety in food, so Choices (A) and (D) — *to contradict the main point of the passage* and *to create a focus in the paragraph* — are incorrect. The sentence in question actually supports the claim in the second sentence of the passage, so Choice (C), *to provide evidence against the second sentence,* is incorrect. No controversy was discussed, so Choice (E), *to add a controversial element,* is out of scope. Choice (B) represents the relationship between the additional information and the first part of the sentence.

175. **C. Whereas the food people ate used to be provided by local farmers and dictated by the seasons, now machines and chemicals are used to create the food feeding more than 95 percent of the world's population.**

Choices (A) and (B) — *the slow food movement isn't just about preserving local foods that are fresh, clean, and humanely acquired* and *it is also about preserving a way of life that is almost obsolete in the heavily industrialized agribusiness of the 20th and 21st centuries* — clearly provide an understanding about what part of the movement is about, but they don't encompass its entire principle. Together, these sentences provide one-half of the ideology of the slow food movement. The answer you're looking for must provide a unified, holistic principle. Choice (D), *variety in foods and flavors has been replaced by ease of mass production as the priority of eating, with just approximately 30 types of food making up a majority of the products sold in America's grocery stores,* is tempting but only gives evidence to support the principle of the slow food movement; it does not represent the principle itself. Only Choice (C) provides the origin of why this movement is deemed necessary.

176. **C. Food prepared using the slow food method is better for the body.**

Choice (A), *6.5 billion people can't be wrong,* uses a statistic from the passage in a false way, and Choice (B) makes an assumption not presented in the passage directly — *abiding by the rules of the movement is more convenient than eating processed foods.* Choice (C) makes an assumption based on the phrases "safe and clean manner" and "negative culture and health effects of industrialized food." Choice (C) is the only correct option.

177. **E. the movement needs to grow significantly to make more of an impact.**

The passage doesn't pass judgment on whether the movement is successful or not, as Choice (A), *the movement is not very successful,* suggests. Choices (B) and (C) inflate the information to create global assumptions — *95 percent of the world's population is unhealthy* and *people don't like variety in their food* — which are not valid conclusions to make from the information provided. Choice (D), *the movement is reaching every facet of the world,* is not a logical assumption; thus, Choice (E) is the only choice that juxtaposes the small movement against the large population of people consuming processed food.

178. **E. "Changing the Global Food Paradigm"**

Choice (B), *"Why Slow Food Is Out of Fashion,"* could be considered tempting if you inferred that because of the high consumption of processed food, slow food is out of fashion. But, still, that would only encompass part of the meaning and would not be a representative title. Choice (D), *"The Popularity of the Slow Food Movement,"* is obviously not correct because the small movement wouldn't be considered popular. There is no mention of the movement taking a combative stance, so Choice (A), *"The War Against Processed Food,"* is out of scope. The movement is about more than growing better food, so Choice (C), *"The Effort to Grow Better Food,"* doesn't encompass the main idea. The aspects of slow food encompass a desire to move away from the current industrialized mode of food production and distribution. Because 95 percent of the world's population exists under this mode, moving to a slow food mode would require a complete reconstruction of how we approach food production, distribution, and consumption, or a shift in *paradigm.* Choice (E) is the correct answer.

179. **B. they could not prove the book did not have literary merit.**

None of the choices provided are represented in the passage except for Choice (B). To prove that the book was in breach of the Obscene Publications Act, the prosecution had to close the loophole of literary merit. Because their witnesses did not provide that information, they were not able to prove that point.

180. **C. It broke down strict moral codes of conduct in society.**

The options listed in Choices (A), (B), and (D) — *Penguin became the largest publisher in the world, the victory over the crown of England was the first ever,* and *the Obscene Publications Act was denounced* — are not mentioned in the passage. Whereas the ruling may have paved the way for books such as *Fifty Shades of Grey,* Choice (E), that is not the main impact the author discusses. Only Choice (C) exemplifies the policy and cultural changes that occurred as a result of the trial outcome.

181. **A. The sentiment in society before the book's publication strictly prohibited indecent behavior.**

When the book was first published, it was denounced for its lewd and salacious material, which was controversial during a time when puritan and proper moral ideologies were the norm. Choice (A) signifies this idea well. Choices (B) and (C) — *people were less polite after the book was published* and *the book fell from the bestseller's list* — are not supported in the text. Choice (D), *society was boorish and promiscuous before the book was published,* is opposite of what society was like during the time of publication. There is no evidence that the Obscene Publication Act was a response to the book's publishing, as Choice (E) indicates. Choice (A) is correct.

182. **B. For helping to overturn censorship laws; C. For initiating a movement toward a more liberal view of sexuality**

The era that was shepherded in after the trial saw a renouncing of old moral values and a manifestation of more sexual freedom and open-mindedness. Behavior was no longer mandated by cultural laws. Both Choices (B) and (C) express these ideas. The book was already published at the time of trial, so Choice (A), *for allowing the book to be published,* is out of scope.

183. **E. intrigued by the trial's impact on society.**

By looking at the adjectives used to describe each answer choice, you can determine which answer is correct. The author goes beyond simply providing information or expressing scholarly interest as Choice (D) suggests. However, the tone is not *amazed, excited,* or *annoyed,* as Choices (A), (B), and (C) suggest. The author seems to be intrigued by the series of events surrounding the court trial. Choice (E) is correct.

184. **D. Never**

The point the author is making in the passage is that the zombie apocalypse is a metaphor for other possible realistic atrocities. Therefore, any answer choice that provides a time frame is incorrect, which is all but Choice (D).

185. **A. skeptical that it will happen.**

The author believes the apocalypse is people's way of putting a face on an unknown fear of natural or biological disasters, so he is not *concerned, fearful of zombies,* or *bleak about the prospects of survival,* as Choices (B), (C), and (D) indicate, respectively. Although he does suggest that people are using zombies to channel their fears about other catastrophes, he doesn't *mock* them, Choice (D). He is merely *skeptical* of the entire scenario; thus, Choice (A) is correct.

186. **C. It provides a theory about the fascination with the zombie apocalypse.**

The first two paragraphs describe the zombie craze and the idea of an apocalypse. The third paragraph provides that author's theory of why this craze started. Although the paragraph does mention the author's opinion, it doesn't discuss the CDC, so Choice (E), *it provides the author's opinion about the CDC,* is incorrect. That fact also removes Choices (B) and (D) — *it places blame on the CDC for the apocalypse* and *it synthesizes the research from the CDC and the* Huffington Post. Choice (A), *it provides evidence to support the existence of zombies,* is the opposite of what the author is saying, so Choice (C) remains the best answer.

187. **D. "Society's Fear and Fascination with Zombies"**

All of the choices except for Choice (E), "*The Causes of the Zombie Apocalypse,*" which are not provided in the passage, express some point brought up in the passage — Choice (A), "*Preparing for the Zombie Apocalypse*"; Choice (B), "*How to Prevent the Zombie Apocalypse*"; Choice (C), "*When Zombies Come Calling*"; and Choice (D), "*Society's Fear and Fascination with Zombies.*" But the passage in general discusses more than the details of the apocalypse. It also provides suggestions for why society has created this scenario in its global mind. Choice (D) encompasses all ideas put forth in the passage.

188. **C. Because the methods needed to catch the perpetrators may be unconstitutional**

The passage states that staying abreast of these acts before they happen would require surveillance of private communication sources, which may violate civil rights. Choice (C) is the only answer that mentions the questionable constitutionality of that action.

189. **B. Flash mobs only aim to entertain or innocently disrupt the peace momentarily.**

You can take the answer directly from the first paragraph, which states, "What originally started as a funny trend in the early 2000s, with large groups of people congregating to conduct spontaneous dance routines or other disruptive antics. . . ." It is the deviation from this light intention into a more hurtful and damaging intention that differentiates the flash rob from the flash mob. Choices (A) and (E) — *flash mobs cause the destruction of property* and *flash robs started before flash mobs* — distort the facts from the passage, and Choice (D), *there is no difference,* is clearly wrong. Choice (C), *flash robs are organized by career criminals,* seems logical, but the passage states that teens are the likely culprits; it's not likely that a teen would be considered a career criminal yet. Choice (B) indicates the benign nature of the flash mob, which is contradicted in the passage by describing the violence conducted by flash robs.

190.

E. Flash robs only occur in the evenings.

Choice (A), *the police use secret technologies to track videos of flash robs in action,* is out of scope in relation to the curfew, so it can be removed as an option. If the scenarios in Choices (B), (C), and (D) were legitimate — *parents are able to override the curfew if they see fit, both adults and teens organize flash robs,* and *the curfew is only for teens with previous records,* respectively — the curfew would only reach a certain number of people, so the incidents could likely continue to occur. Only Choice (E) removes all possibilities of flash robs happening because the curfew time would correspond with the time of the incidents.

191.

B. The need for social workers in the health arena is largely due to the diverse demographics of patients requiring services.

Many of the answer choices contain accurate statements or may even seem true based on the passage, but the main idea must encompass the entire passage, not just one aspect. Use the process of elimination to reveal the correct choice. First, look at Choice (A): *Social workers are vital to the healthcare field to help immigrants sign up for insurance under the Affordable Care Act.* Although this action is part of what health social workers will do, it isn't what the passage is about. Choice (C) also presents an idea suggested in the passage, *the immigrant population in the United States is just as big as it was in the early 20th century,* but it doesn't represent what the rest of the passage expresses. Choices (D) and (E) are out of scope: Choice D, *social workers should be providing more services to immigrants who are unable to receive health insurance,* is a judgment that isn't made in the passage, and Choice (E), *the problem with healthcare today is the same as it was in the early 1900s, despite the new Affordable Care Act,* is wrong because this doesn't address the entire passage. However, population diversity is discussed in both the founding and current scenarios of health social work, and Choice (B) fits this idea nicely.

192.

B. To express the similarities between the need for social work in the medical arena then and now; C. To draw attention to the characteristics of the population still experiencing a lack in health services in the current society

Choice (A), *to point out how people without health insurance are living in the same circumstances as the immigrants from Ellis Island,* takes various parts of the passage and puts them together in an illogical way. The passage doesn't mention health insurance in connection with Ellis Island, and the circumstances in today's world aren't paralleled to those in the tenement districts in New York. Therefore, Choice (A) is wrong.

Choice (B) makes a logical interpretation. The passage does state that the need for social work in hospitals came from an increased population of diverse cultures and languages, and it states that increasing immigration populations is one of the biggest challenges for the Affordable Care Act. Choice (B) is correct.

Choice (C) makes an interesting inference. The passage does point out a lack of coverage for a large number of immigrants and individuals from lower demographics, and the sentence is comparing that population with the immigrants from Ellis Island. Choice (C) is also correct.

193. B. Despite changes in the health care system, social work has stayed true to its founding principles.

You can eliminate Choices (A) and (D) immediately because these claims — *without the Affordable Care Act, there would be no social work* and *the history of social work is more important than what is happening today with best practices* — aren't expressed in the passage.

Choice (B) represents an idea provided in the last paragraph of the passage concerning challenges and focus. This choice has direct evidence in the passage and is a likely choice, but look at the remaining choices before you decide.

Choice (C), *social work has made it possible for immigrants and impoverished individuals to receive the care they need,* takes the idea of helping immigrants and lower demographic populations communicate with physicians and have better access to healthcare too far.

Choice (E), *social work has not changed since the first social worker was introduced into the hospital setting,* is a trap. Many references to similarities between "then" and "now" may seem like social work hasn't changed. However, the essay states only that the "preliminary focus" is the same, not the discipline. Therefore, this choice differs from Choice (B) in that the principles haven't changed, but the nature of the work has changed as society has. Choice (B) is correct.

194. D. Because of the Affordable Care Act, health social workers will find themselves needed in ways similar to those of their founding members.

Although most of the answer choices may represent one part of the author's attitude, the question asks for the best choice. Choices (A) and (B) — *the Affordable Care Act was important for revealing a pattern in the healthcare system* and *more jobs will be available to health social workers thanks to the Affordable Care Act* — are alluded to in the passage, but they point out only one minor reflection and are, thus, wrong. Choice (C), *the Affordable Care Act provides an opportunity for health social workers to get back to their roots,* is vague in meaning and isn't a sentiment expressed in the passage. Choice (E) is an opinion that was never provided in the passage — *the Affordable Care Act is only worthwhile if health social workers are involved* — and is, thus, out of scope. Choice (D) takes the information provided in the first paragraph and paraphrases it, so it's the correct choice.

195. D. Social workers will be vital to integrate and coordinate care to improve patient experiences and liaise with hospitals and physicians.

This question may seem tricky at first, but look carefully at what it's asking. Choice (A) — *Specific actions by the government created a system of increasing costs for healthcare in the 1960s that remains the current trend and hinders the ability of social workers to adequately represent their clients* — and Choice (B) — *However, with the Affordable Care Act, vast areas of potential benefit for social workers exist* — do not actually explain why social workers will be important under the Affordable Care Act. Choice (C) — *A staggering 21 million individuals are projected to remain uninsured under the Act by 2015 due to their undocumented status and the barriers involved in purchasing insurance under the new coverage exchanges* — does not mention social workers at all. Choice (D) is the only one that points out exactly how health social workers will be involved. The word *vital* is the key word in this sentence.

196. **E. webmasters figure out how to manipulate the search engine to inflate their ranking.**

The passage states that search engine companies are continuously updating their algorithms, a practice that started after discovering falsely inflated pages. Thus, Choice (A), *it is standard practice,* might be tempting, but the root of the issue began with Choice (E), *webmasters figure out how to manipulate the search engine to inflate their ranking.* Choices (B) and (C) — *the algorithms expire after every few years and must be updated* and *viruses cause the linking mechanism of the algorithms to fail* — are out of scope. Choice (D), *it blocks webmasters from SEO practices,* is the opposite of what search engine companies desire, as exemplified in the last sentence of the passage. Choice (E) is correct.

197. **A. supportive of the practice.**

The author mentions the usefulness and competitive edge SEO provides to companies. The author also uses disparaging remarks when discussing those who try to manipulate SEO. Thus, it can be assumed that the author is in support of fair SEO practices. There is nothing in the passage to suggest he is *distant*, Choice (B), or *bitter*, Choice (C). Choice (D), *excited,* is too extreme, and Choice (E), *uninformed,* is obviously wrong considering the amount of detail in the passage. Choice (A) is the only choice that works and is therefore correct.

198. **B. the efficiency and process involved in search engine optimization.**

The passage doesn't pass any judgment or provide any *pros or cons* about SEO, Choice (A), nor does it provide a ranking of *search engines*, Choice (C). The passage is not a *how to*, so Choice (D) is excluded. Although *unethical practices of webmasters,* Choice (E), are mentioned in the text, this topic does not comprise the main idea. Only Choice (B) provides a general overview of the passage. Choice (B) is the correct answer.

199. **C. Creating a positive relationship with webmasters supports both entities in positive ways**

It is clear from the passage that Choices (A) and (E) — *they create algorithms that allow webmasters to monopolize most of the Internet traffic* and *they manipulate the Internet to make it more difficult for SEO to work* — are opposite of why search engines create algorithms. The last sentence in the passage dismisses the idea in Choice (B), *they are highly competitive with SEO practitioners.* Choice (D), *there are only three search engines left,* is not relevant or mentioned in the text. Thus, Choice (C) is the only inference that makes sense based on the passage, especially the last sentence. Choice (C) is the correct answer.

200. **A. Many companies now hire people skilled solely in this task.**

All of the phrases provide information about SEO, but only Choice (A) mentions the result of the importance of SEO for businesses. Choice (A) is correct.

201. **C. "Creating Your Best Space with Feng Shui"**

What is the passage discussing? The passage discusses the low acceptance rate of Feng Shui as a legitimate practice in modern society. Thus, you can assume a *boom* hasn't happened, Choice (A). Yet, the author doesn't state that Feng Shui is not revered by some, so it would not be considered a *lost art*, Choice (B). There are no instructions about how to Feng Shui, just information, so Choices (D) and (E) — "*Dos and Don'ts of Feng Shui*" and "*How to Create Qi in the Home*" — are out of scope. Choice (C) provides a title that encompasses the ideas presented. Choice (C) is correct.

202. **D. promotional.**

Although the author doesn't explicitly come out and say it, the last paragraph provides the information in a "what if" context, which gives a tone of *promoting* the practice, as does the conversation regarding the importance of finding the right energy for your home. Choices (A), *aloof;* (B), *forceful;* (C), *pushy;* and (E) *defeated* are out of scope of the passage. Choice (D) is correct.

203. **E. describe the factors involved in true Feng Shui.**

The third paragraph discusses the important elements related to creating good Feng Shui in the home, starting with discovering the Qi. Choice (C), criticizing people who don't believe in Feng Shui, is not presented in the passage, so this choice can be excluded. Choice (A), providing a history of Feng Shui, comes earlier in the passage, not in the paragraph in question. Choices (B) and (D), determining which fabrics best suit you and finding the most Qi in your home, are both mentioned in this paragraph, but they do not represent the primary function. The purpose of all the details in this paragraph is to provide a description of what is involved in creating true Feng Shui in the home, Choice (E). Therefore, Choice (E) is correct.

204. **D. understanding the relationship between space and energy could lead to appropriate design of city structures and grounds.**

Choices (A) and (C) — *schools would serve students better if they were located closer to hospitals* and *certain colors should be used for certain types of buildings* — might be part of what good Feng Shui would mean in a city environment, but they are too specific and narrow to be the overall benefit. Likewise, Choices (B) and (E) — *everybody should understand Feng Shui* and *Qi exists everywhere and can be used for great things* — may be true, but they do not represent the ultimate benefit to planners. Only Choice (D) provides the general idea of why city planners might benefit from *understanding* Feng Shui principles. Choice (D) is the correct answer.

205. **A. How your Qi works with the environmental Qi; B. What colors support your Qi; C. Where your Qi is strongest**

The third paragraph discusses the most important aspect of Feng Shui, which is discovering your Qi. The passage then states that all other choices can be made in an informed way once the Qi has been determined. Thus, all three choices are represented in the passage and are correct.

206. **B. He created structures that mimicked the natural world.**

The second paragraph provides information that opposes Choice (A), *he partitioned rooms into separate entities,* as does the third paragraph with Choice (C), *he thought natural light distorted open spaces.* Choice (B) is supported by information in the third paragraph, so this is the only correct choice.

207. **A. His work has influenced how people think about form and function.**

The last sentence of the passage states what Wright's influence is on modern architecture and practitioners. The other choices may be accurate statements, excluding Choice (B), *more people are now creating more natural light in their homes,* but the main influence was his theories on *form and function,* Choice (A). Choice (A) is correct.

208. **B. informing about Wright's past and growth as an architect.**

None of Wright's buildings are mentioned in the passage, so Choice (A), *showcasing the popular buildings Wright designed,* is wrong. Choices (C), (D), and (E) — *Wright's passion for the environment, Wright's life on the family farm,* and *the number of buildings Wright constructed,* respectively — are all mentioned in the text, but they are only small pieces of Wright's life. Choice (B) provides the general idea behind the information in the passage and is correct.

209. **D. Very successful**

The beginning of the passage states that Wright constructed more than 500 structures. Although that number is half of those he designed, it is still a considerable number. Thus, he was very successful at constructing his designs. Choice (D) is the correct answer.

210. **B. Wright believed that form and function were a single entity and space was something to be honored, not partitioned.**

Choices (A), (C), and (E) — *the prowess and vision Wright had for creating grand structures,* students and practitioners attempting *to emulate his style,* and the fact that he experienced *his first taste of structural design on his family farm* — all provide one aspect of Wright's vision or influence, but they do not touch on the underlying theory behind his vision. Choice (D), *his sentimentality came through, displaying a disdain for urban sprawl and a love of the natural environment,* may be tempting because it describes part of his aesthetic, but it is still not representative of the theory. Only Choice (B) provides the theory behind his architectural decisions. Choice (B) is the correct answer.

211. **D. he had hit his creative plateau.**

To find this answer, you must look at the part of the passage discussing Dr. John's albums. The phrase "a dearth of music production" signifies the point where he stopped creating music. The sentence preceding that phrase describes his inability to move past his creative peak. Thus, Choice (D) expresses this idea well. Although he was in trouble with the law, Choice (A), and lost his ability to play guitar, Choice (E), these are not reasons he stopped producing albums. Further, nothing in the passage suggests that he preferred commercials, Choice (B), or producing other people's music more than his own, Choice (C). Choice (D) is correct.

212. **B. Because he found a way to use his talents to remain relevant as an artist.**

The answer to this question is about the larger scope of the passage, because the opening paragraph sets up this idea of his success as a main topic. Choices (A), (C), and (E) — *because his style was unique from other styles of his time, because other musicians still asked him to play on their tracks,* and *because his first album was a major success,* respectively — are all noted in the passage as being true, but they don't explain his overall success. Although Choice (D), *because he made more money doing commercial voiceovers than selling records,* is tempting, the passage never explicitly states he made more money making commercials, just that he was able to continue to find work down that avenue. Only Choice (B) encompasses all of his abilities as an artist that led to success and is, therefore, correct.

213. A. "Succeeding in the Face of Adversity"

The passage never refers to Dr. John as a poet, so you can exclude Choice (B) as an answer. Although the passage discusses Dr. John's Mardi Gras attire, Choice (C), it is not the main point of the passage, nor is the evolution of New Orleans blues, Choice (E). Choice (D), *"Against All Odds,"* is a bit extreme for the content provided in the passage, but Choice (A) expresses the idea of making the best of a difficult situation, which is what Dr. John did when his albums stopped selling well. Choice (A) is the best answer.

214. E. To improve their endurance and strength

Choices (A) and (B), *to heal from injuries* and *to improve their insulin production,* are true as far as what hGH does in the body, but the passage does not state that these are the reasons athletes are using it. The passage clearly states that athletes use hGH to improve their training because of the benefits to stamina and muscular ability. Choice (E) paraphrases this idea well. Choice (C), *because they want to win a medal,* may be true for some athletes, but not all compete in medal games. The passage doesn't mention addiction, so rule out Choice (D). Choice (E) is correct.

215. D. informative.

Although the ending statement may make you think the passage is *cautionary,* Choice (B), when looked at as a whole, the passage is really only providing information about what hGH is and how it functions in the body, Choice (D). Choices (A), (C), and (E), *accusatory, jovial,* and *persuasive,* respectively, are not supported by anything in the passage. Thus, Choice (D) is correct.

216. B. adverse, believing the risks outweigh the benefits.

The statement at the end of the passage is the only sentence where the author deviates from the informative tone of the passage. The opinion given is that hGH ingestion is not worth the negative side effects. Thus, you know that the author's attitude is negative. Choices (A), (C), and (E), *encouraging, neutral,* and *supportive,* respectively, do not express a negative perspective and can be excluded as possibilities. Choice (D), *skeptical,* is a negative emotion, but the author makes a definitive statement and does not express the need for more information. Only Choice (B) states the author's attitude in the last sentence of the passage, and is, therefore, correct.

217. E. highlight the rise and fall of a prosperous avenue for distinction in the black community.

When deciding what the function of a paragraph is, you must look at what role it plays in providing understanding to the reader. The paragraph takes the facts provided in the previous chapters and gives them emotion and shows the significance of this

Answers
201–300

position for the black community. Choice (E) expresses this idea well. Barbering was just one aspect of how black men were able to find work post-slavery, so Choice (B), *summarize the success of the anti-slave movement,* is too extreme. Choices (A) and (C) — *expose the hidden agenda of barbers at the time* and *explain the dangers involved with barbering* — are out of scope. Choice (D), *describe the advent of mustaches in high society,* is not the purpose of the paragraph, despite riding closely to part of the main idea of the passage. Choice (E) is correct.

218. **B. Many were already skilled in the trade from having practiced on their owners as slaves; C. White society felt it was above this type of service position.**

The best way to answer this question is to look for evidence of each answer choice in the passage. For Choice (A), *they surpassed their white counterparts in their skills with straight blades,* the passage states that black men had become skilled with the use of straight blades during their time as slaves. It also states that white men struggled with their own shaving. However, there is no mention of white barbers being less adept at handling the straight blade than black barbers. Choice (A) can be excluded. You already found Choice (B) when searching for Choice (A), so this choice is supported. The last sentence in Paragraph 4 states that white men saw barbering as an inferior position, so Choice (C) is also supported. Both Choices (B) and (C) are correct.

219. **E. They were tired of looking like women.**

Looking for support in the passage for the different choices helps to rule out the one not mentioned. The last paragraph provides information that supports Choices (A), (B), and (C) — *they became intolerant of the daily upkeep of self-barbering, the skills required to use the straight blades were beyond their abilities,* and *facial hair became a symbol of racial dominance* — and the paragraph before it supports Choice (D), *fears of retaliation from black men drove them away from barbershops.* The passage states that men saw their ability to grow facial hair as proof of their difference and dominance over racial groups and women, but it never says they were afraid of looking like women. Choice (E) is not supported, which makes it the correct answer.

220. **C. the history of the trend is a much different reality than the fashionable homage suggests.**

The author is drawing a comparison between today's trend and the past. The final sentence states the conclusion of that comparison: "If the young trendsetters of today understood the legacy they were celebrating, the movement would likely be less popular." None of the answer choices besides Choice (C) refers to this idea. In fact, there is no evidence to support the other choices in the passage. Choice (C) is correct.

221. **A. Paragraph 2**

To find the answer to this question, you must first understand what the main idea of the passage is and what the main idea of each paragraph is. The main idea of the passage is how the history of facial hair trends differs from current motivations for the trend. Paragraph 1, Choice (B), only discusses the current trends in facial hair. Paragraphs 3, 4, and 5, Choices (E), (C), and (D), respectively, discuss the history of barbering and how it changed during the Revolutionary War era. Paragraph 2, Choice (A), expresses the discrepancy between the levity of today's trends with the dark past of facial hair's popularity, which is the main idea. Choice (A) is correct.

222.   **A. the general public.**

Although many of the people mentioned in the choices might be interested in this information, the passage doesn't specify that the content is aimed at a particular group. The passage is informative and general in its discussion, so Choice (A) is the only answer that fits.

223.   **C. Uncommon**

The first sentence of the last paragraph states that cryonics is not taking the world by storm, just that some people are starting to buy into the idea. Thus, Choices (A), (B), and (E) — *about as frequent as death, very common,* and *nonexistent* — are not supported. Choice (D), *common in certain groups,* seems interesting, but the passage doesn't explicitly state that the choice is common with all affluent people. Overall, the process is still a new phenomenon, making it currently *uncommon,* Choice (C). Choice (C) is correct.

224.   **A. untested and far-fetched.**

The author expresses her opinion in the last paragraph in the passage, where she provides information regarding the lack of proof about cryonics success. This idea is included in the term *untested,* Choice (A). Furthermore, the mention of the "sci-fi" nature of the idea in the first paragraph suggests she thinks it is *far-fetched.* Choices (B) and (C), *viable and a good alternative* and *worth the money,* are both opposite of what the last paragraph is stating, and Choices (D) and (E), *dangerous and illegal* and *suspicious and immoral,* are not supported by the passage. Choice (A) is correct.

225.   **C. Cryonics is gaining interest as an alternative to death.**

The passage is about the process and growing popularity of cryonics, especially for people who are financially well off. There is nothing in the passage to suggest that scientists are trying to make the process *cheaper,* Choice (A), or that it is only for *important people,* Choice (E). The last paragraph counters the statements in Choices (B) and (D), *the success of cryonics is indisputable* and *cryonics is a realistic alternative to death,* so Choice (C) is the only answer that comes close to the central idea. Thus, Choice (C) is correct.

226.   **C. Technology**

You can dismiss Choice (D), *better culinary schools,* immediately because culinary schools are not mentioned in the passage. There is also no indication that only *gourmet chefs* can be gastronomes, so Choice (A) is also dismissed. Choices (B) and (E), *gelling agents* and *competition,* are both mentioned in the text, but they are not seen as catalysts to the movement. The first two sentences and the last sentence of the passage support Choice (C), which is correct.

227.   **B. They can become pioneers of innovative techniques rather than part of the pool of talented traditional chefs.**

The part of the passage dealing with aspiring chefs is located in the last paragraph. Looking at the sentence before the one describing the avenue to make a name for themselves, you can see that innovation is what chefs are attempting to achieve, Choice (B), which is why young chefs can make a name for themselves out from under the cloud of so many talented traditional chefs, Choice (A). The other three choices, (C), (D), and (E) — *the public is beginning to demand innovative dishes, traditional styles of cooking are falling out of favor,* and *the practice is relatively uncommon with older chefs, leaving the door open for them* — are all out of scope. Choice (B) is the best answer.

228. **A. prophesize how this form of cooking could affect our culture.**

The author is making a prediction about what the future of eating could look like based on the information given in the passage. Thus, Choice (A) is supported. Because this statement is just a prediction, the author is not attempting to prepare people for anything concrete, as Choice (D), *prepare people for the future,* suggests. Choice (C), *showcase the technology used by gastronomes,* is true for the passage but not for the last sentence. Choices (B) and (E), *dissuade people from trying new foods* and *warn against a movement away from traditional standards,* are not evidenced in the passage. Choice (A) is correct.

229. **E. "The Influence of Science in the Culinary World"**

It is clear from the beginning that Choices (A), (B), and (C) — *"The Outdated Profession of Gourmet Chefs," "Out With the Old and In With Gastronomy,"* and *"How to Turn an Onion into Foam"* — are not adequate representations of what the passage is about. Choice (D), *"The Different Techniques of Molecular Gastronomy,"* is tempting, but techniques are only part of the picture. Choice (E) gives a wider scope of the passage and the connection between the science of molecular gastronomy and the culinary world. Choice (E) is correct.

230. **A. critical.**

Although the author never comes out and says that music pirates are wrong or bad people, the tone of the passage challenges their reasoning and actions. There is no *argument,* so Choice (B) is incorrect. The tone is not *harsh* or mean, so Choice (D) is incorrect. Choices (C) and (E), *passive* and *unaffected,* are not adequate, but the author is pointed about the consequences of music piracy. Thus, he is *critical* of the action. Choice (A) is correct.

231. **B. exposing the problems associated with music piracy.**

Choice (C), defining music piracy, is true for the opening part of the passage, but it is not what is carried through as the main discussion. The author provides an analysis of the negative outcomes associated with file sharing, Choice (B), but she never attempts to provide a solution, Choice (A), or seek to bridge the gap between labels and fans, Choice (D). Choice (E), *explaining how to share music files,* is obviously incorrect. Thus, Choice (B) is the best choice.

232. **B. To point out who is really suffering because of music piracy**

Job losses are presented as one of the main consequences of the music sharing trend. Looking at the passage further, you can see that this statement is countering the statement showing that music fans believe piracy is acceptable because record labels can afford it. Thus, this point about job losses is being made to show how that assumption is incorrect, or, Choice (B), to show *who is really suffering.* Parts of the other choices may ring true, but none of the four answers is supported by the passage. Choice (B) is the correct answer.

233. **C. Their love for music is actually decreasing the ability of musicians to make more.**

The part of the passage discussing this question is at the very end and states that sharing music and destroying the ability for music creation is hypocritical. Looking at the choices, you can see that Choice (C) fits this idea well. The passage doesn't say that jobs are desired, Choice (A), or that certain genres are being hit the hardest, Choice (B). Only Choice (C) is correct.

234. **B. The lasting effects of these losses are layoffs of the subordinate employees working in production or marketing and a lack of new musical talent.**

Figuring out which choice is correct may be a bit difficult if you're not clear what you are looking for. The passage provides many examples of how music piracy affects the music industry, but only one sentence points to the overall consequence when you add these examples together. Choices (A), (C), and (D) — *the people feeling the sting of this loss are the subordinates working in production or marketing and the artists; however, this seemingly liberating move may have done more to destroy the art fans so eagerly celebrated than enhance it;* and *although the belief these dedicated fans have is that the rich labels can handle a loss here or there, what is actually occurring is a gross accumulation of small losses adding up to major economic pitfalls,* respectively — are all tempting because they express part of the problem, but they are too general to serve as the conclusion. Choice (E), *fans were becoming more familiar with digital platforms purported by the growing Internet era,* is not a consequence. Thus, Choice (B) is the only sentence that specifically addresses the end result. The phrase, "The lasting effects," is also a clue. Choice (B) is the correct answer.

235. **A. to improve how society related to black culture.**

Answering this question is as simple as looking at the passage. Only one answer is supported by the information given. The other choices are either assumptions or can be proven wrong. Choice (B), *to replace education with entertainment for America's youth,* is disproven in the first paragraph. Choices (D) and (E), *to portray comedy as a way to make a substantial income* and *to be the most famous black comedian,* make assumptions about Cosby but are not supported by the information. Choice (C), *to push the envelope on race relations,* does discuss his concern with race relations, but the passage doesn't say he wanted to push the envelope. The information only states that he tried to bring awareness and improve the connection between races. Choice (A) is correct.

236. **C. showcase how Cosby changed racial ideologies about black families.**

Right away, Choices (D) and (E) — *attack his obsession with mainstream society* and *exemplify his comedic genius* — are excluded from the choices. Nothing in the passage supports these ideas. The passage does say that he is best known for *The Cosby Show,* but it doesn't say it was his most *notable achievement,* Choice (B). In fact, the passage provides many other achievements in his life that could take that distinction. The passage does *express the popularity of the show,* Choice (A), but that is not the main function. The description of the show highlights how it was the first time an affluent black family was depicted on TV and the way in which people related to them equally. This concept is paraphrased well by Choice (C), making it the correct answer.

237. **B. pioneer.**

All of the choices are mentioned in the passage except for Choice (C), *elitist,* which can be dismissed. The question is which characteristic encompasses all the discussion in the passage. Choices (A), (D), and (E) — *goof, actor,* and *scholar* — make up only part of who Cosby was, but Choice (B), *pioneer,* lends to a greater role achieved through the combination of these characteristics. Thus, Choice (B) is correct.

238. **E. His comedy was accessible to everyone.**

This question is tricky because the answer choices all seem to point to what the question is asking. But, actually, Choices (A) and (C) only express a certain aspect of Cosby's motivation and success — *most of the projects Cosby was famous for were geared toward positive images of African Americans and creating a commonality among families of all races* and *although goofy and lighthearted in character, his savvy business sense and creative vision made him an important player and leader in the social and entertainment spheres,* respectively. Choices (B) and (D) — *his casting to the show was controversial, with certain southern states refusing to run the program because it starred a black character* and *yet, the rest of the nation became loyal fans, and Cosby set the precedent for other black comedians to find the same success in the future* — point to outcomes of certain events during his career. Choice (E) is the only answer that directly expresses why he was able to reach a wide audience and be successful. Choice (E) is correct.

239. **D. He used his multiple skills and talents to help influence social change.**

Inference questions require you to look at the information and form an assumption about what it all means. The best solution is to look at each answer choice separately. Choice (A), *his career suffered because of his fascination with education,* is not supported because there was no mention of Cosby's career suffering when he was in school. Likewise, the author provides information that supports the opposite assumption of what is given in Choice (B), *he was a typical star who sought fame and fortune.* Choices (C) and (E) — *he would have experienced greater success if he had catered to black audiences more* and *he was a better actor than comedian* — could be tricky if you are not careful to examine the evidence well, but when looking at the passage, you can see that these ideas are out of scope of the context. Choice (D) is general enough and in line with the direction of the passage. Choice (D) is correct.

240. **A. To explain how holidays have changed in popular culture**

The author mentions Thanksgiving and Easter as examples of the statement made in the first sentence: "It is not a new trend for holidays to serve as more than just a celebration of the intended meaning of the day." Thus, you are looking for an answer that expresses this idea. Choices (B), (D), and (E) — *because Easter is the holiday that precedes Labor Day, because Easter is almost as popular as Labor Day in the magnitude of celebration,* and *because Labor Day and Easter celebrate the same thing* — are out of scope and false. Choice (C), *to provide an example of a holiday still steeped in tradition,* is the opposite of the meaning you are searching for. Choice (A) expresses the desired idea well. Choice (A) is the correct answer.

241. **C. cynical.**

The author plainly states that the nature of the Labor Day celebration has changed and even goes so far as to give an example of the irony found in forcing people to work on a holiday that is meant to celebrate their efforts. This strong implication is beyond *indifference*, Choice (A), but is not as extreme as being *hateful*, Choice (D). Choices (B) and (E), *excited* and *supportive,* are the opposite of the author's implication. Choice (C) describes the manner in which the author sees the fading of importance for which the holiday was meant. Thus, *cynical*, Choice (C), is the correct answer.

242. **C. provide information about how Labor Day has evolved over time.**

The author doesn't provide a specific intention with the information given in the passage. Although the tone of the passage slants toward the negative, no explicit judgments are made. Thus, Choices (A), (B), and (D) — to *convince retail owners to allow their employees to have time off on Labor Day,* to *criticize society for placing more importance on shopping than honoring the workforce,* and to *show disdain for all holidays* — are out of scope. Choice (E), to *persuade Americans to participate more in parades,* is not supported at all by the passage. Choice (C) expresses the informative nature of the text and is the correct answer.

243. **E. balanced.**

Throughout the passage, the author provides evidence that supports each side of the issue. What is not included is a determination about which side is better. Thus, the only term that describes this objective point of view is *balanced*, Choice (E). Thus, Choice (E) is the correct answer.

244. **C. individuals are accountable for their own drug use.**

Despite staying neutral on the issue of legalization, the author does make a judgment about the individual responsibility in the last sentence. Choice (C) represents this idea well. The other choices are all conclusions relating to the core of the passage, which you already know involves no judgment. Choice (C) is the only viable answer.

245. **D. discussing both sides of the argument.**

The author only provides information about each side of the issue. There is no mention of *support* for either side, Choice (A), or *forming a conclusion* about which side is correct, Choice (B). The precise *dangers* of legal drugs, Choice (C), is mentioned in passing only, and there is no attempt to *persuade* the reader in either direction, Choice (E). The passage merely *shows both sides*, so Choice (D) is correct.

246. **A. Medical marijuana can be used as a front for drug dealing; C. The side effects of marijuana are too dangerous for commercial use.**

When looking at the information given to support the critical side of the argument, the passage expresses how the federal government sees the recreational use and side effects of marijuana use as possible problems involved with legalizing it for medical purposes, Choices (A) and (C), respectively. Choice (B), *the use of marijuana is only necessary in patients who are terminal,* would lean more toward supporting the use, so this choice is incorrect. Both Choices (A) and (C) are correct.

247. **C. cinematic historians.**

The author does not direct this passage toward a specific group or for a specific reason. Rather, the passage discusses the possible theories and trends seen and suggested in *The Shining*. This passage would be of use to someone who is writing a history of cinema in general or a history of this movie. It serves no real benefit to the other categories of people mentioned: *conspiracy theorists,* Choice (A); *students,* Choice (B); *horror novelists,* Choice (D); and *journalists,* Choice (E). Therefore, Choice (C) is correct.

248. **E. It is clear that Kubrick was trying to make a statement with the movie.**

The passage states "what keeps fans buzzing" about *The Shining* is the possible messages Kubrick was sending through the film. Choices (A), (B), and (C) — The Shining *is only as relevant as its theories,* The Shining *was too scary and graphic,* and *it is clear that Kubrick is not the best director of horror films* — are not supported in the passage. Choice (D), The Shining *is just another movie without any special meaning,* is the opposite of what the passage states. However, Choice (E) expresses this buzz and the determination of fans to get to the bottom of the hidden theories. Choice (E) is correct.

249. **B. explain the respect and significance of a popular horror film.**

Before diving into the adamant assertion that *The Shining* contains secret meaning, the author first introduces the film and provides some history about its significance. Choice (B) reflects this idea the best. Choices (A) and (C), *share the results of investigations into the movie's meaning* and *diminish the validity of conspiracy theories,* are not discussed in the passage, and Choice (D), *support the different theories about* The Shining, is too extreme. No *support* is given to any concept. Choice (E), *discuss the plot of* The Shining, seems likely, but the plot is not mentioned, just a few lines about the location and a character in the film. Choice (B) is correct.

250. **D. "Intrigue and Speculation Surrounding *The Shining*"**

What is the passage about? The passage describes the fascination fans of *The Shining* have with the possible hidden meanings the director created through his film. The passage says that the movie is a *cult classic,* Choice (A), and considered by many to be one of the *best horror movies,* Choice (C), but these are not the main points. Choice (C), "*The Best Horror Movie Ever Made,*" is too extreme. Nowhere does the passage state that *Kubrick is better than King,* Choice (B), and the author does not profess to know the *real meaning* of the film, Choice (E). Only Choice (D) provides a general theme for the passage. Therefore Choice (D) is the correct answer.

251. **C. unsympathetic.**

Most of the passage is delivered in an informative tone, with the author simply providing the details of the suit. However, the last paragraph includes a statement about an alternate option to Pearl Jam's problems that puts the responsibility on the band. Thus, you can eliminate all answers that provide other judgments, such as *admiring,* Choice (B), and *irritable,* Choice (D). The author doesn't *compare* anything, so Choice (A) is eliminated. Although the last statement may seem to evoke *skepticism,* Choice (E), there is nothing that explicitly shows the author thinks there is something dubious about the case. However, the author, in pointing out the other option, doesn't seem to be too *sympathetic* to the band's plight; thus, Choice (C) is correct.

252. **A. its ability to forge agreements for performances that smaller companies can't compete with.**

The first sentence of the last paragraph provides the answer to this question. It clearly states that the anti-competitive claim, or the monopolizing action, is in Ticketmaster's ability to do what smaller companies cannot. Choice (A) paraphrases this idea nicely.

253. **D. Thus, if Pearl Jam wanted to support its fans, it always had the option of performing at less grandiose locales than large arenas and concert halls.**

Choice (A) is a sentence describing the band's reason for the suit *(this surcharge, Pearl Jam claimed, took advantage of the fans because there was no competition to keep the level of service fees stable)*, so this choice can be excluded quickly. Choice (B) discusses Ticketmaster's operations rather than Pearl Jam's actions or beliefs *(. . . in a roundabout fashion, the organization of Ticketmaster's operations actually benefited fans more than it hurt them)*. Choice (C) is merely stating why Ticketmaster was able to dominate ticket sales and does not address Pearl Jam's actions or beliefs: *The fact that smaller ticketing agencies do not have the revenue to support venues in this way was where the anti-competitive claim took shape.* Choice (D) suggests an approach that would actually help its fans if Pearl Jam were to comply. However, because the band doesn't, the fans suffer. Choice (D) is correct.

254. **D. Ticketmaster procures big-name concerts that would likely not be possible otherwise.**

The passage states that the critics believe Ticketmaster may benefit fans by supporting the venues in financing the performance. So, you are looking for an answer that matches this idea. Choice (A) makes a judgment call about the extra fees *(Ticketmaster has a right to charge service fees because they are the best at what they do)*, which is not part of the passage. Choices (B) and (C) — *paying a service fee is a small price to pay for convenience* and *the fans are indebted to Ticketmaster, without which no performances would ever happen* — are a bit out of scope. The passage never mentions *convenience* or that the fans are *indebted* to Ticketmaster. *Record sales,* Choice (E), are also not mentioned. However, part of the issue is that smaller companies can't afford to support venues in the same way, and without the support, shows would be cancelled. Thus, Choice (D) emulates this idea and is correct.

255. **C. The band is not able to perform at major venues while keeping ticket prices low.**

As stated at the end, if Pearl Jam wanted to sell tickets without Ticketmaster, it could play at smaller venues. But, the band is too popular for small venues, and would not profit well because of the reduced attendance. Therefore, the problem is that it has to perform at big venues, but it doesn't want fans to have to pay the extra expense. Choices (A) and (D) — *the fans can't afford to attend shows* and *the band is too popular for small venues* — suggest only part of this problem. Choices (B) and (E) — *the band wants part of Ticketmaster's profits* and *the band is not able to form productive relationships with smaller ticketing agencies* — are out of scope of the passage. Choice (C) suggests both aspects of the problem and is correct.

256. **A. The cinematograph was invented; C. Computers improved certain aspects of animation.**

The invention of the cinematograph is presented as a groundbreaking technology that sparked a new approach to animation, so Choice (A) is correct. It might be true that Mickey Mouse became a household name, Choice (B), but the passage does not state this as a factor that influenced the popularity of animation. The last paragraph describes how CGI has changed not only animated films, but living pictures, as well, which expanded the field. Thus, both Choices (A) and (C) are correct.

257. **D. It gives an account of contemporary animation practices.**

The last paragraph describes the use of current CGI animation in modern films of all kinds. The focus is only on contemporary animation. Thus, any choice that hints at the past, Choices (B) and (E) — *it provides a history of animation* and *it compares old technology to new technology* — can be excluded. No opinions were given about contemporary films, ruling out Choices (A) and (C): *it forms an opinion about the quality of today's films* and *it promotes films that use CGI animation.* Thus, Choice (D) is the only choice that simply addresses the information about modern films and is correct.

258. **C. Motion pictures have been improved through the use of animation.**

The strategy here is to find a statement that is valid based on the information in the passage. If you compare the meaning of each statement to the passage, you quickly see that all of the choices besides (C) make statements that are too extreme for what is provided. The author does not make any judgments about motion pictures, so Choices (A) and (D), *motion pictures are better when animation is used* and *animation is the best thing to happen to the cinema,* are out. Nor does it suggest that animation is more popular than living pictures, as Choice (E) indicates: *The animation industry has taken over Hollywood.* Choice (B), *stop-motion animation is antiquated and ineffective,* is out of scope. Thus, it is clear that Choice (C) is correct.

259. **C. show how far animation has come.**

The sentence begins with "A lot has happened" since the flipbook, which gives the impression that the flipbook is the foundation of animation. The rest of the passage describes how animation changed and advanced as a field and art. Thus, it is possible to compare the advances against the foundation of the flipbook, or *show how far animation has come,* Choice (C). Choices (D) and (E) — *exhibit early forms of technology* and *describe a popular animation technique* — are related to the flipbook but are out of scope as far as its use is concerned. Choices (A) and (B) — *provide an example of CGI* and *set the tone of the passage* — are out of scope as well. Choice (C) is correct.

260. **E. allowing pictures to seemingly move on the big screen.**

Right away, you can eliminate Choice (B), *creating sound to accompany movement from pictures,* because the use of *sound* is not mentioned until much later in the passage. Choice (C), *producing the* X-Men *series,* can likewise be eliminated because it is a clear misrepresentation of the information. Don't be fooled by Choice (D), *making inanimate objects appear to move,* which describes the stop-motion technique. Both Choices (A) and (E) — *using light to create movement in pictures* and *allowing pictures to seemingly move on the big screen* — relate to the use of the cinematograph, but the focus is on *moving pictures on a big screen,* not the use of *light.* Choice (E) is correct.

261. **B. It provides evidence to support the effectiveness of the parkway project.**

The last statement leads to the assumption that the parkway project is a good thing for the homeless community. The sentence in boldface provides two points of evidence to highlight this benefit. Thus, it *supports the effectiveness of the project*, Choice (B). You can see that nothing *negative* is stated in the passage, so Choice (A), *it discusses the negative aspects of the parkway project,* can be eliminated. The first sentence explains the project, so Choice (C), *it explains what the parkway project is about,* is eliminated. Choice (D), *it highlights the struggles faced by the homeless population,* is out of scope of what is provided, and Choice (E), *it shows the environmental impact of the parkway project,* although tempting, only offers one part of the evidence provided. Thus, Choice (B) is the best answer.

262. C. The only cause for longevity in China is acupuncture.

In order to add up the information provided to reach a conclusion, it would have to be assumed that the health outcomes in China are directly related to acupuncture, because no other cause is provided. Thus, the same practice in the United States would have the same effect. Choice (A), *people do not consider acupuncture to be a suitable mode of healing,* would not lead to better outcomes if people do not use the procedure. Choice (B), *acupuncture is a new therapy gaining ground in many countries around the world,* may be correct, but it does not relate to the assumption in the passage. Choice (C) restates the assumption above accurately. Both Choices (D) and (E) — *the Chinese are more progressive than the United States* and *the AMA supports alternative therapy for certain illnesses* — are out of scope of the passage. Thus, Choice (C) is correct.

263. E. This exposure will cause businesses to flourish.

The assumption is that the high exposure of direct-mail campaigns creates more business. Each of the sentences in Choices (A), (B), and (D) — *billboards are typically overlooked or blend into the surrounding environment, everyone checks their mail once a day and looks at every piece before deciding what to throw away,* and *television commercials are often muted or abandoned while the viewer flips to a different channel or walks away for a moment* — provide some piece of evidence that leads to this assumption, but only one states the assumption. Choice (C), *launching a direct-mail campaign is the smartest move a business can make,* is tempting, but it falls short of stating the whole assumption. Choice (E) provides the end result of this move to direct-mail marketing and is the correct choice.

264. C. Local citizens should not be responsible for the wear and tear caused by visitors.

The argument is that roads are being used by more than taxpaying citizens in certain areas; thus, a statement supporting that fact would strengthen the idea that tolls are more advantageous. Saying that the local citizens should not be responsible for all the wear and tear of the busy roads, Choice (C), states this idea well. Choice (A), *local taxpayers use the roads just as much as tourists use them,* may be true, but it does not support the reasoning behind the argument. Rural roads, as noted in Choice (B), *rural roads require more maintenance than urban roads,* are not part of the question. Both Choices (D) and (E) — *the state is responsible for maintaining the condition of all roads* and *tolls only contribute a small portion of the funds required for maintenance* — may also be true, but they do not directly provide evidence to support one way or another whether tolls or taxes are more appropriate for the busy roads. Choice (C) is the only choice that fits.

265.

D. The high prices of organic foods deter many people from being able to experience these positive attributes of food.

If more people were able to lead healthier lives by eating organically, and if that ability were supported by the government to lower the price of organic foods, then the only thing keeping people from eating organic foods is the price. Which sentence provides the best restatement of this idea? Choice (A) is the assumption *(if the government provided financial assistance to these producers, more people could lead healthier lives),* so it does not support itself. Choices (B), (C), and (E) all provide facts about the issue related to organic food consumption — *the organic food movement was designed to provide healthier food options without the use of pesticides or unnatural substances, such as growth hormones; part of this financial burden must fall to the consumers;* and *manufacturers say the cost of certifying their produce as organic is high* — but only Choice (D) gives the reason why these foods are not being consumed. Thus, Choice (D) provides the appropriate evidence to support the assumption.

266.

B. Studies have proven that afterschool programs increase the decision-making abilities of students; C. Afterschool programs provide structure and stability for students.

The assumption is that afterschool programs keep children out of trouble and improve graduation rates. If these programs were *criticized,* Choice (A), they would not be seen as beneficial. However, if they *improve decision-making abilities* and *provide structure and stability,* Choices (B) and (C), respectively, then the argument would be strengthened. Both Choices (B) and (C) are correct.

267.

D. Rescue shelters frequently turn down adoption offers from foster parents.

The assumption is that the description of the relationship between rescue shelters and foster care parents is what leaves so many animals in limbo. Thus, the author is presupposing that shelters often turn down offers of adoption from foster parents. Which answer choice fits this idea? No judgment is made about the level of care foster parents can provide, as Choices (A) and (B) imply *(the level of care needed for permanent placement is more than foster parents can provide* and *foster parents are not good permanent parents),* so those can be eliminated. Choice (C), *rescue shelters know what is best for each animal,* may be correct, but it is not specific enough. Choice (E), *rescue shelters avidly reach out to foster parents for adoption,* is a distortion of the information. Only Choice (D) creates the proper relationship to fit the assumption and is correct.

268.

B. People who create their own profiles do not create quality profiles.

The middle sentence clearly states that profiles that are not professionally created are not quality and, thus, make the person less marketable. Which statement supports this idea? If Choices (A), (C), and (E) were true — *LinkedIn is only used for networking, LinkedIn is predominantly used to post photos,* and *job providers do not consider LinkedIn a legitimate website* — there would be no need for marketable profiles. The assumption is that the profiles are worth it, so Choice (D), *professional profiles are not worth the money required to create them,* weakens the argument. Choice (C) clearly states what you are looking for and is correct.

269. **A. These goals demonstrate the seriousness with which they view their lives.**

If students without the plan will not be considered, and the plan is important as evidence of the seriousness with which the students take their lives, then it must be assumed that students who do not have a plan do not take their lives seriously. Harvard doesn't want these students. Which sentence supports this idea the most? Both Choices (B) and (C) simply provide details about the application process: *Along with the current requirements of high school GPA, standardized test scores, and letters of recommendation, each prospective incoming freshman will be required to submit a five-year plan describing their academic pursuits and career development post-graduation,* and *the admissions policies for entrance into Harvard University have changed, beginning with the class of 2016.* Choice (D), *students without this plan will not be taken into consideration,* is the conclusion. Choice (E), although addressing the issue, is providing advice: *Although this information will only be used to get a sense of each student's ambitions, students are encouraged to set high goals.* Only Choice (A) gives the reason for the assumption being made and is correct.

270. **C. Producers of reality television look for ways to exploit child labor.**

The conclusion is that children on reality television are more vulnerable to exploitation. Which choice, if true, supports this idea? If Choice (A), *child labor laws are antiquated,* is true, the conclusion is off the table as viable. If Choice (B), *chaperones are always present during the filming of reality shows using children,* is true, then the children would be protected, thus weakening the conclusion. If Choice (C) were true, it is undoubted that the children are more vulnerable, which strengthens the conclusion. If Choice (D), *reality television does not use child actors,* is true, there is no problem to begin with, making it out of scope. Choice (E), *the government is not responsible for the care of child actors,* addresses a different issue and is also out of scope. Choice (C) is the best choice.

271. **E. Games that require physical movement help keep children in shape.**

The discussion about inactivity and video games provides a caveat for the detrimental effects it purports. The caveat is that games promoting movement might be beneficial. This is the conclusion you are looking for. Choice (A), *all video games are detrimental to children's health,* does not provide this caveat, and the educational content of games is not discussed, ruling out Choice (B), *video games are more educational than active.* The popularity of movement games, Choice (C), is not questioned, and Choice (D), *technology has caused a health crisis in today's youth,* is too extreme. Choice (E) expresses the caveat, or the conclusion, and is, hence, correct.

272. **B. No other factors beyond the firewall screen can be attributed to the restaurant's success.**

The link between the use of a firewall screen and increased sales for the restaurant is direct. No other factors are provided to explain the increase. Thus, Choice (B), if true, makes the assumption true. Choice (A), *a new chef created a better menu at the restaurant in China,* provides an alternative cause of the increased sales, which would weaken the assumption. Choices (C), (D), and (E) — *studies show that people do not use their cellphones during meals, a peaceful environment is not the ideal for a night out,* and *cellphone use has decreased over the past decade* — are all out of scope, making assertions that are not supported. Choice (B) is correct.

273. **B. It gives the reason for the revote request.**

The revote has been requested to avoid favoritism. The suspicion of favoritism stems from the winner being related to one of the judges. Thus, the sentence in bold provides the information that led to the request, or the reason. This relationship is only described accurately in Choice (B), which is correct.

274. **B. Companies lucky enough to get one of these slots see immediate increases in sales.**

The assumption is that companies that advertise during the Super Bowl gain more business, and small businesses should get these spots because they need the business more. Which statement supports this idea? Choices (A) and (C), *more than 100,000 people tuned in for the big game last year* and *the Super Bowl is the biggest event of the year for sports fans,* do not address the assumption. Choices (D) and (E) explain the intricacies of the ad slots: *Advertising slots during the game are a high-priced ticket due to the extreme exposure to the public* and *thus, smaller companies do not benefit from this tremendous audience, which perpetuates their status as a small company.* Only Choice (B) supports the reasoning behind why these slots are important, especially for growing businesses, and is correct.

275. **A. It supports the assumption.**

The assumption is that deodorants without aluminum will not lead to Alzheimer's disease. In order to understand why, we need the boldfaced sentence to support the claim. Only Choice (A) describes this relationship and is correct.

276. **A. It is clear that green tea is the better option than coffee in the morning.**

The assumption is that green tea is better than coffee as a morning beverage. Choice (A) presents this idea nicely. All of the other choices provide evidence to support this assumption but are not the actual assumption. Choice (A) is correct.

277. **A. Members of congress state the wage is fair for both employees and employers, finding the balance to allow both to thrive.**

The passage mostly discusses the low wage and the detrimental effects it has on individuals and the economy. Thus, you are looking for a statement that says the opposite of that. Choices (B) and (D) discuss other aspects of the topic — the fact that Seattle has increased the minimum wage locally and that this action could start a nationwide trend — and can be eliminated. Choices (C) and (E) both address the inadequacies of the wage: *The U.S. economy will crash if its citizens are not able to put money back into it* and *with inflation and a growing national debt, this amount barely equals a living wage for many Americans.* Choice (A) provides the counter-argument by the U.S. Congress, believing the wage is fair. Thus, this statement weakens the assumptions made and is correct.

278. **D. College dining facilities provide only healthy food.**

The question asks for the answer that wouldn't support the assumption in the argument if it were true. The assumption is that college students would make better choices and be healthier if they had more information about their food. Choices (A), (B), (C), and (E), if true, all support the assumption that labels make the difference between choosing food that's good for you and food that's bad for you. However, if Choice (D) were true, and all the food options in dining facilities were already healthy, then the students' poor health would have nothing to do with labeling, and changing the label would have no effect on whether they chose good or bad food. Therefore, Choice (D) is the correct choice.

279. **B. If the price of acquiring a CNG car were lower, more Americans would be driving them.**

The assumption can be found in the question stated in the middle of the passage about why more people aren't driving CNG cars with the cost and gas benefits. The answer points to the cost of the vehicles. Thus, if the prices for CNG vehicles were not so high, more people would be driving them, Choice (B). Choices (A) and (E), *Converting a car to run on CNG is not worth the savings in gas* and *the upfront cost of CNG vehicles is less than what an average person spends on gas,* are not accurate assumptions because the passage provides evidence of the savings. Choice (C), *if regular cars were more fuel efficient, there would be no need for CNG cars,* is out of scope. The passage points to environmental motivations as well as savings. Choice (D), *Americans are attached to their old cars,* is not supported by the information given. Choice (B) is correct.

280. **C. It provides the reasoning behind the assumption made about the new advisor.**

A false conclusion is presented in this argument. The idea that what someone does in college affects who they are as an adult is not substantiated. But, the athletic director is drawing that conclusion based on the information in bold, so the boldfaced sentence is providing evidence to support the assumption. Looking at the choices, only one fits this description. Choice (C) gives the best explanation and is correct.

281. **D. The small business incentives are solely motivated by a desire to boost the national economy.**

The assumption made at the end only relates to what small businesses can do for the national economy. It does not provide any other motive for why the issue of small business growth is important. Which choice restates this conclusion? Choice (C), *the national economy is thriving,* is not an issue in this discussion, and Choices (A) and (E), *small business owners are not held to the same level of employee support as larger corporations* and *people work harder for small businesses than for larger corporations,* are out of scope. Choice (B), *the Obama administration believes in free enterprise,* may be true, but this is not evidenced in the passage. Choice (D) states the only motivation provided by this information and is correct.

282. **C. The study providing the statistic was conducted in a school district located in a high-crime neighborhood.**

The statement to most weaken the argument provides evidence that works against the idea that school uniforms are the only factor that lead to violence. Choices (A) and (B), *school uniforms provide a sense of unity among the students* and *the federal government is considering a bill to require school uniforms in all schools,* focus on the uniforms, not the choices of teens, so they can be eliminated. Both Choices (D) and (E) provide evidence that support the claim that student clothing choices are a problem: *Public schools have placed a ban on wearing labels on your clothing* and *the most recent incident in the public school in question involved a pair of basketball shoes.* If Choice (C) were true, then one could conclude that violence is common in this school district and not necessarily related to clothing, which would weaken the assumption. Choice (C) is correct.

283. **A. Lawrence lost the case because he did not attain enough signatures on the petition.**

If the signatures were not enough to persuade the judges or provide sufficient support, then the assumption is that there were not enough signatures. Choice (A) states this assumption well. Choice (C), *the petition was only part of the dossier of evidence gathered by the plaintiff,* would leave room for other evidence or a lack of it, but other evidence is not mentioned. Choice (E), *the Constitution has strict rules about unlawful termination,* may be correct, but that does not relate directly to this assumption. Choices (B) and (D), *the courts don't consider petitions when hearing testimony* and *participating in a protest makes a person ineligible for fair treatment,* are out of scope. Choice (A) is correct.

284. **B. The firewall protection used in the breached department store is representative of all firewall security on the Internet; C. Most retailers' in-store transaction networks are more secure than online shopping networks.**

If Choice (A), *the department store that was breached used poor security software to firewall their website,* is true, then it is likely that this site was vulnerable and does not make a generalized statement about the security of all Internet shopping. This answer can be eliminated. However, if the breached security is a common form of security used, Choice (B), this would make the situation vulnerable, in general. Also, the less secure online networks presented in Choice (C) would also deter many from online shopping. Both Choices (B) and (C) are correct.

285. **A. Gender roles are not clearly distinguished in modern society; B. It is the responsibility of the media to shape the cultural values of society.**

If Choice (A) were false, it would mean that gender roles are distinguished, so the media would be right in portraying different roles for the sexes. That weakens the argument. If Choice (B) were false, it would also weaken the argument by removing the responsibility of the media in shaping values. If Choice (C), *gender roles are clearly distinguished in modern society,* were false, the opposite of Choice (A) would be true; thus, the argument would be strengthened. Choices (A) and (B) are correct.

286. **D. It represents a contradiction.**

The passage makes a big point of stating the volunteers must be protected against and are responsible for all accidents and injuries on the job. However, the phrase "ensure the safety" signifies that no injuries will occur. Thus, that phrase, and the surrounding sentence, Choice (D), serve to contradict the information regarding injury liability. None of the other choices relate to what the sentence is saying or how it fits in the passage. Thus, Choice (D) is the only close option.

287. **A. The first provides the evidence to support the assumption; the second provides part of the assumption.**

The assumption is that he will have to hold more sales because he is not willing to adapt to the new way people read, which is why he is losing business. The first sentence provides this insight into his attitude, and the second makes the assumption. The combination you are looking for is evidence (support)/assumption. You can eliminate any choices that do not fit this description. Only Choice (A) comes close to this relationship, so it is the clear choice.

Answers
201–300

288.

C. The betterment of the choir has no effect on the rest of the student body.

The assumption is that supporting the choir supports the student body as a whole. Thus, you are looking for a choice that weakens this idea. Choice (A), *the school has a policy against fundraising,* is out of scope. Choice (B), *all of the students enjoy singing in the choir,* would strengthen the assumption, as might Choice (D), *the choir is the school's most successful club,* in that it relates to the whole school. Choice (E), *success at choir competitions is a priority of the administration,* would also strengthen the argument. Only Choice (C) weakens the argument that school funds should be allocated for choir use and is correct.

289.

D. Yellow Cab could lower its rates to remain competitive.

If there were another option beyond raising taxes to even the playing field, then that option would weaken the argument. You are looking for an answer choice that provides that logic. Yellow Cab may pay more taxes, Choice (A), but there is no evidence that this is unfair. They are a larger company, and that could be completely within the law. Choice (C), *higher tax rates will force the other companies out of business,* creates a different conclusion than the one you are trying to weaken, so that choice can be eliminated. Choices (B) and (E), *the burden to improve Yellow Cab's business is on the state* and *taxi service use is at an all-time low,* may be true, but they don't relate to the assumption at hand. Choice (D) gives an alternative solution that could solve Yellow Cab's problems, so it weakens their argument. Choice (D) is correct.

290.

C. Newspapers and magazines are more widely viewed by voters than other news outlets.

If the most important role is not to cover the debates, than what does that say about the media? There must be another important role or another factor that plays into voter decision making. Look at the choices to see what fits. In Choices (A), (B), and (E) — *the debates are the only source of coverage elections get, the media provides informed coverage of the debates,* and *voters always vote according to the outcomes of the debates* — the media coverage of the debates is set up as a vital element in the information receiving and voting processes. Thus, if these statements are true, the assumption would also be true. So, eliminate those choices. If Choice (C) is true, another news outlet may play an important role, meaning the statement about the media is false. If Choice (D), *voters consider the media to be a trustworthy source of information,* is true, then the assumption is also true. Choice (C) is the only choice that makes the assumption false.

291.

D. The federal government does not consider social media as a legitimate publishing venue.

The last sentence lends to the idea that the federal government does not consider copyright infringement in social media to be as serious as music piracy. Are there any choices that match that description? Choice (D) seems to fit that description well. The other choices do not match the information in the passage. Thus, Choice (D) is the best choice.

292.

E. It provides support for the assumption.

The assumption is that money spent on exams is not worth it because test scores are not the primary deciding factor for enrollment. Thus, the boldfaced sentence provides this statement as evidence, or support. Only Choice (E) presents this sentence in this light and is correct.

293.   **C. Students who do not know Spanish will be at a disadvantage.**

The population of Spanish speakers is increasing in the United States. That is the premise for the assumption. Thus, if this is true, children who grow up without learning Spanish will be at a disadvantage in the future. Choice (C) expresses this assumption well. Choices (A) and (D) — *there is no indication that learning Spanish will increase a student's chances for future success* and *there are just as many opportunities for non-Spanish speakers as there are for Spanish speakers,* might be true, but the information leads to a different assumption. If Choice (B), *Spanish is declining in popularity,* were assumed, there would be no need for the discussion. Choice (E), *English is the most important language in the world,* is not supported in the text. Choice (C) is the best choice.

294.   **C. Many families rely on hunting to survive during difficult times.**

Activists want to ban hunting, so that action would negatively affect a family's ability to survive if they relied on hunting to support them. Choice (A), *hunting is not the only way needy families can get food,* weakens the argument. Choice (B), *animal activists understand the need for families to be independent of government subsidies,* is opposite of what the information provides. Choice (C) provides a good example of what a family would lose if they couldn't hunt. Choice (D), *federal subsidies effectively provide support for impoverished families,* would also weaken the argument. Choice (E), *hunting is mostly done recreationally,* does not relate to families. Choice (C) is the best choice.

295.   **D. It states the problem leading to the assumption.**

The boldfaced sentence provides the law that the assumption claims is unfair. The law, then, is the problem. Only Choice (D) presents this relationship. All of the other choices are false connections. Choice (D) is correct.

296.   **A. Graphics and other animation techniques created mind-blowing visual effects that stunned audiences.**

Despite the assumption that other, more standard films are not interesting to viewers, the question is about the reason *Avatar* was so successful. Choices (B) and (E) — *other movies released at the same time did not contain visual effects and did not do as well at the box office* and *it is clear that moviegoers are not interested in standard film production anymore* — discuss other movies, so they can be eliminated. Choices (C) and (D) — *the special effects used in the movie were a new development by the director* and *Avatar grossed more sales than any other movie in history* — provide mere information about the movie. Choice (A) presents the aspects of the film that enchanted the audiences, hence, leading to success at the box office. Choice (A) is correct.

297.   **E. The consumption of beef has increased over the last 15 years.**

In order for the increased rate of cancer to be related to the concerns from the CDC about hormones used in cows, the consumption of beef would have to have increased, Choice (E). Look for choices that are not supported in the passage. The *peril due to the advent of cancer in cows,* Choice (A), and Americans' consumption of *white meat,* Choice (B), are not supported by the information. The passage clearly states that hormones are a concern, so they would not be assumed beneficial or cancer-fighting agents, as Choice (C), *hormones provide the body with cancer-fighting agents,* suggests. Don't be fooled by Choice (D), *the CDC has determined that there is no connection between beef consumption and cancer.* This may be true, but the passage is structured in a way that leads to a different conclusion. Only Choice (E) provides a possible connection to the information given.

298. **A. Worsening environmental conditions will lead to increased sea levels.**

The assumption that those living close to bodies of water should invest in flood insurance suggests that the detrimental effects to the environment will increase the world's sea levels. Look for a choice that restates this assumption. Choice (A) restates it perfectly. Choice (B), *humans are incapable of stopping the negative effects to the environment,* is out of scope of the passage. Choices (C) and (D) — *fossil fuels cause floods* and *the polar caps are not affected by greenhouse gases* — both address the water issues, but they do not represent the assumption made in the passage, with Choice (D) providing the opposite and Choice (C) making a false conclusion. Choice (E), *fossil fuels and methane gases are the only factors affecting the environment,* is too extreme and not supported in the text. Thus, Choice (A) is the best answer.

299. **B. It ruins the whole experience.**

In this question, you must first decide what the dog park users' assumption is and then find the choice that matches. If dog park users will boycott the park simply because they have to pick up the dog poop, then it can be assumed that the only reason they use the park is to allow their dogs free access to poop wherever. Therefore, the sentence that best relates this will encompass all of this idea. Only Choices (B) and (D) relate to the negative view the users have about the new regulations. Choice (D), however, only points out an annoyance with the rules — *they claim it would require them to follow their dogs around the whole park* — whereas Choice (B) relates an overall judgment about the rules. The other choices do not relate to the assumption. Thus, Choice (B) is the best answer.

300. **D. The amount of work required during the additional two months of remote work is the same load as someone working full-time onsite.**

The assumption is that fairness equals everyone getting what they need and deserve. In this instance, a mother may need more time after giving birth to stay home with her child. It is fair that the company will allow her to do that at a reduced rate of pay while working from home. However, if the work they do at home is the same as would have been done in the office, the benefit of staying at home is lost and the compensation is not suitable. Look for an answer that hinders this idea. What other companies do is not in question in this argument, so Choice (A), *most companies only allow two months of leave before requiring unpaid time for an extended leave,* is out of scope. Whether or not policies are required by law is also not in question, so Choice (B), *maternity policies are not required by law,* may be eliminated. Choice (C), *the amount of work required during the additional two months of remote work is proportional to the reduced salary,* would create balance, thus not casting doubt. Choice (D) restates the imbalance mentioned in the above assumption, so this choice may work. Choice (E), *employees wishing to return to work after two months can use vacation days to take additional time off,* does not directly relate to the policy in question. Choice (D) is correct.

301.

A. The first statement presents the problem, and the second statement expresses a solution.

The problem presented is that lactose intolerance has led to an increase in soy milk consumption, which may lead to a decline in cow milk production on dairy farms. This, lactose intolerance, is the first problem; the non-dairy option is the solution, and the solution creates a possible second problem. Thus, the first sentence states the problem, and the second sentence provides an alternative to the problem. You are looking for problem/solution answers. Lactose intolerance is not the *conclusion,* so Choice (B) is out. It is also not the *solution,* so Choice (E) is out. Both Choices (C) and (D) present the second sentence as a contradiction rather than a solution, so they can be eliminated. Only Choice (A) sets up the proper relationship between these sentences and is correct.

302.

B. Car manufacturers can increase sales by catering certain vehicles to a certain audience.

The text in bold shows that certain people drive certain cars for certain reasons. It categorizes them into specific interests, thus suggesting that car manufacturers can use these categories to reach appropriate markets. Choice (A), *focusing car promotions on the more expensive, flashy vehicles will increase sales the most,* distorts the information and can be eliminated. Choice (C), *although the motivations are different, the types of cars chosen are similar,* makes a false conclusion based on the information. Choices (D) and (E) — *people use their emotions when deciding what car to purchase* and *young drivers are less responsible than older drivers* — are out of scope of the information. Choice (B) expresses the assumption well and is correct.

Answers
301–400

303.

E. The return from the investment will be matched by the company to equal what would have been earned through a raise at the end of 5 years.

The information in the passage doesn't provide any evidence to clearly make this claim, so you have to find your own evidence that will make this claim true. If Choice (A), *employees should prioritize their financial interests over those of the company,* were true, it would lead to the opposite conclusion. If Choice (B), *the salary earned from incremental raises during the five year period is equal to the return on shares,* were true, there would be no need to take the risk of investing. If Choice (C), *the stock market is at its lowest point in history,* were true, taking the risk would be a poor decision. If Choice (D), *the shares will increase in value at the end of 10 years,* were true, making the investment might be a good idea, but it is not in the best interest of the deal offered in the letter. If Choice (E) were true, employees could be sure to recoup at least what they would have had if they'd taken the raise. This would be a good incentive to take the risk; thus, Choice (E) strengthens the argument.

304.

E. She was unable to compete with the conglomerate's low prices.

What is the assumption? Well, despite what your logic might be telling you, the assumption is that banking on loyalty was the best option for Annie May. So, what would strengthen this argument? There is no obvious answer, so taking each sentence separately is the best solution. Choices (A), (B), and (C) — *a reduction of that proportion would have caused her to lose money, Annie May was forced to close the doors of her bakery after a Krispy Donuts opened across the street,* and *she would have had to reduce her prices by 25 percent to remain in line with her competition* — provide the intricate details of her business in relation to Krispy Donuts but they do not relate to her chosen path. Again, Choice (D), *that sort of loss would have run the business into the ground,* although more pointed in providing a conclusion, is about a different path than loyal customers. Choice (E) shows that because she couldn't reduce her prices to compete, she had to rely on loyal customers willing to pay the same prices as before. Choice (E) is correct.

305. **B. Being judged by one's appearance leads to psychological trauma.**

The linkage between beauty pageants and depression in this passage does not make room for other factors that could be related. Thus, the assumption is that the mindset dictated by these pageants creates a situation where depression is likely to follow. Which choice expresses this idea? Choices (A) and (D) — *pageant judges are harsh toward the contestants* and *depression is a serious disease with many causes* — are out of scope. Choice (C), *the desire to be beautiful is the only motivation for women,* makes a generalization that is not supported in the passage. Choice (E), *many young women gain confidence from competing in beauty pageants,* discusses a different topic related to pageants. Only Choice (B) creates the assumed linkage between pageants and mental state. Choice (B) is correct.

306. **A. They both represent the assumption.**

The last part of the passage provides evidence to support the assumption that food processes lead to poor health. Both the boldfaced sentences express this idea: one generally and one specifically. Thus, they both represent the assumption, Choice (A). Any choices suggesting a weakening effect, as Choices (C), (D), and (E) do, can be eliminated immediately, and Choice (B), *they contradict each other in supporting the assumption,* creates a false relationship. Choice (A) is correct.

307. **E. Anything brought onto school property is subject to searches.**

The student claims that his rights were violated when his phone was searched. If Choice (A), *a rash of bullying has occurred at the school,* were true, it still wouldn't necessarily dictate a phone search, so it does nothing to the argument. If Choice (B), *only school-affiliated materials are the property of the school,* were true, it would strengthen the argument, as would Choices (C) and (D) — *the principal has a history of overstepping his bounds* and *school policies do not state any regulations regarding cellphones.* Only Choice (E) weakens the student's claim and is correct.

308. **D. Many college athletes are not able to meet their financial needs with the stipends.**

The basic idea is that athletes are financially poor, and because they are not able to enjoy any of the money profited from the use of their status, they may decide to head to greener pastures instead of college. Do not get bogged down by the details. Only one statement clearly expresses the position of the athlete at its core. Choices (A) and (C) — *an athlete who plays at the college level is not eligible to receive income from sponsorships, public appearances, interviews, or the use of his name and likeness in advertisements and on merchandise* and *the flash of dollar signs can be a hard thing to ignore for a budding athlete with dreams of professional stardom* — provide information about the issue. Choices (B) and (E) — *if professional athletes didn't make so much money, the amateur athletes would not be enticed in the same way* and *this inability to make a living off their status is the reason that many athletes choose to turn pro right out of high school or after one year* — show the cause and effect of the issue. Choice (D) gives the main issue relating to finances and college athletes that leads to this issue in the first place. Choice (D) is correct.

309. **C. Reports of stressful flight experiences have never been attributed to a lack of smoking.**

The assumption is that passengers are uncomfortable because they cannot smoke. If this was a new issue, the FAA would need to address it. Thus, any information indicating that passengers have managed this issue before would weaken the assertion. Choice (A), *smoking on planes is common in other countries,* is out of scope. Choice (B), *smoking was not allowed on flights even before the advent of e-cigarettes,* makes a case against needed action. Choice (E), *e-cigarettes do not produce harmful second-hand smoke like cigarettes do,* even if false, is a good point, but it doesn't address the assumption. Choice (C) would strengthen the argument, as would Choice (D), *the FAA does not support smoking anywhere in the airport.* Choice (C) is the best choice, however, because it supports the issue as being a new issue.

310. **C. These preschools, though pricey, give these children an advantage in elementary school over children who haven't attended preschool.**

The assumption is that families from lower economic statuses will not be able to take advantage of the same preschool systems that more affluent families are able to. Choice (A), *this phenomenon has created a difficult predicament for families in lower socioeconomic classes,* is the assumption, so it wouldn't support itself. Choices (B) and (D) — *a study of 100 children followed from birth to 13 years old shows a surprising trend in high test scores for children who attended preschool* and *social work researchers have determined that cognitive development begins within the first five years of life* — provide the study and outcome, respectively, that sparked the interest in preschools, which is not related to the assumption directly. Choice (E), *this report has prompted more parents to shell out thousands of dollars to enroll their kids in private preschools,* presents the motivation but does not address the assumption. Choice (C) relates the reasons why preschool is desirable and out of reach of families with less income. Choice (C) is correct.

311. E. –10

The distance between two numbers on a number line is equal to the absolute value of the difference of the two numbers. The absolute value of the difference between 1 and –10, Choice (E), is 11, the greatest value and thus the farthest from the number 1 on the number line.

312. 43

If Tabitha is 32nd in line, it means that there are 31 people to one side of her. Counting from the other end, she is 12th in line, so there are 11 people on the other side.

The number of people in line is calculated like this:

$$31 + 11 + 1 = 43$$

313. 28

The positive integer factors of 12 are 1, 2, 3, 4, 6, and 12.

Their sum is 28:

$$1 + 2 + 3 + 4 + 6 + 12 = 28$$

314. **C. 12; D. 18; F. 36**

First, identify the multiples of 2: 8, 12, 18, and 36.

Next, identify the multiples of 3: 9, 12, 18, 21, and 36.

Your answer is those numbers that the multiples of 2 and 3 have in common, which are Choices (C), (D), and (F), 12, 18, and 36, respectively.

315. **B. and C.** $-10, 2^{-4}$

The product of the pair must be negative, so the possible products are

$$(-20)(2^{-4}) = -\frac{5}{4} < -1$$
$$(-20)(3^{-2}) = -\frac{20}{9} < -1$$
$$(-10)(2^{-4}) = -\frac{5}{8} > -1$$
$$(-10)(3^{-2}) = -\frac{10}{9} < -1$$

Only the product of Choices (B) and (C) is between -1 and 0. The other choices result in numbers less than -1.

316. **A.** $2n$; **B.** n^2; **C.** $2 - n$

The simplest approach is to plug in some random numbers:

If n is -1, then $2n = -2$, which is less than n.

If n is $\frac{1}{2}$, then $n^2 = \frac{1}{4}$, which is less than n.

If n is 2, then $2 - n = 0$, which is less than n.

Thus, Choices (A), (B), and (C) could all have a value less than n.

317. **A. 14**

The smallest value for n such that $5n$ is a square is 5.

$75np$ can now be written as $75 \times 5 \times p$. This gives prime factors of $3 \times 5 \times 5 \times 5 \times p$.

To make the expression a perfect cube, p has to have factors of 3×3; hence, $p = 9$.

$$n + p =$$
$$5 + 9 = 14$$

318. **E. 12**

The sets can be written as:

1st set: $n + (n+1) + (n+2) + (n+3)$

2nd set: $(n+3) + (n+4) + (n+5) + (n+6)$

Each term in the 2nd set is three more than the equivalent term in the 1st set. Because there are four terms, the total of the differences is:

$$4 \times 3 = 12$$

319.

A. 17; B. 28; D. 39; E. 50

The fence will consist of one more post than chains; therefore, a total length has to be a multiple of the length of the chains plus one post (5.5 ft.), plus one additional post.

Length $= (5.5n + 0.5)$

If $n = 3$, the length = 17, Choice (A).

If $n = 5$, the length = 28, Choice (B).

If $n = 7$, the length = 39, Choice (D).

If $n = 9$, the length = 50, Choice (E).

There is no whole number that will give 35; therefore, all answers are correct except Choice (C).

320.

2,550

If you write out part of each series, you will see that every term in the second series is one more than the corresponding term in the first series:

1, 3, 5, 7...

2, 4, 6, 8...

Because there are 50 terms, the second sum will be 50 more than the first sum:

$$2,500 + 50 = 2,550$$

321.

B. 6; C. 7

John > 2 × Sean

Sean > Randy + 4

Select numbers that are less than 16 for John's age and check the equations:

If John is 15, then Sean could be 7, 6, or 5.

Randy cannot be less than 1, which means that Sean cannot be less than 6. Choices (B) and (C), 6 and 7, are the correct answers.

322.

101

Four consecutive integers can be written as: $n + (n+1) + (n+2) + (n+3) = 410$

Solve for n:

$$n + (n+1) + (n+2) + (n+3) = 410$$
$$4n + 6 = 410$$
$$4n = 404$$
$$n = 101$$

323.   3

n must be a factor if the result of dividing 81 by n is a whole number.

If each person gets $x, then each person gets the same number of dollars. The factors of 81 are 3, 9, and 27, so n can take three different values.

324.   5

Let the number of wrong answers = x, and the number of right answers = $50 - x$.

Subtracting twice the wrong answers from the right answers gives you 35, so:

$$(50 - x) - 2x = 35$$
$$50 - 3x = 35$$
$$-3x = -15$$
$$3x = 15$$
$$x = 5$$

325.   12

The easiest way to approach this problem is to look for a simple relationship between the numbers. If you multiply by 2, then 145 becomes 290, to which you need to add 10 to make 300. Doubling 300 gives 600 and adding 10 equals 610. So, $x = 2$ and $y = 10$.

$$x + y =$$
$$2 + 10 = 12$$

326.   A. 1

A prime number is a positive whole number that can only be divided by itself and by 1. The numbers 2 and 4, Choices (B) and (D), will result in products with a and b, and the sum of two even products is always even. The sum of any two multiples of 3 is itself divisible by 3; therefore, Choice (C) is not correct. That leaves Choice (A), which is the right answer.

327.   A. Even; B. Odd

The simplest way to approach the solution is to select some prime numbers and solve:

If $x = 3$, then $3 \times 3 = 9$, which is *odd*, Choice (B).

If $x = 2$, then $3 \times 2 = 6$, which is *even*, Choice (A).

Any number multiplied by 3 is itself divisible by 3; therefore, Choice (C), *prime number*, is not correct.

Only multiples of 12 are divisible by both 3 and 4, and 12 is not a prime number; therefore, Choice (D), *divisible by 4*, is not correct.

328. E. $\frac{3}{5}$

The smallest prime number is 2, and the least common multiple of 5 and 10 is 10.

$$\frac{3x}{y} = \frac{3(2)}{10}$$
$$= \frac{6}{10}$$
$$= \frac{3}{5}$$

Choice (E) is the correct answer.

329. E. $1\frac{1}{5}$

The smallest odd prime number is 3 and the second smallest odd prime number is 5.

$$\frac{2x}{y} = \frac{2(3)}{5}$$
$$= \frac{6}{5}$$
$$= 1\frac{1}{5}$$

Choice (E) is thus the correct answer.

330. C. 27.5

The third smallest prime number is 5 and the smallest two-digit prime number is 11.

$$\frac{1}{2}x(y) = \frac{1}{2}5(11)$$
$$= \frac{55}{2}$$
$$= 27.5$$

Choice (C) is the answer you're looking for.

331. C. 22

$$\left| x^3 + 5 \right| = \left| (-3)^3 + 5 \right|$$
$$= \left| -27 + 5 \right|$$
$$= \left| -22 \right|$$
$$= 22$$

Choice (C) is the right answer.

332. **B. 1**

The smallest whole number greater than 1 is 2.

$$\begin{aligned}
\left|2x^2 - 7\right| &= \left|2(2)^2 - 7\right| \\
&= \left|2(4) - 7\right| \\
&= \left|8 - 7\right| \\
&= \left|1\right| \\
&= 1
\end{aligned}$$

The resulting answer is 1, Choice (B).

333. **A. 5**

$$\begin{aligned}
\left|\frac{3}{4}x - 2\right| &= \left|\frac{3}{4}(-4) - 2\right| \\
&= \left|\frac{-12}{4} - 2\right| \\
&= \left|-3 - 2\right| \\
&= \left|-5\right| \\
&= 5
\end{aligned}$$

Choice (A), 5, is the solution.

334. **B. 5; E. –9**

The equation within the absolute value bars needs to be solved as both a positive and a negative:

$$\begin{aligned}
\left|x + 2\right| &= 7 \\
(x + 2) &= 7 \\
x + 2 &= 7 \\
x &= 5
\end{aligned}$$

And

$$\begin{aligned}
-\left|x + 2\right| &= 7 \\
\left|x + 2\right| &= -7 \\
(x + 2) &= -7 \\
x + 2 &= -7 \\
x &= -9
\end{aligned}$$

Choices (B), 5, and (E), –9, are the correct answers.

335. **B. 5; D. –2**

The equation within the absolute value bars needs to be solved as both a positive and a negative:

$$|2x-3|-4=3$$
$$|2x-3|=7$$
$$(2x-3)=7$$
$$2x=10$$
$$x=5$$

And

$$-|2x-3|-4=3$$
$$-|2x-3|=7$$
$$-(2x-3)=7$$
$$-2x+3=7$$
$$-2x=4$$
$$x=-2$$

Choices (B), 5, and (D), –2, are the right answers.

336. **A. 7.5; C. –4.5**

The equation within the absolute value bars needs to be solved as both a positive and a negative:

$$\left(\frac{|2x-3|}{4}\right)^2=9$$
$$\left(\frac{|2x-3|}{4}\right)=\sqrt{9}$$
$$\left(\frac{|2x-3|}{4}\right)=3$$
$$|2x-3|=12$$
$$(2x-3)=12$$
$$2x=15$$
$$x=7.5$$

And

$$\left(\frac{|2x-3|}{4}\right)^2 = 9$$

$$\left(\frac{|2x-3|}{4}\right) = \sqrt{9}$$

$$\left(\frac{|2x-3|}{4}\right) = 3$$

$$|2x-3| = 12$$

$$-(2x-3) = 12$$

$$-2x+3 = 12$$

$$-2x = 9$$

$$x = -4.5$$

The correct answers are Choices (A), 7.5, and (C), –4.5.

337. **B. 2; C. 3; D. 4; E. 5; F. 6**

The equation within the absolute value bars needs to be solved as both a positive and a negative, with the inequality sign being flipped with the negative solution:

$$|x-4| < 3$$

$$(x-4) < 3$$

$$x < 7$$

And

$$|x-4| < 3$$

$$-(x-4) < 3$$

$$-x+4 < 3$$

$$-x < -1$$

$$x > 1$$

x can be any number > 1 and < 7, so Choices (B), (C), (D), (E), and (F), the numbers 2 to 6, respectively, are possible values. Choice (A), 1, is not greater than 1, and Choice (G), 7, is not less than 7.

338. **A. 1; B. 0.5; C. 0; D. –1; E. –2; F. –3.5**

The equation within the absolute value bars needs to be solved as both a positive and a negative, with the inequality sign being flipped with the negative solution:

$$|2x+3| < 6$$

$$(2x+3) < 6$$

$$2x < 3$$

$$x < \frac{3}{2}$$

$$x < 1.5$$

And

$$|2x+3| < 6$$
$$-(2x+3) < 6$$
$$-2x-3 < 6$$
$$-2x < 9$$
$$x > \frac{9}{-2}$$
$$x > -4.5$$

x can be any number < 1.5 and > -4.5, so all the choices are possible values.

---

339.   **B.** $|x-1| < 3$

There are six units between -2 and 4, and half of 6 is 3. Adjust the inequality so that it relates to -3 and 3:

$$-2-1 < x-1 < 4-1$$
$$-3 < x-1 < 3$$

This can be converted to $|x-1| < 3$, which is Choice (B).

---

340.   **A. 7; B. 5; C. 2; D. 0; E. –1; F. –2; G. –3**

All of the answer choices are possible values, because the absolute value of any number will always be greater than a negative number.

---

341.   **$39.50**

First, calculate the cost of 18 pencils:

$$18 \times \$0.25 = \$4.50$$

Next, calculate the cost of 100 erasers:

$$100 \times \$0.35 = \$35.00$$

Finally, calculate the total cost:

$$\$4.50 + \$35.00 = \$39.50$$

---

342.   **B. 1.5**

First, find the area of Box A:

$$\text{area} = \text{length} \times \text{width}$$
$$= 20 \times 3$$
$$= 60$$

Next, find the area of Box B:

$$\text{area} = \text{length} \times \text{width}$$
$$= 9 \times 10$$
$$= 90$$

$$(\text{area of box } A)x = \text{area of box } B$$
$$60x = 90$$
$$x = 1.5$$

Multiplying the area of Box A by 1.5, Choice (B), results in the area of Box B.

343. 0.318

The difference between 0.326 and 0.312 is divided into seven equal units; therefore, each unit is 0.002:

$$\frac{(0.326 - 0.312)}{7} = 0.002$$

P comes three units after 0.312, so:

$$0.312 + 3(0.002) = 0.318$$

344. C. $30

The car gets 33 miles for each gallon of gas:

$$\left(\frac{350}{33}\right)(\$2.95) = \frac{\$1,032.50}{33}$$
$$= \$31.29$$
$$\Rightarrow \$30$$

The approximate cost of the gas is Choice (C), $30.

345. D. 0.2025

First, convert the numbers to decimals:

$$\frac{4}{10} = 0.4$$

$$\frac{5}{1,000} = 0.005$$

Next, calculate the average:

$$= \frac{(0.4 + 0.005)}{2}$$
$$= \frac{(0.405)}{2}$$
$$= 0.2025$$

Choice (D) is the solution.

346.   **A. 0.008206**

A number in scientific notation is written as a number, usually having a decimal, multiplied by a power of 10.

10^{-3} means that the decimal point must be moved three places to the left:

$8.206 \to 0.8206 \to 0.08206 \to 0.008206$

$0.008206 = 8.206 \times 10^{-3}$, making Choice (A) the correct answer.

347.   **E. 0.0000585**

A number in scientific notation is written as a number, usually having a decimal, multiplied by a power of 10.

10^{-5} means that the decimal point must be moved five places to the left:

$5.85 \to 0.585 \to 0.0585 \to 0.00585 \to 0.000585 \to 0.0000585$

$0.0000585 = 5.85 \times 10^{-5}$, which is Choice (E).

348.   **C. 12,756.2**

A number in scientific notation is written as a number, usually having a decimal, multiplied by a power of 10.

10^4 means that the decimal point must be moved four places to the right:

$1.27562 \to 12.7562 \to 127.562 \to 1,275.62 \to 12,756.2$

$12,756.2 = 1.27562 \times 10^4$, making Choice (C) the correct answer.

349.   **C.** $1-(0.04)^{\frac{1}{2}}$; **E.** $1-0.04^3$; **G.** $\left(1-0.04^3\right)^2$

Solve each expression:

Choice (A) is too great: $1+0.04 = 1.04$

Choice (B) is also too great:

$$(1-0.04)2 = (0.96)2$$
$$= 1.92$$

Choice (C) is within the range:

$$1-(0.04)^{\frac{1}{2}} = 1-0.2$$
$$= 0.8$$

Choice (D) is too great: $1+0.04^2 = 1.042$

Choice (E) is within the range: $1-0.04^3 = 0.957$

Choice (F) is too low:

$$\frac{(1-0.04^3)}{2} = \frac{0.957}{2}$$
$$= 0.4785$$

Choice (G) is within the range:

$$(1-0.043)^2 = (0.957)^2$$
$$= 0.915849$$

Choices (C), (E), and (G) fall within this range.

350.

D. 74

Divide the total weight by the weight of 1 gallon:

$$\frac{614.2}{8.3} = 74$$

The result, Choice (D), is the right answer.

351.

A. 1.94

Four and ninety nine one-hundredths = 4.99

Three and five one-hundredths = 3.05

$$4.99 - 3.05 = 1.94$$

Choice (A) is the correct answer.

352.

C. $29.11

First, find the total cost of each food item:

steak 4($3.89) = $15.56
eggs 4($1.05) = $4.20
milk 2($1.99) = $3.98
bread 3($1.79) = $5.37

Next, add all of the food items together:

$$= \$15.56 + \$4.20 + \$3.98 + \$5.37$$
$$= \$29.11$$

Choice (C) is the total cost of the items.

353.

B. 1,145

The weight will be 250g plus $\frac{(1.55-0.65)}{0.10}$ units of 100g

$$250 + 900 = 1,150$$

This is the maximum weight that can be sent at that price. Weights exceeding 250 + 800 will also get charged this amount, so a package that weighs 1,145 grams, Choice (B), will be charged $1.55.

354. **C. 0.4**

Let the weight of the empty tin = w.

The weight of the cookies = $(2 - w)$.

One quarter of the cookies weigh $\dfrac{(2-w)}{4}$.

One quarter of the cookies + tin = 0.8.

$$0.8 = \frac{w + (2 - w)}{4}$$
$$3.2 = 4w + 2 - w$$
$$1.2 = 3w$$
$$0.4 = w$$

The weight of the empty tin is 0.4 pounds, Choice (C).

355. **A. and E.** $\dfrac{2}{5}$, $\dfrac{2}{3}$

Convert all the fractions to decimals:

$$\frac{2}{5} = 0.4$$

$$\frac{1}{4} = 0.25$$

$$\frac{5}{16} = 0.31$$

$$\frac{1}{3} = 0.33$$

$$\frac{2}{3} = 0.67$$

Only Choices (A) and (E) fall within the range $0.33 < x < 0.76$.

356. **B.** $\dfrac{bm}{60a}$

Divide the required number of labels (the number of boxes) by the labels per hour to get time taken in hours:

$$= \frac{\#\text{ of labels needed}}{\dfrac{60 \text{ labels}}{\text{minute}}}$$

$$= \frac{b}{\dfrac{60a}{m}}$$

$$= \frac{bm}{60a}$$

Choice (B) is the correct answer.

357. 5

If $x = \frac{1}{5}$ of the sum, then $8 + 6 + 4 + 2 = \frac{4}{5}$ of the sum. So,

$20 = \frac{4}{5}$ of S, and $20 \div 4$ is $\frac{1}{5}$ of S, so $S = 5$.

358. B; F; G. $\frac{4}{7}, \frac{8}{15}, \frac{9}{17}$

Convert all the fractions to decimals:

$$\frac{2}{5} = 0.4$$

$$\frac{4}{7} = 0.57$$

$$\frac{4}{9} = 0.44$$

$$\frac{5}{11} = 0.45$$

$$\frac{6}{13} = 0.46$$

$$\frac{8}{15} = 0.53$$

$$\frac{9}{17} = 0.53$$

Choices (B), (F), and (G) are greater than $\frac{1}{2}$.

359. 61

There are 10 marks for each inch on the ruler:

$$6 \times 10 = 60$$

Add an additional mark for zero:

$$60 + 1 = 61$$

360. D. $\frac{1}{500}$

0.127 written as a fraction is $\frac{127}{1,000}$.

1/8 can be written as $\frac{(1 \times 125)}{(8 \times 125)} = \frac{125}{1,000}$.

Find the difference:

$$\frac{127}{1,000} - \frac{125}{1,000} = \frac{2}{1,000}$$

$$= \frac{1}{500}$$

Choice (D) is therefore the correct answer.

361.   E. $\dfrac{x-y}{x}$

Let the salary $= x$.

The amount saved $= x - y$.

The amount saved $= \dfrac{x-y}{x}$.

Choice (E) is the right answer.

362.   C. $1\dfrac{1}{2}$

First, change the mixed fractions to improper form:

$$2\dfrac{1}{7} = \dfrac{15}{7}$$
$$1\dfrac{3}{7} = \dfrac{10}{7}$$

Next, set up the equation and solve:

$$\dfrac{15}{7} \div x = \dfrac{10}{7}$$
$$\dfrac{15}{7} = \dfrac{10}{7}x$$
$$\left(\dfrac{7}{10}\right) \times \left(\dfrac{15}{7}\right) = x$$
$$\dfrac{105}{70} =$$
$$\dfrac{3}{2} =$$
$$1\dfrac{1}{2}$$

Choice (C) is the solution.

363.   D. $2\dfrac{14}{19}$

First, change the mixed fractions to improper form:

$$3\dfrac{4}{5} = \dfrac{19}{5}$$
$$10\dfrac{2}{5} = \dfrac{52}{5}$$

Next, set up the equation and solve:

$$\left(\frac{19}{5}\right)x = \frac{52}{5}$$

$$x = \left(\frac{52}{5}\right)\left(\frac{5}{19}\right)$$

$$= \frac{260}{95}$$

$$= 2\frac{70}{95}$$

$$= 2\frac{14}{19}$$

The solution is Choice (D).

364. **C. 10**

John had one candy left, plus the extra piece that he gave to Bruce (= two candies). This was half of what he had before he gave any to Bruce (= four candies). He gave an extra piece to Jerry (= five candies). This was half of what he started with, so he started with ten pieces:

$$2\big((2(1+1))+1\big) = 10$$

The correct answer is Choice (C).

365. **D. 46**

He had 22 fish before eating one for lunch (= 23). This number is half of what he sold, so he started with 46 fish:

$$2(22+1) = 46$$

Choice (D) is the correct answer.

366. **A. $\frac{2}{3}$ hour**

Pipe #1 can fill the tank in twice the amount of time that it takes Pipe #2 to fill the tank:

Pipe #1 = $2x$

Pipe #2 = x

In 40 minutes, Pipe #1 will fill the tank $\frac{2}{3}$ full and Pipe #2 will fill the tank $\frac{1}{3}$ full.

40 minutes = $\frac{2}{3}$ hour

Choice (A) is the correct answer.

367. **B. 6 p.m.**

Let x represent the amount of time passed.

Time left $= \frac{1}{3}x$

Set the equation equal to 24 hours:

$$\frac{1}{3}x + x = 24$$
$$\frac{4}{3}x = 24$$
$$x = 24\left(\frac{3}{4}\right)$$
$$= \frac{72}{4}$$
$$= 18 \text{ hours}$$

Eighteen hours have gone by, so the time is 6 p.m., Choice (B).

368. **D. 2 hours 41 minutes**

There are 60 minutes in 1 hour.

First, convert the minutes to fraction form:

$$2{:}32 \text{ p.m.} = 2\frac{32}{60}$$
$$5{:}13 \text{ p.m.} = 5\frac{13}{60}$$

Now, rewrite the mixed fractions to improper form and subtract:

$$2\frac{32}{60} = \frac{152}{60}$$
$$5\frac{13}{60} = \frac{313}{60}$$
$$\frac{313}{60} - \frac{152}{60} = \frac{161}{60}$$
$$= 2\frac{41}{60}$$

The solution is the equivalent of 2 hours 41 minutes, Choice (D).

369. **C. and D.** $\frac{-2}{5}, \frac{-3}{4}$

Because the x^3 lies between the number and its square on the number line, x must be a negative fraction. Only $\frac{-2}{5}$ and $\frac{-3}{4}$ are negative fractions within the range of $\frac{-5}{2}$ and -1.

Thus, Choices (C) and (D) are correct.

370.

A. $\dfrac{36}{68}$

Consider this a ratio of n (numerator) to d (denominator), where $n + d = 104$. Set it up as such:

$$9x + 17x = 104$$
$$36x = 104$$
$$x = 4$$

Now, multiply 9 and 17 by 4, respectively, to find n and d.

$$9(4) + 17(4) = 104$$
$$36 + 68 = 104$$
$$\Rightarrow \dfrac{36}{68}$$

Choice (A) is the correct answer.

371.

A. $6\frac{1}{12}$ tons; B. $6\frac{1}{2}$ tons; D. $6\frac{1}{4}$ tons; F. 7 tons; G. $6\frac{1}{3}$ tons

First, add up the amount of metal already collected and then subtract that answer from the company's goal:

$$6\frac{2}{3} + 7\frac{3}{4} + 4\frac{1}{2} = 18\frac{11}{12} \text{ received}$$
$$25 - 18\frac{11}{12} = 6\frac{1}{12} \text{ needed}$$

Any answer $\geq 6\frac{1}{12}$ tons is correct.

Choices (A), (B), (D), (F), and (G) meet this requirement.

372.

E. $\dfrac{2}{21}$

The total work done by two adults and two children

$$= \frac{2}{3.5} + \frac{1}{6} + \frac{1}{6}$$
$$= \frac{2}{3.5} + \frac{2}{6}$$
$$= \frac{24}{42} + \frac{14}{42}$$
$$= \frac{38}{42}$$
$$= \frac{19}{21}$$

So, the unfinished work that remains is:

$$\left(1 - \frac{19}{21}\right) = \frac{2}{21}$$

Choice (E) is the one you're looking for.

373.   A. $\frac{1}{3}$

Three small hoses = Two large hoses:

$$\frac{2}{3}+\frac{2}{3}+\frac{2}{3}=\frac{3}{3}+\frac{3}{3}$$

Three small hoses + One large hose = Three large hoses:

$$\frac{2}{3}+\frac{2}{3}+\frac{2}{3}+\frac{3}{3}=\frac{3}{3}+\frac{3}{3}+\frac{3}{3}$$

So, the pool will be filled in $\frac{1}{3}$ of the time, Choice (A).

374.   B. 25

Let x represent red candies.

Green candies = $x+10$

Blue candies = $\frac{1}{3}(x+10)$

Total candies = $5x$

Set up an equation:

$$5x = x+(x+10)+\frac{1}{3}(x+10)$$
$$7x-15x = -40$$
$$-8x = -40$$
$$x = 5$$

There are five red candies in the bag. Use this value to find the total number of candies:

$$\text{Total} = 5x$$
$$= 5 \times 5$$
$$= 25$$

Choice (B) is the solution.

375.   A. $\frac{6}{8}$

If the fraction and its reciprocal total $\frac{25}{12}$, then separate the $\frac{25}{12}$ into two fractions that are equivalent to reciprocals:

$\frac{16}{12}+\frac{9}{12}=\frac{25}{12}$, which reduces to $\frac{4}{3}+\frac{3}{4}=\frac{25}{12}$. Now you know the fraction is $\frac{3}{4}$, but to make the numerator 2 less than the denominator, multiply top and bottom by 2:

$$\frac{3}{4}=\frac{6}{8}$$

Choice (A) is the correct answer.

376. **E. 40,000**

Let the total number of votes polled be x.

$$40\% \text{ of } x = 16,000$$
$$0.4x = 16,000$$
$$x = 40,000$$

The total number of votes polled was 40,000, Choice (E).

377. **1,000**

First, find 25% of 600:

$$0.25 \times 600 = 150$$

Next, set 15% of the number equal to 150:

$$0.15 \times n = 150$$
$$n = \frac{150}{0.15}$$
$$= 1,000$$

378. **25**

If the team won 80%, then it lost 20% of its games. 20% is 5 games, so 100% is 25 games.

379. **33**

The percent profit is:

$$\left(\frac{5}{15}\right) \times 100 = \frac{500}{15}$$
$$= 33.33\overline{3}$$
$$= 33\%$$

Disregard the percent symbol and type in 33.

380. **D. 125**

If the diameter of the old label is 100, the diameter of the new label will be 150. This gives a ratio of 2:3. The areas of the labels will be in the ratio $(2)^2:(3)^2$, or 4:9.

This is an increase in area of five units for every four units:

$$\frac{5}{4} = 125\%$$

381. **3,240**

A 20% increase equals 120%:

$$= 1.2 \times 45$$
$$= 54$$

To calculate the words per hour, multiply by 60:

$$54 \times 60 = 3,240$$

382. **E. 87.5%**

$$x = 8y, \text{ so } y = \frac{1}{8}x$$

First, calculate the % y is of x:

$$\frac{\left(\left(\frac{1}{8}x\right)(100)\right)}{x} = \frac{100}{8}$$
$$= 12.5\%$$

Next, calculate the % that y is less than x:

$100\% - 12.5\% = 87.5\%$, Choice (E).

383. **B. 40%**

S = 150% of T, so:

$$S = \frac{150T}{100}$$
$$S = \frac{3}{2}T$$

Substitute this answer for S into the equation:

$$S + T = \frac{3}{2}T + T$$
$$S + T = \frac{5}{2}T$$
$$\frac{2}{5}(S+T) = T$$
$$\frac{2}{5} \Rightarrow 0.40 \Rightarrow 40\% \text{ of } (S+T)$$

The solution is 40%, Choice (B).

384. **B. 40%**

Let the original price of the TV be 100. After the first reduction, the price will be 75.

This new price is then reduced by 20%:

$$= 0.8 \times 75$$
$$= 60$$

60 represents a reduction of 40% on the original:

$$100 - 60 = 40$$

Choice (B) is the correct answer.

385. **C. $300**

Let x be the total number of people the church will ask for donations.

People already solicited $= 0.6x$

First, calculate the amount of money already raised:

$$(600)(0.6x) = 360x$$

$360x$ constitutes 75% of the total amount needed, so 25% $= 120x$.

Next, calculate the average donation needed from the remaining people:

$$\frac{120x}{0.4x} = 300$$

The average donation needed from the remaining parishioners is $300, Choice (C).

386. **B. 0.25**

Rewrite $\sqrt{5}$% of $5\sqrt{5}$:

$$\frac{\sqrt{5}}{100}\left(5\sqrt{5}\right) = \frac{5 \times 5}{100}$$
$$= \frac{25}{100}$$
$$= 0.25$$

Choice (B) is the correct answer.

387. **C. 0.765D**

If the price is reduced by 15%, then the new price $= 0.85D$

If this new price is further reduced by 10%, the discounted price

$$= 0.9 \times 0.85D$$
$$= 0.765D$$

The employee will have to pay 0.765D, Choice (C).

388.   C. 15

First, find what 150% of 6 is:

$$1.5 \times 6 = 9$$

Next, add this answer to 6 to find the number:

$$9 + 6 = 15$$

The correct answer is Choice (C).

389.   D. 1,200

Let the total number of sugar cones received = x.

The total number of waffle cones received = $3x$.

Calculate the number of sugar cones received:

$$(10\% \text{ of } x) + (4\% \text{ of } 3x) = 66$$
$$(0.1x) + ((.04)(3x)) = 66$$
$$(0.1x) + (0.12x) = 66$$
$$0.22x = 66$$
$$x = 300$$

Now, calculate the total number of all cones received:

$$= x + 3x$$
$$= 4x$$
$$= 4(300)$$
$$= 1,200$$

The shop received a total of 1,200 cones, Choice (D).

390.   C. $450

Let x be the cost price.

Selling price:

$$= x - 0.19x$$
$$= 0.81x$$

Calculate the cost price:

$$0.81x + 162 = x + 0.17x$$
$$162 = 0.36x$$
$$450 = x$$

The cost price of the product is $450, Choice (C).

391.

1.67

Let participation in team sports be t.

Let participation in individual sports be i.

At the beginning of the year, the ratio is $\frac{t}{i}$.

At the end of the year, t increases to $1.25t$, and i decreases to $0.75i$.

The new ratio is $\frac{1.25t}{0.75i} = 1.666\frac{t}{i}$.

Rounded to the nearest two decimal places, the correct answer is 1.67.

392.

E. 12 cups of flour and 8 cups of milk

The ratio of flour to milk is $3:2$.

Multiply the ratio by 4:

$$3 \times 4 : 2 \times 4 = 12:8$$

The recipe will need 12 cups of flour and 8 cups of milk, Choice (E).

393.

C. $7:8$

Five minutes and 50 seconds is not 5.5 minutes, which is why Choice (A) is a trap answer.

First, change both times into seconds:

Karen's time = 350 seconds

Cameron's time = 400 seconds

The ratio of Karen's time to Cameron's time is $350:400$. This can be simplified to $7:8$, Choice (C).

394.

C. $54°$

A right angle is $90°$. Divide $90°$ by the ratio $2:3$.

$$2+3 = 5$$
$$\angle AOB = \frac{2}{5} \times 90°$$
$$= 36°$$
$$\angle BOC = \frac{3}{5} \times 90°$$
$$= 54°$$

Choice (C) is the correct answer.

395. **A.** $3:5$

$$\text{Ratio} = 1.8\text{m} : 3\text{m}$$
$$= 18 : 30$$
$$= 3 : 5$$

Choice (A) is the correct answer.

396. **2.5**

If three painters take five days, then in five days, one painter paints $\frac{1}{5}$, and in one day, paints $\frac{1}{15}$ of the wall. This means that working by himself, the painter takes 15 days to paint the wall. Two painters take 7.5 days, which is 2.5 days longer than the original 5 days.

397. **B.** $1:500,000$

First, convert kilometers to centimeters:

$$25 \text{ km} = 25 \times 1,000 \text{ m} = 25,000 \text{ m}$$
$$25,000 \text{ m} = 25,000 \times 100 \text{ cm} = 2,500,000 \text{ cm}$$

The scale of the map is $5:2,500,000$ and that can be reduced to $1:500,000$, Choice (B).

398. **D. 132°**

A straight line is $180°$. Divide $180°$ by the ratio $4:11$:

$$4 + 11 = 15$$
$$\text{Angle } AOB = \frac{4}{15} \times 180°$$
$$= 4 \times 12°$$
$$= 48°$$

The correct response is Choice (D).

399. **E. 1 cup**

3 cups of flour are used, not 24.

$$24 \div 3 = 8$$

Divide each number by 8:

$$24 \div 8 = 3$$
$$8 \div 8 = 1$$
$$3 \div 8 = \frac{3}{8}$$

$$24 : 8 : 3 = 3 : 1 : \frac{3}{8}$$

1 cup of butter, Choice (A), should be used.

400. C. 16.56 cm

First, convert meters into centimeters:

$$828 \text{ m} \times 1,000 = 82,800 \text{ cm}$$

Next, divide by the 5,000 ratio:

$$82,800 \text{ cm} \div 5,000 = 16.56 \text{ cm}$$

The solution is 16.56 centimeters, Choice (C).

401. D. 12

The segment AC can be found by adding segment AB and segment BC.

$$AB + BC = AC$$
$$7 + 5 = 12$$

Choice (D) is the correct answer.

402. C. 8

The midpoint is the center of the segment.

$$16 \div 2 = 8$$

Choice (C) represents AM.

403. 6

Two lines have one point of intersection. A third line can cut through the other two to give two new points of intersection. (Total = 3.) A fourth line can cut through the other three giving three new points of intersection (Total 3 + 3 = 6).

404. 84

In triangle ABC, angles CAB and CBA are equal and both are 28, making angle ACB equal 124 and angle ACD 56.

Angles ACD and CDA are equal, so

$$\text{Angle } DAC = 180 - 56 - 56$$
$$= 68$$

The angle marked x =

$$180 - 68 - 28 = 84$$

405.   **6**

The description tells us that *l* and *m* are parallel lines with the circle lying between and touching both.

The area of the circle = $\pi r^2 = 9\pi$.

The radius = 3 and the diameter = 6.

406.   **A. 35°**

A bisecting ray divides the angle into two equal halves.

$$\angle XYZ \div 2 = \angle XYW$$
$$70° \div 2 = 35°$$

Choice (A) is the correct answer.

407.   **C. 114°**

Same-side interior angles equal 180° when added together. To find the measurement of angle *4*, you subtract the measurement of angle *1* from 180°.

$$180° - \angle 1 = \angle 4$$
$$180° - 66° = 114°$$

The correct answer is Choice (C).

**Answers
401–500**

408.   **B. 1**

One and only one line can be drawn parallel to line *AB* through a point not on line *AB*. Thus, the correct answer is Choice (B).

409.   **60°**

Let the smallest angle = *x*.

The sum of two vertically opposite angles = 2*x*.

The sum of the other pair of vertically opposite angles = 360 – 2*x*.

Because they are double the measure of angle *x*, their sum also = 4*x*.

$$360 - 2x = 4x$$
$$360 = 6x$$
$$60 = x$$

410.   **3**

First, rearrange the second equation to fit the form *y* = *mx* + *b*, where *m* = slope:

$$y = \frac{9x - 7}{n}$$

Parallel lines have the same slope. From the first equation, slope = n. From the second equation, slope = $\dfrac{9}{n}$. Equating the two slopes gives:

$$n = \frac{9}{n}$$
$$n^2 = 9$$
$$n = 3$$

411. **C. 33 cm**

The area is found by using the formula

$$\text{Area} = \frac{1}{2} \times \text{base} \times \text{height}$$

Substitute the values from the diagram into the formula:

$$\text{Area} = \frac{1}{2} \times bh$$
$$\text{base} = 11 \text{ cm}$$
$$\text{height} = 6 \text{ cm}$$

$$\text{Area} = \frac{1}{2} \times 11 \times 6$$
$$= 33$$

The area is 33 centimeters, Choice (C).

412. **E. 70 m**

The area is found by using the formula

$$\text{Area} = \frac{1}{2} \times \text{base} \times \text{height}$$

Substitute the values from the diagram into the formula:

$$\text{Area} = \frac{1}{2} \times bh$$
$$\text{base} = 14 \text{ cm}$$
$$\text{height} = 10 \text{ cm}$$

$$\text{Area} = \frac{1}{2} \times 14 \times 10$$
$$= 70$$

The area is 70 meters, Choice (E).

413. 5

Half the perimeter = length + breadth = 7

The length = $\frac{2}{7}(14) = 4$

The breadth = $7 - 4 = 3$

The length and the breadth form the legs of a 3-4-5 right triangle with the diagonal of the rectangle forming the hypotenuse, so the diagonal = 5.

414. 6

Area of the rectangle = $3x^2$

Area of the right isosceles triangle = $\frac{1}{2}x^2$

Divide the area of the rectangle by the area of the triangle:

$$\frac{3x^2}{\frac{1}{2}x^2} = 6$$

415. 54

First, find the height:

$$\text{area} = \frac{1}{2}b \times h$$
$$108 = \frac{1}{2}(24) \times h$$
$$108 = 12h$$
$$9 = h$$

Each triangle formed by half the base is a 3-4-5 right triangle; therefore, $a = 15$.

Next, find the perimeter:

$$= 24 + 15 + 15$$
$$= 54$$

416. C. 25

Use the formula

$$a^2 + b^2 = c^2$$

and substitute the values from the diagram into the formula:

$$a^2 + b^2 = c^2$$
$$(24)^2 + (7)^2 = c^2$$
$$576 + 49 = c^2$$
$$625 = c^2$$
$$\sqrt{625} = c$$
$$25 = c$$

The length of c is 25, Choice (C).

417.   **C.** $\sqrt{135}$

Use the formula

$$a^2 + b^2 = c^2$$

and substitute the values from the diagram into the formula:

$$a^2 + b^2 = c^2$$
$$a^2 + (11)^2 = (16)^2$$
$$a^2 + 121 = 256$$
$$a^2 = 256 - 121$$
$$a^2 = 135$$
$$a = \sqrt{135}$$

The correct answer is Choice (B).

418.   **D. 4 cm**

Use the formula

$$a^2 + b^2 = c^2$$

to find the second leg:

$$a^2 + b^2 = c^2$$
$$a^2 + (3)^2 = (5)^2$$
$$a^2 + 9 = 25$$
$$a^2 = 25 - 9$$
$$a^2 = 16$$
$$a = \sqrt{16}$$
$$a = 4$$

The correct answer is 4 centimeters, Choice (D).

419.   **C. 18.8 miles**

The directions can be thought of as sides of a right triangle. Use the formula

$$a^2 + b^2 = c^2$$

and substitute the values from the problem into the formula:

$$a^2 + b^2 = c^2$$
$$(8)^2 + (17)^2 = c^2$$
$$64 + 289 = c^2$$
$$353 = c^2$$
$$18.8 = c$$

The two towns are 18.8 miles apart, Choice (C).

420.   **D. 8 cm**

First, find the hypotenuse:

$$6\text{ cm} + 4\text{ cm} = 10\text{ cm}$$

Use the formula

$$a^2 + b^2 = c^2$$

to find the second leg:

$$a^2 + b^2 = c^2$$
$$a^2 + (6)^2 = (10)^2$$
$$a^2 + 36 = 100$$
$$a^2 = 100 - 36$$
$$a^2 = 64$$
$$a = \sqrt{64}$$
$$a = 8$$

The second leg is 8 centimeters, Choice (D).

421.   **D. 600**

First, use the formula

$$a^2 + b^2 = c^2$$

to find the second leg:

$$a^2 + b^2 = c^2$$
$$a^2 + (40)^2 = (50)^2$$
$$a^2 + 1,600 = 2,500$$
$$a^2 = 2,500 - 1,600$$
$$a^2 = 900$$
$$a = \sqrt{900}$$
$$a = 30$$

Now, calculate the area:

$$\text{Area} = \frac{1}{2} \times bh$$
$$\text{base} = 40$$
$$\text{height} = 30$$

$$\text{Area} = \frac{1}{2} \times 40 \times 30$$
$$= 600$$

The area is 600, Choice (D).

422.   2.4

Hypotenuse $AC = 5$

Leg $CB = 3$

Leg $AB = 4$

Calculate the area:

$$= \frac{1}{2} b \times h$$
$$= \frac{1}{2} 4 \times 3$$
$$= 6$$

Line segment DB is the height of triangle ADB:

$$\text{Area} = \frac{1}{2}(AC)(DB)$$
$$6 = \frac{1}{2} 5(DB)$$
$$\frac{6}{2.5} = DB$$
$$2.4 = DB$$

423.   **D. 36 cm**

First, use the formula

$$a^2 + b^2 = c^2$$

to find the second leg:

$$a^2 + b^2 = c^2$$
$$a^2 + (12)^2 = (15)^2$$
$$a^2 + 144 = 225$$
$$a^2 = 225 - 144$$
$$a^2 = 81$$
$$a = \sqrt{81}$$
$$a = 9$$

Now, calculate the perimeter by finding the sum of the three sides:

$$9 + 12 + 15 = 36 \text{ cm}$$

The perimeter is 36 centimeters, Choice (D).

424. **D. 24 cm**

First, find the hypotenuse:

$$6 \text{ cm} + 4 \text{ cm} = 10 \text{ cm}$$

Use the formula

$$a^2 + b^2 = c^2$$

to find the second leg:

$$a^2 + b^2 = c^2$$
$$a^2 + (6)^2 = (10)^2$$
$$a^2 + 36 = 100$$
$$a^2 = 100 - 36$$
$$a^2 = 64$$
$$a = \sqrt{64}$$
$$a = 8$$

Now, calculate the perimeter by finding the sum of the three sides:

$$6 + 8 + 10 = 24 \text{ cm}$$

The perimeter is 24 centimeters, Choice (D).

425. **C. $\sqrt{13}$**

The rectangle can be divided into two right-angled triangles. Use the formula

$$a^2 + b^2 = c^2$$

and substitute the values from the problem into the formula:

$$a^2 + b^2 = c^2$$
$$(3)^2 + (2)^2 = c^2$$
$$9 + 4 = c^2$$
$$13 = c^2$$
$$\sqrt{13} = c$$

The correct answer is Choice (C).

426. **A. 75 yards**

The rectangular field can be divided into two right-angled triangles. Use the formula

$$a^2 + b^2 = c^2$$

and substitute the values from the problem into the formula:

$$a^2 + b^2 = c^2$$
$$a^2 + (100)^2 = (125)^2$$
$$a^2 + 10,000 = 15,625$$
$$a^2 = 15,625 - 10,000$$
$$a^2 = 5,625$$
$$a^2 = \sqrt{5,625}$$
$$a = 75$$

427. **B. $\sqrt{2}$**

The square can be divided into two right-angled triangles. Use the formula

$$a^2 + b^2 = c^2$$

and substitute the values from the problem into the formula:

$$a^2 + b^2 = c^2$$
$$(1)^2 + (1)^2 = c^2$$
$$1 + 1 = c^2$$
$$2 = c^2$$
$$\sqrt{2} = c$$

Choice (B) is the correct answer.

428. **B. 38.5**

The area is found by using the formula

$$\text{Area} = \frac{1}{2} \times \text{base} \times \text{height}$$

Substitute the values from the diagram into the formula:

$$\text{Area} = \frac{1}{2} \times bh$$
$$\text{base} = 8 + 3 = 11$$
$$\text{height} = 7$$

$$\text{Area} = \frac{1}{2} \times 11 \times 7$$
$$= 38.5$$

The area is 38.5, Choice (B).

429. A. 17.4

The area is found by using the formula

$$\text{Area} = \frac{1}{2} \times \text{base} \times \text{height}$$

Substitute the values from the diagram into the formula:

$$\text{Area} = \frac{1}{2} \times bh$$
$$\text{base} = 6$$
$$\text{height} = 5.8$$

$$\text{Area} = \frac{1}{2} \times 6 \times 5.8$$
$$= 17.4$$

The area is 17.4, Choice (A).

430. C. 7

Use the formula for area

$$\text{Area} = \frac{1}{2} \times \text{base} \times \text{height}$$

and substitute the values from the diagram into the formula:

$$\text{Area} = \frac{1}{2} \times bh$$
$$\text{base} = 12$$
$$\text{area} = 42$$

$$42 = \frac{1}{2} \times 12 \times h$$
$$6 \times h = 42$$
$$h = 42 \div 6$$
$$= 7$$

The height of the triangle is 7, Choice (C).

Answers
401–500

431. D. 9

Use the formula for area

$$\text{Area} = \frac{1}{2} \times \text{base} \times \text{height}$$

and substitute the values from the diagram into the formula:

$$\text{Area} = \frac{1}{2} \times bh$$
$$\text{area} = 22.5$$
$$\text{height} = 5$$

$$22.5 = \frac{1}{2} \times b \times 5$$
$$45 = b \times 5$$
$$b = 45 \div 5$$
$$= 9$$

The base of the triangle is 9, Choice (D).

432. C. 120

Use the formula

$$a^2 + b^2 = c^2$$

to find the second leg:

$$a^2 + b^2 = c^2$$
$$a^2 + (40)^2 = (50)^2$$
$$a^2 + 1,600 = 2,500$$
$$a^2 = 2,500 - 1,600$$
$$a^2 = 900$$
$$a = \sqrt{900}$$
$$a = 30$$

Now, calculate the perimeter by finding the sum of the three sides:

$$30 + 40 + 50 = 120$$

The perimeter is 120, Choice (C).

433. E. 30 cm

First, find the hypotenuse:

$$12 \text{ cm} + 1 \text{ cm} = 13 \text{ cm}$$

Use the formula

$$a^2 + b^2 = c^2$$

to find the second leg:

$$a^2 + b^2 = c^2$$
$$a^2 + (12)^2 = (13)^2$$
$$a^2 + 144 = 169$$
$$a^2 = 169 - 144$$
$$a^2 = 25$$
$$a = \sqrt{25}$$
$$a = 5$$

Now, calculate the perimeter by finding the sum of the three sides:

$$5 + 12 + 13 = 30 \text{ cm}$$

The perimeter is 30 centimeters, Choice (E).

434. **E. 12 cm**

Use the formula

$$a^2 + b^2 = c^2$$

to find the second leg:

$$a^2 + b^2 = c^2$$
$$a^2 + (3)^2 = (5)^2$$
$$a^2 + 9 = 25$$
$$a^2 = 25 - 9$$
$$a^2 = 16$$
$$a = \sqrt{16}$$
$$a = 4$$

Now, calculate the perimeter by finding the sum of the three sides:

$$3 + 4 + 5 = 12 \text{ cm}$$

The perimeter is 12 centimeters, Choice (E).

435. **B. 54**

First, use the formula

$$a^2 + b^2 = c^2$$

to find the second leg:

$$a^2 + b^2 = c^2$$
$$a^2 + (12)^2 = (15)^2$$
$$a^2 + 144 = 225$$
$$a^2 = 225 - 144$$
$$a^2 = 81$$
$$a = \sqrt{81}$$
$$a = 9$$

Now, calculate the area:

$$Area = \frac{1}{2} \times b \times h$$
$$base = 9$$
$$height = 12$$

$$Area = \frac{1}{2} \times 9 \times 12$$
$$= 54$$

The area is 54, Choice (B).

436.   D. 21

Use the formula

$$a^2 + b^2 = c^2$$

and substitute the values from one of the top triangles into the formula:

$$a^2 + b^2 = c^2$$
$$a^2 + (8)^2 = (10)^2$$
$$a^2 + 64 = 100$$
$$a^2 = 100 - 64$$
$$a^2 = 36$$
$$a = \sqrt{36}$$
$$a = 6$$

Using the same formula, now substitute the values from one of the bottom triangles into the formula:

$$a^2 + b^2 = c^2$$
$$(8)^2 + b^2 = (17)^2$$
$$64 + b^2 = 289$$
$$b^2 = 289 - 64$$
$$b^2 = 225$$
$$b^2 = \sqrt{225}$$
$$b = 15$$

Lastly, add the two sides together:

$$AC = a + b$$
$$= 6 + 15$$
$$= 21$$

The length of AC is 21, Choice (D).

---

437. C. $2\sqrt{11}$

Use the formula

$$a^2 + b^2 = c^2$$

and substitute the values from the bottom triangle into the formula:

$$a^2 + b^2 = c^2$$
$$(6)^2 + (8)^2 = c^2$$
$$36 + 64 = c^2$$
$$100 = c^2$$
$$10 = c$$

Using the same formula, now substitute the values from the top triangle into the formula:

$$a^2 + b^2 = c^2$$
$$x^2 + (10)^2 = (12)^2$$
$$x^2 + 100 = 144$$
$$144 - 100 = x^2$$
$$44 = x^2$$
$$\sqrt{44} = x^2$$
$$\sqrt{4 \times 11} = x^2$$
$$2\sqrt{11} = x$$

The solution is Choice (C).

---

438. A. 12 cm

This triangle is a 3-4-5 triangle. Calculate the perimeter by finding the sum of the three sides:

$$3 + 4 + 5 = 12 \text{ cm}$$

The perimeter is 12 centimeters, Choice (A).

Answers
401–500

439. 45

First, calculate the base of the triangle:

$$\frac{1}{2}\text{base} \times \text{height} =$$

$$\frac{1}{2}\text{base} \times 12 = 72$$

$$\frac{1}{2}\text{base} = 6$$

$$\text{base} = 12$$

This means that this is an isosceles right triangle, so $x = 45$.

440. **C. 10 cm**

Because 8 is a multiple of 4, this could be a 3-4-5 triangle. Adjust the 3-4-5 ratio to 6-8-10, and the sides total 24.

The hypotenuse is 10 centimeters, Choice (C).

441. $\frac{1}{4}$

First, calculate the perimeter of R:

$30 + 10 + 30 + 10 = 80$

Next, calculate the perimeter of S:

$5 + 5 + 5 + 5 = 20$

So, the perimeter of S is $\frac{20}{80}$ of the perimeter of R.

$\frac{20}{80}$ reduces to $\frac{1}{4}$.

442. **C. 55°**

The interior angles of a quadrilateral add up to 360°. Add all of the known angles and subtract from 360°:

$$83° + 107° + 115° = 305°$$
$$\text{Angle } D = 360° - 305°$$
$$\text{Angle } D = 55°$$

The correct answer is Choice (C).

443.   **E. 129°**

The interior angles of a quadrilateral add up to 360°. Angle D and angle B are equal. Subtract the sum of angle D and angle B from 360°:

$$\text{Angle } A + \text{Angle } C = 360° - 51° - 51°$$
$$= 360° - 102°$$
$$= 258°$$

Because $A = C$, divide the last answer by 2 to find the measurement of angle A:

$$258° \div 2 = 129°$$

You have your answer — Choice (E).

444.   **21%**

If the correct side length and width of the card are each 10, then the correct area is 100. However, if the sides are 10% too long, then the length and width are each 11, for an area of 121. 121 is 21% larger than 100.

445.   **D. 121°**

The interior angles of a quadrilateral add up to 360°. Subtract the sum of angle D and angle C from 360°:

$$\text{Angle } D + \text{Angle } C = 360° - 59° - 59°$$
$$= 360° - 118°$$
$$= 242°$$

Because $A = B$, divide the last answer by 2 to find the measurement of angle A:

$$242° \div 2 = 121°$$

The correct answer is Choice (D).

446.   **C. 62.8 feet**

Use the formula for the circumference of a circle:

$$C = 2\pi r$$
$$\pi = 3.14$$
$$C = 2 \times 10 \times 3.14$$
$$= 62.8$$

The circumference is 62.8 feet, Choice (C).

447.   **B. 44 inches**

Use the formula for the circumference of a circle:

$$C = \pi d$$

$$\pi = \frac{22}{7}$$
$$d = 14$$

$$C = \pi d$$
$$= (\frac{22}{7})(14)$$
$$= 44$$

---

448. **B. 154 cm²**

Use the formula for the area of a circle:

$$A = \pi r^2$$

$$\pi = \frac{22}{7}$$
$$r = 7$$

$$A = \pi r^2$$
$$= \frac{22}{7}(7)^2$$
$$= 22 \times 7$$
$$= 154$$

The correct answer is Choice (B).

---

449. **A. 4.52 m²**

Use the formula for the area of a circle:

$$A = \pi r^2$$

$$\pi = 3.14$$
$$r = 1.2$$

$$A = \pi r^2$$
$$= 3.14 \times (1.2)^2$$
$$= 3.14 \times 1.44$$
$$= 4.52$$

The correct answer is Choice (A).

---

450. **C. 10**

Use the formula for the circumference of a circle:

$$C = 2\pi r$$

$$\pi = 3.14$$
$$C = 62.8$$

Rewrite the equation to solve for d:

$$C = 2\pi r$$
$$\frac{C}{\pi} = 2r$$
$$\frac{62.8}{3.14} = 2r$$
$$20 = 2r$$
$$10 = r$$

The approximate radius of the circle is 10, Choice (C).

451.

B. 132 cm

Use the formula for the circumference of a circle:

$$C = 2\pi r$$
$$= (\frac{22}{7})(2 \times 21)$$
$$= (22)(2 \times 3)$$
$$= 132$$

The circumference is 132 centimeters, Choice (B).

452.

D. 16a²

If the area of the circle is $4a^2\pi$, the radius is the square root of $4a^2 = 2a$, making the diameter $4a$. The diameter is also the side of the square.

$$\text{Area of square} = s^2$$
$$= \left(4a\right)^2$$
$$= 16a^2$$

Choice (D) is the correct answer.

453.

A. 1; B. 3; C. 4; D. 7; E. 10; F. 11

Make a diagram with Town A and Town B 5 miles apart. Draw a circle centered on Town B, with a radius of 6. Town C could be anywhere on this circle. The minimum distance would be 1 and the maximum distance would be 11, but anywhere in between is also possible. All of the choices are correct.

454.

E. 34π

Use the formula for the area of a circle:

$$A = \pi r^2$$

First, find the area of the top circle:

$$A = \pi r^2$$
$$= \pi 3^2$$
$$= 9\pi$$

Next, find the area of the bottom circle:

$$A = \pi r^2$$
$$= \pi 5^2$$
$$= 25\pi$$

Add the area of the top circle to the area of the bottom circle.

Top circle = 9π

Bottom circle = 25π

$$9\pi + 25\pi = 34\pi$$

Choice (E) is correct.

455. **C. 154 in²**

Use the formula for the area of a circle:

$$A = \pi r^2$$

$$\pi = \frac{22}{7}$$
$$r = \frac{d}{2} = \frac{14}{2}$$
$$= 7$$

$$A = \pi r^2$$
$$= \frac{22}{7} \times (7)^2$$
$$= 22 \times 7$$
$$= 154$$

Choice (C) represents the area of the circle.

456. **A. 5π**

Arc $AQB = \frac{1}{4}$ the perimeter of the circle.

The diagonal SQ of the rectangle is the radius of the circle.

Find the diagonal:

$$r^2 = 8^2 + 6^2$$
$$r^2 = 64 + 36$$
$$r^2 = 100$$
$$r = 10$$

Find the length of the arc:

$$\frac{1}{4} 20\pi = 5\pi$$

Choice (A) is the correct answer.

457.   **D.** 5π

The diagonal of the rectangle is the diameter of the circle. The diagonal is the hypotenuse of a 3-4-5 triangle and is therefore 5.

$$\text{Circumference} = \pi(\text{diameter})$$
$$= 5\pi$$

The answer you're looking for is Choice (D).

458.   **C.** 77 cm^2

Use the formula for the area of a circle: $a = \pi r^2$

$$\pi = \frac{22}{7}$$
$$r = \frac{d}{2} = \frac{14}{2}$$
$$= 7$$

Because the problem uses a semicircle, you divide the area in half:

$$A = \frac{\pi r^2}{2}$$
$$= \frac{\frac{22}{7}(7)^2}{2}$$
$$= \frac{22(7)}{2}$$
$$= 11(7)$$
$$= 77$$

Choice (C) represents the area of the semicircle.

459.   **B.** 5π

Use the formula for the area of a circle:

$$A = \pi r^2$$

First, find the area of the outer circle:

$$A = \pi r^2$$
$$= \pi(3^2)$$
$$= 9\pi$$

Next, find the area of the inner circle:

$$A = \pi r^2$$
$$= \pi(2^2)$$
$$= 4\pi$$

Subtract the area of the inner circle from the area of the outer circle:

Outer circle $= 9\pi$

Inner circle $= 4\pi$

$$9\pi - 4\pi = 5\pi$$

The solution is Choice (B).

460.   **5.39**

Angles DAB and ABC are right angles. Because the areas of the circles are in the ratio of 4:1, the radii must be in the ratio of $\sqrt{4} : \sqrt{1}$, which is 2:1.

Radius $BC = 4$, so the radius $AD = 2$.

Drawing a perpendicular line from D to BC will divide $ABCD$ into a rectangle and a right triangle. The right triangle has sides of 5 (because it is equal to AB), 2 (half of BC), and DC.

$$5^2 + 2^2 = DC^2$$
$$25 + 4 = DC^2$$
$$29 = DC^2$$
$$\sqrt{29} =$$
$$5.3852 =$$
$$5.39$$

461.   **C.** 125 in^3

Use the formula for volume of a cube:

$$\text{Volume} = (\text{Length of one Edge})^3$$
$$= (5 \text{ in} \times 5 \text{ in} \times 5 \text{ in})$$
$$= 125 \text{ in}^3$$

462. **B.** 150 cm^2

Use the formula for surface area of a cube:

$$\text{Surface Area} = 6 \times \left(\text{Length of one Edge}\right)^2$$
$$= 6\left(5 \text{ cm}\right)^2$$
$$= 6\left(25 \text{ cm}^2\right)$$
$$= 150 \text{ cm}^2$$

Choice (B) is the correct answer.

463. **108**

First, find the volume of one cube:

$$\frac{54}{2} = 27$$

To find the side of each cube, find the cube root:

$$\sqrt[3]{27} = 3$$

If the side of the cube is 3 units, the area of one face is 9 units. There are six faces on a cube, so the surface area equals $6 \times 9 = 54$.

There are two cubes, so the total surface area is

$$2 \times 54 = 108$$

464. **144**

If the side of one cube is 6 inches, the surface area = 6×6^2.

Because there are three of these cubes, their total surface area = $3 \times 6 \times 6^2$.

The four cube faces that are glued together to form the rectangular box will cause the surface area of the rectangular box to be 4×6^2 less than the surface area of the cubes:

$4 \times 6^2 = 144$

465. **A.** 24π

Use the formula for surface area of a cylinder:

$$\text{Surface Area} = 2\pi r(r + h)$$

diameter $= 4$, so $r = 2$
$h = 4$

$$\text{Surface Area} = 2\pi r(r+h)$$
$$= 2\pi \times 2(2+4)$$
$$= 2\pi \times 2(6)$$
$$= 2\pi \times 12$$
$$= 24\pi$$

The correct answer is Choice (A).

466. **B. 8**

Total volume of water:

$$= 12 \text{ liters}$$
$$= 12 \times 1,000 \text{ cm}^3$$
$$= 12,000 \text{ cm}^3$$

Volume $= l \times w \times h$

$$12,000 = 50 \times 30 \times h$$
$$12,000 = 1,500 \times h$$
$$8 = h$$

Choice (B) is the right answer.

467. **B. 40**

Surface area of one cube = 6

Total number of cubes = 12

Total surface when disassembled $= 6 \times 12 = 72$

Surface of larger structure = area of four larger faces + area of two smaller faces

$$= (4 \times 6) + (2 \times 4)$$
$$= 24 + 8$$
$$= 32$$

$$72 - 32 = 40$$

This is an increase of 40 units, Choice (B).

468. **D. 25:18**

Let r be the side of the large cube.

First, calculate the volume of the larger cube, which equals the sum of the volumes of the smaller cubes:

$$r^3 = 3^3 + 4^3 + 5^3$$
$$r^3 = 27 + 64 + 125$$
$$r^3 = 216$$
$$r = 6$$

The total surface area of the large cube = 216.

Next, find the total surface area of the smaller cubes:

$$= 6\left(3^2 + 4^2 + 5^2\right)$$
$$= 6(9 + 16 + 25)$$
$$= 6(50)$$
$$= 300$$

The ratio:

$$300 : 216 = 25 : 18$$

Choice (D) is your answer.

469.   **E. 184 in^2**

Find the surface area of the rectangular solid using the formula:

Surface area $= 2wl + 2lh + 2hw$

$l = 8$ in
$w = 5$ in
$h = 4$ in

Surface area $= 2wl + 2lh + 2hw$
$$= (2 \times 5 \text{ in} \times 8 \text{ in}) + (2 \times 8 \text{ in} \times 4 \text{ in}) + (2 \times 4 \text{ in} \times 5 \text{ in})$$
$$= 80 \text{ in}^2 + 64 \text{ in}^2 + 40 \text{ in}^2$$
$$= 184 \text{ in}^2$$

The correct answer is Choice (E).

470.   **E. 360**

Find the volume of the rectangular solid using the formula:

Volume = height $\times$ weight $\times$ length

$l = 12$
$w = 6$
$h = 5$

$$\text{Volume} = \text{height} \times \text{weight} \times \text{length}$$
$$= 5 \times 6 \times 12$$
$$= 360$$

The volume is 360, Choice (E).

471. **C.** $(3a-1)^2$

$$9a^2 - 6a + 1$$
$$(3a)^2 + 2(3a)(-1) + (-1)^2$$
$$(3a-1)^2$$

The correct answer is Choice (C).

472. **C.** $\dfrac{a^3}{b^6}$

$$\frac{a^0 b^{-5}}{a^{-3}b} = \frac{1}{b^5 a^3 b}$$
$$= \frac{1}{b^5 b a^3}$$
$$= \frac{a^3}{b^6}$$

The correct answer is Choice (C).

473. **C.** xy^2

$$3x^2 y^3 (15x^3 y^2) \times 5x^2 y = \frac{3x^2 y^3}{15x^3 y^2} \times 5x^2 y$$
$$= \frac{3x^2 y}{15x^3} \times 5x^2 y$$
$$= xy^2$$

The correct answer is Choice (C).

474. **A.** $(x+y)(x+y-z)$

$$x^2 + 2xy + y^2 - xz - yz = (x+y)^2 + z(-x-y)$$
$$= (x+y)(x+y-z)$$

The correct answer is Choice (A).

475. **B. –1**

The exponent is –5, so multiply the base number by itself, five times. Because the exponent is a negative number, the answer is the reciprocal:

$$(-1)^{-5} = \frac{1}{(-1)(-1)(-1)(-1)(-1)}$$
$$= \frac{1}{-1}$$
$$= -1$$

Choice (B) is the correct answer.

476. **D. 1**

Any number to the power of 0 equals 1:

$$(-10)^0 = 1$$

Therefore, Choice (D) is the right answer.

477. **B. 3.75**

First, find the value of 2^2:

$$2^2 = 2 \times 2 = 4$$

Next, find the value of 2^{-2}:

$$2^{-2} = \frac{1}{2 \times 2} = \frac{1}{4}$$
$$= 0.25$$

Lastly, add the two answers together:

$$2^2 - 2^{-2} =$$
$$4 - 0.25 = 3.75$$

The solution is Choice (B).

478. **C.** $\dfrac{x^2 - 2xy + 2xz + y^2 + z^2}{xyz}$

$$\frac{x-y+z}{yz} + \frac{y+z-x}{zx} + \frac{z+x-y}{xy} = \frac{x(x-y+z) + y(y+z-x) + z(z+x-y)}{xyz}$$
$$= \frac{(xx-xy+xz) + (yy+yz-yx) + (zz+zx-zy)}{xyz}$$
$$= \frac{x^2 - 2xy + 2xz + y^2 + z^2}{xyz}$$

The correct answer is Choice (C).

479. D. $\dfrac{-25}{8}$

$$(-2)^{-3}5^2 = (-2^{-3})25$$
$$= \left(\dfrac{-1}{2^3}\right)25$$
$$= \dfrac{-25}{8}$$

The correct answer is Choice (D).

480. B. $-\dfrac{1}{4}$

$$8 = 16^{x+1}$$
$$8 = (2^4)^{x+1}$$
$$8 = 2^{4(x+1)}$$
$$x = -\dfrac{1}{4}$$

The solution is Choice (B).

481. A. $-x^{6ab}$

$$(-x^{2a})^{3b} = -(x^{2a})^{3b}$$
$$= -x^{6ab}$$

The correct answer is Choice (A).

482. B. 1

The smaller n becomes, the greater $\dfrac{1}{2^n}$ becomes. The smallest nonnegative integer is 0.

$$\dfrac{1}{2^n} = \dfrac{1}{2^0}$$
$$= \dfrac{1}{1}$$
$$= 1$$

Choice (B) is the correct answer.

483. A. $5 - 2\sqrt{6}$

Expand $\left(\sqrt{2} - \sqrt{3}\right)^2$.

$$\left(\sqrt{2} - \sqrt{3}\right)\left(\sqrt{2} - \sqrt{3}\right)$$
$$= 2 - 2\left(\sqrt{2} + \sqrt{3}\right) + 3$$
$$= 5 - 2\sqrt{6}$$

The correct answer is Choice (A).

484.   **C.** 2^{32}

All four terms are identical:

$$4\left(2^{30}\right)$$
$$=\left(2^{2}\right)\left(2^{30}\right)$$
$$=2^{32}$$

The correct answer is Choice (C).

485.   **E.** 6^{4}

$$\frac{6^{5}-6^{4}}{5}=\frac{6^{4}\left(6-1\right)}{5}$$
$$=\frac{6^{4}(5)}{5}$$
$$=6^{4}$$

Choice (E) is correct.

486.   **A. 1; B. 3; D. 7; E. 9**

The units digit of 57^{n} is the same as the units digit of 7^{n} for all positive integers n. The units digits of 7 are:

$$7^{1}=7$$
$$7^{2}=49=9$$
$$7^{3}=343=3$$
$$7^{4}=2,401=1$$
$$7^{5}=16,807=7$$

The pattern of 7, 9, 3, and 1 repeats without end; therefore, these four digits are the only possible units digits of 57^{n}.

Choices (A), (B), (D), and (E) are correct.

487. -2

$$0.1^{x}=100$$
$$\left(\frac{1}{10}\right)^{x}=100$$
$$\left(\frac{1}{2\times5}\right)^{x}=100$$
$$x=-2$$

488. 2

8 is 2 raised to the power of 3, so:

$$n + 1 = 3$$
$$n = 2$$

489. 4

First, simplify the equation:

$$\frac{1}{3}f\left(y^2\right) = 5$$
$$f\left(y^2\right) = 15$$

Next, plug y^2 for x in the original function:

$$f(x) = x - 1$$
$$f\left(y^2\right) = y^2 - 1$$

If $f\left(y^2\right) = y^2 - 1$ and $f\left(y^2\right) = 15$, then $y^2 - 1 = 15$. Solve for y:

$$y^2 - 1 = 15$$
$$y^2 = 16$$
$$y = 4$$

490. B. 1

The equation always produces a negative number if n is odd. Because all prime numbers greater than 2 are odd, the number in the middle will always be negative. Thus, the only instance in which the inequality holds true is if $n = 2$.

The number of integer values that make the equation true is 1, Choice (B).

491. B. 90

Given $x \times y = (3x)(2y)$

Evaluate 3×5

Substitute 3 for x and 5 for y in the given equation:

$$3 \times 5 = 3(3) \times 2(5)$$
$$= 9 \times 10$$
$$= 90$$

The correct answer is Choice (B).

492. E. 11

Given $x \odot y = x + 2y$

Evaluate $3 \odot 4$

Substitute 3 for x and 4 for y in the given equation:

$$3 \odot 4 = 3 + 2(4)$$
$$= 3 + 8$$
$$= 11$$

Choice (E) is correct.

493. E. 0

Given $x \cup y = x - 2y$

Evaluate $4 \cup 2$

Substitute 4 for x and 2 for y in the given equation:

$$4 \cup 2 = 4 - 2(2)$$
$$= 0$$

The correct answer is Choice (E).

494. D. 9

Given $x \otimes y = 3x + 2y$

Evaluate $1 \otimes 3$

Substitute 1 for x and 3 for y in the given equation:

$$1 \otimes 3 = 3(1) + 2(3)$$
$$= 3 + 6$$
$$= 9$$

Choice (D) is correct.

495. A. 28

Given $x \oplus y = \frac{1}{2}xy$

Evaluate $8 \oplus 7$

Substitute 8 for x and 7 for y in the given equation:

$$7 \oplus 8 = \frac{1}{2}(8 \times 7)$$
$$= 4 \times 7$$
$$= 28$$

The correct answer is Choice (A).

496. D. 40

Given $x \oslash y = \left(\sqrt{x}\right)(2y)$

Evaluate $16 \oslash 5$

Substitute 16 for x and 5 for y in the given equation:

$$x \oslash y = \left(\sqrt{x}\right)(2y)$$
$$16 \oslash 5 = \left(\sqrt{16}\right)(2 \times 5)$$
$$= (4)(10)$$
$$= 40$$

The correct answer is Choice (D).

497. B. 13.5

Given $x \mp y = 3y\left(\dfrac{1}{2x}\right)$

Evaluate 3 ∓ 27

Substitute 3 for x and 27 for y in the given equation:

$$3 \mp 27 = 3 \times 27\left(\dfrac{1}{2 \times 3}\right)$$
$$= \dfrac{81}{6}$$
$$= 13.5$$

Choice (B) is the correct answer.

498. A. 2.5

Given $x \therefore y = \dfrac{1}{y}x + \dfrac{1}{x}y$

Evaluate $10 \therefore 5$

Substitute 10 for x and 5 for y in the given equation:

$$10 \therefore 5 = \dfrac{1}{5}(10) + \dfrac{1}{10}(5)$$
$$= 2 + 0.5$$
$$= 2.5$$

The correct answer is Choice (A).

499. D. 40

Given $x \odot y = 2xy$

Evaluate $4 \odot 5$

Substitute 4 for x and 5 for y in the given equation:

$$4 \odot 5 = 2(4 \times 5)$$
$$= 2(20)$$
$$= 40$$

Choice (D) is the correct answer.

500. 144

Given $x \spadesuit y = (x+y)^2$

Evaluate $(1 \spadesuit 2) \spadesuit 3$

First, substitute 1 for x and 2 for y in the given equation:

$$1 \spadesuit 2 = (x+y)^2$$
$$= (1+2)^2$$
$$= 3^2$$
$$= 9$$

Next, substitute the answer above (9) for x and 3 for y in the given equation:

$$9 \spadesuit 3 = (x+y)^2$$
$$= (9+3)^2$$
$$= 12^2$$
$$= 144$$

501. 7

$(x + 1)$ on the left side of the equation occurs in exactly the same place as 8 on the right side of the equation, so:

$$x+1 = 8$$
$$x = 7$$

502. A. –4

$$5x + 32 = 4 - 2x$$

Whatever is done on one side must be done on the other side:

$$5x + 32 = 4 - 2x$$
$$5x + 28 = -2x$$
$$28 = -7x$$
$$-4 = x$$

x is equal to –4, Choice (A).

503. C. $9 per hour

Total hours worked:

$$= (8 \times 3) + (6 \times 2)$$
$$= 24 + 12$$
$$= 36$$

Total earned = $324

Hourly wage:

$$= \frac{\$324}{36}$$
$$= \$9$$

Roberto earned $9 per hour, Choice (C).

504. A. $\dfrac{Vr}{12-V}$

Rearrange the equation to solve for R:

$$V = \frac{12R}{(r+R)}$$
$$V(r+R) = 12R$$
$$Vr + VR = 12R$$
$$Vr = 12R - VR$$
$$Vr = R(12-V)$$
$$\frac{Vr}{12-V} = R$$

The correct answer is Choice (A).

505. B. 9

$$\frac{x-3}{3} = \frac{x-5}{2}$$

Rewrite the equation without fractions by cross multiplying:

$$\frac{x-3}{3} = \frac{x-5}{2}$$
$$2(x-3) = 3(x-5)$$
$$2x - 6 = 3x - 15$$
$$2x - 3x = -15 + 6$$
$$-x = -9$$
$$x = 9$$

The value of x is 9, Choice (B).

506.   A. 15

$$\frac{2x-3}{9}+\frac{x+1}{2}=x-4$$

First, rewrite the equation without fractions by multiplying both sides of the equation by the least common multiple (LCM) of the denominators. The LCM of 2 and 9 is 18:

$$18\left(\frac{2x-3}{9}\right)+18\left(\frac{x+1}{2}\right)=18(x-4)$$

Now, simplify the cleaned equation. Whatever is done on one side must be done on the other side:

$$4x-6+9x+9=18x-72$$
$$13x-18x=-72-3$$
$$-5x=-75$$
$$x=15$$

The value of x is 15, Choice (A).

507.   B. –5

$$\frac{x-3}{x-1}=\frac{x+1}{x+2}$$

Rewrite the equation without fractions by cross multiplying and then simplify:

$$\frac{x-3}{x-1}=\frac{x+1}{x+2}$$
$$(x-3)(x+2)=(x-1)(x+1)$$
$$x^2-x-6=x^2-1$$
$$-x=-1+6$$
$$-x=5$$
$$x=-5$$

The value of x is –5, Choice (B).

508.   E. 2

$$5-\frac{(x+1)}{3}=2x$$
$$-(x+1)+3\times\frac{5}{3}=2x$$
$$-x-1+5=2x$$
$$x=2$$

The correct answer is Choice (E).

509.   A. $\dfrac{cst}{abu(v+w)}$

$$\frac{ab}{c}=\frac{st}{u(v+w)x}$$

Rewrite the equation without fractions by cross multiplying and then simplify:

$$\frac{ab}{c} = \frac{st}{u(v+w)x}$$

$$cst = abu(v+w)x$$

$$\frac{cst}{abu(v+w)} = x$$

Choice (A) represents the value of x.

510. 50

Let the number of $2.50 cards be n and the number of $10 packs = $75 - n$.

Total sales $= n(2.5) + (75-n)10$

$$375 = n(2.5) + (75-n)10$$
$$375 = 2.5n + 750 - 10n$$
$$375 = -7.5n + 750$$
$$-375 = -7.5n$$
$$50 = n$$

The store sold 50 of the $2.50 cards that day.

511. A. –2; F. 3

Factor $x^2 - x + 6 = 0$ into $(x+2)(x-3) = 0$.

To make the equation true, x has to equal either –2 or 3, Choices (A) and (F).

512. D. 1; E. 2

Factor $x - 5\sqrt{x} + 4 = 0$ into $(\sqrt{x} - 4)(\sqrt{x} - 1) = 0$.

To make the equation true, $\sqrt{x}$ has to equal either 4 or 1, making x equal to either 2 or 1. Because a square root can only be on a positive number, x cannot equal –2 or –1.

Thus, Choices (D) and (E) are correct.

513. A. 5

Using the FOIL method, multiply the first term in the first set of parentheses by each term in the second set of parentheses. Then, multiply the second term in the first set of parentheses by each term in the second set of parentheses. Lastly, combine like terms.

$$(3x+2)(2x-5) = 6x^2 - 15x + 4x - 10$$
$$= 6x^2 - 11x - 10$$

So,

$$a = 6$$

$$k = -11$$

$n = -10$

Now, solve the equation:

$$a - n + k = 6 - (-10) + (-11)$$
$$= 6 + 10 - 11$$
$$= 5$$

The value of $a - n + k$ is 5, Choice (A).

514. **C. 0; D. 1**

Factor $3x^2 - 3x + 0 = 0$ into $3(x-1)(x+0) = 0$.

To make the equation true, x has to equal either 0 or 1, Choices (C) and (D).

515. **C. –1; G. 4**

Factor $x^2 - 3x - 4 = 0$ into $(x-4)(x+1) = 0$.

To make the equation true, x has to equal either –1 or 4, Choices (C) and (G).

516. **E. 144**

a^4 can be factored to create a simple multiplication problem:

$$a^4 = (a^2)(a^2)$$
$$= 12 \times 12$$
$$= 144$$

The correct answer is Choice (E).

517. **C. $5y(y+3)$**

The terms $5y^2$ and $15y$ are both divisible by 5 and y. Therefore, the highest common factor is $5y$.

$$5y^2 + 15y = 5y(y) + 5y(3)$$
$$= 5y(y+3)$$

Choice (C) is correct.

518. **B. $3y(y+4)$**

The terms $3y^2$ and $12y$ have the common factor of $3y$.

$$3y^2 + 12y = 3y(y+4)$$

Choice (B) is the correct answer.

519. **A. $(2x+3)(2x-3)$** $4x^2 - 9 = (2x)^2 - (3)^2$

This is the difference of squares. Use $(a+b)(a-b) = a^2 - b^2$, with $a = 2x$ and $b = 3$.

$$a^2 - b^2 = (a+b)(a-b)(2x)^2 - (3)^2$$
$$= (2x+3)(2x-3)$$

The correct answer is Choice (A).

---

520. **B.** $-(a+b)$

$$\frac{-(a^2-b^2)}{a-b} = \frac{-(a-b)(a+b)}{a-b}$$
$$= -(a+b)$$

The correct answer is Choice (B).

---

521. **A.** $(x+y-5)(x+y+5)$

This is the difference between two squares.

$$x^2 + 2xy + y^2 - 25 = (x+y)^2 - 25$$
$$= (x+y-5)(x+y+5)$$

Choice (A) is the correct answer.

---

522. **D.** $(x+3)(x+1)$

$$x^2 + 4x + 3 = (x+3)(x+1)$$

The correct answer is Choice (D).

---

523. **C.** $2(y+3)$

Both $2y$ and 6 have a common factor of 2:

$$2y + 6 = 2(y+3)$$

Choice (C) is the correct answer.

---

524. **B.** $(y^m + 6x)(y^m - 6x)$

The equation can be factored:

$$y^{2m} - 36x^2 = (y^m + 6x)(y^m - 6x)$$

The correct answer is Choice (B).

---

525. **E.** $(x-6)(x+5)$

The equation can be factored:

$$x^2 - x - 30 = (x-6)(x+5)$$

The correct answer is Choice (E).

526. D. $2\sqrt{10}$

First, factor the value within the radical and then simplify:

$$\begin{aligned}\sqrt{40} &= \sqrt{2 \times 4 \times 5}\\ &= 2\sqrt{2 \times 5}\\ &= 2\sqrt{10}\end{aligned}$$

Choice (D) is the correct answer.

527. A. $7\sqrt{2}$

First, factor the value within the radical and then simplify:

$$\begin{aligned}\sqrt{98} &= \sqrt{2 \times 7 \times 7}\\ &= 7\sqrt{2}\end{aligned}$$

Choice (A) is correct answer.

528. C. $6\sqrt{3}$

First, factor the value within the radical and then simplify:

$$\begin{aligned}\sqrt{108} &= \sqrt{3 \times 3 \times 3 \times 2 \times 2}\\ &= 6\sqrt{3}\end{aligned}$$

The correct answer is Choice (C).

529. D. $6\sqrt{2}$

First, factor the value within the radical and then simplify:

$$\begin{aligned}\sqrt{72} &= \sqrt{2 \times 6 \times 6}\\ &= 6\sqrt{2}\end{aligned}$$

Choice (D) is the correct answer.

530. A. $30\sqrt{5}$

First, factor the value within the radical and then simplify:

$$\begin{aligned}\sqrt{4,500} &= \sqrt{5 \times 9 \times 10 \times 10}\\ &= 30\sqrt{5}\end{aligned}$$

The correct answer is Choice (A).

531. E. $5\sqrt{3}$

The radical is the same in each term, so the terms can be combined:

$$\begin{aligned}2\sqrt{3} + 3\sqrt{3} &= (2+3) \times \sqrt{3}\\ &= 5\sqrt{3}\end{aligned}$$

Choice (E) is the right answer.

532.

C. $4\sqrt{3}+2\sqrt{5}$

Combine the like radicals:

$$3\sqrt{3}+2\sqrt{5}+\sqrt{3}=4\sqrt{3}+2\sqrt{5}$$

The correct answer is Choice (C).

533.

A. $-9\sqrt{2}$

Simplify and combine the like radicals:

$$3\sqrt{50}-2\sqrt{8}-5\sqrt{32}=3\sqrt{25\times2}-2\sqrt{4\times2}-5\sqrt{16\times2}$$
$$=15\sqrt{2}-4\sqrt{2}-20\sqrt{2}$$
$$=-9\sqrt{2}$$

Choice (A) is the correct answer.

534.

D. $-9\sqrt{2}-3\sqrt{3}$

Simplify and combine like terms:

$$\sqrt{18}-2\sqrt{27}+3\sqrt{3}-6\sqrt{8}$$
$$=\sqrt{(3\times3\times2)}-2\sqrt{(3\times3\times3)}+3\sqrt{3}-6\sqrt{(2\times2\times2)}$$
$$=3\sqrt{2}-(2\times3)\sqrt{3}+3\sqrt{3}-(6\times2)\sqrt{2}$$
$$=3\sqrt{2}-6\sqrt{3}+3\sqrt{3}-12\sqrt{2}$$
$$=-9\sqrt{2}-3\sqrt{3}$$

Choice (D) is the correct answer.

535.

E. $10\sqrt{2}+4\sqrt{6}$

Simplify and combine the like terms:

$$8\sqrt{8}+2\sqrt{24}-2\sqrt{18}=8\sqrt{2\times4}+2\sqrt{6\times4}-2\sqrt{2\times9}$$
$$=16\sqrt{2}+4\sqrt{6}-6\sqrt{2}$$
$$=10\sqrt{2}+4\sqrt{6}$$

The correct answer is Choice (E).

536.

C. 15

First, solve the first term:

$$\sqrt{25}=\sqrt{5\times5}$$
$$=5$$

Next, solve the second term:

$$\sqrt{9} = \sqrt{3 \times 3}$$
$$= 3$$

Lastly, multiply the two answers:

$$5 \times 3 = 15$$

The correct answer is Choice (C).

537. C. 16

First, solve the first term:

$$\sqrt{16} = \sqrt{4 \times 4}$$
$$= 4$$

Next, solve the second term:

$$\sqrt{16} = \sqrt{4 \times 4}$$
$$= 4$$

Lastly, multiply the two answers:

$$4 \times 4 = 16$$

The correct answer is Choice (C).

538. D. 2

First, solve the division problem inside of the square root. Then, solve the square root:

$$\sqrt{\left(\frac{8}{2}\right)} = \sqrt{4}$$
$$= 2$$

Choice (D) is the correct answer.

539. E. $\frac{\sqrt{3}}{5}$

Separate the terms inside of the square root and solve each, if possible:

$$\sqrt{\left(\frac{3}{25}\right)} = \frac{\sqrt{3}}{\sqrt{25}}$$
$$= \frac{\sqrt{3}}{\sqrt{5 \times 5}}$$
$$= \frac{\sqrt{3}}{5}$$

Choice (E) is the correct answer.

540.   A. $2\sqrt{5}$

First, rationalize the denominator by multiplying both the top and the bottom by the radical and then simplify:

$$\frac{10}{\sqrt{5}} = \left(\frac{10}{\sqrt{5}}\right)\left(\frac{\sqrt{5}}{\sqrt{5}}\right)$$
$$= \frac{10\sqrt{5}}{\sqrt{5} \times \sqrt{5}}$$
$$= \frac{10\sqrt{5}}{\sqrt{25}}$$
$$= \frac{10\sqrt{5}}{5}$$
$$= 2\sqrt{5}$$

The correct answer is Choice (A).

541.   E. $3 + \sqrt{15} - 3\sqrt{2} - \sqrt{30}$

Use the FOIL method to simplify and then combine like terms:

$$\left(\sqrt{3} + \sqrt{5}\right)\left(\sqrt{3} - \sqrt{6}\right)$$
$$= \sqrt{9} + \sqrt{15} - \sqrt{18} - \sqrt{30}$$
$$= 3 + \sqrt{15} - \sqrt{(9 \times 2)} - \sqrt{30}$$
$$= 3 + \sqrt{15} - 3\sqrt{2} - \sqrt{30}$$

The correct answer is Choice (E).

542.   A. –2

Use the FOIL method to simplify and then combine like terms:

$$\left(\sqrt{3} + \sqrt{5}\right)\left(\sqrt{3} - \sqrt{5}\right)$$
$$= \sqrt{9} + \sqrt{15} - \sqrt{15} - \sqrt{25}$$
$$= 3 + \sqrt{15} - \sqrt{15} - 5$$
$$= 3 - 5$$
$$= -2$$

Choice (A) is the correct answer.

543.   D. $x\sqrt{6y}$

$$\sqrt{2x}\left(\sqrt{3xy}\right) = \sqrt{2x(3xy)}$$
$$= \sqrt{6x^2y}$$
$$= \sqrt{2(3)(x)(x)(y)}$$
$$= x\sqrt{6y}$$

Choice (D) is the correct answer.

544.   **D.** $2\sqrt{3}$

$$\frac{14\sqrt{27}}{7\sqrt{9}} = \frac{14}{7} \times \frac{\sqrt{27}}{\sqrt{9}}$$
$$= 2\sqrt{3}$$

Choice (D) is the correct answer.

545.   **B.** $9\sqrt{2}$

$$\frac{18\sqrt{60}}{2\sqrt{30}} = \frac{18}{2} \times \frac{\sqrt{60}}{\sqrt{30}}$$
$$= 9\sqrt{2}$$

The correct answer is Choice (B).

546.   **A.** -1

Use the FOIL method to simplify and then combine like terms:

$$\left(\sqrt{4} + \sqrt{5}\right)\left(\sqrt{4} - \sqrt{5}\right)$$
$$= \sqrt{16} + \sqrt{20} - \sqrt{20} - \sqrt{25}$$
$$= 4 + \sqrt{20} - \sqrt{20} - 5$$
$$= 4 - 5$$
$$= -1$$

The correct answer is Choice (A).

547.   **D.** $6 + \sqrt{15}$

Use the distributive property to multiply and then combine like terms:

$$\sqrt{3}\left(2\sqrt{3} + \sqrt{5}\right) = \sqrt{3}\left(2\sqrt{3}\right) + \sqrt{3}\left(\sqrt{5}\right)$$
$$= 2\sqrt{3 \times 3} + \sqrt{3 \times 5}$$
$$= 2 \times 3 + \sqrt{15}$$
$$= 6 + \sqrt{15}$$

Choice (D) is the correct answer.

548.   **E.** $1 + 2\sqrt{2}$

Use the FOIL method to simplify and then combine like terms:

$$\left(1 + \sqrt{2}\right)\left(3 - \sqrt{2}\right)$$
$$= 3 - \sqrt{2} + 3\sqrt{2} - \sqrt{4}$$
$$= 3 + 2\sqrt{2} - 2$$
$$= 1 + 2\sqrt{2}$$

The correct answer is Choice (E).

549. **C.** $16 - 8\sqrt{3}$

First, rewrite the expression: $\left(\sqrt{12} - 2\right)^2 = \left(\sqrt{12} - 2\right)\left(\sqrt{12} - 2\right)$ Use the FOIL method to simplify and then combine like terms:

$$= \left(\sqrt{12} - 2\right)\left(\sqrt{12} - 2\right)$$
$$= \left(\sqrt{12} \times \sqrt{12}\right) - 2\sqrt{12} - 2\sqrt{12} + 4$$
$$= \sqrt{144} - 4\sqrt{12} + 4$$
$$= 12 - 4\sqrt{12} + 4$$
$$= 16 - 4\sqrt{12}$$
$$= 16 - 4\sqrt{4 \times 3}$$
$$= 16 - 8\sqrt{3}$$

The correct answer is Choice (C).

550. **B.** $2\sqrt{10} - 4$

Use the FOIL method to simplify and then combine like terms:

$$\left(\sqrt{2} + \sqrt{2}\right)\left(\sqrt{5} - \sqrt{2}\right) = \sqrt{10} - \sqrt{4} + \sqrt{10} - \sqrt{4}$$
$$= 2\sqrt{10} - 2\sqrt{4}$$
$$= 2\sqrt{10} - 2\sqrt{2 \times 2}$$
$$= 2\sqrt{10} - 2(2)$$
$$= 2\sqrt{10} - 4$$

Choice (B) is the correct answer.

551. **C.** –2

For the line represented by $y = mx + b$, the slope is m and the y-intercept is b. In this equation, $m = -2$ and $b = 3$.

The slope = –2, Choice (C).

552. **D.** 3

For the line represented by $y = mx + b$, the slope is m and the y-intercept is b. In this equation, $m = -2$ and $b = 3$.

The y-intercept = 3, Choice (D).

553.   C. $\frac{1}{2}$

Rewrite the equation to put it into $y = mx + b$ form:

$$x = 2y - 3$$
$$x + 3 = 2y$$
$$2y = x + 3$$
$$y = \frac{1}{2}x + 1\frac{1}{2}$$

For the line represented by $y = mx + b$, the slope is m and the y-intercept is b.
In this equation, $m = \frac{1}{2}$ and $b = 1\frac{1}{2}$.

$$slope = \frac{1}{2}$$

Choice (C) is the correct answer.

554.   E. $1\frac{1}{2}$

Rewrite the equation to put it into $y = mx + b$ form:

$$x = 2y - 3$$
$$x + 3 = 2y$$
$$2y = x + 3$$
$$y = \frac{1}{2}x + 1\frac{1}{2}$$

For the line represented by $y = mx + b$, the slope is m and the y-intercept is b.
In this equation, $m = \frac{1}{2}$ and $b = 1\frac{1}{2}$.
The y-intercept $= 1\frac{1}{2}$, Choice (E).

555.   C. $y = -\frac{4}{3}x - 4$

First, find the slope:

$$\text{Slope} = \frac{(\text{change in } y)}{(\text{change in } x)}$$
$$= -\frac{4}{3}$$

Next, find the y-intercept:

$$y\text{-intercept} = -4$$

for the line $y = mx + b$.

The equation for this line is $y = -\frac{4}{3}x - 4$
The correct answer is Choice (C).

556. A. $y = 4$

Every point on the line has a y-coordinate equal to 4; therefore, the equation of the line is $y = 4$, Choice (A).

557. D. $x = -3$

Every point on the line has an x-coordinate equal to -3; therefore, the equation of the line is $x = -3$, Choice (D).

558. B. $y = -0.6x + 2.5$

First, find the slope:

$$\text{Slope} = \frac{(\text{change in } y)}{(\text{change in } x)}$$

$$= -\frac{3}{5}$$

$$= -0.6$$

Next, find the y-intercept:

y-intercept $= 2.5$

for the line $y = mx + b$.

The equation for this line is $y = -0.6x + 2.5$.

Choice (B) is the correct answer.

559. D. $y = \frac{1}{2}x - 2$

First, find the slope:

$$\text{Slope} = \frac{(\text{change in } y)}{(\text{change in } x)}$$

$$= \frac{2}{4}$$

$$= \frac{1}{2}$$

Next, find the y-intercept:

y-intercept $= -2$

for the line $y = mx + b$.

The equation for this line is $y = \frac{1}{2}x - 2$.

The correct answer is Choice (D).

560. D. $y = -4x + 2$

First, find the slope:

$$\text{Slope} = \frac{(\text{change in } y)}{(\text{change in } x)}$$

$$= -\frac{4}{1}$$

$$= -4$$

Next, find the y-intercept:

y-intercept $= 2$

for the line $y = mx + b$.

The equation for this line is $y = -4x + 2$.

The correct answer is Choice (D).

561. D. $x = 3, y = 0$

First, add the two equations to eliminate the y variable and solve for x:

$$(4x + 3x) + (5y - 5y) = 12 + 9$$

$$7x + 0 = 21$$

$$7x = 21$$

$$x = 3$$

Next, substitute the x value in the first equation and solve for y:

$$4x + 5y = 12$$

$$4(3) + 5y = 12$$

$$12 + 5y = 12$$

$$5y = 0$$

$$y = 0$$

The correct answer is Choice (D).

562. E. $x = 1, y = 3$

First, substitute the value of y into the second equation and solve for x:

$$x + (x + 2) = 4$$

$$2x + 2 = 4$$

$$2x = 4 - 2$$

$$2x = 2$$

$$x = 1$$

Next, substitute the x value in the first equation and solve for y:

$$y = x + 2$$
$$y = 1 + 2$$
$$= 3$$

The correct answer is Choice (E).

563. **A.** $x = -5$, $y = -7$

First, add the two equations to eliminate the y variable and solve for x:

$$x + y = -12$$
$$\underline{x - y = 2}$$
$$2x = -10$$
$$x = -5$$

Next, substitute the x value in the first equation and solve for y:

$$x + y = -12$$
$$-5 + y = -12$$
$$y = -7$$

Choice (A) is the correct answer.

564. **D.** $x = 9, y = -3$

First, multiply the first equation by -7, then add the result to the second equation to eliminate x and solve for y:

$$-7(x + 8y) = -15(-7)$$
$$-7x - 56y = 105$$
$$\underline{7x + 8y = 39}$$
$$-48y = 144$$
$$y = -3$$

Next, substitute the y value in the first equation and solve for x:

$$x + 8y = -15$$
$$x + 8(-3) = -15$$
$$x - 24 = -15$$
$$x = 9$$

The correct answer is Choice (D).

565. **B.** $x = -7, y = 1$

First, multiply the second equation by -1, and then add the result to the first equation to eliminate y and solve for x:

$$-1(0.8x + 0.6y) = (-5)(-1)$$
$$-0.8x - 0.6y = 5$$
$$\underline{-0.1x + 0.6y = 1.3}$$
$$-0.9x = 6.3$$
$$x = -7$$

Next, substitute -7 for x in the first equation and solve for y:

$$-0.1x + 0.6y = 1.3$$
$$-0.1(-7) + 0.6y = 1.3$$
$$0.7 + 0.6y = 1.3$$
$$0.6y = 0.6$$
$$y = 1$$

Choice (B) is the correct answer.

566. **C.** $x = 3, y = -1$

First, rewrite the first equation to solve for y:

$$2x + y = 5$$
$$y = 5 - 2x$$

Then, substitute the rewritten equation into the second equation and solve for x:

$$x + 2y = 1$$
$$x + 2(5 - 2x) = 1$$
$$x + 10 - 4x = 1$$
$$-3x = -9$$
$$x = 3$$

Next, substitute 3 for x in the first equation and solve for y:

$$2x + y = 5$$
$$2(3) + y = 5$$
$$6 + y = 5$$
$$y = -1$$

The correct answer is Choice (C).

567.

C. $x = -11, y = 9$

First, make the coefficients of y additive inverses of each other by multiplying the first equation by 3 and the second equation by –2:

$$3(x + 2y = 7)$$
$$3x + 6y = 21$$

$$-2(2x + 3y = 5)$$
$$-4x - 6y = -10$$

Then, add the equations together:

$$3x + 6y = 21$$
$$\underline{-4x - 6y = -10}$$
$$-x = 11$$
$$x = -11$$

Next, substitute –11 for x in the first equation and solve for y:

$$x + 2y = 7$$
$$-11 + 2y = 7$$
$$2y = 18$$
$$y = 9$$

The correct answer is Choice (C).

568.

E. $x = 6, y = 4$

First, rewrite the first equation to solve for x:

$$x - 6y = -18$$
$$x = 6y - 18$$

Then, substitute $6y - 18$ for x in the second equation and solve for y:

$$2x - 7y = -16$$
$$2(6y - 18) - 7y = -16$$
$$12y - 36 - 7y = -16$$
$$5y - 36 = -16$$
$$5y = 20$$
$$y = 4$$

Next, substitute 4 for y into the first equation and solve for x:

$$x - 6y = -18$$
$$x - 6(4) = -18$$
$$x - 24 = -18$$
$$x = 6$$

---

569. **A. $x = 6, y = 0$**

First, rewrite the first question to solve for x:

$$x + 5y = 6$$
$$x = 6 - 5y$$

Then, substitute $6 - 5y$ for x in the second equation and solve for y:

$$-2x + 6y = -12$$
$$-2(6 - 5y) + 6y = -12$$
$$-12 + 10y + 6y = -12$$
$$-12 + 16y = -12$$
$$16y = 0$$
$$y = 0$$

Next, substitute 0 for y into the first equation and solve for x:

$$x + 5y = 6$$
$$x + 5(0) = 6$$
$$x + 0 = 6$$
$$x = 6$$

Choice (A) is the correct answer.

---

570. **$x = 4, y = -4$**

First, rewrite the second equation to solve for x:

$$x - y = 8$$
$$x = 8 + y$$

Then, add the result to the first equation to eliminate the x variable and solve for y:

$$4x + 5y = -4$$
$$4(8 + y) + 5y = -4$$
$$32 + 4y + 5y = -4$$
$$32 + 9y = -4$$
$$9y = -36$$
$$y = \frac{-36}{9}$$
$$y = -4$$

Next, substitute –4 for y in the first equation and solve for x:

$$x - y = 8$$
$$x - (-4) = 8$$
$$x + 4 = 8$$
$$x = 4$$

Choice (D) is the correct answer.

571. **B. –192; C. 0; E. 200; F. 440; G. 668; I. 816**

All terms in the sequence are multiples of 4.

Choices (B), (E), (F), (G), and (I) are all multiples of 4, and the series would reach 0, which is Choice (C).

572. **B. 192**

To find the sixth term, replace n with 6:

$$x_n = 3 \times (2)^n$$
$$x_6 = 3 \times (2)^6$$
$$= 3 \times 64$$
$$= 192$$

The sixth term of the sequence is 192, Choice (B).

573. **D. 81**

To find the 21st term, replace n with 21:

$$x_n = 4n - 3$$
$$x_{21} = (4 \times 21) - 3$$
$$= 84 - 3$$
$$= 81$$

The 21st term of the sequence is 81, Choice (D).

574. **D. $\frac{1}{25}$**

To find the third term, replace n with 3:

$$\{a_n\} = \left\{ \left(\frac{1}{n} \right)^{n-1} \right\}$$
$$\{a_3\} = \left\{ \left(\frac{1}{5} \right)^{3-1} \right\}$$
$$= \left\{ \left(\frac{1}{5} \right)^2 \right\}$$
$$= \frac{1}{25}$$

Choice (D) represents the third term of the sequence.

575.   C. 31

If n is a positive integer less than 5, it could be 1, 2, 3, or 4. The squares of these are:

$$1^2 = 1$$
$$2^2 = 4$$
$$3^2 = 9$$
$$4^2 = 16$$

Next, add all of these together: $1 + 4 + 9 + 16 = 31$, Choice (C).

576.   D. 66

$$h_n = n(2n-1)$$

Replace n with 6:

$$h_n = n(2n-1)$$
$$h_6 = 6(2 \times 6 - 1)$$
$$= 6(12-1)$$
$$= 6 \times 11$$
$$= 66$$

The sixth hexagonal number is 66, Choice (D).

577.   C. 3

Set up the equation and solve for n:

$$x_n = 26$$
$$3n^2 - 1 = 26$$
$$3n^2 = 27$$
$$n^2 = 9$$
$$n = 3$$

Choice (C) is the correct answer.

578.   16

There will be four doubling periods. After the first period, the population will be two times greater. After the second period, it will be 2^2, and after the third period, it will be $2n^3$, and so forth.

After the fourth period, it will be 2^4 greater, which equals 16.

579. **C. The seventh term**

$$\text{If } x_n = 4$$
$$\frac{n^2 - 1}{n + 5} = 4$$
$$n^2 - 1 = 4(n - 5)$$
$$n^2 - 1 = 4n + 20$$
$$n^2 - 4n - 21 = 0$$

This quadratic equation can be factored into $(n - 7)(n + 3) = 0$, which has solutions of $n = 7$ or $n = -3$.

Because n can't be negative, $n = 7$. The correct answer is therefore Choice (C).

580. **D. 5**

Given $a_n = n^2 - 5n + 2$, try values for n until a_n is positive.

$$a_1 = 1^2 - 5 \times 1 + 2$$
$$= 1 - 5 + 2$$
$$= -4 + 2$$
$$= -2, \text{ which is negative}$$

$$a_2 = 2^2 - 5 \times 2 + 2$$
$$= 4 - 10 + 2$$
$$= -6 + 2$$
$$= -4, \text{ which is negative}$$

$$a_3 = 3^2 - 5 \times 3 + 2$$
$$= 9 - 15 + 2$$
$$= -6 + 2$$
$$= -4, \text{ which is negative}$$

$$a_4 = 4^2 - 5 \times 4 + 2$$
$$= 16 - 20 + 2$$
$$= -4 + 2$$
$$= -2, \text{ which is negative}$$

$$a_5 = 5^2 - 5 \times 5 + 2$$
$$= 25 - 25 + 2$$
$$= 0 + 2$$
$$= 2, \text{ which is positive}$$

The smallest value of n for which a_n is positive is 5. Thus, Choice (D) is correct.

581. **B. 60 miles**

First, determine how many hours are in 120 minutes. Next, multiply the number of hours by the speed.

$$120 \text{ minutes} = 2 \text{ hours}$$

$$\frac{30 \text{ miles}}{\text{hour}} \times 2 \text{ hours} = 60 \text{ miles}$$

The correct answer is Choice (B).

582. **A.** $10\frac{m}{s}$

A kilometer has 1,000 meters, and an hour has 3,600 seconds, so 36 kilometers per hour is:

$$\frac{36km}{1h} \times \frac{1,000\frac{m}{km}}{3,600\frac{s}{h}} = \frac{36,000m}{3,600s}$$

$$= 10\frac{m}{s}$$

Choice (A) represents the boat's speed in meters per second.

583. **D. 10 a.m.**

After t hours, the distances $D1$ and $D2$, in miles per hour, traveled by the two cars are given by:

$$D1 = 40t$$
$$D2 = 50t$$

After t hours, the distance D separating the two cars is given by:

$$D = D1 + D2$$
$$= 40t + 50t$$
$$= 90t$$

Distance D will be equal to 450 miles when

$$90t = 450 \text{ miles}$$
$$t = 5 \text{ hours}$$

$$5{:}00 \text{ a.m.} + 5 \text{ hours} = 10{:}00 \text{ a.m.}$$

The two cars will be 450 miles apart at 10 a.m., Choice (D).

584. **E. 12 p.m.**

After t hours, the distance traveled by Car 1 is given by:

$$D1 = 40t$$

Car 2 leaves at 10 a.m. and will have spent one hour less than Car 1 when it passes it. After $t-1$ hours, the distance traveled by Car 2 is given by:

$$D2 = 60(t-1)$$

When Car 2 passes Car 1, they are at the same distance from the starting point, so $D1 = D2$:

$$D1 = D2$$
$$40t = 60(t-1)$$

Solve for t:

$$40t = 60(t-1)$$
$$40t = 60t - 60$$
$$-20t = -60$$
$$t = 3$$

$$9:00 \text{ a.m.} + 3 \text{ hours} = 12:00 \text{ p.m.}$$

Car 1 will pass Car 2 at 12 p.m., Choice (E).

585. **C. 6 p.m.**

The two cars are traveling in directions that create a right angle. Let x be the distance traveled by Car 1 and y be the distance traveled by Car 2 in t hours:

$$x = 30t$$
$$y = 40t$$

Because the two directions create a right angle, the Pythagorean theorem can be used to find the distance between the two cars:

$$D^2 = x^2 + y^2$$
$$(500)^2 = (30t)^2 + (40t)^2$$
$$250,000 = 900t^2 + 1,600t^2$$
$$250,000 = 2,500t^2$$
$$100 = t^2$$
$$10 = t$$
$$10 \text{ hours} = t$$

$$8:00 \text{ a.m.} + 10 \text{ hr} = 6:00 \text{ p.m.}$$

The two cars will be 500 miles apart at 6 p.m., Choice (C).

586. **C. 9**

The mean is the average of the numbers. To find the mean, add the numbers in the data set together and then divide the sum by the number of values in the set. There are 6 numbers in the set, so:

$$\frac{\text{sum}}{\text{\# of values}} = \text{mean}$$

$$\frac{3+12+4+x+12}{5} = 8$$

$$\frac{31+x}{5} = 8$$

$$31+x = 40$$

$$x = 9$$

The correct answer is Choice (C).

---

587. **D. 15**

The mean is the average of the numbers. To find the mean, add the numbers in the data set together and then divide the sum by the number of values in the set. There are 6 numbers in the set, so:

$$\frac{\text{sum}}{\text{\# of values}} = \text{mean}$$

$$\frac{7+12+7+12+7+x}{6} = 10$$

$$\frac{45+x}{6} = 10$$

$$45+x = 60$$

$$x = 15$$

Choice (D) is the correct answer.

---

588. **C. 11.2**

The mean is the average of the numbers. To find the mean, add the numbers in the data set together and then divide the sum by the number of values in the set. There are 6 numbers in the set, so:

$$\frac{\text{sum}}{\text{\# of values}} = \text{mean}$$

$$\frac{3.4+-2.2+1+x+5.2+6.6}{6} = 4.2$$

$$\frac{14+x}{6} = 4.2$$

$$14+x = 25.2$$

$$x = 11.2$$

The correct answer is Choice (C).

---

589. **E. 17**

The median is the middle number when the numbers in the data set are arranged in numerical order. First, arrange the numbers from least to greatest:

10, 13, 14, 17

To make 14 the middle number in the data set, x must be greater than 14. Of the answer choices, only 17 is greater than 14, so Choice (E) is your answer.

590.   **D. 10**

The mode is the number that appears the most in a data set. First, arrange the numbers from least to greatest:

3, 4, 5, 10, 20

To make 10 the number that appears most often in the data set, x must be 10, Choice (D).

591.   **C. 8**

The range is the difference between the greatest number and the lowest number. First, arrange the numbers from least to greatest:

5, 8, 9

Subtract the least number from the greatest number:

$$9 - 5 = 4$$

The range of the data set is already 4, so x must be a number between 5 and 9. The only answer choice between 5 and 9 is 8, Choice (C).

592.   **B. 9; E. 13**

The range is the difference between the greatest number and the lowest number. First, arrange the numbers from least to greatest:

10, 11, 12, 12

If 10 is the lowest number, then for a range of 3, x is 13, Choice (E). If 12 is the highest number, then for a range of 3, x is 9, Choice (B).

593.   **E. 17**

The mean is the average of the numbers. To find the mean, add the numbers in the data set together and then divide the sum by the number of values in the set. There are 5 numbers in the set, so:

$$\frac{\text{sum}}{\text{\# of values}} = \text{mean}$$
$$\frac{3+8+x+x+5}{5} = 10$$
$$\frac{16+2x}{5} = 10$$
$$16 + 2x = 50$$
$$2x = 34$$
$$x = 17$$

The correct answer is Choice (E).

594. A. 6

The mean is the average of the numbers. To find the mean, add the numbers in the data set together and then divide the sum by the number of values in the set. There are 5 numbers in the set, so:

$$\frac{\text{sum}}{\text{\# of values}} = \text{mean}$$
$$\frac{2+3+(x+1)+x+2}{5} = 4$$
$$\frac{(x+1)+x+7}{5} = 4$$
$$(x+1)+x+7 = 20$$
$$(x+1)+x = 13$$
$$2x = 12$$
$$x = 6$$

The correct answer is Choice (A).

595. C. 14

The mean is the average of the numbers. To find the mean, add the numbers in the data set together and then divide the sum by the number of values in the set. There are 7 numbers in the set, so:

$$\frac{\text{sum}}{\text{\# of values}} = \text{mean}$$
$$\frac{6+3+x+4+3+5+y}{7} = 5$$
$$\frac{21+x+y}{7} = 5$$
$$21+x+y = 35$$
$$x+y = 14$$

Choice (C) is the correct answer.

596. C. 3.0

Because the numbers are weighted, each number in the set must be multiplied by its weighted value:

$$(0.1\times1)+(0.2\times2)+(0.3\times3)+(0.4\times4) =$$
$$0.1+0.4+0.9+1.6 = 3.0$$

The answer you're looking for is Choice (C).

597. **A. 2.5**

Because the numbers are weighted, each number in the set must be multiplied by its weighted value:

$$(0.5\times1)+(0.1\times2)+(0.1\times3)+(0.1\times4)+(0.1\times5)+(0.1\times6)=$$
$$0.5+0.2+0.3+0.4+0.5+0.6=2.5$$

The correct answer is Choice (A).

598. **B. 48**

Because the numbers are weighted, each number in the set must be multiplied by its weighted value. To find the exact values, divide by the sum of the weights. The sum of the weights = 15, so:

$$\frac{\text{sum}}{\text{\# of values}}=\text{mean}$$

$$\frac{(40\times1)+(45\times2)+(80\times3)+(75\times4)+(10\times5)}{15}=$$

$$\frac{720}{15}=48$$

The weighted mean is 48, Choice (B).

599. **C. 56**

Because the numbers are weighted, each number in the set must be multiplied by its weighted value. To find the exact values, divide by the sum of the weights. The sum of the weights = 20, so:

$$\frac{\text{sum}}{\text{\# of values}}=\text{mean}$$

$$\frac{(90\times6)+(35\times5)+(20\times4)+(55\times2)+(70\times2)+(75\times1)}{20}=$$

$$\frac{1{,}120}{20}=56$$

The weighted mean is 56, Choice (C).

600. **B. 70.4%**

First, convert each of the percentage weights into decimals:

$$30\%=0.3$$
$$20\%=0.2$$
$$50\%=0.5$$

Next, multiply each category grade by its weighted value:

$$(0.3\times85)+(0.2\times72)+(0.5\times61)=$$
$$25.5+14.4+30.5=70.4$$

The overall grade for the assignments was 70.4%, Choice (B).

601.   E. 70%

Convert each percentage into a decimal and multiply each by the appropriate number of matches. Add them together:

$$(0.8 \times 10) + (0.5 \times 5) = 8 + 2.5$$
$$= 10.5$$

Next, divide by the total number of matches:

$$10.5 \div 15 = 0.7$$

The percent of her first serves for the season was thus 70%, Choice (E).

602.   C. 79.5%

First, convert each of the percentage weights into decimals:

$$10\% = 0.1$$
$$20\% = 0.2$$
$$70\% = 0.7$$

Next, multiply each category grade by its weighted value:

$$(0.1 \times 92) + (0.2 \times 68) + (0.7 \times 81) =$$
$$9.2 + 13.6 + 56.7 = 79.5$$

The course grade was 79.5%, Choice (C).

603.   B. 7 pounds

Multiply each weight by the appropriate number of boxes and add them together:

$$(10 \times 6) + (5 \times 9) = 60 + 45$$
$$= 105$$

Next, divide by the total number of boxes:

$$105 \div 15 = 7$$

The average box weight is 7 pounds, Choice (B).

604.   D. 68%

First, multiply each average by the number of students who had that average and find the sum:

$$80 \times 10 + 60 \times 15 = 800 + 900$$
$$= 1,700$$

Next, divide this by the total number of students:

$$\frac{1,700}{25} = 68\%$$

The entire class average on the test was 68%, Choice (D).

605.   **B. 8.3**

Let the score for difficulty be x:

Convert each weighted percentage into a decimal and multiply each by the appropriate score. Add them together and set the equation equal to the overall score of 9.5:

$$(0.8)(9.8)+(0.2)(x) = 9.5$$
$$7.84 + 0.2x = 9.5$$
$$0.2x = 1.66$$
$$x = 8.3$$

The correct answer is Choice (B).

606.   **D. $100**

The formula for calculating simple interest is $I = Prt$.

$P = \$1,000$

$r = 10\% = 0.10$

$t = 1$ year

$$I = Prt$$
$$= 1,000 \times 0.10 \times 1$$
$$= 100$$

The interest paid was $100, Choice (D).

607.   **E. 9%**

The formula for calculating simple interest is $I = Prt$.

$I = \$1,350$

$P = \$5,000$

$t = 3$ years

$$I = Prt$$
$$1,350 = 5,000 \times r \times 3$$
$$1,350 = 15,000r$$
$$\frac{1,350}{15,000} = r$$
$$0.09 = r$$

The annual interest rate was 9%, Choice (E).

608. **C. 7%**

The formula for calculating simple interest is $I = Prt$.

$I = \$630$

$P = \$4,500$

$t = 2$ years

$$I = Prt$$
$$630 = 4,500 \times r \times 2$$
$$630 = 9,000r$$
$$\frac{630}{9,000} = r$$
$$0.07 = r$$

The annual interest rate was 7%, Choice (C).

609. **E. 4**

The formula for calculating simple interest is $I = Prt$.

$I = \$840$

$P = \$7,000$

$r = 3\% = 0.03$

$$I = Prt$$
$$840 = 7,000 \times 0.03 \times t$$
$$840 = 210t$$
$$\frac{840}{210} = t$$
$$4 = t$$

The amount of time on the loan was thus 4 years, Choice (E).

610. **B. 9%**

The formula for calculating simple interest is $I = Prt$.

$I = \$840$

$P = \$7,000$

$r = 3\% = 0.03$

$$I = Prt$$
$$1,350 = 5,000 \times r \times 3$$
$$1,350 = 15,000r$$
$$\frac{1,350}{15,000} = r$$
$$0.09 = r$$

The annual interest rate was 9%, Choice (B).

611. C. 7%

Convert each percentage into a decimal and multiply each by the appropriate number of liters. Add them together:

$$(0.06 \times 10) + (0.09 \times 5) = 0.6 + 0.45$$
$$= 1.05$$

Next, divide by the total number of liters:

$$1.05 \div 15 = 0.07$$

The correct answer is Choice (C), 7%.

612. C. $4/pound

Multiply each price by the appropriate number of pounds. Add them together:
$$(5 \times 2) + (3 \times 2) = 10 + 6$$
$$= 16$$

Next, divide by the total number of pounds:

$$16 \div 4 = 4$$

The price of the nut mixture was therefore $4 per pound, Choice (C).

613. C. 25 liters

To turn her 50% soap solution into a 25% soap solution, Cheyenne has to double the volume of her solution. If she has 25 liters of the mix, an additional 25 liters will dilute the 50% mixture into 25%.

The correct answer is therefore Choice (C), 25 liters.

614. D. 80 liters

Let x represent the amount of the 20% alcohol solution and $(40 + x)$ represent the total solution amount. Convert each percentage to a decimal. Multiply each solution by the appropriate amount of each and add them together. Set the equation equal to the total solution amount, multiplied by the percent concentration of the new alcohol solution:

$$(0.2)(x) + (0.5)(40) = (0.3)(40 + x)$$
$$0.2x + 20 = 12 + 0.3x$$
$$0.2x = -8 + 0.3x$$
$$-0.1x = -8$$
$$x = 80$$

The number of liters needed is 80, Choice (D).

615.   **A. 5 pounds Coffee A and 15 pounds Coffee B**

Let x represent the amount of Coffee A and $(60-x)$ represent the amount of Coffee B. Multiply each price by the appropriate number of pounds. Add them together and set the equation equal to the cost and amount of the new mixture:

$$5x + 3(20-x) = 3.50 \times 20$$
$$5x + 60 - 3x = 70$$
$$2x + 60 = 70$$
$$2x = 10$$
$$x = 5$$

Coffee A = 5 pounds

Coffee B = $20 - x$, or $20 - 5$, which is 15 pounds

Choice (A) is the correct answer.

616.   **A. 200 kg**

Let x represent the amount of water and $(x+100)$ represent the amount of 10% solution. First, convert each percentage to a decimal. Then, multiply each amount by the appropriate percentage and set the equation equal to the percentage and amount of the new mixture:

$$(0.3)(100) = (0.1)(x+100)$$
$$30 = 0.1x + 10$$
$$20 = 0.1x$$
$$200 = x$$

The amount of water needed is 200 kilograms, Choice (A).

617.   **B. 100 adult tickets and 300 child tickets**

Let x represent the number of adult tickets and $(400-x)$ represent the number of child tickets. Multiply each price by the appropriate type of ticket. Add them together and set the equation equal to the total ticket sales:

$$5x + 2(400-x) = 1,100$$
$$5x + 800 - 2x = 1,100$$
$$3x = 300$$
$$x = 100$$

Adult tickets = 100

Child tickets = $400 - x$, or $400 - 100$, which is 300

Therefore, the correct answer is Choice (B).

618. **C. 50 peanuts and 50 chocolate candies**

Let x represent the amount of peanuts and $(100 - x)$ represent the amount of chocolate candies. Multiply each price by the appropriate item. Add them together and set the equation equal to the new price:

$$(2.49)(x) + (3.89)(100 - x) = (3.19)(100)$$
$$2.49x + 389 - 3.89x = 319$$
$$-1.40x + 389 = 319$$
$$-1.40x = -70$$
$$x = 50$$

Peanuts = 50

Chocolate candies = $100 - x$, or $100 - 50$, which is 50

The mixture contains 50 peanuts and 50 chocolate candies, Choice (C).

619. **E. 15 gallons**

Let x represent the amount of cranberry juice used and $(40 - x)$ represent the amount of apple juice used. First, convert each percentage to a decimal. Then, multiply each juice amount by the appropriate percentage and set the equation equal to the percentage and amount of the new juice mixture:

$$x + (0.2)(40 - x) = (0.5)(40)$$
$$x + 8 - 0.2x = 20$$
$$0.8x = 12$$
$$x = 15$$

The amount of 100% concentrate needed is 15 gallons, Choice (E).

620. **D. 200 grams**

Let x represent the amount of sterling silver and $(500 - x)$ represent the amount of alloy. First, convert each percentage to a decimal. Next, multiply each amount by the appropriate percentage. Add them together and set the equation equal to the percentage and amount of the new mixture:

$$(0.925)(x) + (0.9)(500 - x) = 0.91 \times 500$$
$$0.925x + 450 - 0.9x = 455$$
$$0.925x - 0.9x = 455 - 450$$
$$0.025x = 5$$
$$x = 200$$

The correct answer is Choice (D).

621. **D. $\frac{1}{3}$**

The probability of an event happening can be found by dividing the number of ways the event can happen by the total number of outcomes. There are 6 faces on a die, and two have what you are looking for: 4 or 3. The probability is $\frac{2}{6} = \frac{1}{3}$, which is Choice (D).

622. 154

The total number of chocolates is 22. The first person has a chance of $\frac{5}{22}$ of taking a soft center. The second person has 21 sweets left, of which four could be soft, making the chance $\frac{4}{21}$. The third person has a chance of $\frac{3}{20}$.

The total probability is obtained by multiplying all these chances together:

$$\left(\frac{5}{22}\right)\left(\frac{4}{21}\right)\left(\frac{3}{20}\right) = \frac{1}{154}$$

623. E. $\frac{3}{5}$

The probability of an event happening can be found by dividing the number of ways the event can happen by the total number of outcomes. There are three odd numbers (1, 3, and 5), so the number of ways the event can happen is 3. There are five numbers altogether, so the probability is $\frac{3}{5}$, which is Choice (E).

624. A. $\frac{4}{11}$

The probability of an event happening can be found by dividing the number of ways the event can happen by the total number of outcomes. There are 4 I's in the word MISSISSIPPI, so the number of ways the event can happen is 4. There are 11 letters altogether, so the probability the letter chosen is an I is $\frac{4}{11}$, which is Choice (A).

625. B. $\frac{2}{13}$

The probability of an event happening can be found by dividing the number of ways the event can happen by the total number of outcomes. There are four queens and four kings, so the number of ways the event can happen is 8. There are 52 cards altogether, so the probability the card chosen is a queen or a king is $\frac{8}{52}$, which reduces to $\frac{2}{13}$.

Choice (B) is the one you're looking for.

626. $\frac{2}{7}$

The probability is the ratio of the area of the beds to the total area.

The sides of the square beds = $4y - 2y = 2y$

Area of one bed = $4y^2$

Area of two beds = $8y^2$

Total garden area = $4y \times 7y = 28y^2$

Probability = $\frac{8y^2}{28y^2} = \frac{2}{7}$

627. D. $\frac{2}{3}$

The probability of an event happening can be found by dividing the number of ways the event can happen by the total number of outcomes. The factors of six are 1, 2, 3, and 6, so the number of ways the event can happen is 4.

There are 6 possible scores when a die is thrown, so the probability is $\frac{4}{6}$, which reduces to $\frac{2}{3}$.

Choice (D) represents the probability that the face shown is a factor of 6.

628. C. $\frac{3}{8}$

The probability of an event happening can be found by dividing the number of ways the event can happen by the total number of outcomes. Let H represent "heads up" and let T represent "tails up." There are eight possible ways the coins can land: (H, H, H), (H, H, T), (H, T, H), (H, T, T), (T, H, H), (T, H, T), (T, T, H) and (T, T, T).

Of these ways, three have one "heads up" and two "tails up": (H, T, T), (T, H, T) and (T, T, H). This means that the number of ways the event can happen is 3, and the total number of outcomes is 8. The probability of the event happening is $\frac{3}{8}$, Choice (C).

629. $\frac{3}{8}$

The probability of an event happening can be found by dividing the number of ways the event can happen by the total number of outcomes. n can be four different values, each of which can be combined with the four possible values for p. This gives 16 possible pairs.

To find out how many of these pairs can give a value for $\frac{n}{2p}$, which is in set P:

If $n = 12$ and $p = 2$, $\frac{12}{4} = 3$, which is in set P.

Similarly, if $n = 12$ and p = 3, $\frac{12}{6} = 2$, which is in set P.

If $n = 18$, p can be 3. If $n = 2$, p can be 1. If $n = 6$, p can be 1 or 3.

This gives 6 pairs out of 16 total possible:

$$\frac{6}{16} = \frac{3}{8}$$

630. B. $\frac{1}{2}$

The probability of an event happening can be found by dividing the number of ways the event can happen by the total number of outcomes. After the first marble is drawn and found to be blue, there are now six marbles left in the bag, three of which are blue. The probability of the second marble being blue is $\frac{3}{6}$, which reduces to $\frac{1}{2}$.

Choice (B) is the correct answer.

631. **B. 2**

There are two classifications: students taking English and students taking Chemistry. There are five students who are taking both English and Chemistry. Subtract the five students who are taking both English and Chemistry from each class total:

Both = 5

English only = 14 − 5 = 9

Chemistry only = 29 − 5 = 24

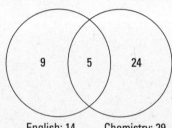

English: 14   Chemistry: 29

Add all the numbers together to get the total number of students taking either English or Chemistry:

$$9 + 5 + 24 = 38$$

There are 40 students in the group, so subtract 38 students from 40 to get the number of students who are *not* taking either of the two classes:

$$40 − 38 = 2$$

Choice (B) is the correct answer.

632. **C. 33**

There are two classifications: students taking English and students taking Chemistry. There are five students who are taking both English and Chemistry. Subtract the five students who are taking both English and Chemistry from each class total:

Both = 5

English only = 14 − 5 = 9

Chemistry only = 29 − 5 = 24

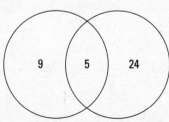

English: 14   Chemistry: 29

Add the class numbers together to get the total number of students taking only 1 class:

$$9 + 24 = 33$$

The correct answer is Choice (C).

---

633. C. 3

There are two classifications: children with a dog and children with a cat. There are eight children who have both a dog and a cat. Subtract the eight children who have both a dog and a cat from each total:

Both = 8

Dog only = $12 - 8 = 4$

Cat only = $18 - 8 = 10$

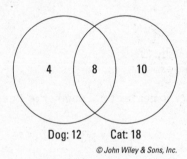

Dog: 12   Cat: 18

© John Wiley & Sons, Inc.

Add all the numbers together to get the total number of children who have a pet:

$$4 + 8 + 10 = 22$$

There were 25 children surveyed, so subtract 22 children from 25 to get the number of children who *do not* have a pet at home:

$$25 - 22 = 3$$

The number of children who do not have a pet at home is 3, Choice (C).

---

634. E. 14

There are two classifications: children with a dog and children with a cat. There are eight children who have both a dog and a cat. Subtract the eight children who have both a dog and a cat from each total:

Both = 8

Dog only = $12 - 8 = 4$

Cat only = $18 - 8 = 10$

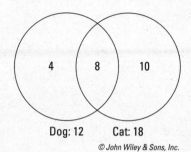

Dog: 12   Cat: 18
© John Wiley & Sons, Inc.

Add the two pet numbers together to get the total number of students having only 1 pet at home:

$$10 + 4 = 14$$

The correct answer is Choice (E).

635.   **B. 16**

There are two classifications: those who like cream and those who like sugar. There are 20 coffee drinkers who like both. Subtract the 20 coffee drinkers who like both cream and sugar from the number of drinkers who like cream:

Both = 20

Cream only = $36 - 20 = 16$

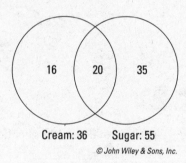

Cream: 36   Sugar: 55
© John Wiley & Sons, Inc.

The number of coffee drinkers who like cream only is 16, Choice (B).

636.   **C. 35**

There are two classifications: those who like cream and those who like sugar. There are 20 coffee drinkers who like both. Subtract the 20 coffee drinkers who like both cream and sugar from the number of drinkers who like sugar:

Both = 20

Sugar only = $55 - 20 = 35$

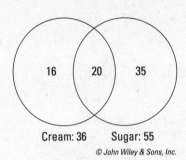

Cream: 36   Sugar: 55

© John Wiley & Sons, Inc.

The number of coffee drinkers who like sugar only is 35, Choice (C).

637.   **C. 35**

There are two classifications: those who like cream and those who like sugar. There are 20 coffee drinkers who like both. Subtract the 20 coffee drinkers who like both cream and sugar from each of the categories:

Both = 20

Cream only = $36 - 20 = 16$

Sugar only = $55 - 20 = 35$

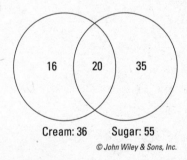

Cream: 36   Sugar: 55

© John Wiley & Sons, Inc.

Add all the numbers together to get the total number of coffee drinkers who like either cream or sugar:

$$16 + 20 + 35 = 71$$

There were 100 coffee drinkers surveyed, so subtract 71 from 100 to get the number of coffee drinkers who *do not like* cream or sugar:

$$100 - 71 = 29$$

The correct answer is Choice (C).

638.   **A. 9**

There are three classifications: those who studied French, those who studied Spanish, and those who studied Latin. There were 4 people who studied all three languages, 9 people who studied French and Latin, and 11 people who studied Spanish and Latin. Subtract the four people who studied all three languages from the number of people who studied French and Latin:

All languages = 4

French and Latin = $9 - 4 = 5$

Subtract the four people who studied all three languages from the number of people who studied Spanish and Latin:

Spanish and Latin = $11 - 4 = 7$

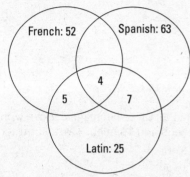

© John Wiley & Sons, Inc.

Add the people who studied all three languages, those who studied French and Latin, and those who studied Spanish and Latin. Then, subtract the sum from those who studied Latin:

$$25 - (5 + 4 + 7) = 25 - 16$$
$$= 9$$

Choice (A) is the correct answer.

639. D. 23

There are three classifications: those who studied French, those who studied Spanish, and those who studied Latin. There were 4 people who studied all three languages, 9 people who studied French and Latin, 11 people who studied Spanish and Latin, and 24 people who studied French and Spanish. Subtract the four people who studied all three languages from the number of people who studied French and Latin:

All languages = 4

French and Latin = $9 - 4 = 5$

Subtract the four people who studied all three languages from the number of people who studied French and Spanish:

French and Spanish = $24 - 4 = 20$

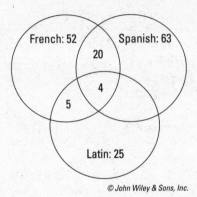

© John Wiley & Sons, Inc.

Add the people who studied all three languages, those who studied French and Latin, and those who studied French and Spanish. Then, subtract the sum from those who studied French:

$$52 - (20 + 5 + 4) = 52 - 29$$
$$= 23$$

Choice (D) is the correct answer.

640.   **D. 32**

There are three classifications: those who studied French, those who studied Spanish, and those who studied Latin. There were 4 people who studied all three languages, 9 people who studied French and Latin, 11 people who studied Spanish and Latin, and 24 people who studied French and Spanish. Subtract the four people who studied all three languages from the number of people who studied Spanish and Latin:

All languages = 4

Spanish and Latin = $11 - 4 = 7$

Subtract the four people who studied all three languages from the number of people who studied French and Spanish:

French and Spanish = $24 - 4 = 20$

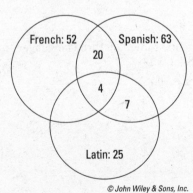

© John Wiley & Sons, Inc.

Add the people who studied all three languages, those who studied Spanish and Latin, and those who studied French and Spanish. Then, subtract the sum from those who studied Spanish:

$$63 - (20 + 7 + 4) = 63 - 31$$
$$= 32$$

Choice (D) is the correct answer.

641. **E. 12**

The total combinations can be found by multiplying each of the numbers of items. There are three shirts and four pairs of pants, so $3 \times 4 = 12$ outfits that can be made. The correct answer is Choice (E).

642. **D. 18**

The total combinations can be found by multiplying each of the numbers of items. There are six flavors of ice cream and three different types of cones, so $6 \times 3 = 18$ ice-cream cone combinations that can be made. The correct answer is Choice (D).

643. **E. 42**

The total combinations can be found by multiplying each of the numbers of items. There are two pizza sizes, seven different toppings, and three different crusts, so $2 \times 7 \times 3 = 42$ different single-topping pizza combinations that can be made. The correct answer is Choice (E).

644. **E. 63,000**

The total combinations can be found by multiplying each of the numbers of items. There are nine different skirts, seven different tops, ten different pairs of shoes, two different necklaces, and five different bracelets, so $9 \times 7 \times 10 \times 2 \times 5 = 63,000$ outfits that can be made. Choice (E) is the correct answer.

645. **A. 329**

The total combinations can be found by multiplying each of the numbers of items. Including "none" as an option, there are 6 choices of appetizer, 11 choices of entree, and 5 choices of dessert. Thus, the total number of choices is $6 \times 11 \times 5 = 330$. However, one of these is not a meal (no appetizer, no main meal, and no dessert), so there are 329 possible meals. The correct answer is Choice (A).

646. **C. 240**

The ! symbol means to multiply a series of descending integers, beginning with the number that precedes that ! symbol.

$$5!2! = (5 \times 4 \times 3 \times 2 \times 1)(2 \times 1)$$
$$= (120)(2)$$
$$= 240$$

Choice (C) is the correct answer.

647. **D. 336**

The ! symbol means to multiply a series of descending integers, beginning with the number that precedes that ! symbol.

$$\frac{8!}{5!} = \frac{8 \times 7 \times 6 \times 5 \times 4 \times 3 \times 2 \times 1}{5 \times 4 \times 3 \times 2 \times 1}$$

$$= \frac{8 \times 7 \times 6}{1}$$

$$= 336$$

The correct answer is Choice (D).

648. **A. 126**

The ! symbol means to multiply a series of descending integers, beginning with the number that precedes that ! symbol.

$$\frac{9!}{5!4!} = \frac{9 \times 8 \times 7 \times 6 \times 5 \times 4 \times 3 \times 2 \times 1}{(5 \times 4 \times 3 \times 2 \times 1)(4 \times 3 \times 2 \times 1)}$$

$$= \frac{9 \times 8 \times 7 \times 6}{4 \times 3 \times 2 \times 1}$$

$$= \frac{9 \times 7 \times 2}{1}$$

$$= 126$$

Choice (A) is the correct answer.

649. **C.** $\dfrac{1}{x^2 + 5x + 6}$

The ! symbol means to multiply a series of descending integers, beginning with the number that precedes that ! symbol.

$$\frac{(x+1)!}{(x+3)!} = \frac{(x+1)!}{(x+3)(x+2)(x+1)!}$$

$$= \frac{1}{(x+3)(x+2)}$$

$$= \frac{1}{x^2 + 3x + 2x + 6}$$

$$= \frac{1}{x^2 + 5x + 6}$$

The correct answer is Choice (C).

650.   E. $\dfrac{n}{n+1}$

The ! symbol means to multiply a series of descending integers, beginning with the number that precedes that ! symbol.

$$\frac{(n!)^2}{(n-1)!(n+1)!} = \frac{(n!)(n!)}{(n-1)!(n+1)!}$$

$$= \frac{(n!)}{(n-1)!} \times \frac{(n!)}{(n+1)!}$$

$$= \frac{n(n-1)!}{(n-1)!} \times \frac{(n!)}{(n+1)(n!)}$$

$$= n\frac{1}{(n+1)}$$

$$= \frac{n}{n+1}$$

The correct answer is Choice (E).

651.   50

Every packet must have ten mints, so ten is the limiting factor. The maximum number of packets:

$$\frac{500}{10} = 50$$

652.   189

There are seven choices for a, three choices for b, and nine choices for c:

$$7 \times 3 \times 9 = 189$$

653.   E. 120

Imagine that there are five spots on the shelf and you place the novels one by one. The first novel to be placed could go in any one of the five spots.

The second novel to be placed could then go in any one of the four remaining spots. The third novel to be placed could then go in any one of the three remaining spots, and so on. There are a total of five novels and five places to be chosen, so the total number of ways the five novels could be placed on the shelf is:

$$^5P_5 = 5 \times 4 \times 3 \times 2 \times 1$$

$$= 120$$

The correct answer is Choice (E).

654. E. 720

There is a total of ten people and three are to be chosen at random, in order, with no replacement. The total number of permutations is:

$$^{10}P_3 = 10 \times 9 \times 8$$
$$= 720$$

Choice (E) is the correct answer.

655. C. 210

There is a total of seven books and three books are to be chosen, so the total number of ways to arrange three books is:

$$^{7}P_3 = 7 \times 6 \times 5$$
$$= 210$$

The correct answer is Choice (C).

656. C. 60

There is a total of five digits and three numerals to be chosen, so the total number of different three-digit numerals that can be made is:

$$^{5}P_3 = 5 \times 4 \times 3$$
$$= 60$$

The correct answer is Choice (C).

657. B. 24

There is a total of four friends and four places to walk, so the total number of different patterns is:

$$^{4}P_4 = 4 \times 3 \times 2 \times 1$$
$$= 24$$

Choice (B) is the correct answer.

658. B. 650

There is a total of 26 letters and 4 letters to be chosen, so the total number of permutations is:

$$^{26}P_2 = 26 \times 25$$
$$= 650$$

Choice (B) is the correct answer.

659. **B. 5,040**

There is a total of seven different letters to be used, so the total number of arrangements is:

$$^7P_7 = 7 \times 6 \times 5 \times 4 \times 3 \times 2 \times 1$$
$$= 5,040$$

The correct answer is Choice (B).

660. **B. 720**

There is a total of six different letters to be used, so the total number of arrangements is:

$$^6P_6 = 6 \times 5 \times 4 \times 3 \times 2 \times 1$$
$$= 720$$

Choice (B) is the correct answer.

661. **B. 15**

The first person will shake hands with each of the other five people. The second person will shake hands with the other five, but he/she has already shaken with the first person. This means that there are only four new handshakes. The third person will have to shake with 5 – 2 = 3 people, and so on.

Total handshakes:

$$= 5 + 4 + 3 + 2 + 1$$
$$= 15$$

The correct answer is Choice (B).

662. **12**

First, imagine B in the second position. This gives a choice of one out of three for first place, and one out of two for third place. This is equivalent to six possible combinations.

Putting C in the second place results in six more combinations, for a total of 12 combinations.

663. **A. 126**

John is already chosen, so you need to choose another four people from nine. In choosing a committee, order doesn't matter, so you only need the number of combinations of four people chosen from nine:

$$^9C_4 = \frac{9 \times 8 \times 7 \times 6}{4 \times 3 \times 2 \times 1}$$
$$= \frac{9 \times 2 \times 7}{1}$$
$$= 126$$

Choice (A) is the correct answer.

664. **A. 252**

The order doesn't matter, so you only need the number of combinations of five people chosen from ten:

$$^{10}C_5 = \frac{10 \times 9 \times 8 \times 7 \times 6}{5 \times 4 \times 3 \times 2 \times 1}$$
$$= \frac{2 \times 9 \times 2 \times 7}{1}$$
$$= 252$$

The correct answer is Choice (A).

665. **C. 5**

The order doesn't matter, so you only need the number of combinations of four candies chosen from five:

$$^5C_4 = \frac{5 \times 4 \times 3 \times 2}{4 \times 3 \times 2}$$
$$= 5$$

The correct answer is Choice (C).

666. **C. 35**

The order doesn't matter, so you only need the number of combinations of four shirts chosen from seven:

$$^7C_4 = \frac{7 \times 6 \times 5 \times 4}{1 \times 2 \times 3 \times 4}$$
$$= 7 \times 5$$
$$= 35$$

Choice (C) is the correct answer.

667. **E. 120**

The order doesn't matter, so you only need the number of combinations of three students chosen from ten:

$$^{10}C_3 = \frac{10 \times 9 \times 8}{3 \times 2 \times 1}$$
$$= 10 \times 3 \times 4$$
$$= 120$$

The correct answer is Choice (E).

668. **A. 36**

The order doesn't matter, so you only need the number of combinations of two teams chosen from nine schools:

$$^9C_2 = \frac{9\times 8}{1\times 2}$$
$$= 9\times 4$$
$$= 36$$

The correct answer is Choice (A).

669. **C. 1,326**

The order doesn't matter, so you only need the number of combinations of 2 cards chosen from 52:

$$^{52}C_2 = \frac{52\times 51}{1\times 2}$$
$$= 26\times 51$$
$$= 1,326$$

The correct answer is Choice (C).

670. **C. 31**

There are two teams that are to play out of four pools, so the number of matches played in each pool is:

$$^4C_2 = \frac{4\times 3}{1\times 2}$$
$$= 6$$

With four pools, the total number of pool matches is:

$$4\times 6 = 24$$

The winners and second-place teams play four further matches; then there are two semi-finals and one final match. So, the total number of matches is:

$$24 + 4 + 2 + 1 = 31$$

The correct answer is Choice (C).

671. **B. 0.3**

To find the median, arrange the numbers in numerical order and find the middle term:

0.0003, 0.003, 0.3, 0.31, 0.33

The median is 0.3, Choice (B).

672. C. 6

To find the median, arrange the numbers in numerical order and find the middle term:

3, 3, 4, 5, 6, 7, 10, 11, 12

The median is 6, Choice (C).

673. D. 70

To find the median, arrange the numbers in numerical order:

44, 56, 65, 67, 69, 71, 75, 77, 80, 83

Average the two middle numbers: 69 and 71.

$$\frac{69+71}{2} = \frac{140}{2}$$
$$= 70$$

The median is 70, Choice (D).

674. D. $2,000

To find the median, arrange the numbers in numerical order and find the middle term:

1,000, 1,000, 2,000, 2,000, 3,000

The median is 2,000, Choice (D).

675. B. 22

To find the median, arrange the numbers in numerical order and find the middle term:

3, 5, 7, 12, 13, 14, 21, 23, 23, 23, 23, 29, 40, 56

There are two middle numbers: 21 and 23. Add these numbers together and divide by 2:

$$\frac{21+23}{2} = \frac{44}{2}$$
$$= 22$$

The median is 22, Choice (B).

676. C. 1.5

The median is the middle number when ranked in numerical order. There are 60 drivers, so the median will come between the value for the 30th and 31st drivers.

There are two middle numbers: 1 and 2. Add these numbers together and divide by 2:

$$= \frac{1+2}{2}$$
$$= \frac{3}{2}$$
$$= 1.5$$

The median is 1.5, Choice (C).

677.   **B. 25**

The squares of the ten lowest positive integers are:

$$1^2, 2^2, 3^2, 4^2, 5^2, 6^2, 7^2, 8^2, 9^2$$
$$= 1, 4, 9, 16, 25, 36, 49, 64, 81$$

The middle number is 25, Choice (B).

678.   **B. 12; C. 13; D. 14; E. 15; F. 16**

The median is the middle value when put in numerical order. Besides Z, there are eight numbers in the set. That means that arranged in order, four numbers are to the left of Z and four numbers are to the right.

      5, 7, 9, 12, Z, 16, 18, 23, 44

So, Z must equal or fall between 12 and 16. Choices (B), (C), (D), (E), and (F) are possible values of Z.

679.   **A. 7**

To find the median, arrange the numbers in numerical order and find the middle term:

2, 3, 5, 7, 11, **13**, 17

The median is 7, Choice (A).

680.   **D. 13**

First, put the list of numbers in order:

2, 7, 11, 16, 24

The median of these five numbers is 11. To increase the median by 1, the mean of the middle two numbers must be 12. The mean of 11 and 13 is 12, so the extra number must be 13, Choice (D).

681.   **A. 5**

First, put the numbers in order:

3, 4, 5, 5, 5, 6, 7, 7, 8, 9

The mode is the number that appears most often, which is 5, Choice (A).

682.   **E. 19**

First, put the numbers in order:

8, 15, 19, 19, 28, 29, 35

The mode is the number that appears most often, which is 19, Choice (E).

683.   **B. 3 and 6**

The mode is the number that appears most often. In this set, there are two numbers that both appear three times: 3 and 6, Choice (B), so there are two modes.

684.   E. 7

There are two 6s and two 7s in the list, but there is only one mode, so x must be either **6** or **7**.

If $x = 6$, then the numbers in order are:

2, 5, 6, 6, 6, 7, 7, 10, 13

Mean $= \dfrac{62}{9} = 6.89$

Median = 6

Mode = 6

The mean, median, and mode are not all equal.

If $x = 7$, then the numbers in order are:

2, 5, 6, 6, 7, 7, 7, 10, 13

Mean $= \dfrac{63}{9} = 7$

Median = 7

Mode = 7

The mean, median, and mode are all equal; therefore, $x = 7$, Choice (E).

685.   E. 18

There are seven numbers in the list and the mean = 13. So, the sum of the numbers must be:

$$7 \times 13 = 91$$

The sum of the numbers shown is 73:

$$= 11 + 18 + 5 + 24 + 12 + 3 + x = 73 + x$$

Therefore:

$$73 + x = 91$$
$$x = 91 - 73$$
$$x = 18$$

So, the numbers are 11, 18, 5, 24, 12, 3, and 18. In order, they are:

3, 5, 11, 12, 18, 18, 24

The mode is the number that appears the most often, which is 18, Choice (E).

686.   C. $1.08

The range is the difference between the lowest and highest values. Subtract the smallest number from the largest number:

$$\$2.06 - \$0.98 = \$1.08$$

The correct answer is Choice (C).

687.

A. 80

The range is the difference between the lowest and highest values. Subtract the smallest number from the largest number:

$$91 - 11 = 80$$

The correct answer is Choice (A).

688.

E. 87

The range is the difference between the lowest and highest values. Subtract the smallest number from the largest number:

$$82 - (-5) = 82 + 5$$
$$= 87$$

Choice (E) is the correct answer.

689.

D. 5

The range is the difference between the lowest and highest values. Subtract the smallest number from the largest number:

$$6 - 1 = 5$$

The correct answer is Choice (D).

690.

D. 4

The range is the difference between the lowest and highest values. Subtract the smallest number from the largest number:

$$8 - 4 = 4$$

The correct answer is Choice (D).

691.

C. 7 minutes per mile

The total time spent by the athlete was 24 minutes. If two of the miles took 10 minutes, then the other two took 14.

$\frac{14}{2}$ = 7 minutes per mile, Choice (C).

692.

A. 60

$$\frac{8 + 11 + 25 + x}{4} = 15$$
$$8 + 11 + 25 + x = 60$$

The correct answer is Choice (A).

693.   B. 2.4

The mean is calculated by finding the sum of the values and dividing by the number of values:

$$\frac{3+(-7)+5+13+(-2)}{5} = \frac{12}{5}$$
$$= 2.4$$

Choice (B) is the correct answer.

694.   D. 16

$$\frac{8+11+25+x}{4} = 15$$
$$8+11+25+x = 60$$
$$x = 16$$

The correct answer is Choice (D).

695.   C. 3

The mean is calculated by dividing the sum of the values by the number of values:

$$\frac{3+1+6+2+3+3}{6} = \frac{18}{6}$$
$$= 3$$

The correct answer is Choice (C).

696.   A. 74.5%

The mean is calculated by dividing the sum of the values by the number of values:

$$\frac{86+67+62+72+84+76}{6} = \frac{447}{6}$$
$$= 74.5$$

The correct answer is Choice (A).

697.   C. 100

The average of an evenly spaced series of numbers is equal to the value of the middle term. The middle term out of 19 is the tenth term in the series, which is 100, Choice (C).

698.   A. 25

The mean is calculated by dividing the sum of the values by the number of values:

$$\frac{500}{20} = 25$$

Choice (A) is the correct answer.

699. **E. 180**

The mean is calculated by dividing the sum of the values by the number of values. Let x represent the sum of the values:

$$\frac{x}{30} = 6$$
$$x = 6(30)$$
$$= 180$$

Choice (E) is the correct answer.

700. **C. 40**

The mean is calculated by dividing the sum of the values by the number of values. Let x represent the number of values:

$$\frac{1,200}{x} = 30$$
$$1,200 = 30(x)$$
$$\frac{1,200}{30} = x$$
$$40 = x$$

The correct answer is Choice (C).

701. **C. $1,800**

The mean is calculated by dividing the sum of the values by the number of values:

$$\frac{(1,000+2,000+3,000+2,000+1,000)}{5} = \frac{9,000}{5}$$
$$= 1,800$$

The mean is $1,800, Choice (C).

702. **E. 6**

The mean is calculated by dividing the sum of the values by the number of values:

$$\frac{6+8+4}{3} = \frac{18}{3}$$
$$= 6$$

The mean tree height is 6, Choice (E).

703. **D. 11**

The mean is calculated by dividing the sum of the values by the number of values:

$$\frac{10+3+20}{3} = \frac{33}{3}$$
$$= 11$$

The mean number of Italian recipes that each person makes is 11, Choice (D).

704. **B. 45**

First, find the sum of the original set of 6 numbers:

$$= 20 \times 6$$
$$= 120$$

Next, find the sum of the new set of 5 numbers:

$$= 15 \times 5$$
$$= 75$$

Subtract the sums:

$$120 - 75 = 45$$

The number that's removed is 45, Choice (B).

705. **D. 5.5**

The mean of the two largest numbers is 9; therefore, their sum $= 9 \times 2 = 18$.

The mean of all three numbers is 7; therefore, their sum $= 7 \times 3 = 21$.

So, the third number must be:

$$21 - 18 = 3.$$

The three numbers written on the piece of paper were 3, 8, and 10. So, the mean of the two smallest numbers is:

$$\frac{3+8}{2} = \frac{11}{2}$$
$$= 5.5$$

Choice (D) is the correct answer.

706. **B. 7**

Let the smaller number be x. The larger number must be $x + 6$.

The mean is:

$$\frac{x + x + 6}{2} = \frac{2x + 6}{2}$$
$$= x + 3$$

The mean is 10, so:

$$x + 3 = 10$$
$$x = 7$$

The smaller of the two numbers is 7, Choice (B).

707. **50%**

The mean score from a class of 30 students was 55%, so:

$$30 \times 55 = 1{,}650$$

The mean score from a class of 25 students was 44%, so:

$$25 \times 44 = 1{,}100$$

So, the total score of all 55 students is:

$$1{,}650 + 1{,}100 = 2{,}750$$

The mean for all 55 students is:

$$2{,}750 \div 55 = 50$$

The correct answer is Choice (D).

708. **B. $\frac{1}{2}x$**

$$\frac{x+y+z}{3} = \frac{x + \frac{1}{3}x + \frac{1}{6}x}{3}$$
$$= x\left(1 + \frac{1}{3} + \frac{1}{6}\right)\left(\frac{1}{3}\right)$$
$$= \frac{1}{2}x$$

Choice (B) is your answer.

709. **D. 28**

The mean of 15 numbers is 12; therefore, the total of 15 numbers is:

$$15 \times 12 = 180$$

The mean of 16 numbers is 13; therefore, the total of 16 numbers is:

$$16 \times 13 = 208$$

So, the extra number must be:

$$208 - 180 = 28$$

The extra number is 28, Choice (E).

710. B. 2

The mean is calculated by dividing the sum of the values by the number of values, so:

$$\frac{1+2+4+5+6+6+7+8+9+10+12+x}{12}=6$$

$$\frac{70+x}{12}=6$$

$$70+x=72$$

$$x=2$$

If the mean is 6, the value of x is 2, Choice (B).

711. C. 50%

Under a normally distributed curve, the mean divides the population in half. The area under the curve that is below the mean represents 50% of the population. The correct answer is Choice (C).

712. C. N

Standard deviation is a measure of how dispersed the data is. Data set N, Choice (C), has values that are more clumped together, so it has the smallest standard deviation.

713. E. The standard deviation stays the same.

If each number is increased by 2, then the mean is also increased by 2. The distance between the numbers would be unchanged, so the standard deviation would also be unchanged, Choice (E).

714. C. The standard deviation triples.

If each number is multiplied by 3, then the mean is also multiplied by 3. The values of the differences are also multiplied by 3. Therefore, the standard deviation triples, Choice (C).

715. C. 3.5

The standard deviation is based on the distance each value is from the mean. A value of 3.5, Choice (C), would be closest to the mean, causing the least change in the standard deviation.

716. C. C

Data set C, Choice (C), has values that are farther away from the mean compared to sets A and B, so set C has the largest standard deviation.

717. **A. The standard deviation of the set is equal to 4; B. The standard deviation of the set is less than 4; C. The standard deviation of the set is greater than 4; D. The standard deviation of the set is the same with or without the inclusion of values of *x*, *y*, and *z*.**

The standard deviation is based on the distance each value is from the mean. The exact values of *x*, *y*, and *z* are not known, so the standard deviation is not known; therefore, any of the statements could be true and all the answer choices are correct. A wide range of values for *x*, *y*, and *z* would result in a high standard deviation, while a narrow range of values for *x*, *y*, and *z* would result in a low standard deviation.

718. **B. 16%**

Between the mean and the mean minus one standard deviation (5 centimeters) is about 34% of the population. The randomly chosen dog would have to be farther than one standard deviation from the mean if it has a height that is less than 60 centimeters. The area under the curve that is farther than one standard deviation from the mean represents 16% of the population, Choice (B).

719. **C. 95**

Because the mean is 65 centimeters and the standard deviation is 5 centimeters, this question is focusing on the area between the mean and two standard deviations above the mean. The area under the curve between the mean and two standard deviations above the mean represents 47.5% of the population. There are 200 dogs, so $200 \times 0.475 = 95$, Choice (C).

720. **E. 98%**

Because the mean is 70% and the standard deviation is 12 points, the student's score of 95% puts the student just over two standard deviations above the mean. The area under the curve below two standard deviations above the mean represents 97.5% of the population. The closest answer is 98%, Choice (E).

721. **D. 3–4 standard deviations**

The standard deviation is 0.021, so the reaction time of 0.205 seconds is 3–4 standard deviations from the 0.135 average:

$$0.205 - 0.135 = 0.07$$

$$\frac{0.07}{0.021} \approx 3.3$$

The answer you want is Choice (D).

722. **B. 30**

If the mean is 60 and the standard deviation is 15:

Above the mean by two standard deviations =

$$60 + 2(15) = 90$$

Below the mean by two standard deviations =

$$60 - 2(15) = 30$$

This is the lowest possible score, making Choice (B) the right answer.

723. **E. 30.6**

The standard deviation is based on the distance each value is from the mean. If the passenger numbers are tripled, the differences in averages will also triple. Multiply 10.2 by 3 and you get 30.6, Choice (E).

724. **C. 9, 11**

The numbers 9 and 11, Choice (C), are closest to 10, so they reduce the average distance from the mean the most.

725. **B. 93%**

The standard deviation is 8, so 2.5 standard deviations above the average would be 92%:

$$2.5 \times 8 = 20$$
$$20 + 72 = 92$$

To be considered "exceptional," the test score has to be greater than 2.5 standard deviations above the mean, so the lowest score would be 93%, Choice (B).

726. **C. C, A, B**

Set C consists of all the same number, so the standard deviation is zero. In Set A, the mean is 5. Two of the numbers equal 5 and no number is more than two units from the mean. In Set B, the mean is also 5, but every number is three units away from the mean, making the standard deviation of Set B larger than the standard deviation of Set A. Choice (C) is the correct answer.

727. **E. 2%**

The mean is 10, so one standard deviation below the mean is $10 - 2 = 8$. A second standard deviation below the mean is $8 - 2 = 6$. All values below 6 would fall more than two standard deviations below the mean. The area below the mean minus three standard deviations is about 2% of the population, Choice (E).

728. **B. 16%**

First, find the mean weight:

$$\frac{21,600}{300} = 72$$

A weight of 84 pounds is the mean plus 1 standard deviation. The area above the mean plus 1 standard deviation is about 16% of the population, Choice (B).

729.   **A. 0**

The standard deviation is based on the distance each value is from the mean. If the same value is added to every number in the set, the standard deviation will not change. Thus, the correct answer is 0, Choice (A).

730.   **A. Set *R*; C. Set *T***

Each number in Set *R* is 30 more than each number in Set *A*. The numbers have shifted, but the spacing has not changed, so the standard deviation is not changed. Set *R* has the same standard deviation as Set *A*, making Choice (A) correct. Set *T* has the same spacing as Set *A*, just in the opposite direction, so Set *T* has the same standard deviation as Set *A* and Choice (C) is also correct.

731.   **6,000**

The number of large cars sold was 20, and the sales total for large cars was $120,000. Thus the average sale price per car was

$$\frac{\$120,000}{20} = \$6,000.$$

732.   **E. 2:1**

# of small cars offered = 32

# of small cars sold = 16

The ratio = 3:16, which reduces to 2:1, Choice (E).

733.   **C. 56%**

Total # of cars sold:

$$16 + 20 = 36$$

Percent of large cars:

$$\frac{20}{36} = \frac{5}{9}$$
$$= 0.556$$
$$= 56\%$$

Choice (C) is right on target.

734.   **C. 60%**

The sector representing Asia is bigger than half (50%) but smaller than three quarters (75%), so 60%, Choice (C), is the best answer.

735.   **B. 15%**

The sector representing Africa is bigger than a 5% slice but smaller than a quarter slice, so 15%, Choice (B), is the best answer.

736. **B. 11**

The number of students greater than or equal to 60 inches tall is shown in the bars representing the groups $60-65$, $65-70$, $70-75$ and $75-80$:

$$5+2+3+1=11$$

Choice (B), 11, is the right answer.

737. **B. 13**

The number of students greater than or equal to 55 inches tall, but less than 70 inches tall, is shown in the bars representing the groups $55-60$, $60-65$ and $65-70$:

$$6+5+2=13$$

Choice (B) is the answer you're looking for.

738. **C. 66**

The number of eggs less than 23 millimeters in length is found by adding the frequencies for the groups $19-20$, $20-21$, $21-22$ and $22-23$:

$$1+8+17+40=66$$

Choice (C) is the correct answer.

739. **E. 100**

The number of eggs measured is found by adding all the frequencies:

$$1+8+17+40+26+8=100$$

Choice (E) is the right answer.

740. **A. 0**

The bar heights for the English column and History column extend to the same height, so Tom earned 0 more points in English than in History. Choice (A) is the one you want.

741. **E. 15**

The bar heights for the Science and History columns extend to 95 and 80, respectively. Subtract the History score from the Science score for the difference:

$$95-80=15$$

Tom earned 15 more percentage points in Science than in History, Choice (E).

742. **A. The temperature is about 30°F at 9 p.m.; B. The range of temperatures is 40°F.**

Choice (A) is correct — the recorded temperature at 8 p.m. is 35°F, and the recorded temperature at 10 p.m. is 25°F. The temperature is dropping at a regular rate; therefore, at 9 p.m. the temperature is about 30°F.

Choice (B) is also correct — the highest temperature recorded is 50°F at 4 p.m., and the lowest temperature recorded is 10°F at midnight. The difference between the highest and the lowest temperatures is:

$$50°F - 10°F = 40°F$$

Choice (C) is incorrect — without actually calculating the average, it is clearly higher than 25°F.

Choice (D) is also incorrect — without actually calculating the percent of change, the drop from 45°F to 35°F is far less than 60%.

743. **B. 25%**

The recorded temperature at noon is 40°F, and the recorded temperature at 4 p.m. is 50°F. That's a 10° increase:

$$50°F - 40°F = 10°F$$

Find the percentage change:

$$\frac{10°F}{40°F} = \frac{1}{4}$$
$$= 0.25$$
$$= 25\%$$

The increase in temperature from noon to 4 p.m. is 25%, Choice (B).

744. **B. 1940–1980; D. 1910–1940**

1910 = 800 people

1920 = 1,200 people

1940 = 2,000 people

1960 = 3,000 people

1980 = 4,000 people

2000 = 5,400 people

1940–1960:

$$3,000 - 2,000 = 1,000$$

$$\frac{1,000}{2,000} = \frac{1}{2} = 0.5 = 50\%$$

1940–1980:

$$4,000 - 2,000 = 2,000$$

$$\frac{2,000}{2,000} = 1 = 100\%$$

1910–1920:

$1,200 - 800 = 400$

$$\frac{400}{800} = \frac{1}{2} = 0.5 = 50\%$$

1910–1940:

$2,000 - 800 = 1,200$

$$\frac{1,200}{800} = \frac{3}{2} = 1.5 = 150\%$$

1980–2000:

$5,400 - 4,000 = 1,400$

$$\frac{1,400}{4,000} = \frac{7}{20} = 0.35 = 35\%$$

Choices (B) and (D) are correct.

745.   **E. 7,400**

Follow the curved line upward until it is above the year 2020. Follow that point left to the y-axis and approximate the y value of that point. It is approximately 7,400, Choice (E).

746.   **B. 2,800**

Every five squares on the vertical axis represent a population of 1,000, so each square represents 200. The point for the year 1920 is 1 square above 1,000; therefore, the population in 1920 was 1,200. The population in 1980 was 4,000.

$$4,000 - 1,200 = 2,800$$

So the population increased by 2,800, Choice (B), between 1920 and 1980.

747.   **C. 90°**

First, find the total number of times the die was rolled by adding all of the frequencies:

$$2 + 6 + 1 + 3 + 5 + 3 = 20$$

Of these, the score 5 was obtained 5 times; therefore, the fraction of the scores that were 5 is $\frac{5}{20}$. To find the angle of the sector, multiply the above fraction by 360°:

$$\frac{5}{20} \times 360° = 0.25 \times 360°$$
$$= 90°$$

The angle of the sector of the pie chart representing the score of 5 is 90°, Choice (C).

748. E. 45%

First, find the total number of times the die was rolled by adding all the frequencies:

$$2+6+1+3+5+3=20$$

Of these, the score 2 was obtained 6 times:

$$\frac{6}{20}=0.3=30\%$$

The score 6 was obtained 3 times:

$$\frac{3}{20}=0.15=15\%$$

The sum:

$$30\%+15\%=45\%$$

Therefore, the sum of the percentages of rolls that resulted in the die landing on a 2 or a 6 is 45%, Choice (E).

749. C. 14.4°

First, find the total percent for all the other types of pets:

$$39\%+30\%+8\%+7\%+12\%=96\%$$

Next, subtract this percentage amount from 100%:

$$100\%-96\%=4\%$$

The angle for the sector of the pie chart representing fish is found by multiplying the percentage of fish by 360°:

$$0.04\times360°=14.4°$$

The right answer is Choice (C).

750. E. 32

First, find the total percent for all the other types of pets:
$$39\%+30\%+8\%+7\%+12\%=96\%$$

Next, subtract this percentage amount from 100%:

$$100\%-96\%=4\%$$

The number who said their favorite pet was fish can be found by multiplying the percentage of fish by the total number of students:

$$0.04\times800=32$$

Therefore, Choice (E) is the one you want.

751. **D. 64**

First, find the total number of students surveyed:

39% of students said their favorite pet was a dog, so 39% of those surveyed is 312.

$$312 \div 0.39 = 800$$

The number of students whose favorite pet was a rabbit can be found by multiplying the number of those surveyed by 8%:

$$8\% \times 800 = 0.08 \times 800$$
$$= 64$$

A rabbit was the favorite pet of 64 children, Choice (D).

752. **E. 9.6**

Work represents 40% of the chart. Forty percent of 24 hours is:

$$0.4 \times 24 \text{ hours} = 9.6 \text{ hours}$$

Choice (E) is the correct answer.

753. **C. 3.5 hours**

Sport represents 14% of the chart. Fourteen percent of 24 hours is:

$$0.14 \times 24 \text{ hours} = 3.36 \text{ hours}$$
$$\approx 3.5 \text{ hours}$$

Susan spends approximately 3.5 hours per day playing sports, Choice (C).

754. **B. 2 hours 38 minutes**

Sleep represents 25% of the chart. Twenty-five percent of 24 hours is:

$$0.25 \times 24 \text{ hours} = 6 \text{ hours}$$

Morning prep represents 6% of the chart. Six percent of 24 hours is:

$$0.06 \times 24 \text{ hours} = 1.44 \text{ hours}$$

Eating represents 8% of the chart. Eight percent of 24 hours is:

$$0.08 \times 24 \text{ hours} = 1.92 \text{ hours}$$

The total time spent on morning prepping and eating is:

$$1.44 + 1.92 = 3.36 \text{ hours}$$

Sleep – (Eat + Morning prep) is:

$$6 - 3.36 = 2.64 \text{ hours}$$
$$\approx 2 \text{ hours } 38 \text{ minutes}$$

Thus, Susan spends about 2 hours and 38 minutes more time sleeping than engaging in morning prep and eating each day. Choice (B) is your answer.

755. **A. 59%**

Schizophrenia has the largest number of patients.

$$\frac{24{,}651}{41{,}674} = 0.59 = 59\%$$

So schizophrenia is the largest disease category with 59% of patients, Choice (A).

756. **D. 7%**

Schizophrenia = 24,651

Psychotic diseases = 10,279

First, find the reduction of patients in each category:

$$24{,}651 \times 0.1 = 2{,}465$$

$$10{,}279 \times 0.05 = 514$$

Next, find the total reduction:

$$2{,}465 + 514 = 2{,}979$$

Finally, find the percent of reduction:

$$\frac{2{,}979}{41{,}674} = 0.07 = 7\%$$

Choice (D), 7%, is the correct answer.

757. **A. Neuroses and Drug dependence; B. Alcoholism and Others; C. Neuroses and Alcoholism; D. Neuroses and Others; F. Drug dependence and Others**

Calculate the percentage for each category:

Neuroses: $\dfrac{1{,}122}{41{,}674} = 0.027 = 3\%$

Drug dependence: $\dfrac{996}{41{,}674} = 0.02 = 2\%$

Alcoholism: $\dfrac{692}{41{,}674} = 0.02 = 2\%$

Others: $\dfrac{1{,}052}{41{,}674} = 0.025 \doteq 3\%$

Find the sums of the percentages. All the answers are correct except Choice (E).

758.

B. Both companies have the same mode percent profit; C. Both companies have the same median percent profit; E. The mode percent profit for Company X is equal to the median percent profit for Company Y.

The median is the middle value when put in numerical order:

Company X median = 40, 45, 50, 50, 55, 65 = 50

Company Y median = 35, 45, 50, 50, 55, 60 = 50

The mode is the value that appears the most often:

Company X mode = 50

Company Y mode = 50

Choices (B), (C), and (E) can correctly be deduced from the data in the graph.

759.

B. 37.5%

1996 = 40%

1998 = 55%

Increase = 15%

Calculate percentage increase:

$$\frac{15}{40} = 0.375 = 37.5\%$$

Choice (B), 37.5%, represents the increase in profit from 1996 to 1998.

760.

B. The difference between percent profit for Company X and percent profit for Company Y was less than 15% in more than half the years shown; C. The percent profit for Company X was never less than 75% of the percent profit for Company Y.

The difference between percent profit for Company X and percent profit for Company Y was less than 15% during all but one year, so Choice (B) is correct.

The percent profit for Company X is less than the percent profit for Company Y in only three years, but it is never less than 75% of the percent profit for Company Y. Choice (C) is correct.

Choice (A) is not correct; because the percent profit for Company X dipped in 1999 and 2001.

761. **A. Quantity A is greater.**

$$-1(-1) = 1$$
$$-1 + (-1) = -1 - 1$$
$$= -2$$

Thus, Choice (A) is the correct answer.

762. **A. Quantity A is greater.**

To the nearest hundredths place, 62,210 becomes 62,200.

To the nearest thousandths place, 62,210 becomes 62,000.

Thus, Choice (A) is the correct answer.

763. **B. Quantity B is greater.**

A positive integer is a whole number equal to or greater than 1. Any positive integer multiplied by 2 will be greater than the integer itself.

The correct answer is Choice (B).

764. **D. It cannot be determined from the information given.**

The easiest approach to this problem is to simply select a few random, even integers to test. For example, if n is 10, the remainder for Quantity A is 1, and the remainder for Quantity B is 0. But if n is 12, the remainder for Quantity A is 0 and the remainder for Quantity B is 2. Thus, the answer must be Choice (D).

765. **D. It cannot be determined from the information given.**

The easiest approach to this problem is to simply select a few random, positive integers to test. For example, if the integer n is 1, Quantity A is 2. If n is 3, Quantity A is $3\frac{1}{3}$, which is greater than 2. Thus, the answer must be Choice (D).

766. **B. Quantity B is greater.**

The first number of the series of multiples of 3 is 51 and the last is 99; therefore, the number of integers that are multiples of 3 is 17.

The first number of the series of multiples of 4 is 12 and the last is 80; therefore, the number of integers that are multiples of 4 is 18.

Thus, Choice (B) is the correct answer.

767. **D. It cannot be determined from the information given.**

"More than twice" is not specific enough. It could mean two and a half, three, four, or even twenty times what Sara and Tina have. Hence, the number of candies that Robbi has could be less or more than three times Sara and Tina's total. The relationship cannot be determined from the information given, Choice (D).

768.

D. It cannot be determined from the information given.

No limits are placed on the upper size of the odd integers, so it's easy to pick examples where Quantity A or Quantity B can be greater. Hence, the relationship cannot be determined from the information given, Choice (D).

769.

C. The quantities are equal.

If the rate at $10°$ is x, the rate will be $2x$ at $20°$ and $4x$ at $30°$.

Therefore, twice the rate at $10°$ ($2x$) and half the rate at $30°$ ($1/2$ of $4x$) will be the same. Choice (C) is the correct answer.

770.

D. It cannot be determined from the information given.

If the product of the three consecutive integers is 0, one of the numbers must be zero. But which one? The numbers could be -2, -1, 0; they could be -1, 0, 1; or they could be 0, 1, 2. Therefore, the relationship cannot be determined from the information given, Choice (D).

771.

C. The quantities are equal.

Prime factors of 36 are 3 and 2. Prime factors of 48 are 3 and 2 also. The greatest prime factor in both cases is 3. Choice (C) is the correct answer.

772.

A. Quantity A is greater.

Prime factors of 40 are 5 and 2. Prime factors of 24 are 3 and 2. So, the greatest prime factor is 5 in Quantity A. The correct answer is Choice (A).

773.

C. The quantities are equal.

Prime factors of 540 are 5, 3, and 2. Prime factors of 90 are 5, 3, and 2 also. The greatest prime factor in both cases is 5. Choice (C) is the correct answer.

774.

B. Quantity B is greater.

Prime factors of 252 are 7, 3, and 2. Prime factors of 3,150 are 7, 5, 3, and 2. So, Quantity B has the greater number of different prime factors. The correct answer is Choice (B).

775.

C. The quantities are equal.

Prime factors of 2,500 are 5 and 2. Prime factors of 1,215 are 5 and 3. Thus, both quantities have two different prime factors. Choice (C) is the correct answer.

776. **B. Quantity B is greater.**

Absolute value means how far a number is from 0.

$$|-5| = 5$$
$$|7| = 7$$

Thus, Quantity B is greater, making Choice (B) the correct answer.

777. **A. Quantity A is greater.**

Absolute value means how far a number is from 0.

$$|-3| = 3$$

Thus, Quantity A is greater, making Choice (A) the correct answer.

778. **A. Quantity A is greater.**

Absolute value means how far a number is from 0.

$$|-3| + |-2| = 3 + 2$$
$$= 5$$
$$-3 + (-2) = -3 - 2$$
$$= -5$$

Thus, Quantity A is greater, making the correct answer Choice (A).

779. **C. The quantities are equal.**

Absolute value means how far a number is from 0.

$$|8 - 3| = |5| = 5$$
$$|3 - 8| = |-5| = 5$$

Thus, the two quantities are equal, and the correct answer is Choice (C)..

780. **A. Quantity A is greater.**

Absolute value means how far a number is from 0.

$$|-3 \times 6| = |-18| = 18$$
$$-|-12| = -12$$

Thus, Quantity A is greater, making Choice (A) the correct answer.

781. **A. Quantity A is greater.**

Absolute value means how far a number is from 0.

$$|2 \times 7| = |14| = 14$$
$$\left|\frac{3}{1} + 7\right| = |3 + 7| = |10| = 10$$

Thus, Quantity A is greater, and the correct answer is Choice (A).

782. **A. Quantity A is greater.**

Absolute value means how far a number is from 0.

$$|5 \times -3| = |-15| = 15$$
$$-|5 - 9| = -|-4| = -4$$

Thus, Quantity A is greater, and the correct answer is Choice (A).

783. **A. Quantity A is greater.**

Absolute value means how far a number is from 0.

$$-|-6| \div |-2| = -6 \div 2$$
$$= -3$$
$$|-6| \times -|2| = 6 \times -2$$
$$= -12$$

Thus, Quantity A is greater, making Choice (A) the correct answer.

784. **B. Quantity B is greater.**

Absolute value means how far a number is from 0.

$$\frac{-4 \times |3 - 8|}{|1 + 3|} = \frac{-4 \times |-5|}{|4|}$$
$$= \frac{-4 \times 5}{4}$$
$$= \frac{-20}{4}$$
$$= -5$$
$$\frac{4 \times |8 - 3|}{|-2|} = \frac{4 \times |5|}{2}$$
$$= \frac{4 \times 5}{2}$$
$$= \frac{20}{2}$$
$$= 10$$

Thus, Quantity B is greater, and Choice (B) is the right answer.

785. **B. Quantity B is greater.**

Absolute value means how far a number is from 0.

$$\left|\frac{-4 \div 2}{6 - 8}\right| \times \frac{-3}{4} = \left|\frac{-2}{-2}\right| \times \frac{-3}{4}$$

$$= |1| \times \frac{-3}{4}$$

$$= 1 \times \frac{-3}{4}$$

$$= \frac{-3}{4}$$

$$\left|\frac{-4 \times 2}{8 - 6}\right| \times \frac{3}{4} = \left|\frac{-8}{2}\right| \times \frac{3}{4}$$

$$= |-4| \times \frac{3}{4}$$

$$= 4 \times \frac{3}{4}$$

$$= \frac{12}{4}$$

$$= 3$$

Thus, Quantity B is greater, making Choice (B) the right answer.

786. **B. Quantity B is greater.**

Each place value to the right is 10 times smaller than the value to its left. For Quantity A, the 2 is three place values to the right of the ones place, making the 2 in a place value that is 1/1,000. For Quantity B, the 2 is two place values to the right of the ones place, making the 2 in a place value that is 1/100.

Thus, Quantity B is greater, making Choice (B) the correct answer.

787. **C. The quantities are equal.**

A percent is a fraction of 100, so 1,000% equals 10. Choice (C) is the correct answer.

788. **A. Quantity A is greater.**

$$1.01(-1.01) = -1.0201$$

$$-1.01 + (-1.01) = -1.01 - 1.01$$

$$= -2.02$$

Thus, Quantity A is greater, and Choice (A) is the correct answer.

789. **C. The quantities are equal.**

To the nearest hundredths place, 2.2740 becomes 2.27.

To the nearest thousandths place, 2.2704 becomes 2.270.

Thus, the two quantities are equal, Choice (C).

---

790. **B. Quantity B is greater.**

To find the maximum difference between x and y, make x as large as possible (just less than 8.3) and make y as small as possible (just greater than 3.1). The maximum difference is a little less than 5.2; therefore, Quantity B is greater. The correct answer is Choice (B).

---

791. **B. Quantity B is greater.**

The top number (numerator) in a fraction represents the number of parts that you have. The bottom number (denominator) in a fraction represents the number of parts the whole is divided into. Two parts is greater than 1 part; therefore, Quantity B is greater. Choice (B) is the correct answer.

---

792. **A. Quantity A is greater.**

Quantity A can be matched to Quantity B by multiplying the top and bottom of the fraction by 6: $\frac{5}{6} = \frac{30}{36}$, which is greater than $\frac{29}{36}$. Thus, Quantity A is greater, and Choice (A) is the correct answer.

---

793. **D. It cannot be determined from the information given.**

The top number (numerator) in a fraction represents the number of parts that you have. The bottom number (denominator) in a fraction represents the number of parts the whole is divided into. Because the denominator is not mentioned in the problem, the relationship cannot be determined, Choice (D).

---

794. **D. It cannot be determined from the information given.**

The easiest way to solve this problem is to convert the fractions to decimals:

$$\frac{7}{8} = 0.875$$

$$\frac{5}{6} = 0.8333$$

$$\frac{6}{7} = 0.857 \, (approx.)$$

Both x and Quantity B lie between $\frac{7}{8}$ and $\frac{5}{6}$, so the relationship cannot be determined from the information given. Choice (D) is the correct answer.

---

795. **B. Quantity B is greater.**

The denominator is the number on the bottom of the fraction. To get an equivalent fraction with a denominator of 12, multiply the denominator (3) by 4.

Next, multiply the numerator (2) by 4:

$$\frac{2}{3} = \frac{2 \times 4}{3 \times 4} = \frac{8}{12}$$

The numerator is the number on the top of the fraction. To get an equivalent fraction with a numerator of 12, multiply the numerator (1) by 8.

Next, multiply the denominator (2) by 8:

$$\frac{1}{2} = \frac{1 \times 8}{2 \times 8} = \frac{8}{16}$$

The denominator in Quantity B is greater than the numerator in Quantity A. Choice (B) is the correct answer.

796. **C. The quantities are equal.**

The denominators in Quantity A are the same, so only the numerators are added:

$$\frac{2}{7} + \frac{3}{7} = \frac{5}{7}$$

The denominators in Quantity B need to be made the same:

$$\frac{1}{4} + \frac{3}{8} = \frac{1 \times 2}{4 \times 2} + \frac{3}{8}$$
$$= \frac{2}{8} + \frac{3}{8}$$
$$= \frac{5}{8}$$

Thus, the two quantities are equal, and Choice (C) is the correct answer.

797. **A. Quantity A is greater.**

The multiples of 9 are: 9, 18, 27, **36**, 45, . . .

The multiples of 12 are: 12, 24, **36**, 48, . . .

The multiples of 36 are: **36**, 72, . . .

Thus, the least common multiple of 9, 12, and 36 is **36**.

The multiples of 3 are: 3, 6, 9, 12, 15, 18, 21, **24**, 27, . . .

The multiples of 12 are: 12, **24**, 36, . . .

The multiples of 8 are: 8, 16, **24**, 32, . . .

Thus, the least common multiple of 3, 12, and 8 is **24**.

Therefore, Quantity A is greater, and Choice (A) is the correct answer.

798. **A. Quantity A is greater.**

The multiples of 12 are: 12, 24, **36**, 48, . . .

The multiples of 9 are: 9, 18, 27 **36**, 45, . . .

Therefore, the least common multiple of 12 and 9 is **36**.

The correct answer is Choice (A).

799. **B. Quantity B is greater.**

Multiply the bottom numbers and multiply the top numbers:

$$\frac{5}{8} \times \frac{4}{5} = \frac{5 \times 4}{8 \times 5}$$

$$= \frac{20}{40}$$

$$= \frac{1}{2}$$

$$\frac{2}{7} \times \frac{4}{3} = \frac{2 \times 4}{7 \times 3}$$

$$= \frac{8}{21}$$

The number 8 is greater than 1; thus, Quantity B is greater. The correct answer is Choice (B).

800. **B. Quantity B is greater.**

The easiest way to solve this problem is to convert the fractions to decimals:

$$\frac{1}{3} = 0.333$$

$$\frac{4}{5} = 0.8$$

$$\frac{3}{11} = 0.273$$

$$\frac{1}{2} = 0.5$$

The smallest fraction is $\frac{3}{11}$ and the largest fraction is $\frac{4}{5}$, which when multiplied by $\frac{2}{3}$ is $\frac{8}{15}$ (0.533). Thus, Quantity B is greater, and Choice (B) is the correct answer.

801. **C. The quantities are equal.**

A 15% discount means that you get the item at 85% of its original price. Eighty-five percent of p is the equivalent of $0.85p$. Thus, the two quantities are equal, Choice (C).

802. **A. Quantity A is greater.**

$$75\% = \frac{75}{100} = 0.75$$

$$0.75 \times 60 = 45$$

$$55\% = \frac{55}{100} = 0.55$$

$$0.55 \times 55 = 30.25$$

Thus, Quantity A is greater. Choice (A) is the correct answer.

803.   **A. Quantity A is greater.**

As a fraction,

$$\frac{16}{20} = \frac{80}{100} = 80\%$$

As a fraction,

$$\frac{27}{50} = \frac{54}{100} = 54\%$$

Thus, Quantity A is greater, and Choice (A) is the correct answer.

804.   **A. Quantity A is greater.**

The difference between 14 and 26 is:

$$26 - 14 = 12$$

The average is:

$$\frac{(26 + 14)}{2} = \frac{40}{2} = 20$$

So, the percentage difference is:

$$\left(\frac{12}{20}\right)100\% = 60\%$$

The difference between 26 and 38 is:

$$38 - 26 = 12$$

The average is:

$$\frac{(38 + 26)}{2} = \frac{64}{2} = 32$$

So, the percentage difference is:

$$\left(\frac{12}{32}\right)100\% = \left(\frac{3}{8}\right)100\% = 37.5\%$$

Therefore, Quantity A is greater. The correct answer is Choice (A).

805.   **C. The quantities are equal.**

If 45% of m is 54, then m equals 120, as $m = \dfrac{54}{0.45} = 120$.

If 90% of n is 108, then n also equals 120, as $n = \dfrac{108}{0.9} = 120$.

Thus, the two quantities are equal. Choice (C) is the correct answer.

806. **B. Quantity B is greater.**

The only multiples of 2 that are multiples of 5 are the multiples of 10. So, only 1 in 5 multiples of 2 are multiples of 5 (2, 4, 6, 8, 10, 12, 14, 16, 18, 20. . . .).

The multiples of 5 that are multiples of 2 are also the multiples of 10. But this time, half the multiples of 5 are multiples of 2 (5, 10, 15, 20, 25, 30, . . .).

Therefore, Quantity B is greater, and Choice (B) is the correct answer.

807. **A. Quantity A is greater.**

From 1989 to 1991, the rise is 2,000. From 1991 to 1993 the fall is 2,000.

The percent increase is:

$$\left(\frac{2,000}{1,000}\right)100 = 2 \times 100$$
$$= 200$$

The percent fall is:

$$\left(\frac{2,000}{3,000}\right)100 = \frac{2,000}{3,000} \times \frac{100}{1}$$
$$= \frac{200,000}{3,000}$$
$$= 66.67$$

Therefore, the percent rise is greater. Choice (A) is the correct answer.

808. **A. Quantity A is greater.**

40 gallons at $1.152 = $46.08
40 gallons at $1.245 = $49.80
The savings will be $49.80 − $46.08 = $3.72

Therefore, Quantity A is greater, and Choice (A) is the correct answer.

809. **D. It cannot be determined from the information given.**

You don't have the totals for each class; therefore, you can't assume that the sizes of the classes are equal.

If they are both equal (in other words, 100 each), then the combined percentage is 21.

But, you can make the percentage less than 20 by making Class B much larger than Class A. Thus, Choice (D) is the correct answer.

810.   **A. Quantity A is greater.**

Because 50% of the students study Spanish, 16 students study Spanish. The number of boys in the class is 25%, and 25% of 32 is 8. Assume that all the boys in the class study Spanish. That leaves 8 girls who study Spanish, which would be the minimum number of girls taking Spanish. If fewer boys study Spanish, the number of girls will increase; hence, the number of girls studying Spanish cannot be less than 8. Choice (A) is the correct answer.

811.   **C. The quantities are equal.**

First, find the number of boys in the class:

$$32 - 12 = 20$$

So, the ratio of girls to boys is $12 : 20$. This ratio can be reduced by dividing by 4:

$$12 : 20 = \frac{12}{4} : \frac{20}{4} = 3 : 5$$

Thus, the two quantities are equal, Choice (C).

812.   **C. The quantities are equal.**

$$4 : 5$$
$$= 4(2) : 5(2)$$
$$= 8 : 10$$

Choice (C) is the correct answer.

813.   **C. The quantities are equal.**

First, find the number of other-colored cars:

$$10 - 3 = 7$$

So, the ratio of red cars to other-colored cars is $3 : 7$. The correct answer is Choice (C).

814.   **D. It cannot be determined from the information given.**

The length of the equal parts could be 3, in which case the leftover part would be 1 foot long. But, nothing says that the equal parts have to be integer values. For example, if the equal parts were 3.1 feet each, then the leftover part would be 0.7 feet.

The relationship cannot be determined from the information given, Choice (D).

815. **B. Quantity B is greater.**

To divide into the ratio 4 to 5, first add the parts of the ratio:

$$(4 + 5 = 9)$$

Then, divide the money by 9 to get one part of the ratio:

$$\left(\frac{153}{9} = 17\right)$$

To find X's share, multiply by 4:

$$(17 \times 4 = 68)$$

$70.00 is greater than $68.00; therefore, Quantity B is greater. Choice (B) is the correct answer.

816. **B. Quantity B is greater.**

At 10:05, the hour hand points to the 10 and the minute hand points to the 1. This makes a 90-degree angle. At 10:30, the minute hand points to the 6 and the hour hand points halfway between the 10 and the 11. This makes an angle greater than 90 degrees. The correct answer is Choice (B).

817. **A. Quantity A is greater.**

BC = AC – AB

CD = CE – DE, but AC and CE are both equal. Because DE is greater than AB, CD must be less than BC. (A smaller amount is taken from half the segment when AB is subtracted from AC.) The correct answer is Choice (A).

818. **C. The quantities are equal.**

Because l, m, and n are parallel, x must be equal to the angle between AB and line m (corresponding angles) and y must be equal to the angle between BC and line m. So,

$$\angle B = x + y = 90°$$

Choice (C) is the correct answer.

819. **B. Quantity B is greater.**

The perimeter is found by adding the three sides of the triangle:

$$4 + 5 + 6 = 15$$

So, Quantity B is greater, making Choice (B) the correct answer.

820. **C. The quantities are equal.**

The perimeter is found by adding the three sides of the triangle. An equilateral triangle has three equal sides:

$$6 + 6 + 6 = 18$$

So, the two quantities are equal. Choice (C) is the correct answer.

821. **D. It cannot be determined from the information given.**

The area of a triangle is found with the formula $\frac{1}{2} b \times h$. Without knowing the heights, the areas of the triangles cannot be calculated. Choice (D) is the correct answer.

822. **A. Quantity A is greater.**

The perimeter is found by adding the three sides of the triangle. Even though you only know the length of two of the sides, a scalene triangle has no equal sides. The third side must be any number greater than 2. Thus, Quantity A is greater. The correct answer is Choice (A).

823. **A. Quantity A is greater.**

The longest side of a triangle is opposite the largest angle.

Hence, $b > a > c$. Thus, Quantity A is greater, and Choice (A) is the correct answer.

824. **A. Quantity A is greater.**

The value of angle 4 must be more than the value of angle 2 because angle 4 is an external angle of the triangle. Therefore, angle 4 is equal to the sum of the two opposite interior angles (angle 1 + angle 2).

Choice (A) is the correct answer.

825. **A. Quantity A is greater.**

Because two angles are given, you can find the third:

$$180 - 59 - 61 = 60$$

The largest angle is opposite the longest side. Because AB is opposite angle ACB, side AB is the largest. Choice (A) is the correct answer.

826. **B. Quantity B is greater.**

Use the following rule:

"The length of the third side of a triangle will lie between the sum and the difference of the other two sides."

In this case, $2 < x < 10$, so the third side has to be less than 10. Choice (B) is the correct answer.

827. **B. Quantity B is greater.**

The total area of the upper triangles is less than the area of the lower triangles. The more triangles that you cut the semicircle into, the more of the circle that is occupied. Therefore, Choice (B) is the correct answer.

828. **B. Quantity B is greater.**

First, determine the area of the triangle:

$$area = \frac{1}{2} b \times h$$
$$base = 6$$
$$height = 3$$
$$area = \frac{1}{2} 6 \times 3$$
$$= 9$$

Next, determine the maximum area possible for the rectangle by assuming the rectangle is a square:

$$area = l \times h$$
$$length = 2.5$$
$$height = 2.5$$
$$area = 2.5 \times 2.5$$
$$= 6.25$$

The area of the triangle is greater than the area of the rectangle. Choice (B) is the correct answer.

829. **A. Quantity A is greater.**

The curved path must be longer than the straight-line distance between A and C.

The straight-line distance is the hypotenuse of a 3-4-5 triangle, and is therefore 5. Thus, Quantity A is greater, and the correct answer is Choice (A).

830.   **B. Quantity B is greater.**

First, notice that *MO, ON, OP,* and *QO* are all radii. If we assume that the radius equals 1, then *MN* equals 2.

PQ is the hypotenuse of a right triangle (*POQ*) with the other sides both equal to 1. This is a special triangle with sides in the ratio of $x : x : x\sqrt{2}$. Since *PQ* is $\sqrt{2}$, the ratio of $MN : PQ = 2 : \sqrt{2}$, which is less than 2 : 1. Choice (B) is the correct answer.

831.   **B. Quantity B is greater.**

The largest angle in a right triangle is the right angle of 90°; therefore, Quantity B is greater, Choice (B).

832.   **A. Quantity A is greater.**

An isosceles right triangle has angles of 90°, 45°, and 45°. A scalene right triangle has one angle of 90° and two other angles that are unequal. Because the sum of the interior angles is equal to 180°, you know that one of the angles in the scalene right triangle must be greater than 45° and the other must be less than 45°. Thus, the smallest angle of an isosceles right triangle is larger. Choice (A) is the correct answer.

833.   **A. Quantity A is greater.**

The area of the triangle for Quantity A is:

$$\frac{1}{2}6\times 8 = 24$$

The area of one of the Quantity B triangles is:

$$\frac{1}{2}3\times 4 = 6$$

So, two of them have an area of 12, which is smaller than Quantity A. Choice (A) is the correct answer.

834.   **D. It cannot be determined from the information given.**

The diagonal of the square can be calculated because we know that the length of each side is 4, but the diagonal of the rectangle can't be calculated because we know the length of only two of the sides. The other two sides could be greater than or less than the known sides. Therefore, Choice (D) is the correct answer.

835.   **B. Quantity B is greater.**

The triangle is right-angled, so we know two of its angles: 67° and 90°. The third angle is calculated by subtracting the known angles from 180°:

$$180° - (67° + 90°) = 180° - 157°$$
$$= 23°$$

Thus, Quantity B is greater, Choice (B).

836. C. The quantities are equal.

The interior angles of a quadrilateral add up to 360°. We know three angles: 83°, 107°, and 115°. Their sum is:

$$83° + 107° + 115° = 305°.$$
$$\text{Angle } D = 360° - 305° = 55°.$$

Thus, the quantities are equal, Choice (C).

837. C. The quantities are equal.

The interior angles of a quadrilateral add up to 360°; therefore, the two quantities are equal, Choice (C).

838. A. Quantity A is greater.

1cm^2 is the equivalent of 100mm^2, so the Quantity B is much less, because it's only 10mm^2. Choice (A) is the correct answer.

839. B. Quantity B is greater.

The diagonal of a rectangle cuts the rectangle into two equal triangles. The diagonal is the hypotenuse of either of these triangles and must be less than the sum of the other two sides. The other two sides make up half the perimeter, which is greater. Choice (B) is the correct answer.

840. B. Quantity B is greater.

A line QS (not shown) divides the quadrilateral into two right-angle triangles. The triangle QRS is a 3-4-5 triangle with a hypotenuse of 5.

In triangle QSP, the hypotenuse is 5 and side PQ must be less than 5. (There is no need to calculate the exact value.) Choice (B) is the correct answer.

841. C. The quantities are equal.

The circumference of a circle is $2\pi r$, so the circumference of a circle with a radius of $5 = 10\pi$ The correct answer is Choice (C).

842. B. Quantity B is greater.

The circumference of a circle is $2\pi r$. Because π is more than 3, this makes the circumference greater than $6r$. Choice (B) is the correct answer.

843. B. Quantity B is greater.

The diameter of a circle is 2 times the radius. Choice (B) is the correct answer.

844. **C. The quantities are equal.**

The line can cut through the circle at a maximum of two points; therefore, the two quantities are equal, Choice (C).

845. **C. The quantities are equal.**

The sectors next to the 7 must be assigned 8. Next to these 8s, there must be 7s. Between the 7s, there must be an 8 = x. The right answer is Choice (C).

846. **D. It cannot be determined from the information given.**

If *BC* were a diameter, then the marked angle would be 90°.

Because it's not a diameter, the measure of the angle could be less or more, depending on where you draw the chord. Therefore, the answer cannot be determined from the information given, Choice (D).

847. **A. Quantity A is greater.**

The easiest approach to this is to draw a sketch. Put a point for the city. Draw a circle with a radius of 2 centered on the city, on which the beach resort can lie. Draw a circle with a radius of 10 centered on the city, on which the sports center can lie. Wherever you put the resort and the sports center on these circles, they can never be closer than 8 kilometers, which is the shortest distance between the circles. Choice (A) is the correct answer.

848. **A. Quantity A is greater.**

A cube has 12 edges and a triangular prism has 9 edges. Hence, Quantity A is greater, Choice (A).

849. **B. Quantity B is greater.**

A cube with a side of 1 has the volume of 1 cubic unit.

A cube with a side of 2 has the volume $2 \times 2 \times 2 = 8$ cubic units. This is greater than twice the volume of the cube with a side of 1, so Choice (B) is the correct answer.

850. **D. It cannot be determined from the information given.**

You can find the volume of a rectangular block by multiplying the area of the base by the height. But in this case, the height isn't known. You can't assume that the sides of the faces must be squares. If they are squares, the volume is $16 \times 5 = 80$. But if one face is 16×1 and the other face is 20×1, then the volume becomes $16 \times 20 \times 1 = 320$. Thus, the correct answer is Choice (D).

851. **D. 1**

Any number raised to the power of zero is 1. The correct answer is Choice (D).

852. **A. 7**

When converting a value to or from scientific notation, the exponent tells you how many places to adjust the decimal point to the right (or to the left if the exponent is negative).

$$3.0 \times 10^7 = 3.0 \times 10,000,000$$
$$3.0 \times 10,000,000 = 30,000,000$$

30,000,000 has seven zeroes, Choice (A).

853. **B.** $\dfrac{1}{x^6}$

Any number raised to a negative exponent is the reciprocal of the same number to a positive exponent.

$$x^{-6} = \frac{1}{x^6}$$

The correct answer is Choice (B).

854. **C. The quantities are equal.**

When multiplying like bases, simply add the exponents:

$$3^5 \times 3^2 = 3^{5+2} = 3^7$$

Thus, the correct answer is Choice (C).

855. **A. Quantity A is greater.**

When dividing like bases, subtract the exponents:

$$5^9 \div 5^3 = 5^{9-3} = 5^6$$
$$5^6 > 5^3$$

The correct answer is Choice (A).

856. **A. Quantity A is greater.**

When raising a power to a power, multiply the exponents:

$$\left(4^3\right)^4 = 4^{3\times4}$$
$$= 4^{12}$$
$$\approx 17,000,000$$

When multiplying unlike bases with like exponents, multiply the bases and keep the exponent:

$$4^4 \times 3^4 = (4\times3)^4$$
$$= 12^4$$
$$\approx 21,000$$

Thus, the correct answer is Choice (A).

857.   **C.** $16x^3 + 8y^2$

To add or subtract like bases with like powers, add or subtract the coefficients:

$$21x^3 - 17x^3 + 14y^2 + 12x^3 - 6y^2$$
$$(21 - 17 + 12)x^3 + (14 - 6)y^2$$
$$(16)x^3 + (8)y^2$$

Choice (C) is the correct answer.

858.   **D. It cannot be determined from the information given.**

Without knowing what x is, you can't determine the value of x^{16}. Choice (D) is the correct answer.

859.   **D. It cannot be determined from the information given.**

This one is tricky both ways. First, you may think that 2,126 is a big number, no matter what power it is raised to, but then (hopefully) you remember that anything to the power of 0 is 1.

Then you think that x^2 must be bigger than 1, but without knowing what x is, you have no way of knowing what x^2 is either.

The answer cannot be determined without more information, so Choice (D) is the right answer.

860.   **D. It cannot be determined from the information given.**

This one is tricky. If you recall that $x^{-2} = \dfrac{1}{x^2}$, it might seem clear that x^{14} would always be bigger.

What if x is a fraction, though? Look what happens if $x = \dfrac{1}{10}$:

$$\left(\frac{1}{10}\right)^{14} = 0.00000000000001$$
$$\left(\frac{1}{10}\right)^{-2} = \left(\frac{10}{1}\right)^2 = 100$$

Therefore, the answer cannot be determined without more information, Choice (D).

861.   **B. 11**

To solve a function for a given value of the variable, substitute the value in place of the variable in the function:

$$f(3) = 2(3) + 5$$
$$= 6 + 5$$
$$= 11$$

Choice (B) is the correct answer.

862. **E. 16**

The question specifies that $x \otimes 3 = 3x + 1$, so to evaluate $5 \otimes 3$, substitute 5 in for x in the original equation:

$$x \otimes 3 = 3x + 1$$
$$(5) \otimes 3 = 3(5) + 1$$
$$(5) \otimes 3 = 16$$

Choice (E) is the correct answer.

863. **A. 4**

To solve a function for a given value of the variable, substitute the value in place of the variable in the function:

$$f(6) = \frac{(6)}{3} + 2$$
$$= 2 + 2$$
$$= 4$$

The correct answer is Choice (A).

864. **D.** $\frac{10}{21}$

This one looks much harder than it is. Just substitute 7 for x, and 3 for y and solve the equation:

$$x \odot y = \frac{x + y}{xy}$$
$$7 \odot 3 = \frac{7 + 3}{(7)(3)}$$
$$= \frac{10}{21}$$

Choice (D) is your answer.

865. **D. 100**

Substitute 6 for x and 8 for y and solve the equation:

$$x \oplus y = x^2 + y^2$$
$$6 \oplus 8 = (6)^2 + (8)^2$$
$$= 36 + 64$$
$$= 100$$

The correct answer is Choice (D).

866.   E. $x = -\frac{5}{4}$

Begin by collecting all the x variables on one side and all the constants (the numbers) on the other. Then divide both sides by the coefficient of (the number before) x:

$$7x + 5 = 3x$$
$$7x - 3x = -5$$
$$4x = -5$$
$$x = -\frac{5}{4}$$

Choice (E) is the correct answer.

867.   D. $x = \frac{15}{11}$

This equation already has all the x variables on one side; don't let the fact that they're on the right side confuse you. Just add the x – coefficients and divide both sides by the total number of x's:

$$15 = 13x - 2x$$
$$15 = 11x$$
$$\frac{15}{11} = x$$
$$x = \frac{15}{11}$$

The answer you want is Choice (D).

868.   C. $x = 6$

Begin by collecting all the variables on one side and all the constants (numbers) on the other side; then divide by the coefficient (the number in front of the x):

$$3x + 5 = 5x - 7$$
$$3x - 5x = -7 - 5$$
$$-2x = -12$$
$$x = \frac{-12}{-2}$$
$$x = 6$$

Choice (C) is the correct answer.

869.

E. $x = -\dfrac{42}{29}$

Begin by multiplying both sides by the common denominator (44), and collecting all the variables on one side and all the constants (numbers) on the other side; then divide by the coefficient (the number in front of the x):

$$\frac{(x-5)}{11} = \frac{(3x+2)}{4}$$
$$44 \times \frac{(x-5)}{11} = \frac{(3x+2)}{4} \times 44$$
$$4 \times (x-5) = (3x+2) \times 11$$
$$4x - 20 = 33x + 22$$
$$-42 = 29x$$
$$x = \frac{-42}{29}$$

The correct answer is Choice (E).

870.

C. $x = \dfrac{388}{69}$

Begin by multiplying both sides by the common denominator (7). Then distribute the 35, and collect all the variables on one side and all the constants on the other side. Finally, divide by the coefficient (the number in front of the x):

$$5(2x-11) = \frac{(x+3)}{7}$$
$$35(2x-11) = (x+3)$$
$$70x - 385 = x + 3$$
$$69x = 388$$
$$x = \frac{388}{69}$$

Choice (C) is the correct answer.

871.

B. $ab + 3a - 5b - 15$

FOIL is an acronym, used to help remember the steps to multiply binomials: First two terms, Outer two terms, Inner two terms, Last two terms. Multiply the terms of each binomial in this order.

$$\text{Multiply}: (a-5)(b+3)$$
$$\text{First } (a)(b) = ab$$
$$\text{Outer } (a)(3) = 3a$$
$$\text{Inner } (-5)(b) = -5b$$
$$\text{Last } (-5)(3) = -15$$
$$\text{Answer} = ab + 3a - 5b - 15$$

The answer you're looking for is Choice (B).

872.   A. $6x^2 + 8x - 14$

Multiply the binomials using FOIL, then collect the like terms: in this case $14x$ and $-6x$.

$$\text{Multiply} : (2x - 2)(3x + 7)$$
$$\text{First } (2x)(3x) = 6x^2$$
$$\text{Outer } (2x)(7) = 14x$$
$$\text{Inner } (-2)(3x) = -6x$$
$$\text{Last } (-2)(7) = -14$$
$$\text{Answer} = 6x^2 + 8x - 14$$

The correct answer is Choice (A).

873.   A. $3x^2 + 8xy - 3y$

Multiply the binomials using FOIL; then include all the terms in the final expression. Remember that x^3 and x^2 are not like terms.

$$\text{Multiply} : (3x - y)(x + 3y)$$
$$\text{First } (3x)(x) = 3x^2$$
$$\text{Outer } (3x)(3y) = 9xy$$
$$\text{Inner } (-y)(x) = -yx = -xy$$
$$\text{Last } (-y)(3y) = -3y$$
$$\text{Answer} = 3x^2 + 8xy - 3y$$

The correct answer is Choice (A).

874.   B. $2x^2 - 9x - 18$

Multiply the binomials using FOIL; then include all the terms in the final expression. Don't let the fractions concern you; just multiply straight across and simplify as necessary.

$$\text{Multiply} : \left(\tfrac{1}{2}x - 3\right)(4x + 6)$$
$$\text{First } \left(\tfrac{1}{2}x\right)(4x) = 2x^2$$
$$\text{Outer } \left(\tfrac{1}{2}x\right)(6) = 3x$$
$$\text{Inner } (-3)(4x) = -12x$$
$$\text{Last } (-3)(6) = -18$$
$$\text{Answer} = 2x^2 - 9x - 18$$

Choice (B) is the correct answer.

875.

D. $15x^2 - 11xy - 14y^2$

Multiply the binomials using FOIL; then include all the terms in the final expression. Don't let the fractions concern you; just multiply straight across and simplify as necessary.

$$\text{Multiply}: (3x + 2y)(5x - 7y)$$
$$\text{First } (3x)(5x) = 15x^2$$
$$\text{Outer } (3x)(-7y) = -21xy$$
$$\text{Inner } (2y)(5x) = 10yx = 10xy$$
$$\text{Last } (2y)(-7y) = -14y^2$$
$$\text{Answer} = 15x^2 - 11xy - 14y^2$$

The correct answer is Choice (D).

876.

A. $(x+3)(x-6)$

Because the first term is x^2, you know that the first two terms in the binomials must both be x. Then you need to identify two numbers that multiply to be –18, and add to be –3. To get a product of –18, one number must be negative and the other positive, and $(6)(3) = 18$. The two binomials must be either $(x+3)(x-6)$ or $(x-3)(x+6)$. Because the middle (added) term is negative, the larger value is the negative one, and the answer is $(x+3)(x-6)$, Choice (A).

877.

D. $(2x-5)(x+4)$

Because the first term is $2x^2$, you know that the first two terms in the binomials must be x and $2x$. Next, identify two numbers that multiply to be –20 and add to be +3 when one of them has been multiplied by 2. To get a product of –20, one number must be negative and the other positive, and $(5)(4) = 20$. The two binomials could be one of four options:

$$(2x+5)(x-4) \text{ or } (2x-5)(x+4)$$
$$\text{Or}$$
$$(2x+4)(x-5) \text{ or } (2x-4)(x+5)$$

Try each combination to discover that $2(4) = 8$ and $8 + -5 = +3$. The answer is $(2x-5)(x+4)$, Choice (D).

878.

A. $x = \{-4, 6\}$

Begin by factoring the trinomial. You know you need to find two numbers that multiply to be –24 and add to be –2. The factored binomials are $(x-6)(x+4)$:

Because $(x-6)(x+4) = 0$, the two possible values for x must be the values that solve $x - 6 = 0$ and $x + 4 = 0$.

The answers are –4 and +6, Choice (A).

---

879.   A. $x = \{-11, 2\}$

Begin by factoring the trinomial. You know you need to find two numbers that multiply to be 44 and add to be 15 when one has been multiplied by 2. The factored binomials are $(2x + 4)(x + 11)$:

Because $(2x + 4)(x + 11) = 0$, the two possible values for x must be the values that solve $2x + 4 = 0$ and $x + 11 = 0$.

The answers are –11 and +2, Choice (A).

---

880.   A. $x = \{-9, 5\}$

Begin by setting the equation equal to zero: $x^2 + 4x - 45 = 0$

Next, factor the trinomial: $(x - 5)(x + 9) = 0$

Finally, set each binomial equal to zero and solve for x:

$$\begin{array}{ccc} x - 5 = 0 & & x + 9 = 0 \\ x = 5 & \text{and} & x = -9 \end{array}$$

The correct answer is Choice (A).

---

881.   D. 2.6

The square root of 7 is between the roots of 4 and 9. Because the root of 4 is 2 and the root of 9 is 3, the root of 7 must be between 2 and 3. To be even more accurate, you may note that the root of 7 must be a little closer to 3 than 2 because 7 is a little closer to 9 than 4.

The only answer between 2 and 3 is 2.6, Choice (D).

---

882.   C. 4.6

The square root of 21 is between the roots of 16 and 25. Because the root of 16 is 4 and the root of 25 is 5, the root of 21 must be between 4 and 5. To be even more accurate, you may note that the root of 21 must be a little closer to 5 than 4 because 21 is a little closer to 25 than 16.

The only answer between 4 and 5 is 4.6, Choice (C).

---

883.   D. 11.2

The square root of 125 is between the roots of 121 and 144. Because the root of 121 is 11 and the root of 144 is 12, the root of 125 must be between 11 and 12. To be more accurate, note that the root of 125 must be quite a bit closer to 11 than 12 because 125 is a lot closer to 121 than 144. The only answer that makes sense is 11.2, Choice (D).

884. B. 5.2

The square root of 27 is between the roots of 25 and 36. Because the root of 25 is 5 and the root of 36 is 6, the root of 27 must be between 5 and 6. To be more accurate, note that the root of 27 must be quite a bit closer to 5 than 6 because 27 is a lot closer to 25 than 36.

The only possibilities between 5 and 6 are 5.2 and 5.8. Since you know the answer must be closer to 5 than 6, the only answer that makes sense is 5.2, Choice (B).

885. B. 7.9

The square root of 63 is between the roots of 49 and 64. Because the root of 49 is 7 and the root of 64 is 8, the root of 63 must be between 7 and 8. To be more accurate, note that the root of 63 must be quite a bit closer to 8 than 7 because 63 is a lot closer to 64 than 49.

The only possibilities between 7 and 8 are 7.1 and 7.9. Since you know the answer must be closer to 8 than 7, the only answer that makes sense is 7.9, Choice (B).

886. A. $11\sqrt{17}$

To add like radicals (the same value under the radical in both terms), simply add the coefficients, in this case the 4 and the 7, to get the coefficient of the answer:

$$4\sqrt{17} + 7\sqrt{17}$$
$$(4+7)\sqrt{17}$$
$$11\sqrt{17}$$

Choice (A) is the correct answer.

887. B. $7\sqrt{2}$

To subtract like radicals (the same value under the radical in both terms), simply subtract the coefficients, in this case the 13 and the 6, to get the coefficient of the answer:

$$13\sqrt{2} - 6\sqrt{2}$$
$$(13-6)\sqrt{2}$$
$$7\sqrt{2}$$

The correct answer is Choice (B).

888. **C.** $5\sqrt{7}$

To combine like radicals, add or subtract the coefficients, in this case the 4, 7, and –6, to get the coefficient of the answer:

$$4\sqrt{7}+7\sqrt{7}-6\sqrt{7}$$
$$(4+7-6)\sqrt{7}$$
$$5\sqrt{7}$$

The correct answer is Choice (C).

889. **D.** $5\sqrt{5}$

Before combining the radicals, you need to simplify them to identify like radicals:

$$\sqrt{125}+3\sqrt{5}-\sqrt{45}$$
$$\sqrt{25\cdot5}+3\sqrt{5}-\sqrt{9\cdot5}$$
$$5\sqrt{5}+3\sqrt{5}-3\sqrt{5}$$
$$5\sqrt{5}$$

Choice (D) is the correct answer.

890. **E.** $11\sqrt{11}-15\sqrt{2}$

Before combining the radicals, you need to simplify them to identify like radicals:

$$4\sqrt{11}-\sqrt{128}+\sqrt{77}-\sqrt{98}$$
$$4\sqrt{11}+\sqrt{77}-\sqrt{128}-\sqrt{98}$$
$$4\sqrt{11}+7\sqrt{11}-8\sqrt{2}-7\sqrt{2}$$
$$11\sqrt{11}-15\sqrt{2}$$

The correct answer is Choice (E).

891. **A.** $\sqrt{14}$

To multiply the radicals, collect all the values under one radical and multiply:

$$(\sqrt{7})(\sqrt{2})$$
$$\sqrt{(7)(2)}$$
$$\sqrt{14}$$

Choice (A) is the correct answer.

892. **A.** $8\sqrt{30}$

To multiply the radicals, collect all the radical values under one radical and then multiply the values under the radical together. Multiply the values outside of the radical together:

$$\left(2\sqrt{3}\right)\left(4\sqrt{5}\right)\left(\sqrt{2}\right)$$
$$\left((2)(4)(1)\right)\left(\sqrt{(3)(5)(2)}\right)$$
$$(8)\left(\sqrt{30}\right)$$
$$8\sqrt{30}$$

The correct answer is Choice (A).

893. **B.** $3\sqrt{7}$

To divide the radicals, divide the coefficients and divide the values under the radical. Then recombine the quotients and simplify as necessary:

$$\left(9\sqrt{14}\right) \div \left(3\sqrt{2}\right)$$
$$\left(\frac{9}{3}\right)\left(\sqrt{\frac{14}{2}}\right)$$
$$3\sqrt{7}$$

The correct answer is Choice (B).

894. **E.** $120\sqrt{2}$

To multiply the radicals, collect the coefficients, collect the values under the radicals, and multiply each group separately. Then simplify by rearranging the values under the radical into values that have even roots. Finally, combine like terms and/or multiply any remaining values.

$$\left(2\sqrt{18}\right)\left(5\sqrt{32}\right)$$
$$\left(2\sqrt{(9)(2)}\right)\left(5\sqrt{(16)(2)}\right)$$
$$\left(6\sqrt{2}\right)\left(20\sqrt{2}\right)$$
$$120\sqrt{2}$$

The correct answer is Choice (E).

895.   **A.** $\dfrac{10\sqrt{2}}{3}$

$$\left(10\sqrt{128}\right) \div \left(3\sqrt{64}\right)$$

$$\dfrac{10\sqrt{(64)(2)}}{3\sqrt{64}}$$

$$\dfrac{(10)(8)\sqrt{2}}{(3)(8)}$$

$$\dfrac{10\sqrt{2}}{3}$$

The resulting answer is Choice (A).

896.   **C.** 2

When you encounter operations inside of radicals, complete the operations first; then deal with the radical:

$$\sqrt{2 + \dfrac{3}{8} + \dfrac{13}{8}}$$

$$\sqrt{2 + \dfrac{16}{8}}$$

$$\sqrt{2 + 2}$$

$$\sqrt{4}$$

$$2$$

Choice (C) is the right answer.

897.   **D.** 3

Complete the operations under the radical first; then simplify the radical.

$$\sqrt{2(3+5) - 7}$$

$$\sqrt{2(8) - 7}$$

$$\sqrt{16 - 7}$$

$$\sqrt{9}$$

$$3$$

The correct answer is Choice (D).

898. D. $\dfrac{4\sqrt{11}}{3}$

Begin by simplifying the fractions under the radical; then take the square root of the denominator.

$$4\sqrt{\frac{2}{3}+\frac{5}{9}}$$

$$4\sqrt{\frac{6}{9}+\frac{5}{9}}$$

$$4\sqrt{\frac{11}{9}}$$

$$\frac{4\sqrt{11}}{3}$$

Choice (D) is the correct answer.

899. D. 4

First complete the operations under the radical in the numerator; then combine the numerator and denominator under the same radical. Next, divide and take the square root of the quotient.

$$\frac{\sqrt{4(5+3)}}{\sqrt{2}}$$

$$\frac{\sqrt{(4)(8)}}{\sqrt{2}}$$

$$\frac{\sqrt{32}}{\sqrt{2}}$$

$$\sqrt{\frac{32}{2}}$$

$$\sqrt{16}$$

$$4$$

The result is Choice (D).

900. E. $\dfrac{4}{5\sqrt{2}}$

First complete the operations in the numerator and evaluate the root of the result. Then simplify the root in the denominator.

$$\frac{\sqrt{4(2+2)}}{\sqrt{50}}$$

$$\frac{\sqrt{16}}{\sqrt{2(25)}}$$

$$\frac{4}{5\sqrt{2}}$$

The correct answer is Choice (E).

901.   **E. (1, –3)**

The equation $3x - 74 = 24$ is linear. There are infinite solutions, but only one pair from the multiple-choice options works. Substitute the values from each pair in for x and y in the given equation until you find the pair that works:

A. $(5,2): 3(5) - 7(2) = 24$

$15 - 14 = 24$: untrue

B. $(3,-7): 3(3) - 7(-7) = 24$

$9 - 49 = 24$: untrue

C. $(-3,7): 3(-3) - 7(7) = 24$

$-9 - 49 = 24$: untrue

D. $(-3,1): 3(-3) - 7(1) = 24$

$-9 - 7 = 24$: untrue

E. $(1,-3): 3(1) - 7(-3) = 24$

$3 + 21 = 24$: *TRUE*

The only pair that yields a true statement is (1, –3), Choice (E).

902.   **A. (5, 4)**

The equation $-2x + 3y = 2$ is linear. There are infinite solutions, but only one pair from the multiple-choice options works. Substitute the values from each pair in for x and y in the given equation until you find the pair that works:

A. $(5,4): -2(5) + 3(4) = 2$

$-10 + 12 = 2$: *TRUE*

The ordered pair (5, 4), Choice (A), works.

903.   **B. (6, 0) and (0, 3)**

To find the x and y intercepts, first substitute 0 in for x in the equation and solve for y. Then substitute 0 in for y and solve for x.

$$2x + 4(0) = 12 \quad 2(0) + 4y = 12$$
$$2x = 12 \qquad 4y = 12$$
$$x = 6 \qquad y = 3$$

When $y = 0$, $x = 6$ and when $x = 0$, $y = 3$.

Choice (B) is the correct answer.

904.

C. $-2y = -2x + 14$

To find the equation that includes the given point, substitute the point into each equation until you identify the one that yields a true statement:

$$A. \ -2(-2) = (5) + 14$$
$$4 = 19 \text{: untrue}$$
$$B. \ 5(5) - (-2) = 0$$
$$25 + 2 = 0 \text{: untrue}$$
$$C. \ -2(-2) = -2(5) + 14$$
$$4 = -10 + 14 \text{: } TRUE$$

The equation $-2y = -2x + 14$ is the only one that yields a true statement when the point (5, –2) is substituted. Choice (A) is correct.

905.

B. $6x + 3y = 9$

To find the equation that includes the given point, substitute the point into each equation until you identify the one that yields a true statement:

$$A. \ 3(-2) + 9(7) = -8$$
$$-6 + 63 = 8.1 \text{: untrue}$$
$$B. \ 6(-2) + 3(7) = 9$$
$$-12 + 21 = 9 \text{: } TRUE$$

The equation $6x + 3y = 9$, Choice (B), is the only one that yields a true statement when the point (–2, 7) is substituted.

906.

A. (5, 2)

These two equations are excellent candidates for the addition method. Note that the y term is already opposite in value between the two equations, –3 in one and +3 in the other. Just set the equations on top of each other and add vertically to cancel out the y term:

$$\begin{array}{r} x - 3y = -1 \\ -3x + 3y = -9 \\ \hline -2x + 0y = -10 \end{array}$$

Then solve for x:

$$-2x = -10$$
$$x = 5$$

Substitute 5 in for x and solve either of the original equations:

$$(5) - 3y = -1$$
$$-3y = -6$$
$$y = 2$$

So $x = 5$ and $y = 2$.

Written in coordinate form, that's (5, 2), Choice (A).

907.   **D. (–4, 1)**

These two equations can be solved with substitution. Note that the second one is already solved for y. Substitute the y-equivalent from the second equation in for y in the first equation; then solve for x:

$$-3x + (-x - 3) = 13$$
$$-4x - 3 = 13$$
$$-4x = 16$$
$$x = -4$$

Now substitute –4 for x in the original second equation to solve for y:

$$y = -(-4) - 3$$
$$y = 4 - 3$$
$$y = 1$$

Written in coordinate form, the answer is (–4, 1), Choice (D).

908.   **B. (3, 2)**

This pair can be solved by substitution or the addition method. With the addition method, start by multiplying the top equation by 2 so that x will cancel when the equations are added together:

$$(2)(-2x + 3y) = 0(2)$$
$$-4x + 6y = 0$$

$$\begin{array}{r} -4x + 6y = 0 \\ 4x + 1y = 14 \\ \hline 7y = 14 \end{array}$$
$$y = 2$$

Now substitute 2 in for y in either of the original equations to solve for x:

$$4x + 2 = 14$$
$$4x = 12$$
$$x = 3$$

Written in coordinate form, the answer is (3, 2), Choice (B).

909.   **C. (–3, 2)**

This one can be solved by substitution or the addition method. To use the substitution method, begin by solving the second equation for y since it is nearly done already.

$$y - 2 = 3(x + 3)$$
$$y = 3x + 11$$

Substitute $3x+11$ for y in the other equation and solve for x:

$$6x+2(3x+11)=-14$$
$$6x+6x+22=-14$$
$$12x=-36$$
$$x=-3$$

Now substitute -3 for x in the second equation to solve for y:

$$y=3x+11$$
$$y=3(-3)+11$$
$$y=-9+11$$
$$y=2$$

Written in coordinate form, the answer is $(-3, 2)$, Choice (C).

910. **A. 10 movies and 15 games**

This is really a simultaneous equation problem. Let m be the number of movies Brian bought and g be the number of games. Using the data from the question, you know:

$m+g=25$: The number of movies and games together is 25.

$5m+11g=215$: The cost of movies and the cost of games together is \$215.

Solve the equations for both variables. To use the addition method, first multiply the top equation by -5 and add the equations together to eliminate m:

$$-5m-5g=-125$$
$$\underline{5m+11g=+215}$$
$$6g=90$$
$$g=15$$

Now substitute 15 in for g in the other equation to solve for m:

$$m+(15)=25$$
$$m=10$$

Brian purchased 10 movies and 15 games, Choice (A).

911. **D. 16**

This is a "missing-term average" problem. Recall that the mean of a set is equal to the sum of the values in the set divided by the number of items in the set:

$$\text{mean}=\frac{\text{sum}}{\text{count}}$$
$$15=\frac{(14+14+14+15+15+15+16+16+x)}{9}$$
$$15=\frac{119+x}{9}$$
$$135=119+x$$
$$16=x$$

The correct answer is Choice (D).

912.

C. 15

This is a "missing-term average" problem. Recall that the mean of a set is equal to the sum of the values in the set divided by the number of items in the set:

$$mean = \frac{sum}{count}$$

$$16 = \frac{(6+8+12+19+19+20+21+24+x)}{9}$$

$$16 = \frac{129+x}{9}$$

$$144 = 129+x$$

$$15 = x$$

Choice (C) is the correct answer.

913.

A. 50

To calculate the correct answer, sum all the values individually; then divide by 13:

$$26 = \frac{(12(24)+x)}{13}$$

$$26 = \frac{288+x}{13}$$

$$338 = 288+x$$

$$50 = x$$

The missing value is 50, Choice (A).

914.

B. 80%

The highest score Jennifer can get without extra credit is 100%, so calculate the average using that score:

$$x = \frac{(4(75)+100)}{5}$$

$$x = \frac{300+100}{5}$$

$$x = \frac{400}{5}$$

$$x = 80\%$$

The best grade she could get for the course is 80%, Choice (B).

915.

B. 61%

To calculate the minimum score Sayber needs, first find the average of Tuscany's scores:

$$\frac{72\%+85\%+86\%+94\%+97\%+58\%}{6} = 82\%$$

Sayber needs an average greater than 82%. Calculate the final score that yields that average:

$$82\% = \frac{76\% + 82\% + 88\% + 91\% + 94\% + x}{6}$$
$$492\% = 431\% + x$$
$$61\% = x$$

Sayber only needs to score above 61%, Choice (B), to have a higher overall grade than Tuscany.

916.　**D. $161.50**

To estimate the weighted average using percentages (the answers are far enough apart that an estimate is sufficient), multiply each rounded sales price by the percentage of sales at that price and then add the products:

$$.25 \times 100 \approx 25$$
$$.25 \times 150 \approx 37.5$$
$$.5 \times 200 \approx 100$$
$$\overline{TOTAL \quad \approx 162.50}$$

The weighted average sales price is about $162.50. Choice (D) is the only one that makes sense.

917.　**A. $5.00**

To calculate the weighted average using frequencies, first multiply the number of instances of each sale by the sales price:

$$16 \times 4 = 64$$
$$21 \times 5 = 105$$
$$13 \times 5 = 65$$
$$8 \times 7 = 56$$

Then divide the sum by the total number of sales:

$$64 + 105 + 65 + 56 = 290$$
$$\frac{290}{(16 + 21 + 13 + 8)} =$$
$$\frac{290}{58} =$$
$$= 5.00$$

The average sales price of lunch at Soup and Sandwich is $5.00, Choice (A).

918. C. 6

To calculate the weighted average using frequencies, first multiply the number of instances of each frequency by the value associated with it:

$$4 \times 8 = 32$$
$$7 \times 7 = 49$$
$$2 \times 9 = 18$$
$$7 \times 3 = 21$$

Then, divide the sum by the total number of values:

$$32 + 49 + 18 + 21 = 120$$
$$\frac{120}{(4+7+2+7)} =$$
$$\frac{120}{20} =$$
$$= 6$$

The weighted average is 6, Choice (C).

919. B. 12

Multiply the number of instances of each frequency by the value associated with it:

$$4 \times 12 = 48$$
$$6 \times 10 = 60$$
$$1 \times 14 = 14$$
$$5 \times 14 = 70$$

Then divide the sum by the total number of values:

$$48 + 60 + 14 + 70 = 192$$
$$\frac{192}{(4+6+1+5)} =$$
$$\frac{192}{16} =$$
$$= 12$$

The weighted average is 12, Choice (B).

920. A. 17

Multiply the number of instances of each frequency by the value associated with it:

$$1 \times 26 = 26$$
$$12 \times 7 = 84$$
$$9 \times 16 = 144$$
$$2 \times 9 = 18$$

Then divide the sum by the total number of values:

$$26 + 84 + 144 + 18 = 272$$

$$\frac{272}{(1 + 12 + 9 + 2)} =$$

$$\frac{272}{24} =$$

$$= 11\frac{1}{3}$$

Choice (A) represents the weighted average.

921. **D. 3.7**

Multiply each value by the decimal equivalent of the percentage associated with it:

$$.10 \times 12 = 1.20$$
$$.25 \times 16 = 4$$
$$.30 \times 20 = 6$$
$$.35 \times 10 = 3.5$$

The sum of the products is the weighted average:

$$1.20 + 4 + 6 + 3.5 = 14.7$$

$$\frac{14.7}{4} = 3.67$$

922. **D. 29.5**

Multiply each value by the decimal equivalent of the percentage associated with it:

$$.75 \times 32 = 24$$
$$.15 \times 10 = 1.5$$
$$.06 \times 50 = 3$$
$$.04 \times 25 = 1$$

The sum of the products is the weighted average:

$$24 + 1.5 + 3 + 1 = 29.5, \text{ Choice (D)}$$

923. **B. $4.45**

Multiply each cost by the fraction of the group that spent it:

$$\frac{1}{2} \times 5.50 = 2.75$$

$$\frac{1}{4} \times 4 = 1.00$$

$$\frac{3}{16} \times 3.20 = 0.20$$

$$\frac{1}{16} \times 8 = 0.50$$

The sum of the products of the costs is the weighted average snack cost:

$2.75 + 1 + .20 + .5 = 4.45$, Choice (B)

924. **C. $0.70**

Start with the price per pound from each supermarket:

Food-2-Go: 0.60

SuperSaver: 0.90 (2.70/3)

Speedy Mart: 0.60 (3.60/6)

$$0.60 + 0.90 + 0.60 = 2.10$$
$$\frac{2.10}{3} = 0.70$$

The average price per pound is $0.70, Choice (C).

925. **D. 2.4**

Multiply the number of students in each grade by the average time spent by students in that grade:

$$15 \times 2 = 30$$
$$15 \times 1 = 15$$
$$20 \times 3 = 60$$
$$25 \times 3 = 75$$

Divide the sum by the total number of values:

$$\frac{(30 + 15 + 60 + 75)}{15 + 15 + 20 + 25} = \frac{180}{75}$$
$$\frac{180}{75} = 2.4$$

The correct answer is Choice (D).

926. **C. 8%**

To solve simple interest problems, use the formula $I = P \cdot r \cdot t$ to solve for the missing value, in this case r.

$$r = \frac{I}{P \cdot t}$$
$$r = \frac{\$100}{\$1,250 \cdot 1}$$
$$r = 0.08$$
$$r = 8\%$$

The correct answer is Choice (C).

927. E. $15,000

To solve simple interest problems, use the formula $I = P \cdot r \cdot t$ to solve for the missing value, in this case P.

$$P = \frac{I}{r \cdot t}$$
$$P = \frac{600}{(0.04)(1)}$$
$$P = 15,000$$

Ryan invested $15,000, Choice (E).

928. E. 8 years

To solve simple interest problems, use the formula $I = P \cdot r \cdot t$ to solve for the missing value, in this case t.

$$t = \frac{I}{P \cdot r}$$
$$t = \frac{8,000}{(20,000)(0.05)}$$
$$t = 8 \text{ years}$$

929. A. $2,700

To solve simple interest problems for interest, use the formula $I = P \cdot r \cdot t$.

$$I = P \cdot r \cdot t$$
$$I = (15,000)(0.03)(6)$$
$$I = (450)6$$
$$I = \$2,700$$

The interest paid was $2,700, Choice (A).

930. C. $55,000.00

To solve simple interest problems for interest, use the formula $I = P \cdot r \cdot t$.

$$I = P \cdot r \cdot t$$
$$I = (250,000)(0.02)(11)$$
$$I = (5,000)(11)$$
$$I = 55,000$$

The interest paid was $55,000.00, Choice (C).

931.   **A. 1.25 pounds**

Start by assigning a variable to the missing value. Let c be the number of pounds of chips in the final mixture, since that's what you're trying to identify. Now you can say that the cost of the 4 pounds of peanuts at \$1.25 per pound plus c pounds of chips at \$2.25 per pound is equal to the cost of the number of pounds of the mixture at \$2.00 per pound:

$$4(\$1.25) + c(\$2.25) = (5 + c)\$2.00$$

Drop the \$ signs from both sides for simplification, and solve for c.

$$4(1.25) + c(2.25) = (5 + c)2.0$$
$$5 + 2.25c = 10 + 2c$$
$$.25c = 5$$
$$c = 1.25$$

You need 1.25 pounds of chips, Choice (A).

932.   **D. 25**

Start by assigning a variable to the missing value. Let f be the number of footballs, since that's what you're trying to identify. Now you can say that the cost of the 25 soccer balls at \$4.00 each plus f footballs at \$6.00 per ball is equal to the cost of the total number of balls at \$5.00 per ball:

$$25(\$4.00) + f(\$6.00) = (25 + f)\$5.00$$

Drop the \$ signs from both sides for simplification, and solve for f.

$$25(4) + f(6) = (25 + f)5$$
$$100 + 6f = 125 + 5f$$
$$f = 25$$

The school should buy 25 footballs, Choice (D).

933.   **C. $6\frac{2}{3}$ liters**

Begin by assigning x to be the number of liters of the low salt solution, since that's the value you need for the answer.

Since the final solution will be 20 liters in volume, the high salt solution volume must be $20 - x$ liters.

Now you can say that x liters of the 20% solution added to $20 - x$ liters of the 50% solution is equal to 20 liters of the 40% solution:

$$2x + .5(20 - x) = .4(20)$$

Now solve for x:

$$.2x + .5(20 - x) = .4(20)$$
$$.2x + 10 - .5x = 8$$
$$-.3x = -2$$
$$x = 6\frac{2}{3}$$

You need $6\frac{2}{3}$ liters, Choice (C).

---

934. **D. 50 gallons**

Assign a variable to the value you are looking for, which is the number of gallons of 25% sugar mixture: s = gal of 25% solution.

The total number of gallons then is $s + 100$. Now you can say that the number of gallons of 25% solution plus 100 gallons of the 10% solution equals the number of gallons in the final 15% mixture. Further, you can say that the amount of *sugar* in the 25% mixture is $0.25(s)$ gallons, added to the *sugar* in the 10% mixture, $0.1(100)$ gallons, equals the *sugar* in the final solution, $0.15(100 + s)$:

$$0.25(s) + 0.1(100) = 0.15(100 + s)$$

Now solve for s to get the answer:

$$0.25(s) + 0.1(100) = 0.15(100 + s)$$
$$0.25s + 10 = 15 + .15s$$
$$.10s = 5$$
$$s = 50$$

You need 50 gallons of the 25% sugar mixture, Choice (D).

---

935. **C. 12 hours**

It may not exactly look like it, but this is a mixture problem. Assign a variable to the value you are looking for, the number of hours of 75% on-task time: m = time at 75% time-on-task.

The total number of hours is $m + 12$. Now you can say that the number of hours that Mary works plus the 12 hours that Paul works equals the total number of hours. Further, you can say that the amount of *on-task hours* that Mary puts in, $0.75(m)$ hours, added to the *on-task hours* that Paul contributes, $0.25(12)$ hours, equals the *on-task hours* together, $0.50(12 + m)$:

$$0.75(m) + 0.25(12) = 0.5(12 + m)$$

Now solve for m to get the answer:

$$0.75(m) + 0.25(12) = 0.5(12 + m)$$
$$0.75m + 3 = 6 + 0.5m$$
$$0.25m = 3$$
$$m = 12$$

Mary needs to work 12 hours, Choice (C).

936. A. $\frac{4}{25}$

The probability of pulling a yellow marble is equal to the number of yellow marbles divided by the total number of marbles in the bag:

$$P = \frac{4}{(11+3+4+7)}$$
$$P = \frac{4}{25}$$

The probability of pulling a yellow marble from the bag is 4 out of 25 or $\frac{4}{25}$. Choice (A).

937. B. $\frac{1}{3}$

There are a total of six colors on the wheel, and the probability of landing on any one is the same as landing on any other, since the spacing is equal. The probability of a favorable outcome occurring is:

$$\frac{red+violet}{red+orange+yellow+green+blue+violet}$$
$$\frac{2}{6} = \frac{1}{3}$$

Choice (B) is the correct answer.

938. C. $\frac{1}{64}$

The probability of the spinner landing on green three times in a row is the product of the probability of it landing on green multiplied by itself three times:

$$\frac{1}{4} \times \frac{1}{4} \times \frac{1}{4} = \frac{1}{64}$$

The correct answer is Choice (C).

939. E. $\frac{1}{210}$

The tricky part of this question is the part about keeping each card as it is drawn, because as each card is pulled from the deck, the probability of each successive card changes.

The first card probability is pretty easy — any one of the four from a deck of 10: $\frac{4}{10}$

The second card probability is any of the three remaining pulled from a deck of 9, since one card is already gone: $\frac{3}{9} = \frac{1}{3}$

The third card is either of the two remaining desired cards pulled from a deck of 8: $\frac{2}{8} = \frac{1}{4}$

The fourth card is pulled from a deck of 7: $\frac{1}{7}$

The probability of pulling all four in a row is the product of all four separate probabilities:

$$\frac{2}{5} \times \frac{1}{3} \times \frac{1}{4} \times \frac{1}{7} = \frac{2}{420}$$
$$= \frac{1}{210}$$

Choice (E) is the correct answer.

940. B. $\frac{2}{39}$

The probability of both occurrences is the same as the product of the individual probabilities. The probability of pulling a 4 or a 5 from a standard deck is 8/52, or 2/13. The probability of rolling a 3 or a 4 on a standard die is 2/6, or 1/3. The product of the two is the answer:

$$\frac{2}{13} \times \frac{1}{3} = \frac{2}{39}$$

The correct answer is Choice (B).

941. C. 54

There are three groups: red vehicles (cars and trucks), red trucks, and trucks of all colors.

There are a total of 28 red vehicles and a total of 40 trucks. Fourteen of the trucks are also red vehicles, so the total number of unique vehicles includes 40 trucks and the remaining 14 red vehicles that aren't trucks:

$$40 + 14 = 54 \text{ total vehicles}$$

The correct answer is Choice (C).

942. D. 26

There are 40 trucks total, and 14 trucks are red. If there are 14 red trucks, then there must be $40 - 14 = 26$ trucks that are not red, Choice (D).

943. A. 14

There are 40 trucks total, and 14 trucks are red. If there are 28 red vehicles, 14 of which are trucks, then there must be $28 - 14 = 14$ red vehicles that are not trucks, Choice (A).

944. D. 33.3%

The probability of a randomly chosen student wearing a red shirt is equal to the number of red-shirted students divided by the total number of students:

$$\frac{12}{12+8+6+10}$$
$$\frac{12}{36} = 33.3\%$$

Choice (D) is the correct answer.

945.   **E. 80%**

The probability of a randomly chosen student not wearing a striped shirt is equal to the number of not-striped-shirted students divided by the total number of students:

$$\frac{10+6+8}{10+6+6+8}$$
$$\frac{24}{30} = \frac{4}{5} = 80\%$$

The other way to handle this problem is to solve for the probability of a student wearing a striped shirt and finding the complement:

$$\frac{6}{10+6+6+8} = \frac{6}{30}$$
$$\frac{6}{30} = 20\%$$
$$100\% - 20\% = 80\%$$

Either way, Choice (E) is the correct answer.

946.   **E. 135**

The number of different desserts is the product of the number of flavors of ice cream, the types of cones, and the different toppings:

$$(9 \text{ flavors})(3 \text{ cones})(5 \text{ toppings}) = 135$$

There are 135 different desserts, Choice (E).

947.   **C. 216**

Each die has six sides and there are three dice, so the number of possible combinations is $6 \times 6 \times 6 = 216$. Choice (C) is the correct answer.

948.   **B. 40**

To find the total number of outfits, simply multiply the number of pairs of jeans by the number of shirts. Multiply the product by the number of pairs of shoes:

$$(2)(4)(5) = 40$$

There are 40 possible different outfits, Choice (B).

949.   **C. 56**

Larame has a total of $(2)(5)(14)(2) = 280$ different outfits. If he wears five different outfits each week, he can go to work for $\frac{280}{5} = 56$ weeks, or a year and a month or so, before repeating an outfit. Choice (C) is the correct answer.

950.   C. 864

The number of possible combinations is the product of each number of possibilities at every step:

$$(2)(2)(6)(6)(6) = 864$$

Thus, Choice (C) is the correct answer.

951.   E. 10!

The first card in the new stack could be any one of the 10 with which you start. The second card could be any of the 9 remaining, the third any of the 8 remaining, and so on. The total number of possibilities, then, is 10!, Choice (E).

952.   B. Quantity B is greater.

Quantity A is 8!, or $(8)(7)(6)(5)(4)(3)(2)(1) = 40,320$

Quantity B is 8^8 or $(8)(8)(8)(8)(8)(8)(8)(8) = 16,777,216$

Therefore, Quantity B is greater, Choice (B).

953.   A. Quantity A is greater.

Quantity A is $\dfrac{(7)(6)(5)(4)(3)(2)(1)}{(5)(4)(3)(2)(1)} = \dfrac{(7)(6)(5)(4)(3)(2)(1)}{(5)(4)(3)(2)(1)} = 42$

Quantity B is $2! = (2)(1) = 2$

Therefore, Quantity A is greater, Choice (A).

954.   B. Quantity B is greater.

Quantity A is $(7!)(5!) = (5,040)(120) = 604,800$

Quantity B is $12! = 479,001,600$

Therefore, Quantity B is greater, Choice (B).

955.   B. Quantity B is greater.

Quantity A is $9+8+7+6+5+4+3+2+1 = 45$

Quantity B is 81

Therefore, Quantity B is greater, Choice (B).

956. **E. 10!**

This is a factorial question. Because there are ten players, there are ten possibilities for first place. Once one of the players is assigned to first, there will be nine remaining possibilities for second place, then eight for third, and so on. Mathematically, that looks like $(10)(9)(8)(7)(6)(5)(4)(3)(2)(1)$, which is 10 factorial.

There are 10! ways that ten players could be ranked in the top ten places, so the correct answer is Choice (E).

957. **D. 60**

If there were 13 competitors and 13 places, this would be a simple factorial question, but only the top 3 places will get a job, and their bonus depends on rank. This is a permutation question. Use the permutation formula $P_r^n = \dfrac{n!}{(n-r)!}$, where P is the number of permutations, n is the number of items (competitors) to choose from, and r is the number chosen (the number of jobs available).

$$P_r^n = \frac{n!}{(n-r)!}$$
$$= \frac{5!}{(5-3)!}$$
$$= \frac{5!}{2!}$$
$$= 60$$

Choice (D) is the correct answer.

958. **D. 930**

Because the order of the scoops is important, use the permutations formula to solve:

$$P_r^n = \frac{n!}{(n-r)!}$$
$$= \frac{31!}{(31-2)!}$$
$$= \frac{31!}{29!}$$
$$= (31)(30)$$
$$= 930$$

Choice (D) is the correct answer.

959. D. 1,056

This is a permutations problem, picking 2 from a pool of 33: P_2^{33}.

Use the permutations formula to calculate the answer:

$$P_2^{33} = \frac{33!}{(33-2)!}$$
$$= \frac{33!}{31!}$$
$$= (33)(32)$$
$$= 1,056$$

The correct answer is Choice (D).

960. C. 1,716

Use the permutations formula to solve P_3^{13}:

$$P_3^{13} = \frac{13!}{(13-3)!}$$
$$= \frac{13!}{10!}$$
$$= (13)(12)(11)$$
$$= 1,716$$

Choice (C) is the correct answer.

961. C. 20

The competitor's ranking is not important, since all three top contenders will get a job and there is no starting bonus difference. This is a combinations problem; use the combinations formula:

$$C_3^5 = \frac{5!}{3!(5-3)!}$$
$$= \frac{5!}{3!2!}$$
$$= \frac{(5)(4)}{2}$$
$$= 20$$

The correct answer is Choice (C).

962. **C. 220**

Since the triangles will each be the same regardless of the order of the pencils forming the sides, this is a combinations question. Use the combinations formula:

$$C_{12}^3 = \frac{12!}{3!(12-3)!}$$
$$= \frac{12!}{6(9!)}$$
$$= \frac{(12)(11)(10)}{6}$$
$$= 220$$

The correct answer is Choice (C).

963. **C. 190**

Since the order in which the cards are picked or held does not affect the hand, the number of hands is equal to the number of combinations possible by picking two things from a pool numbering 20, that is C_2^{20}. Use the combinations formula to solve:

$$C_2^{20} = \frac{20!}{2!(20-2)!}$$
$$= \frac{20!}{2!(18!)}$$
$$= \frac{(20)(19)}{2}$$
$$= \frac{380}{2}$$
$$= 190$$

Choice (C) is the correct answer.

964. **D. 455**

A given set of coins is the same regardless of the order of the coins, so this is a combinations question. Use the combinations formula:

$$C_3^{15} = \frac{15!}{3!(15-3)!}$$
$$= \frac{15!}{3!(12!)}$$
$$= \frac{(15)(14)(13)}{(6)}$$
$$= (5)(7)(13)$$
$$= 455$$

The correct answer is Choice (D).

965.

C. 300

The question does not state that the order of the cars is important, so this is a combinations question. Use the combinations formula:

$$C_2^{25} = \frac{25!}{2!(25-2)!}$$
$$= \frac{25!}{2!(23!)}$$
$$= \frac{(25)(24)}{2}$$
$$= \frac{600}{2}$$
$$= 300$$

The correct answer is Choice (C).

966.

C. $52,000

The median income is the middle value when all five are listed in ascending or descending value: $27,000, $34,000, $52,000, $64,000, and $71,000.

Since there are an odd number of values, the middle number, which is $52,000, is the median income. Therefore, Choice (C) is the correct answer.

967.

D. 48.5

The median value is the middle number when the data is arranged in ascending or descending order: 12, 13, 25, 31, 66, 66, 70, 71.

The number of values in this set is even, so the median is actually the mean of the two middle numbers, 31 and 66: 48.5, which is Choice (D).

968.

B. $100.00

The median price is the middle price when all applicable prices are arranged by ascending or descending price: $200, $200, $100, $100, $100, $100, $20, $0

The number of prices here is even, but since both middle values are $100, you don't need to worry about finding a mean.

The median price is $100.00, Choice (B).

969.

E. It would not change at all.

Sort the values by ascending or descending order: 138, 140, 143, 144, 144, 145, 145, 147, 147, 148, 149. The median is the middle number, 145.

If you add 256 on to the end of the series, you have an even number of values, so the median is the mean of the two middle values. Since both middle values are 145, the median remains unchanged, making Choice (E) the correct answer.

970. **D. 512**

Begin by calculating the population for each hour. You know that the population is increasing, so the data will already be organized in ascending order. You actually only need to calculate halfway since 17 is an odd number (don't forget the starting population), and the population at the end of the ninth hour is the median:

hour	:	population
0	:	1
1	:	2
2	:	4
3	:	8
4	:	16
5	:	32
6	:	64
7	:	128
8	:	256
9	:	512

The correct answer is Choice (D).

971. **E. There is no mode.**

The mode is the most common value in a set of data. Because there are no repeating values in this data, there is no mode, Choice (E).

972. **E. 66**

The mode is the most common value in a set of data. The value 66 is the only one that is repeated, so that is the mode.

973. **C. $100.00 and $200.00**

The modal price is the price that appears most often in the set of data. In the applicable data, the prices $100.00 and $200.00 each appear twice, and all others appear only once. Therefore, $100.00 and $200.00, Choice (C), are both modes of the data.

974. **A. $0.00**

Sort the prices by ascending or descending order: $200, $200, $100, $100, $100, $99, $50, $0, $0, $0, $0, $0.

The modal value(s) appear more often than the others. In this case the only value that appears four or more times is $0.00, Choice (A), so that is the mode.

975. **A. $44,000**

The range is the lowest salary subtracted from the highest salary:

$$71,000 - 27,000 = 44,000$$

The correct answer is Choice (A).

976. **D. It increases significantly.**

The original range is $87 - 42 = 45$.

The new range is $129 - 42 = 87$.

The new range is nearly double the original range, so there is a significant increase, Choice (D).

977. **B. Quantity B is greater.**

The range of Quantity A is $921 - 888 = 33$.

The range of Quantity B is $49 - 14 = 35$.

Therefore, Quantity B is greater, Choice (B).

978. **C. The quantities are equal.**

The range of Quantity A is $243 - 43 = 200$.

The range of Quantity B is $591 - 391 = 200$.

The quantities are equal, Choice (C).

979. **E. 180°F**

The range of temperatures is the lowest temperature subtracted from the highest: $212°F - 32°F = 180°F$.

Choice (E) is the correct answer.

980. **B. $50,000**

The mean income is the average income, which is the total income divided by the number of tiers:

$$\frac{71,000 + 34,000 + 52,000 + 66,000 + 27,000}{5}$$

$$\frac{250,000}{5} = 50,000$$

The correct answer is Choice (B).

981. C. 45

The mean value is the average, so add the values and divide by 8, the number of data points:

$$\frac{71+13+66+31+25+66+76+12}{8}$$

$$\frac{360}{8}=45$$

Choice (C) is the correct answer.

982. C. $126.67

The mean price would be the average price, so add the prices of all the Galaxy phones and divide by 12:

$$\frac{200+200+100+100+100+100+0+20+200+250+150+100}{12}$$

$$\frac{1,520}{12}=126.67$$

The correct answer is Choice (C).

983. B. $43.33

The mean price is the sum of the prices of all Lumia phones divided by the number of Lumia phones in the data. Since there is no available price for a Lumia phone from Sprint, it is not included.

$$\frac{100+0+30}{3}$$

$$\frac{130}{3}=43.33$$

The correct answer is Choice (B).

984. E. 1,861

Begin by calculating the population for each hour; then add the hourly populations and divide by 11, the number of entries:

hour	:	population
0	:	10
1	:	20
2	:	40
3	:	80
4	:	160
5	:	320
6	:	640
7	:	1,280
8	:	2,560
9	:	5,120
10	:	10,240
		20,470

$$\frac{20,470}{11} = 1,861$$

Choice (E) is the correct answer.

985. A. Quantity A is greater.

To estimate the standard deviations of each quantity, use the mean deviation. First find the mean of each set; then calculate the mean distance of the values in each set from its associated mean:

Quantity A mean: $\frac{7+14+25+29+34+35}{6} = 24$

Quantity A difference between each value and the mean:

$$|24-7| = 17$$
$$|24-14| = 10$$
$$|24-25| = 1$$
$$|24-29| = 5$$
$$|24-34| = 10$$
$$|24-35| = 11$$

Quantity A mean deviation: $\frac{7+14+25+29+34+35}{6} = 9$

Quantity B mean: $\frac{10+23+23+25+26+37}{6} = 24$

Quantity B difference between each value and the mean:

$$|24-10| = 14$$
$$|24-23| = 1$$
$$|24-23| = 1$$
$$|24-25| = 1$$
$$|24-26| = 2$$
$$|24-37| = 11$$

Quantity B mean deviation: $\dfrac{14+1+1+1+2+11}{6} = 5$

9 is greater than 5, so Choice (A) is your answer.

986.　　**C. The quantities are equal.**

To estimate the standard deviations of each quantity, use the mean deviation. First find the mean of each set; then calculate the mean distance of the values in each set from its associated mean:

Quantity A mean: $\dfrac{2+4+6+8+10+12}{6} = 7$

Quantity A difference between each value and the mean:

$$|7-2| = 5$$
$$|7-4| = 3$$
$$|7-6| = 1$$
$$|7-8| = 1$$
$$|7-10| = 3$$
$$|7-12| = 5$$

Quantity A mean deviation: $\dfrac{5+3+1+1+3+5}{6} = 3$

Quantity B mean: $\dfrac{1+3+5+7+9+11}{6} = 6$

Quantity B difference between each value and the mean:

$$|6-1| = 5$$
$$|6-3| = 3$$
$$|6-5| = 1$$
$$|6-7| = 1$$
$$|6-9| = 3$$
$$|6-11| = 5$$

Quantity B mean deviation: $\dfrac{5+3+1+1+3+5}{6} = 3$

The standard deviations are equal, Choice (C).

987. **C. Decrease less than 2.0**

To estimate the standard deviation of the original set, use the mean deviation. First calculate the mean; then find the average of the distances of each value from the mean:

$$\frac{5+10+15+20+25}{5} = 15 \qquad \begin{aligned} |15-5| &= 10 \\ |15-10| &= 5 \\ |15-15| &= 0 \\ |15-20| &= 5 \\ |15-25| &= 10 \end{aligned}$$

Original mean deviation: $\frac{10+5+0+5+10}{5} = 6$

By adding the value of 15, which is the same as the mean, the only effective change is to the final calculation, where you will divide by 6 values instead of 5 since the difference between the added value and the mean is 0:

$$\frac{10+5+0+5+10+0}{6} = 5$$

The mean deviation difference is a decrease of 1, so the average deviation will be less than 2.0, Choice (C).

988. **A. Quantity A is greater.**

To estimate the standard deviation, use the mean deviation. First calculate the mean; then find the average of the distances of each value from the mean:

$$\frac{200+200+100+99}{4} \approx 150$$

$$\begin{aligned} |150-200| &= 50 \\ |150-200| &= 50 \\ |150-100| &= 50 \\ |150-99| &= 51 \end{aligned}$$

Standard deviation: $\frac{50+50+50+51}{4} \approx 50$

Clearly, the mean, Quantity A, is significantly greater, so Choice (A) is the correct answer.

989. **A. Quantity A is greater.**

You may be able to simply reason this one through. Just to be sure, estimate the standard deviation, using the mean deviation, and make note of the mean along the way:

Mean: $\frac{4+8+12+16+20+24}{6} = 14$

Apx standard deviation:

$$|14 - 4| = 10$$
$$|14 - 8| = 6$$
$$|14 - 12| = 2$$
$$|14 - 16| = 2$$
$$|14 - 20| = 6$$
$$|14 - 24| = 10$$

$$\frac{10 + 6 + 2 + 2 + 6 + 10}{6} = 6$$

The mean is more than twice the standard deviation, so Choice (A) is correct.

990. Review the following essay.

It would seem illogical to say that the Internet is hindering our ability to think, but I fear that is exactly what is happening. In a time when instant gratification is the norm and quandaries and questions can be addressed immediately, the need to think deeply about an issue is no longer relevant. For those in older generations, this ease of information attainment is a nice addition to their already developed analytical thinking skills. However, younger generations, specifically teens, do not know anything different from this accessibility of information; thus, they were never trained to use critical thinking skills to solve a problem, leaving them at a disadvantage intellectually.

Technological advances are mostly to blame for this dearth of analytical and critical reasoning skills. Computer programs have spell check that removes the need to sound out words or research the proper spelling in reference material, search engines have taken the place of traditional investigations, and phones have calculators that remove the need for basic math ability. In fact, on a number of occasions in retail stores, I have watched a teen struggle to make change from a $20 bill, a task a small child could do by counting on his fingers. The fact that counting on his fingers was not the next logical step for this teen signifies just how little reasoning is happening.

Visual media is also causing a shift in how our brains work. Because of videos, graphics, video games, and other visually stimulating activities, reading, especially literary reading, has been reduced. Reading, which stimulates deep thinking, helps the brain develop imagination, something not needed when the images are presented on the screen. The brain is no longer required to tap into stored information to guide understanding or link ideas together to form a larger picture.

Some argue that the Internet has increased knowledge by making information accessible and further reaching. The ability to conduct research has been advanced due to the advent of electronic files and topic- or field-specific websites. Often, information about one topic will include links to related information, which allows the researcher to find associated information quickly. However, the use of hyperlinks removes the necessity of a person making informed associations on his or her own, which, again, reduces the level of critical thinking. Hyperlinks can serve as a distraction when taking in the initial information, as well.

Thus, despite the advent of new ways of retrieving information quickly and in different formats, the ease and manner in which this information is provided reduces the amount of thinking a person has to do. When thinking is reduced in one realm of life, it is likely to be reduced in others, leading to other, possibly negative, outcomes for humanity and ill equipping our youth with successful decision-making abilities.

This response is very strong and addresses the issue successfully. The writer clearly states the position in the first paragraph and uses clear examples to support that position. The writer also acknowledges the merit of counter arguments.

This essay is strengthened by the use of stimulating language, such as "ill-equipping" and "dearth." Sufficient transitions are used to link the paragraphs, creating a strong tone and flow of the content. Further, a variety of sentence lengths and structures keeps the essay interesting. It is clear this writer organized his thoughts before writing.

991.   Review the following essay.

The way that a society cares for its aging population represents a model for how that society's citizens view each other. Children tend to model the way their parents and other adults in their lives behave. Thus, if the adults of a society deem it a priority to provide loving and appropriate care for their elderly population, children will learn to value their elders and people, in general, more.

Some cultures, such as the Chinese, hold the value of filial piety, the idea that parents and ancestors deserve respect, in high regard. In fact, the government has begun to consider a law that would mandate that adult children spend a certain amount of time with their aging parents. The move for this type of stringent social policy is an attempt to continue the tradition of values and knowledge being passed down through the generations so the values of the culture are maintained.

However, in other cultures, such as the United States, this belief in filial piety is not a priority. It is less common for adult children to serve as caregivers for their parents than it is to house them in an assisted-living facility or nursing home. These actions remove the amount of time spent with the aging family members, which, in turn, reduces the influence they can have on younger generations. As a result, a large gap is created between older and younger generations, leaving each feeling alienated from the other.

In addition to creating a generation gap, leaving the care of aging family members to strangers sends a message to the youth culture about the value of that population. Children who see their grandparents hidden away in facilities begin to believe that after a certain age, you are no longer a productive member of society, and hence, you have nothing to offer. This idea translates to the way that they view all persons older than they are and not only affects the level of respect they give their parents and other persons of authority, but also renders the elderly and their guidance irrelevant. However, in cultures where family care is the norm, children grow up respecting the wisdom of their elders and see them as providing emotional value to their lives, which translates into respect in other parts of society.

The example a culture sets for the younger generations surpasses the simple act of who will take care of grandma and grandpa. It speaks to a larger sense of responsibility, family connectedness, and respect for those from other generations. The policies and morals that guide national policies for older persons should take these factors into consideration if they want to maintain the integrity of their culture.

The writer of this essay was smart in bringing in real-world facts and examples to support the position. The opinion is clear in the thesis statement, and the conclusion relates to the thesis in a new and interesting way, rather than restating what was already presented.

Use of transitions like "However" and "In addition" keep the movement of the essay clear and the information attainable. The writer went beyond what was needed to understand her opinion and created a wider view of the issue.

992.   Review the following essay.

There is an old saying that you have to spend money to make money. Although this saying typically applies to matters of business or personal finances, it is also relevant when analyzing public aid. More specifically, investing in the citizens of a society helps provide them with the means to put money back into that society. If this support is not provided, people will suffer more, increasing the rate of illness and decreasing the quality of life, which brings down the morale of a culture and leads to more intense services than those opposed to begin with.

Consider a single father with two children who is working multiple jobs to support his family. The money he is earning is barely enough to cover the costs of living, and the time taken away from his children leaves them without a role model or proper supervision. No lessons, beyond that of hard work and resilience, are being passed to the children, and the lack of supervision could possibly create an environment where injury or poor judgment is likely. If this father were able to attain partial financial support for his family from the government, he would have more time with his children at home, helping them with their schoolwork and providing them with the proper supervision. Their family unit would be stronger because of it, which leads to more stability as children age.

Opponents contest that taxpayers' money should be put toward an issue that affects everyone. They do not want to experience increases in their taxes to support people they don't know. There is also the idea that people requiring social services are not motivated to change their circumstances or find better employment. The concept is one of "If I can do it, they can do it." Critics point to abusers of the system who are able to work but choose not to, as well.

In addition, some critics feel the government does not manage the services well, using the money appropriated for aid in irresponsible ways. They point to the lack of progress made in putting people back on their feet as a prime example. This argument holds some weight because it is true that the poverty rate and use of services such as food stamps and unemployment has not changed significantly in the last 50 years. Yet, is it the mismanagement of funds that is behind this stagnant statistic or is the cost of living increasing at rates not proportionate to improvements in income generated?

Regardless of the reason for opposition, one fact remains: Without aid, these citizens will continue to suffer, and the help they will need later will outweigh the help they need now. Furthermore, despite the initial costs of increased taxes and resource use, the resulting benefits of people having the ability to put money back into the local and national economies benefits everyone in the end. Society must think holistically to thrive. Supporting programs that provide aid to the needy strengthens the bonds of community and the ability of everyone to prosper.

The opening of this essay is strong and provides a common foundation for the writer's opinion. In this way, the audience is already able to relate to the information. The use of a hypothetical creates a tangible image for the reader to understand the issue, and the writer presents and supports the example astutely.

The writer also provides the opposing view and reasoning to refute it. There is a strong sense of structural organization. The grammar and punctuation are accurate, and the paragraphs are proportional. The language is at a high level, and uses of phrases such as "stagnant statistic" keep the language fresh.

993. Review the following essay.

To determine which is better for a small community — growth in business and property development or protecting wilderness areas — one has to look at the benefits and losses each scenario brings to the equation. The desire to develop land points to a desire to increase the local economy by promoting business growth and collecting the ensuing additional property taxes. Thus, the issue comes down to which venture is more financially beneficial. If the local economy depends on the recreational tourism, it seems that taking away that attraction is counterproductive to improving revenue to support local citizens.

This community may lack certain conveniences, such as large shopping complexes or variety in restaurants or entertainment options. There may also be a dearth of employment opportunities for the local community, leaving families struggling to make ends meet. The benefit of allowing the expansion of businesses and the introduction of mega-stores to solve these issues must be weighed against the losses incurred by the other sector of the economy, which may negate the benefits gained from these actions.

This other sector — the wilderness and recreation sector — may lose business and revenue if it no longer has the facilities to attract tourists or conduct their businesses. If there are no tourists, there are no people to book guided tours, buy recreational equipment, and stay in area hotels. The tourists will not be spending money in the restaurants or grocery stores, spending fees to support wilderness and road maintenance, or buying souvenirs to remember their amazing trip. If these businesses are not able to bring in customers, they will be forced to close their doors, fire their employees, and cease their property tax payments. Such an event would have a profound impact on the local economy. If you look at the proposition in this way, the development of land for economic gain is counterproductive if no one will be around to spend money in those businesses.

Either way, unemployment and inconvenience remain in the lives of community residents, but only one option provides the best hope. Protecting the core resource that creates the most financial support in the community is the smartest choice. For this town, that resource is the main attraction that keeps tourists coming back: the wilderness. There is guaranteed success of this venture, and this source of revenue should be protected for the betterment of the people.

The author uses the technique of restating the issue in a different way before providing an opinion, which allows the reader to understand the writer's perspective. The pros and cons of this issue are thoughtfully presented, and the evidence to support both is clear and organized.

The writer presents both points of view without losing the integrity of his opinion. Terms such as "negate" and "counterproductive" show a high level of understanding academic language. The writer's argument is well reasoned and, thus, accessible.

994. Review the following essay.

When it comes to cutting the budget, the decision by school districts to cut music programs is understandable. Music is seen as an elective, whereas other subjects, such as math and English, are seen as requirements for the educational growth and success of each student. However, what these administrators are missing is the way that music education actually enhances the success of learning these other subjects and that it should be promoted to improve grades and test scores.

Recent discussions about music education have determined a number of benefits to brain functioning from learning to play a musical instrument as a child. Reports have shown that musical training improves the connection and communication between different regions of the brain, and the manner in which sensory information is assimilated and deciphered is improved through learning to play an instrument.

Yet, budgetary concerns are very real for many schools, especially those in rural or low–socio-demographic areas, and money for supplies and resources needs to come from somewhere. How do you compare the need for textbooks with vital improvements in brain development? Government funding is one way, but sanctions and state autonomy regarding education don't make this a viable solution. A reduction in salaries is also not the best solution because good teachers will not accept low-paying jobs.

It is clear that a solution is needed to solve the budget concerns of the public school systems, but there must be recognition of the importance of a well-rounded curriculum. Music enhances our culture and provides great joy to many people. It is used therapeutically for certain behavioral and mental conditions and represents a major industry in the world. Simply cutting music programs because they seem less important academically only leads to cultural problems in the future. Thus, a solution that saves money and music is needed.

Although the writer clearly presents her opinion in the opening paragraph, an understanding of the challenges faced by the opposition is clear. This sort of empathetic understanding gives more value and legitimacy to the argument. It shows that the writer is thoughtful in presenting her opinion, not motivated by personal beliefs.

The author provides unflinching evidence to support her position, but she also provides solutions, which makes for a more productive argument. The mechanics of the writing are near perfect, as is the organization of the information. The conclusion is strong and relates to the whole essay.

995. Review the following essay.

It is impossible to think of voting in this country without feeling frustrated. The memories of the 2000 presidential election are still fresh in people's minds and still serve as a reminder of what can happen when the voter process is tampered with. Although the subsequent elections did not experience the same level of mishaps and misdeeds as the 2000 election did, there is still a sense among the American public that one's vote may or may not be counted accurately. I think it would be wise to look into a new system of voting because it is clear that faith in a fair and balanced election is no longer prevalent.

Part of society's growing distrust over election results is the use of antiquated voting technology. Outdated or complicated software often experience malfunctions that can disrupt or even destroy the ability of the machines to accurately count and store votes. In the case of the 2000 election, the term "chad" was introduced into common vernacular because it represented one of the biggest malfunctions in voter history. The chad is the part of a punch card that is discarded. A hanging chad or pregnant chad are terms used to describe when the chad is still dangling or merely indented but not punched through, respectively. The chad mishap was caused by a malfunction of the machinery used to punch the holes, and many votes in Florida were not counted.

If something as simple as a hole-punch malfunction can shift the results of a national election, the system is severely dysfunctional. Subsequently, a dysfunctional voting system deters voters from participating in elections, which is a poor reason for low voter turnout. Likewise, long lines at voting venues are also a poor reason to lose voter attendance. People stand in line for as many as eight hours so they can take two minutes to make their selection. People who have jobs, small children, or other responsibilities may not be able to take that amount of time to place a vote.

These issues could be addressed if a new policy, such as mandatory mail-in ballots, was in place for national elections. The ballots could be due within a certain timeframe to allow ample time for counting, and voting could be done in a minute from the convenience of your home. Technology would not have an impact on the turnout, nor would people without access to a voting center feel left out of the election.

The mail-in ballots address one of many issues surrounding the accuracy of vote counting during a presidential election. Energy should be put toward finding a solid solution to the voting problem, but the deeper issues lie elsewhere in the government. A review of the entire system is needed.

The author has a very clear opinion about this issue, and it is not a positive opinion. However, the care used in presenting the problems relating to the issue is strong and shows a thorough investigation of the topic. The use of a real example from history strengthens the position and makes the writer's perspective tangible.

Terms such as "vernacular" and "antiquated," and transition words make this essay a high-quality text. The author provides a solution and supports it with possible outcomes. This is a well-crafted argument.

---

996. Review the following essay.

The author makes a large leap in his argument when he proposes that banning snowboarding from ski resorts would reduce skier injuries. Although the information presented seems to lead to that conclusion, there is much left out of this evidence, and further information is needed before a clear solution can be found.

The blame the author attributes to snowboarding is nebulous at best. The data presented do show that more injuries have occurred since allowing snowboarding on the mountain, but there are no categories for the type and severity of the injury or the circumstances surrounding each incident. It is possible that the shapes of skis changed, creating more difficulty for skiers as they became used to the new style of skiing. It is also possible that snow conditions have worsened in the past decade, causing more extreme conditions on the snow. If injuries were resulting from other causes, such as these mentioned, the blame could not be placed entirely on snowboarders.

Moreover, there is no way of knowing the full significance of the data. How many injuries does 33 percent equate to? If the sample population is small, then 33 percent may not be that significant of a number in the big picture. However, if the opposite were true, 33 percent more injuries would be a major problem. Merely providing statistics is not sufficient evidence without a context for those statistics.

Finally, the author provides an example of how snowboarding affects the slopes differently from skiing. This example is used to show that skiers are at an increased risk of injury. However, the author does not link the example with injuries directly. He does not state that more challenging moguls lead to more injuries. Thus, the information is not quantified in the essay and serves no purpose beyond knowledge. The author would need to provide real evidence linking this cause to the effect to make a critical point with this information.

It may be that snowboarding has negatively affected the skiing experience or skier safety. However, the author leaves many unanswered questions in his argument, and the conclusion is not valid based on the information given.

The essay author presents his case clearly. He takes the assumptions made by the essay prompt and logically shows the flaws in the assumptions. Even better, the writer provides examples of further evidence needed to address the flaws. Through the use of these examples, the reader is clearly able to understand what is missing from the argument.

A high level of language and proper mechanics makes this a top-scoring essay.

997. Review the following essay.

The supervisor makes a good case for his feelings regarding the seeming delinquent actions of the employee; however, the logic of the supervisor is faulty regarding the employee's level of ability and concern. The evidence the supervisor presents is not sufficient for the claims she is making, with the proposed solution resting on a number of assumptions. More information is needed to refute or support the supervisor's claims of negligence by the employee before the severe action is taken regarding hours worked and payment.

First, the fact that the employee has had his timesheet updated after the deadline twice in the last six months does not seem to warrant the assumption that he is unable to do so properly. For instance, the supervisor's assumption of inability would be valid if timesheets were turned in once every two months. That frequency would mean the employee has required assistance after the fact more than half of the required times, suggesting a chronic problem. However, if the timesheets are turned in bi-monthly, and the employee had turned in the correct hours all other times, it would mean he completed the task appropriately 10 times. With that average, it wouldn't be valid to say the employee is unable to complete the task successfully.

Second, the reasoning for the lapses in completing the timesheet in a timely manner is not provided. The supervisor assumes that the employee is simply ignoring the appropriate protocol and, therefore, not respecting the policies of the company. Yet, there could be many reasons the employee did not turn in the correct hours. Did the employee work hours beyond his normal schedule that required adjusting? Was the employee asked by payroll to distribute his hours differently to avoid overtime pay? Was the employee sick or involved in a stressful situation that impeded his ability to enter the correct hours? The answers to these questions would help clarify whether the changes were merely the employee's failings or caused by an outside influence.

Furthermore, if no other policies have been broken by this employee, the claim of an overall irresponsibility is not grounded. Is this employee the only one who has ever needed a timesheet update after the deadline? Does this employee frequently fail to complete other tasks designated to him? Are there other signs of incompetence the employee has exhibited? These answers are needed to determine whether he is actually irresponsible or whether these are two isolated incidents to support the supervisor's assumption.

Finally, the solution to only pay the employee for a certain number of hours, regardless of the hours actually worked, is illegal. I'm sure there is something in the Federal Employment Compensation laws that dictates an employer cannot withhold payment for work completed. Thus, taking this kind of action could open the company up to a lawsuit.

It is not acceptable for an employee to disregard the rules of his place of employment, but it is also not acceptable for unfit punishment to be handed down arbitrarily. The human resources department and supervisor should investigate the situation further to find the answers to some of the above questions before assuming the worst and handing down an unjust punishment.

The author is very direct in addressing the opinions presented in the prompt in the first paragraph. The author uses clearly organized paragraphs to break down the vague assumptions made about the employee. Using logic and putting himself in the position of the employee creates a legitimacy and sympathy that causes the reader to think more deeply about the actions suggested by the supervisor. This essay is well organized, well written, and clear. It addresses the argument sufficiently and presents alternative questions that should be asked to find a solution to the problem.

998. Review the following essay.

When considering a massive decision like a complete forbiddance of a certain action by the public, the ins and outs of the legality and equitable aspects of the action must be considered. Banning smoking on public beaches in Hawaii might be a good idea, but the proponents of the law have not provided sufficient information to support their cause. Their evidence contains many holes that legislatures are expected to fill by agreeing with the proponents' assumptions. Yet, some important facts are missing that legislators need to get a real idea about the extent of the cigarette butt problem on beaches before banning public smoking.

The first assumption the author makes is that the number of cigarette butts removed from the beach is so great that it detracts from the beauty of the beach. However, no information is given about the beach where the clean-up took place, how many months or years it has been since the last clean-up, or how significant this litter was compared with other littered items. If the beach was a 50-mile expanse of shoreline on the Big Island, than 10,000 butts may not make such a large aesthetic impact. If it had been years since the last clean-up effort, the daily average of butt litter may be small to insignificant and the problem is actually a lack of clean-up efforts. If other litter, like paper products and bottles, make up more of the litter strewn around the beach, smoking may not cause the biggest littering problem.

Next, although second-hand carcinogens create a compelling argument for anti-smoking legislation, the assumption the author makes is that non-smokers are being put in harm's way by the amount of second-hand smoke on the beach. Yet, how have they accessed this risk? Have locals or tourists complained about second-hand smoke? Has there been an increase in second-hand smoke-related illnesses in the area where the beach resides? Are the breeze and expansive open air sufficient to mitigate the danger of second-hand smoke? If the answers to these questions are no, then the assumption made by the author is not supported.

Finally, the author assumes that the above issues lead to a reduction in tourism to the state's beaches. No information is given to support this claim, such as a dearth in visitation to the island or complaints by tourists about the condition of the beaches. Also, this point is based on the assumption that most visitors are non-smokers. However, there is no evidence suggesting that more non-smokers visit the island than smokers do. If most tourists are smokers, the smoking ban could, in turn, be detrimental to tourism.

Although the legislation may be a good idea, in general, for the public's health and to reduce litter, the assumptions made by the author are not founded in evidence. The proponents of this law need to answer the above-mentioned questions if they are to make a clear argument for banning cigarette smoking on public beaches.

The author provides a generalized statement to set up her position. Keeping both sides of the argument in mind, the writer clearly presents the issues at hand and the validity or lack of validity of the evidence presented to support the conclusion.

Language such as "carcinogens" and "dearth" express a high level of thinking and a strong understanding of the language. Other veins of thinking are presented to address the issue, but they do not detract from the writer's opinion. Use of transitions and topic sentences provides a good framework for this essay.

999. Review the following essay.

It is not legitimate to assume that allowing Virgin Records to enter the town will have detrimental effects on the local businesses and townspeople. The evidence provided by the author makes some good points, but there are many contingent factors that could further support or refute each point.

First, the author states that the city should deny the megastore to save local businesses. However, there is no evidence to suggest that this is the likely outcome. The author would need to show data from other towns where this sort of scenario took place and local businesses were negatively impacted by a corporate competitor. Without this information, the possible outcome is merely one of many possible outcomes.

The author also affirms that local musicians will suffer as a result of the entrance of the Virgin store into their community. However, the type of support the author mentions for local talent from the local music storeowners is nondescript. Do the musicians receive payment for performances at the stores? Are they able to sell their albums at the stores for profit? The type of support offered is important in determining whether the Virgin store is capable of supporting the musicians in the same way.

Finally, the city council represents the entire community. It is not clear from the author's report whether the entire community agrees with the protestors or just a select group. It's possible that other area residents support bringing the store to the town for economic advantages or for a greater selection of music. More information regarding the sentiment of all local residents would shed more light on the author's assertion.

Although the author uses valid arguments against the building of a Virgin record store in Lawrence, there are too many unanswered questions regarding the impact of the store on the community and how the entire community feels about the motion. The city council should take the time to investigate these issues before voting against the Virgin record store.

The author of the essay provides a clear and efficient assessment of the issue regarding the Virgin Record Store. He carefully and clearly dissects the prompt author's assumptions to show where the logic is not stable.

The author's language is clear, his point of view never falters, and his position is supported by a strong conclusion. There is no doubt what the writer thinks, and strong language and mechanics make this a high-level essay.

1,000. Review the following essay.

With statistics such as those presented in the argument, it would seem that the Housing First model is an effective solution to the homeless problem in America. This may be a true statement, but more information is needed before we can understand the full significance of these statistics and whether Housing First is the best solution for the problem of homelessness in many major cities.

The author does a great job of presenting the logic behind Housing First and explaining the usefulness of this model in a few metropolitan areas. Showcasing the programs in Portland and Salt Lake City is a good tactic for implying how successful the program can be, but the author doesn't express the unique aspects of each city that allowed this program to be beneficial. Compared to other U.S. cities, do Portland and Salt Lake City have fewer homeless shelters, more homeless with substance abuse issues, or more support from their local and state policymakers? Are the conditions in these cities representative of other cities? Answers to these questions would be helpful in determining whether success in Portland and Salt Lake City predicts success in other cities.

Next, the author suggests that a 15 percent reduction in the use of public resources is a good result. What is the percent reduction from other shelters? If it's 20 percent, then Housing First is not as effective as the author suggests. Although I think it is obvious, or should be, that any reductions in substance use and use of city resources are positive outcomes, regardless of how large the impact is, it is still necessary for the author to provide comparative information for the reader to assess the efficacy of the program.

Overall, the idea behind what the author is suggesting is that providing the homeless with housing as a first step helps them recover and reenter society more efficiently than other programs. Whereas this may be true, the author does not back this idea up with the necessary support in order to sway legislation. Simply stating that this type of intervention works is not enough. Policymakers want to see research comparing different rehabilitation approaches for homeless populations before they are able to determine which is the most effective for their cities. More results showing the outcomes of different approaches are needed to support the author's claim.

It would be wise for the author to dig deeper into his knowledge bank to provide a more resilient and clear argument regarding the implementation of the Housing First model. As the argument stands, there are too many unanswered questions and vague ideas for it to be sufficient for policy change.

The writer has taken the time to put her thoughts together and try to understand what is missing from this argument. The writer relates the faulty assumptions in a pragmatic way, which leaves little room for doubt that the information is not sufficient for the stated conclusion.

The transitions are strong, as is the language, and the introduction and conclusion make a cohesive message. This writer could have appealed to the sympathies of the reader, but instead, she relied on the evidence to state her case, which makes this essay very strong.

1,001. Review the following essay.

Relocating an entire university is a drastic step toward resolving the issues of crime in the neighborhood. The amount of time and resources required to make such a large-scale move is extraordinary. Therefore, the author needs to provide a compelling argument for the wisdom of such a move. However, many questions are unanswered, and more specific information is needed to provide a clearer picture of the issues related to neighborhood crime and how the university should respond.

One part of the argument needing more information is the comparison made between the neighborhood now and before the school was built. The author suggests that because the university staff and faculty moved farther from campus, the area surrounding campus became diminished. Yet, are there not other neighborhoods close to the school with crime? Is the crime in the more proximal area worse than crime in other areas? Are the new neighborhoods crime-free? If the school is to be moved because of the surrounding area, it should be made clear that the new location has less crime.

Furthermore, the author uses the private school status of McCarther University as a reason why crime is more prevalent near the school. However, there is also crime near public schools. Is the private status of the school the cause of the crime or just an unrelated detail about the university? More information is needed comparing crime among public universities and private universities before one can make such a drastic recommendation as moving to a new campus for this reason alone.

Finally, the author suggests that moving to a nicer area will bolster enrollment. However, how is this claim being measured? Have the enrollment numbers decreased more substantially in the last few years than before the crime became a major issue? Are there other factors affecting enrollment, such as reduced funding and scholarship opportunities or increases in tuition? Additional research is required to support this claim.

It is necessary for university administrators and officials to find answers to these questions before undertaking the expense and inconvenience of moving to a new campus. With such a large action at stake, supporting evidence needs to be much more clear and pointed to determine the best course.

The writer doesn't present an opinion about the appropriate course of action for the university in the introductory paragraph. Rather, the author looks at the issue from a larger perspective and gets to the heart of the assumptions quickly. Alternative questions are asked, which show a depth of thought, and the logic of the school's position is diminished when presented next to these alternatives.

The use of academic language is high, and there is a clear understanding of how elements of an essay work together. Proper grammar and punctuation make this essay readable and the stance clear.

Index

• N •

• O •

Publisher's Acknowledgments

Executive Editor: Lindsay Sandman Lefevere

Project Editor: Tim Gallan

Copy Editor: Christine Pingleton

Contributor: LearningMate Solutions

Contributing Editor: Ron Woldoff

Technical Editor: Karen Berlin Ishii

Art Coordinator: Alicia B. South

Project Coordinator: Kinson Raja

Cover Image: ©iStock.com/barisonal

& Mac

r Dummies,
tion
18-72306-7

For Dummies,
tion
18-69083-3

ll-in-One
mmies, 4th Edition
18-82210-4

avericks
mmies
18-69188-5

ng & Social Media

ok For Dummies,
tion
18-63312-0

Media Engagement
mmies
18-53019-1

ress For Dummies,
tion
18-79161-5

ss

nvesting
mmies, 4th Edition
18-37678-2

ng For Dummies,
tion
470-90545-6

Personal Finance
For Dummies, 7th Edition
978-1-118-11785-9

QuickBooks 2014
For Dummies
978-1-118-72005-9

Small Business Marketing Kit
For Dummies, 3rd Edition
978-1-118-31183-7

Careers

Job Interviews For Dummies,
4th Edition
978-1-118-11290-8

Job Searching with Social
Media For Dummies,
2nd Edition
978-1-118-67856-5

Personal Branding
For Dummies
978-1-118-11792-7

Resumes For Dummies,
6th Edition
978-0-470-87361-8

Starting an Etsy Business
For Dummies, 2nd Edition
978-1-118-59024-9

Diet & Nutrition

Belly Fat Diet For Dummies
978-1-118-34585-6

Mediterranean Diet
For Dummies
978-1-118-71525-3

Nutrition For Dummies,
5th Edition
978-0-470-93231-5

Digital Photography

Digital SLR Photography
All-in-One For Dummies,
2nd Edition
978-1-118-59082-9

Digital SLR Video &
Filmmaking For Dummies
978-1-118-36598-4

Photoshop Elements 12
For Dummies
978-1-118-72714-0

Gardening

Herb Gardening
For Dummies, 2nd Edition
978-0-470-61778-6

Gardening with Free-Range
Chickens For Dummies
978-1-118-54754-0

Health

Boosting Your Immunity
For Dummies
978-1-118-40200-9

Diabetes For Dummies,
4th Edition
978-1-118-29447-5

Living Paleo For Dummies
978-1-118-29405-5

Big Data

Big Data For Dummies
978-1-118-50422-2

Data Visualization
For Dummies
978-1-118-50289-1

Hadoop For Dummies
978-1-118-60755-8

Language &
Foreign Language

500 Spanish Verbs
For Dummies
978-1-118-02382-2

English Grammar
For Dummies, 2nd Edition
978-0-470-54664-2

French All-in-One
For Dummies
978-1-118-22815-9

German Essentials
For Dummies
978-1-118-18422-6

Italian For Dummies,
2nd Edition
978-1-118-00465-4

Math & Science

Algebra I For Dummies,
2nd Edition
978-0-470-55964-2

Anatomy and Physiology
For Dummies, 2nd Edition
978-0-470-92326-9

Astronomy For Dummies,
3rd Edition
978-1-118-37697-3

Biology For Dummies,
2nd Edition
978-0-470-59875-7

Chemistry For Dummies,
2nd Edition
978-1-118-00730-3

1001 Algebra II Practice
Problems For Dummies
978-1-118-44662-1

Microsoft Office

Excel 2013 For Dummies
978-1-118-51012-4

Office 2013 All-in-One
For Dummies
978-1-118-51636-2

PowerPoint 2013
For Dummies
978-1-118-50253-2

Word 2013 For Dummies
978-1-118-49123-2

Music

Blues Harmonica
For Dummies
978-1-118-25269-7

Guitar For Dummies,
3rd Edition
978-1-118-11554-1

iPod & iTunes For Dummies,
10th Edition
978-1-118-50864-0

Programming

Beginning Programming
with C For Dummies
978-1-118-73763-7

Excel VBA Programming
For Dummies, 3rd Edition
978-1-118-49037-2

Java For Dummies,
6th Edition
978-1-118-40780-6

Religion & Inspiration

The Bible For Dummies
978-0-7645-5296-0

Buddhism For Dummies,
2nd Edition
978-1-118-02379-2

Catholicism For Dummies,
2nd Edition
978-1-118-07778-8

Self-Help & Relationships

Beating Sugar Addiction
For Dummies
978-1-118-54645-1

Meditation For Dummies,
3rd Edition
978-1-118-29144-3

Seniors

Laptops For Seniors
For Dummies, 3rd Edition
978-1-118-71105-7

Computers For Seniors
For Dummies, 3rd Edition
978-1-118-11553-4

iPad For Seniors
For Dummies, 6th Edition
978-1-118-72826-0

Social Security For Dummies
978-1-118-20573-0

Smartphones & Tablets

Android Phones
For Dummies, 2nd Edition
978-1-118-72030-1

Nexus Tablets For Dummies
978-1-118-77243-0

Samsung Galaxy S 4
For Dummies
978-1-118-64222-1

Samsung Galaxy Tabs
For Dummies
978-1-118-77294-2

Test Prep

ACT For Dummies,
5th Edition
978-1-118-01259-8

ASVAB For Dummies,
3rd Edition
978-0-470-63760-9

GRE For Dummies,
7th Edition
978-0-470-88921-3

Officer Candidate Test
For Dummies
978-0-470-59876-4

Physician's Assistant E
For Dummies
978-1-118-11556-5

Series 7 Exam For Dur
978-0-470-09932-2

Windows 8

Windows 8.1 All-in-On
For Dummies
978-1-118-82087-2

Windows 8.1 For Dum
978-1-118-82121-3

Windows 8.1 For Dum
Book + DVD Bundle
978-1-118-82107-7

e **Available in print and e-book formats.**

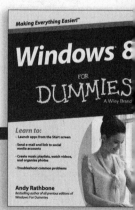